Thomson Nelson
Canadian Dictionary

for the Social Sciences

Gary Parkinson
Thompson Rivers University

Robert Drislane
Thompson Rivers University

THOMSON

NELSON

Australia   Canada   Mexico   Singapore   Spain   United Kingdom   United States

THOMSON

NELSON

Thomson Nelson Canadian Dictionary for the Social Sciences

by Gary Parkinson and Robert Drislane

Associate Vice-President, Editorial Director:
Evelyn Veitch

Executive Editor:
Cara Yarzab

Executive Marketing Manager:
Kelly Smyth

Developmental Editor:
Maya Bahar

Production Editor:
Anne Macdonald

Copy Editor:
June Trusty

Proofreader:
June Trusty

Production Coordinator:
Susan Ure

Interior Design:
Katherine Strain

Cover Design:
Courtney Hellam

Cover Image:
Billy Hustrace / Photographer's Choice / Getty Images

Compositor:
Doris Chan

Printer:
Webcom

Library and Archives Canada Cataloguing in Publication

Parkinson, Gary, 1940–
   Thomson Nelson Canadian dictionary for the social sciences / Gary Parkinson, Robert Drislane.

ISBN 0-17-625237-1

   1. Social sciences—Dictionaries.
I. Drislane, Robert II. Title.
III. Title: Canadian dictionary for the social sciences.

H41.P37 2006   300'.3
C2006-901037-4

Preface

Welcome to the *Thomson Nelson Canadian Dictionary for the Social Sciences*. We hope the 1,400 entries covering the fields of anthropology, sociology, and political science will enhance your studies.

This dictionary is designed for undergraduate students in Canada and covers the main concepts, names, and events with which you should be familiar as you study social sciences.

An important component of your learning is the acquisition of the somewhat specialized language of the social sciences. Each entry is designed to provide you with sufficient information to grasp the basic content of a concept, how the term is used, and its connection to other concepts. Developing a solid grasp of the meaning of key terms will speed and deepen your learning and will lead to greater success.

There are several ways to use this dictionary. The first and most obvious is to use it to investigate puzzling words you encounter in your textbooks or readings. When using the dictionary to locate definitions and explanations, be sure to note the way the word is used in the reading—check whether it is used as a noun, verb, or adjective. Also notice if the term is typically used to modify something else or is related specifically to some other concept. Always investigate the words it may be contrasted with or related to.

You can also use the dictionary as a tool to take control of your own learning. Spend time reading it to see how clusters of concepts or issues are linked together. For example, the "aboriginal peoples" entry will lead you to entries on "C-31 Indians," the "Gladue case," and "over-representation." This may lead you to read the entry on the "*Indian Act*" or on "Oka" or on the "Supreme Court of Canada," or it may stimulate your interest in the idea of "First Nations" and this may lead you to the entry on "nation," then to "self-government," and then perhaps to "sovereignty." You might then be interested in learning about when and how the first peoples arrived on this continent. Always explore the connections.

Another informative approach is to seek out opposing concepts or theoretical perspectives and then investigate how the contrast between them is reflected in many other terms and concepts in your textbook. For example, taking the entry "positivism" as one side and the entry "postmodernism" as the other, you will find many other entries that are connected to these two. Or investigate "consensus perspective" and "critical perspective" and determine what concepts would be connected to this contrast. You will find more examples of these interconnections of terms and concepts as you read. If you wish to explore any concept or event further, please search out the reference provided or go to the Internet and search for more information. In short, take control of your learning.

Another feature of this dictionary is the inclusion of brief descriptions of key events that are important for deepening your analysis of Canadian society. For example you will find descriptions of the "'Persons' case"; the "*Meech Lake Accord*"; "confederation"; the "Calder case"; "Morgentaler, Henry"; "Gustafsen Lake"; the "pipeline debate"; "*Lament for a Nation*"; "Head-Smashed-in-Buffalo Jump"; the "Quiet Revolution"; "referendum"; and the "King–Byng crisis."

You might also want to refer to the *Nelson Criminology Dictionary* (2005) that we also prepared, which contains entries covering the specialized vocabulary and concepts of criminology, as well as brief outlines of the ideas of principal writers and theorists within the discipline. In addition, it provides coverage of historical and recent events important to the study of criminology in Canada.

We wish to acknowledge the continuing support of Thomson Nelson Canada in developing this dictionary. Specifically, we wish to thank Maya Bahar, Cara Yarzab, Anne Macdonald, Katherine Strain, and Laura Armstrong for their work on this project, as well as our copy editor June Trusty.

Robert Drislane (Victoria)
Gary Parkinson (Vancouver)
October 15, 2005

80/20 principle While this ratio should not be considered to be exact, social scientists have found that it applies to many things in the world: On a committee, 80% of the work is done by 20% of the members; 80% of car accidents are the fault of 20% of the drivers; and so on. This principle is also known as *Pareto's principle*. Reference: Koch, R. (1998). *The 80/20 Principle: The Art of Achieving More with Less.* New York: Bantam. *See also* **Pareto's principle**.

A

Abell, Helen C. (1917–2005) Helen C. Abell was the first woman in Canada to be awarded a doctorate in rural sociology. In her varied career, she served in the army for four wartime years, became a senior bureaucrat at the federal Ministry of Agriculture, held senior posts at several universities, and played a prominent role in international agencies administering community and agricultural development programs in Africa.

Aboriginal Justice Inquiry of Manitoba This inquiry was established in 1988 to investigate the events surrounding the shooting death of J.J. Harper and the unrelated death of Helen Betty Osborne, as well as to examine the declining relationship between aboriginal people and the justice system. The inquiry reported in 1991, recommending a series of structural changes to the justice system, and that over the long term, the government move toward a separate justice system for the Métis and native peoples of Manitoba. *See also* **Harper, John Joseph; Osborne, Helen Betty**.

aboriginal peoples In the Americas, aboriginal peoples have descended from the first inhabitants of the continents, before European contact, and include the peoples broadly classified as Indian and Inuit. The synonymous term *native peoples* is also widely used. Section 35(2) of the *Constitution Act, 1982*, declares that "aboriginal peoples" includes "Indian, Inuit, and Métis peoples of Canada." *See also* **C-31 Indians; Gladue case; overrepresentation**.

abortion Abortion was regulated by criminal law in Canada until January 1988, when the Supreme Court of Canada ruled the law unconstitutional on the grounds that it was applied in an arbitrary and discriminatory manner. The law was struck down under Section 7 of the *Canadian Charter of Rights and Freedoms*. No new law has been enacted, so abortion continues to be legal. The invalidated law was an amendment to the *Criminal Code* made in 1969, allowing a hospital committee to authorize a therapeutic abortion if it was deemed that the life or health of the mother was at considerable risk. In the United States, abortion was legalized in 1973 by the U.S. Supreme Court case known as *Roe vs. Wade*. The struggle between pro-life and pro-choice groups over abortion has now shifted to the financing of abortions, hospital policy, and protests outside clinics providing abortions. Conflict over the abortion issue is less intense in Canada, where there is overwhelmingly pro-choice public opinion, than in the United States, where there is a strong pro-life movement linked to fundamentalist religious groups. Reference: *Morgentaler v. R.* [1988] 1 S.C.R. 30. *See also* **Morgentaler, Henry**.

Acadians Today's Acadians are descendents of the original French settlers of the regions of Nova Scotia, New Brunswick, and Prince Edward Island, who arrived as early as 1604. The *Treaty of Utrecht* in 1713 made them permanent British subjects, and in 1730, an agreement was signed by which the Acadians would swear an oath of allegiance to the British crown but would not be forced to take up arms. By 1754, however, things had changed and the Acadians were asked to sign a new oath requiring them to take up arms. When they refused, the Nova Scotia Council decided to deport all Acadians. Approximately 6,000 people were immediately rounded up and dispersed among the American colonies or returned to France. Over the next few years, another 2,000 to 4,000 were deported. Acadians were allowed to return in 1764. Some did return and others had remained hidden, so there are now many Canadians with Acadian ancestry. A vibrant Acadian culture flourishes today in these three maritime provinces. While redress has been sought for the 18th-century injustice, the federal government has acknowledged the wrong but has not apologized. Reference: Jobb, Dean. (2005). *The Acadians: A people's story of exile and triumph.* Toronto: John Wiley & Sons Canada.

accounts As used in the sociology of deviance, *accounts* refers to the rationalizations that people provide for their actions. Two large groups of accounts are distinguished: justifications and excuses. A justification accepts responsibility for an action but denies the wrongfulness of that action. An excuse, on the other hand, denies responsibility while accepting the wrongfulness of the action. These ideas go back to Edwin Sutherland (1924), C.W. Mills (1940), and Donald Cressey (1953). Reference: Sutherland, E.H. (1924). *Principles of Criminology*. Philadelphia: Lippincott [1939]. *See also* **neutralization techniques**.

acculturation This process of cultural transformation is initiated by contacts between different cultures. At a global level, acculturation takes place as societies experience the transforming impact of international cultural contact. The global trend toward modern economic organization and developed market economies has been accompanied by a process of cultural transformation. A key change is toward a transformation of economic organization: The great majority of individuals come to generate their income through employment or running businesses, rather than from economic bonds with family and community. In the modern world, international communication and interaction between cultures is very easy, but sociologists have generally focused attention on the global impact of the capitalist Western world on other societies. While each society experiences a unique process of cultural and economic transformation, some common trends appear to be linked to the development of complex market economies, a wage employment system, and urbanization. Individuals experience acculturation when their social roles and socialization are shaped by norms and values that are largely foreign to their native culture. Educational and occupational experiences are the primary agents of the individual's acculturation process. Some sociologists use the term *acculturation* to refer simply to the process of learning and absorbing a culture, making it synonymous with *socialization*, but *enculturation* is a more appropriate word for that meaning. *See also* **enculturation; socialization**.

acephalous society The literal meaning of *acephalous* is "headless," so this term refers to a society that does not have a formalized or institutionalized system of power and authority. Collective decisions are made in a variety of ways, including informal community gatherings.

Acheulean tool tradition This term refers to the tool-making tradition of *Homo erectus*, with the signature piece being the hand axe.

action theory Action theory is a sociological perspective that focuses on the individual as a subject and views social action as something purposively shaped by individuals within a context to which they have given meaning. This approach has its foundations in German sociologist Max Weber's (1864–1920) "interpretive sociology," which claims that it is necessary to know the subjective purpose and intent of the actor before an observer can understand the meaning of social action. Sociologists who focus on "action" tend to treat the individual as an autonomous subject, rather than as constrained by social structure and culture. As a subject, the individual is seen as exercising agency, taking voluntary action, giving meaning to objects and events, and acting with intent. While Weber insisted on the power of society and historical context in giving shape to human action, some sociologists who have adopted action theory have been accused of neglecting the influence of social structure and culture on people's behaviour. *See also* **agency**.

Adorno, Theodor W. (1903–1969) Theodor Adorno, a German philosopher and critical theorist, was an important member of the Frankfurt School. *See also* **Frankfurt School**.

affect disorder In this form of mental disorder, the individual experiences mood swings greater than normal. This disorder is usually associated with depression and in more severe cases with mania or periods of excitement and overconfidence.

affinal kin Referring to all relatives by marriage, *affinal kin* contrasts with *consanguineal kin*, who are relatives by birth, or blood relatives.

affirmative action This term refers to policies of governments and other institutions that are designed to actively promote and advance the status and the social and occupational participation of groups of people designated by sex, ethnicity, or another shared characteristic. The intent of such policies is to counteract the perceived disadvantagement of such groups. The *Canadian Charter of Rights and Freedoms* (Section 15[2]) allows for the possibility of such a policy without it being subject to challenge on grounds of discrimination against non-designated groups. Affirmative action programs are designed to provide greater equality of opportunity, since it is known that inequality of opportunity can be linked to crime and deviance. *See also* **Merton, Robert**.

Africville A Black community on the edges of Halifax that had been in existence for 150 years, Africville had a population in the 1960s of about 400 people when it was bulldozed to make way for redevelopment. Some residents chose to be moved to public and private housing. The community had never been properly serviced by the municipality of Halifax (e.g., there was no sewer or water service), and the site had became a dumping ground and the location of much deviant activity by the residents of Halifax. Only after its destruction did it become obvious that the redevelopment had reflected the racism of the larger community and had ignored the importance of the neighbourhood for the Black community in Nova Scotia. Africville has now been declared a national heritage site and has served as the symbol for the political and cultural heritage of the Black community. Reference: Clairmont, Donald H., & Magill, D.W. (1999). *Africville: The life and death of a Canadian Black community.* Toronto: Canadian Scholars Press.

ageism The assumption that a person's age should determine his or her social status and roles in society is called *ageism*. This term usually refers to stereotyping and devaluation of seniors. *See also* **stereotype**.

agency This term is linked to sociologies that focus on the individual as a subject and view social action as something purposively shaped by individuals within a context to which they have given meaning. This view is usually contrasted with those sociologies that focus on social structure and imply that individuals are shaped and constrained by the structural environment in which they are located. *See also* **action theory**.

agnatic descent Also referred to as *patrilineal descent* or *male descent*, agnatic descent is a unilineal system of descent through the male line.

agoraphobia This is a form of anxiety disorder in which a person experiences intense fear of open spaces or being in public.

Agricultural Revolution The development of crop and animal raising as a food source among human communities to supplement hunting and gathering, the Agricultural Revolution is thought to have first occurred among human groups in the Neolithic Period (approximately 10,000 to 8,000 B.C.). It is worth noting that an agricultural revolution occurred in the New World independently of those in Europe or Asia. This allowed the civilizations of Mesoamerica to develop cities of at least 150,000 inhabitants long before urban areas of this size appeared in Europe. The staple crops developed in the early days of this revolution still feed most of the world. Reference: MacNeish, R.S. (1992). *The origins of agriculture and settled life.* Norman, OK: University of Oklahoma Press.

Air India disaster On June 22, 1985, an Air India airplane left the Toronto airport with 329 people on board. The majority of the passengers were Canadian women and children of Indian origin. The plane exploded off the coast of Ireland, killing all on board. It was determined that a bomb had been planted on the plane. Authorities investigated a potential link between this terrorist action and some radical groups seeking establishment of an independent Sikh nation separate from India. On June 23, 1985, a second bomb exploded in Tokyo's airport while baggage was being handled, killing two people. It was bound for a plane connecting to an Air India flight travelling to Bangkok. It is thought that this bomb was also planted by Sikh terrorists and had exploded earlier than planned. Inderjit Singh Reyat was charged and convicted for his role in the Tokyo explosion and served 10 years in prison. In October 2000, Ripudaman Singh Malik and Ajaib Singh Bagri were finally charged with this terrible crime; a protracted and difficult trial was expected. In 2001, Inderjit Singh Reyat was added to the list of those charged and the trial of all three was to proceed until Reyat unexpectedly pleaded guilty to his role and received five years in jail. A new trial of Ripudaman Singh Malik and Ajaib Singh Bagri was launched in 2003. This trial was possibly the most complex criminal trial in Canadian history. In June 2005, the judge found both of the accused not guilty. A public inquiry is likely to be called in an attempt to find out why so little success was obtained in this case and why it took so long to conclude. Reference: Bolan, Kim. (2005). *Loss of faith: How the Air India bombers got away with murder.* Toronto: McClelland and Stewart.

alienation Describing a separation of individuals from the control and direction of their social life, *alienation* was used widely in German philosophy in the 18th and 19th centuries, but it has become important for sociology because of the ideas of Karl Marx (1818–1883), German philosopher, social scientist, historian, and revolutionary. Marx claimed that human alienation was created by a socially structured separation between humans and their work.

This separation reached its highest intensity in capitalist society, where the great mass of the population depended for subsistence on working under the direction of others. In the capitalist workplace, individuals were separated from ownership, control, and direction of their work, and were unable to achieve personal creative expression. The competitive nature of the workplace also alienated, or separated, workers from each other. Alienation is of interest to those studying workplace crime, since it is known that alienation may result not only in low productivity but also in theft of employer property or intentional damage to equipment or products.

alterity From the word *alter*—to make a thing different—the term *alterity* is central to postmodern discussions of identity in which the self is given meaning in terms of an "other." This other is posed or imagined in terms of difference. Alterity, then, is a state or condition of otherness. The term is useful for thinking about how many peoples throughout history have been cast in the role of inferior and as the opposite of those who look down on them. Negative qualities are projected onto these "others" and the imagined contrast with them strengthens the sense of one's own rightness and confirms one's sense of identity. For Euro-Canadians, for example, the "Indian" has been a significant expression of the other and hence central to the Euro-Canadian sense of self. "Indian" then is the "other" and has the quality of alterity. *See also* **postmodernism**.

Althusser, Louis (1918–1990) Louis Althusser was a French social philosopher who exerted great influence on many disciplines during the 1960s and 1970s. He set out to rescue Marxism from what he thought was corruption imposed by Stalinism, and this reworking became associated with what is called *structural Marxism*. To everyone's surprise, Althusser was convicted of the murder of his wife and spent his last years in a mental hospital. Reference: Benton, T. (1984). *The rise and fall of structural Marxism*. London: Macmillan.

altruism Social behaviour and value orientation in which individuals give primary consideration to the interests and welfare of other individuals, members of groups, or the community as a whole is called *altruism*. The term was used by French sociologist Émile Durkheim (1858–1917) to describe a suicide committed for the benefit of other individuals or for the community; this would include self-sacrifice for military objectives in wartime. Sociobiologists argue that altruistic behaviour has its roots in self-interest, the unconscious desire to protect one's genetic heritage. Critics of sociobiology respond that altruism is evident between individuals and in social situations where people are completely unrelated genetically, and claim that human conduct and motivations cannot be explained without reference to the values and norms of culture.

Amazon In Greek legend, the Amazon was a female hunter, unusual for occupying a male role. The Amazon River was named after this legendary hunter after early European explorers encountered women who were hunters and in many ways acted like men. Many cultures have acknowledged a masculine role for women. In Hinduism, this role is an aspect of the female *hijras*. The Kaska Indians of the Subarctic sometimes selected a daughter when it appeared the family was going to have no sons and performed a transformation ceremony to symbolically turn the daughter into a son. The dried ovaries of a bear were tied to a belt that she always wore; she dressed like a male and engaged in hunting. The counterpart of this role among men is called *berdache*. Societies with little outlet for nonconventional sexual or gender identities are more likely to have individuals with psychological problems. Reference: Roscoe, Will. (1998). *Changing Ones: Third and Fourth Genders in Native North America*. New York: St. Martin's Press. *See also* **berdache**.

amending formula Until the *Constitution Act, 1982*, Canada was governed by the terms of the *British North America Act, 1867* (now called the *Constitution Act, 1867*), which had been passed by and could be amended only by Britain's Parliament. Although a constitutional convention was established that Britain was always to act as requested by Canada's Parliament, this relationship was still, in legal terms, a colonial one. The 1982 Act achieved patriation and Canada now has complete autonomy to change its *Constitution* under the new rules specified in the amending formula. Some provisions of the *Constitution* can be amended only with the unanimous approval of Parliament and the 10 provincial legislatures. This includes changes to the status and office of the monarch or the governor general and changes to the structure of the Supreme Court and the Senate. Most other changes may be made if agreed to by Parliament and at least seven provinces, and these provinces must have a total of at least 50% of the population.

amino acid racemization dating This is a method of absolute dating in archaeology, which builds on the assumption that the amino acids trapped in organic materials change from left-handed forms to right-handed forms over time. Thus, the ratio of left-handed forms to right-handed forms will determine the age of the material.

Amish A religious sect related to the 16th-century Mennonites but emerging under the leadership of Bishop Jacob Ammon, the Amish arrived in Canada in 1825 and settled in Waterloo County, Ontario. This group is more traditional than many present Mennonites and has kept its religious beliefs alive as well as the traditional ways of living, dressing, and working. *See also* **sect**.

Amnesty International Formed in 1961, this organization has become a widely supported and successful defender of human rights. Its members have given special attention to individuals wrongfully imprisoned.

amplification of deviance Developed by British criminologist Leslie Wilkens (1915–2000), deviance amplification refers to the unintended outcome of moral panics or social policies designed to prevent or reduce deviance. Typically, the attention given to deviance by the media and by moral entrepreneurs serves to attract new recruits and provides them with a definition of what the public expects, thus amplifying the amount of deviance in society. Reference: Wilkins, L.T. (1964). *Social Deviance, Social Policy, Action and Research*. London: Tavistock. *See also* **moral entrepreneur; moral panic**.

androgyny An androgynous personality has a balance of feminine and masculine characteristics, is comfortable with displaying both types of characteristics, and is able to move back and forth between the two. Some feminists have advocated gender androgyny as a source of liberation from polarized cultural ideas of masculine and feminine. This is of interest to those studying male violence, since there appears to be a relationship between societies that place high value on male characteristics (the military, for example) and high rates of crime against women.

animism A belief related to the supernatural, *animism* means seeing the natural world of humans, animals, and plants as animated by spirits.

annulment When a marriage is annulled, it is declared to be invalid. This declaration may be made by a law court in cases such as bigamy or marriage involving fraud. However, the majority of marriage annulments are made by the Catholic Church, based on decisions made by a tribunal of three priest–judges with majority agreement. A positive decision must be confirmed by an appeal court, and if this court does not agree with the initial decision, the case goes to the Roman Rota. The grounds for annulment have to do with the matter of proper consent that might arise from psychopathology or lack of sufficient reason (a criterion that is seldom used). The most contentious criterion is that of "lack of discretion." The majority of cases coming to a tribunal involve Catholics who did not marry in the church—these marriages are considered invalid. The need for annulment usually arises when a divorced Catholic wishes to remarry, since Catholics can do so within the church only if the first marriage can be annulled. Most Catholic annulments worldwide occur in the United States, where about 60,000 marriages are annulled each year.

anomia Distinguished from French sociologist Émile Durkheim's *anomie* (a societal condition), anomia is a social psychological condition in which the individual experiences a loss of moral direction and a sense of disconnection from society. This concept has proved much easier to investigate empirically than has Durkheim's anomie. *See also* **anomie**.

anomic division of labour This term describes a situation in which the division of labour in the workplace is based on power and social and economic status, rather than on differentiations of individual ability or effort. In such circumstances, according to French sociologist Émile Durkheim (1858–1917), the division of labour cannot command normative consensus and may become a source of anomie and breakdown of social solidarity. *See also* **inequality of opportunity**.

anomie French sociologist Émile Durkheim (1858–1917) used this term to describe an absence of clear societal norms and values. Individuals lack a sense of social regulation and feel unguided in the choices they have to make. Anomie can occur in several different situations. For example, the undermining of traditional values may result from cultural contact. The concept can be helpful in partially understanding the experience of colonized aboriginal peoples who, even as their traditional values are disrupted, do not identify with the new cultural values imposed on them: They lose a sense of authoritative normative regulation. Durkheim was also concerned that anomie might arise from a lack of consensus over social regulation of the workplace. American sociologist Robert Merton (1910–2003) used the term more narrowly to refer to a situation in which people's goals—what they wanted to achieve—were beyond their means. Their commitment to their goals was so strong that they would adopt deviant means to achieve them. He argued that American society—perhaps more strongly than other capitalist societies—held out the goal of personal wealth and success to all its citizens. It placed extremely high value on the attainment of wealth and high social status. Materialistic goals were so stressed in society, Merton argued, that those groups in society who did not believe in their chance of success through conventional avenues (a good education, good job, good income, etc.), because they were poor or otherwise lacked opportunity, were induced toward unconventional routes to attain wealth—including crime. The social norms against crime were sometimes too weakly implanted in individuals to restrain them from seeking to achieve economic success through criminal means. They wanted to win the game without regard to the rules. More recently, anomie has been used in a more individually focused way to talk about the problems of immigrant youth when faced with a new culture or about the identity crises that often erupt during the age transition from youth to adult. Durkheim's use of the term "lack of social regulation" remains the standard definition. Reference: Durkheim, Émile. (1951). *Suicide: A Study in Sociology*. Glencoe, IL: The Free Press.

anorexia Anorexia is a form of mental disorder in which people are overly concerned about their weight or their image and starve themselves since, regardless of how thin they become, they still consider themselves to be overweight.

anthropology, applied The field of anthropology that attempts to use the knowledge and methods of anthropology to solve or shed light on practical problems is known as *applied anthropology*. Two significant branches are medical anthropology and forensic anthropology.

anthropology, forensic Forensic anthropology is an area of applied anthropology that applies the knowledge of physical anthropology to the examination of crimes. Methods including DNA analysis and skeletal measurement can be used to determine the sex or race of bodily remains, the age of bones, and the characteristics of injuries.

anthropology, physical A specialization within the discipline of anthropology, physical anthropology is centred on the scientific study of the origins and development of human beings through analysis of fossil and skeletal remains. Many students of physical anthropology were employed during the search for evidence of human remains in the missing women case in Vancouver, British Columbia.

anthropology, social Also referred to as cultural anthropology, social anthropology is conceptually and theoretically similar to sociology. Anthropology originally developed as the study of non-Western cultures, but since many anthropologists now study Western societies, the disciplines of sociology and anthropology have been tending to converge. Social or cultural anthropologists are interested in understanding how crime and deviance are responded to in various cultures and in how notions of justice are institutionalized.

anthropophagy In archaeology and anthropology, this term is used for the practice of cannibalism—the eating of human flesh. *See also* **cannibalism.**

anti-Asian riot In 1907, an anti-Asian riot in Vancouver swept through Chinatown, damaging Chinese and Japanese property. The government, after an inquiry, agreed to pay some compensation. The Asiatic Exclusion League had been formed by members of the Vancouver Trades and Labor Council in the year in which the riot took place, an indication of increasing racial tensions in the city. It has been argued that one result of this inquiry was a new law prohibiting the use and sale of opium. Reference: Comack, Elizabeth. (1985). The Origins of Canadian Drug Legislation: Labelling versus Class Analysis. In T. Fleming (Ed.), *The New Criminologies in Canada*. Toronto: Oxford University Press.

anticombines law In order to protect the principle of competition (valued by all liberal, capitalistic societies), laws have been created to prevent and punish the undermining of free markets by corporate combination. Competition law was first introduced in 1889, but there have been few successful prosecutions in Canada, even though Canada has an unusually high degree of corporate concentration, suggesting at least the potential for abuse of the market. Reference: Goff, C., and Reasons, C. (1978). *Corporate Crime in Canada: A Critical Analysis of Anti-Combines Legislation.* Scarborough: Prentice-Hall; Stanbury, W.T. (1991). Chapter 6: Legislation to Control Agreements in Restraint of Trade in Canada: Review of the Historical Record and Proposals for Reform. In R.S. Khemani & W.T. Stanbury (Eds.), *Canadian Competition Law and Policy at the Centenary.* Halifax: Institute for Research on Public Policy.

anti-Semitism As a migrant people, the Jews have experienced this negative and hostile attitude toward them and their religion within many societies and throughout much of recorded history. The most extreme expression of anti-Semitism was the Holocaust, when six million Jews were murdered in German concentration camps during World War II. This mass killing, carried out in an advanced and intellectually sophisticated society, traumatized Western societies and called into question the then dominant idea that historical development was marked by an increasingly rational commitment to the creation of an enlightened, progressive, and humane society. During recent years, anti-Semitism seems to be increasing in many Western societies, partly associated with continuing political conflict in the Middle East. *See also* **hate crime**.

Anti-Terrorism Act Passed in 2001, Canada's *Anti-Terrorism Act* created new criminal offences linked to terrorism. Among other things, the new law gives police forces greater search powers and creates new criminal offences, including knowingly providing funds to terrorist groups, either in Canada or elsewhere; contributing to or facilitating terrorist activity; instructing a person to carry out terrorist acts or activities; and harbouring or concealing a terrorist. The Act also provides that any indictable offence committed in pursuit of terrorist objectives is punishable with up to life imprisonment with no eligibility for parole. In December 2004, a Senate committee was established to review this Act. Reference: Daniels, R.J., Macklin, P., & Roach, K. (Eds.). (2001). *The Security of Freedom: Essays on Canada's Anti-Terrorism Bill.* Toronto: University of Toronto Press.

apartheid A policy of racial segregation maintained in South Africa from 1948 to 1994, apartheid estab-

lished the doctrine of "separate development," whereby South African Blacks were segregated into reserves known as "homelands" and subjected to residential and occupational restrictions. Apartheid was maintained by a wide range of laws that included the prohibition of interracial sexual intercourse or marriage and outlawed racially integrated political and social organizations. A White minority government, faced with international pressures and internal conflict, began the process of dismantling apartheid in the late 1980s and eventually extended the right to vote on equal terms to all South African adults. A subsequent election in 1994 installed South Africa's first Black majority government, led by Nelson Mandela.

APEC riot The Asia-Pacific Economic Cooperation conference met in Vancouver in 1997, hosted by the federal government. To highlight the "cooperation" aspect of the organization, efforts were made to have President Suharto of Indonesia attend. Suharto was responsible for the invasion of East Timor and a policy of genocide. While the details are not known, it is thought that Suharto attended the conference with a guarantee that he would not be embarrassed by protesters. The protesters did of course turn out, and when it looked like they would get too close to the street on which Suharto's car was travelling, the crowd was first ordered to disband and then sprayed with tear gas by members of the RCMP. The prime minister of Canada was not called to the subsequent inquiry but there was strong evidence that orders to disrupt the protesters came from his office. Reference: Pue, W. Wesley (Ed.). (2000). *Pepper in Our Eyes: The APEC Affair.* Vancouver: University of British Columbia.

archaeology Archaeology is the study of past cultures through the discovery and examination of remaining artifacts (things made by people) and remains of things used by people. In the social sciences, archaeology is one of the main fields of anthropology since it offers the only method for studying lost and forgotten cultures. Archaeological study can uncover a rich store of information about the beliefs, social structure, economic organization, and environmental effects of past societies. Modern archaeologists have enhanced the accuracy of their work with scientific techniques of dating artifacts and with the use of DNA analysis.

Aristotle (384–322 B.C.) Ancient Greece philosopher Aristotle's contribution to political philosophy differed from the idealism of Plato and took a more grounded empirical approach to the question of how society is best governed. His most important work for social scientists is his *Politics*, which deals with ideal states, citizenship, constitutions, and revolutions.

Armenian genocide From 1915 to 1922, approximately 1.5 million Armenians lost their lives as a result of a Turkish government policy of genocide. Many Armenians tried to escape the genocide by emigrating to Canada, only to find they were classified as "Asians" under Canadian immigration policy, making it difficult for them to enter. In 2004, the Canadian House of Commons passed a private member's bill acknowledging the Armenian genocide, which met with much criticism from the Turkish community. *See also* **genocide.**

Arone, Shidane *See* **Somalia, incident in**.

assassins The modern term *assassins* derives from the Arabic word *hashishi* (plural: *hashishiyyin*, meaning those who smoked hemp), and was the name given to a 14th-century radical Islamic sect led by Hasan Sabbah. This group waged war against the orthodox Muslim world by killing authority figures but failed in its mission and eventually disappeared. Reference: Lewis, B. (1967). *Assassins: A radical sect in Islam.* London: Weidenfeld and Nicolson [2001].

assimilation When an ethnic group loses distinctiveness and becomes absorbed into a majority culture, *assimilation* is said to have occurred. Some sociologists suggest that the process can create a new culture resulting from the fusion of the cultures of different ethnic groups into a new blend, but the term *integration* is usually chosen by sociologists to suggest this blending of divergent cultures. The concept of assimilation is useful when discussing the persistence of minority cultures within host societies. In Canada, for example, visible minorities have experienced slower and less comprehensive assimilation than many European ethnic minorities. Canada's official government policy of multiculturalism implies resistance to assimilation and support for a society where people preserve their cultural distinctiveness, yet join together for common pursuits and agree on fundamental values. *See also* **acculturation; integration, social; multiculturalism.**

assisted suicide While suicide itself is no longer a criminal offence, it is an offence to assist or encourage someone to take his or her own life. In the case of Sue Rodriguez, the Supreme Court of Canada did not accept arguments supporting assisted suicide, thus forcing her and an accomplice to break the law in order to terminate her life. In 2005, a federal government backbencher introduced a Bill to allow assisted suicide. *See also* **Rodriguez, Sue.**

Association in Defence of the Wrongfully Convicted This is a Canadian association formed in 1993 to provide assistance to those whom the executive of the association believe to have been wrongfully convicted. The association has been successful in having some prisoners' cases reopened—resulting in acquittals—and this has brought a great deal of public attention to the problem. *See also* **wrongful conviction.**

atavism A tendency to reproduce ancestral type in plants and in animals (e.g., to resemble one's grandparents or great-grandparents more than one's parents), atavism implies a "throwback," using a popular form of speech. This concept was used by Cesare Lombroso (1835–1909) to describe a type of criminal he called the *born criminal*. The atavistic criminal was one representing an earlier stage of human evolution (thus representing the ancestral type more than the parental type). This ancestral type was identified by Lombroso through several stigmatized physical characteristics—including the length of ear lobes and fingers, and the bone structure of the head. This supposed physical degeneracy was associated with moral degeneracy and, thus, more frequent criminal behaviour. These physical stigmata were not found to be especially associated with criminals and this particular theory of criminality was rejected. Lombroso also studied female criminals, and while not finding the stigmata with the same frequency as among men, he did not abandon his theory. Rather, he argued that females were less evolved than men and thus had less far to degenerate: This would explain the infrequency of their criminal behaviour and the nature of the criminal acts they do commit.

attachment Attachment is the degree to which an individual has affective ties to other persons. Reference: Hirschi, Travis. (1969). Aspects of the Social Bond. *Causes of Delinquency.* Berkeley, CA: University of California Press.

audience An audience is a group of individuals paying attention to a common media. Audience members receive communication from the same source, but are not active participants and do not communicate with each other. In sociology, the term is used to draw attention to the way in which media corporations develop audiences of readers, listeners, and viewers with the business objective of selling access to this audience to advertisers. In this perspective, the creation and maintenance of an audience (rather than the activity of communication) is the prime goal of media enterprises. *See also* **consumer culture**.

Augustine Mound Some 2,500 years old, this North American Indian burial site was found in New Brunswick in 1972 by Joseph Mike Augustine after he read a magazine story about burial mounds in the United States. Located on the Miramichi River, the site is now a national historical site and is seen as a sign of the diffusion of cultural elements from the Adena people associated with mound-building in the Ohio valley. The area is home to the Mi'kmaq peoples.

Australopithecus The first well-known hominine, *Australopithecus* has now been identified as a distinct genus with at least five species. The first fossil was found in 1924 at a site in South Africa and dates back about 4 million years. To oversimplify, the genus resembles humans from the waist down and apes from the waist up. Thus, they were bipedal but had a brain similar in size to that of apes.

authority Authority is the power of an individual or institution to secure compliance from others, based on the possession of a recognized right to legitimately claim obedience. Authority is obeyed because the individual or institution issuing commands is believed to have the right to do so. German sociologist Max Weber (1864–1920) defined three ideal types of authority: traditional, which rests on history, myth, and ritual; charismatic, founded on belief in a leader's exceptional qualities and inspirational mission; and rational-legal, founded on democratic principles and a framework of law to which all individuals and institutions are subject.

Autopact Officially known as the *Canada–US Automotive Products Agreement*, the Autopact, signed in January 1965, established a link between the number of vehicles sold in Canada and the amount of automotive manufacturing activity that must be carried out in Canada. The agreement provided that manufacturers must ensure that value added by automotive manufacturing activity in Canada must not fall below the level established in 1964. The agreement also provided for percentages of Canadian manufacturing content to be increased as total Canadian sales values rose. Initially, the agreement was intended to ensure that the Canadian economy gained an appropriate proportion of the manufacturing activity and employment benefits that flowed from car sales, by foreign— chiefly U.S. corporations—to Canadian consumers. Over the years since 1965, Canada has in fact maintained a higher ratio of value-added manufacturing activity to sales than the levels provided in the Autopact. While the pact has helped to ensure a strong automotive manufacturing presence in both Ontario and Quebec, it has entrenched complete foreign domination of an important sector of the Canadian economy. In 2000, the World Trade Organization ruled in favour of Japan and the European community that the Autopact agreement was in violation of trade rules.

autocracy Usually, *autocracy* refers to a situation in which power is controlled by one person: a monarch, religious leader, or political dictator. The term can also be applied to particular social institutions in which one individual has dominant power and authority. *See also* **democracy**; **meritocracy**; **plutocracy**.

automation Methods of production that rely on mechanical or electronic technologies as a replacement for human labour are classed as automation.

avunculocal residence Most often found in matrilineal society, avunculocal residence occurs when the adult sons of a married couple leave their parents' household and go to live in the household of their mother's brother. The sons also bring their wives into the maternal uncle's household. This practice appears to be designed to locate the adult male members of the matrilineage in the same household.

B

baby boom The substantial increase in the birth rate following World War II (from 1947 to approximately 1966), called the *baby boom*, has created a population bulge that is slowly working its way through the age structure of society, affecting everything from classroom space to chances of promotion to pension funds. The baby boom was most apparent in Canada, the United States, Australia, and New Zealand. In 1996, the baby boom generation made up 33% of the Canadian population. This large population "bulge" may partially explain the labour market problems and high unemployment that Canada has had for the past decade or more. The baby boom generation has also been of interest to criminologists, since it is known that crime is strongly correlated with age. It could have been predicted that crime would go up as members of this generation went through their teenage years and into early adulthood, and then declined as they matured. Reference: Foot, David. (2001). *Boom, Bust & Echo*: *Profiting from the Demographic Shift in the 21st Century*. Toronto: Stoddart. *See also* **birth rate; cult of domesticity; echo generation**.

baby bust The rapid decline in Canada's birth rate following the baby boom years of 1947 to 1966 is called the *baby bust*. From 1967 to 1979, the fertility rate of Canadian women declined to less than half of the rate during the boom years. After 1979, women born in the boom years began to have children, leading to an echo boom, or echo generation. *See also* **echo generation**.

backbencher A member of Parliament or a legislature who is neither a member of the government nor an official policy critic for an Opposition party. In Parliamentary systems like Canada's, there is strong party discipline and very few backbenchers have had a successful political career after refusing to support their party and its leaders.

background knowledge As used by ethnomethodologists, *background knowledge* refers to common-sense reasoning and to the way that members of society—and sociologists, as well—use a background knowledge of culture and social structure as an unstated source of guidance in their reasoning.

Badgley Report A 1984 report of the Committee of Enquiry into Sexual Offences against Children and Youth, the *Badgley Report* was commissioned by the federal government of Canada and chaired by Robin Badgley. Research found that more than one-half of girls were victims of unwanted sexual acts and more than one-third of boys were victimized. The committee also examined juvenile prostitution and child pornography. The report's findings were shocking to Canadians, but it took several years for changes to the law to occur.

band A designated group of First Nations individuals, identified in the *Indian Act*, is called a *band*. Band members are usually historically related to each other by kinship and area of residence. Through much of human history, bands were seen as the basic social unit larger than the family, and now are associated with hunting-and-gathering societies.

Banks, Hal It is hard to know where to begin this Canadian tale, but the elements become clear on June 29, 1954, when a one-man inquiry into the status of Hal Banks (often described as a "thug") finds that he should be deported to the United States. The report is sent to the minister of Immigration with this recommendation, but it comes back with the word "Rejected" removed and "Approved" put in its place. Banks, by an order in council of the governor general on the advice of the Cabinet, is now given landed immigrant status in Canada. How did we get to here? Hal Banks entered Canada on a temporary permit in early 1949 at the request of the Liberal government, steamship owners, and unions. He was brought in to "clean up" the Canadian Seamen's Union (CSU), which controlled much of the shipping on the Great Lakes. The CSU had recently led many strikes and was involved in organizing an international strike. The CSU was accused of being run by communists and used for communist purposes, so Bank's job was to wrest control of shipping from this union. Banks had been a local tough on the San Francisco waterfront and had a criminal record. Using violence, he was able to reduce the CSU to an ineffective group and help a breakaway union, the Seafarers International Union (SIU), to get contracts for manning ships on the Great Lakes. Banks quickly took over this union and used gangster tactics to live well, while keeping countless union members who did not support him from finding work. Many opponents were seriously assaulted. The Canadian Labour Congress finally tried to assist the union members who had been hurt and intimidated by Banks by organizing a boycott of goods coming from and going to Canadian ports. This brought shipping on the St. Lawrence Seaway to a standstill. The tactic got the attention of the federal government, which agreed to establish a commission of inquiry into Banks' activities in Canadian ports. The Norris inquiry began August 7, 1962, and after 100 days of investigation, concluded that Banks really was a crook and placed his union under trusteeship. In the meantime, Banks appeared before a criminal court on a serious assault charge. While out on bail, he skipped town and was found in the United States by a reporter (the RCMP and politicians claimed they had no idea where he was). In a precedent-setting case, U.S. Secretary of State Dean Rusk decided not to extradite Banks to Canada. Interestingly, it is reported that a $100,000 donation from the SIU appeared in the campaign coffers of the Democratic Party 10 days after Rusk made his decision. Case closed. However, many questions about the relationship of government officials to Banks remain unanswered. Banks died in the United States in September 1985. Reference: Edwards, Peter. (1987). *Waterfront Warlord*. Toronto: Key Porter Books.

Barbeau, Marius Marius Barbeau (1883–1969) earned a law degree before becoming the first French Canadian Rhodes Scholar at Oxford University, where he earned a degree in anthropology. He returned to Canada to work at the National Museum of Canada, where he began to record the oral histories of First Nations and to collect French Canadian folklore. Reference: Nowry, L. (1995). *Marius Barbeau: Man of Mana*. Toronto: NC Press.

base (or infrastructure) A concept from Marxism, *base* refers to the mode of production of a society: the social and technical organization of its economy. Karl Marx (1818–1883), German philosopher, social scientist, historian, and revolutionary, argued that it is on this base that the superstructure of the society—its institutions and culture—are built. While the social institutions and culture of society are shaped by this base, at the same time, they help to maintain and reproduce the mode of production and may, in certain conditions, contribute to its transformation. *See also* **mode of production**.

battered woman syndrome Although a controversial concept, the psychological aspects of the battered woman syndrome provide an explanation for why some women remain in abusive relationships and why some murder their intimate partners when one might assume they could seek an alternative resolution to violence. This syndrome was accepted by the Supreme Court as a version of self-defence and the criteria for allowing this defence were articulated in a 1990 judgment (*see* **Lavallée case**). A 1998 Supreme Court decision decided that battered woman syndrome was not in itself a defence,

but rather a psychiatric explanation that might help explain a woman's state of mind (*see* **Malott case**). References: Vallee, B. (1986). *Life with Billy*. Toronto: Seal Books; *R. v. Malott* [1998] 1 S.C.R. 123.

Becker, Howard S. (1928–) A professor of sociology at Northwestern University, Howard Becker is famed for the labelling theory developed in his 1963 book, *Outsiders: Studies in the Sociology of Deviance*. He combined elements of symbolic interactionism with structural perspectives to develop his argument that deviance is a social construction created by the responses of others to the acts of individuals. He linked this argument to structural perspectives by demonstrating that the power to label and the chance of being labelled are linked to the socioeconomic status of the individuals or groups involved. Reference: Becker, Howard S. (1963). *Outsiders: Studies in the Sociology of Deviance*. New York: The Free Press of Glencoe.

bedlam In general, *bedlam* refers to a great deal of noise and confusion. The term is a shortening of the name of an "insane asylum" in medieval London, St. Mary of Bethlehem.

belief Belief is acceptance by the mind that something (e.g., conventional values, morality, and the legitimacy of law) is true or real. Reference: Hirschi, Travis. (1969). Aspects of the Social Bond. *Causes of Delinquency*. Berkeley, CA: University of California Press.

bell curve Abraham de Moivre (1667–1754) discovered the bell curve when he noticed that many phenomena cluster around an average value and, in so doing, form a bell-shaped curve. The heights of Canadians, for example, cluster around an average height, and if all heights were graphed, a bell-shaped curve would appear. The normal curve is a similar idea and has a similar shape, but is a theoretical curve (or one derived from mathematical manipulation rather than observation) and was developed by Friedrich Gauss (1777–1855) to depict the effects of random variation. For example, if you collect 100 samples from a population in which you know the average value of a phenomenon (e.g., support for a political party), the means of the 100 samples will cluster around the true mean (the population mean) according to the characteristics of the normal curve. The normal curve is symmetrical, so if you draw a line from the highest point of the curve to the base, half of the curve will lie on one side and half on the other. Further, approximately 68% of the area of the entire curve is located between lines drawn at plus and minus 1 standard deviation (a standardized amount of deviation from the mean), and 95% of the area of the curve lies between lines drawn at plus and minus 2 standard deviations. In the example of drawing 100 samples from a population, it can now be said that 95 of the means obtained from these samples will fall within plus or minus 2 standard deviations of the true mean. Once the calculation of standard deviation is learned, you can then calculate the sampling error when doing sampling and estimate the value of a phenomenon in a population based on one sample. This is what is implied when an opinion poll in the newspaper reports that "a sample of this size is accurate to within plus or minus x%, 19 times out of 20" (i.e., 95% of the time).

Beothuk peoples The Beothuk lived for many years in what is now called Newfoundland and may have been the first aboriginals in North America to encounter European explorers and settlers. Settlement led to several periods of conflict and some mass killings. As a result of disease and a reduction in access to their food supply, the Beothuk eventually died out; the last, Shananditti, died in 1829.

berdache In several early North American First Nations cultures, a male berdache took on the roles of women and might also dress as a woman and engage in sexual intimacy with men. More recently, the term *Two Spirits*, which has traditional roots, has been preferred. Berdache status is interpreted as a way of integrating deviant members into cohesive, small societies. While the term is sometimes used to refer to women who take on male roles, there does not appear to have been female berdache in North America, and authors tend to prefer the term *Amazon* to describe these women. Both of these terms are important parts of the anthropology of gender and sexuality and reveal the social or cultural construction of gender. Reference: Roscoe, Will. (1998). *Changing Ones: Third and Fourth Genders in Native North America*. New York: St. Martin's Press. *See also* **Amazon**.

Berger Report *See* **Mackenzie Valley Pipeline Inquiry**.

Bering Strait theory Also referred to as the *land bridge theory*, the Bering Strait theory relates to the origins of human habitation of North America. On three occasions during the last Ice Age (70,000 to 10,000 years ago), sea levels were so low that the areas of Siberia, Alaska, and the Yukon formed one landmass. Since people were known to have lived in Siberia at least 35,000 years ago, it is postulated that they followed animals into the New World, thus beginning the first human settlement. There is growing debate about the veracity of this theory. Among other competitors is the coastal route theory, claiming that the first inhabitants came by boat along the northern and western coasts of Canada. Another theory, the Atlantic marine theory, claims that the first inhabitants came from Europe by boat. Reference: Dewar, E. (2001). *Bones: Discovering the First Americans*. Toronto: Random House Canada.

Beringia The landmass created during the last Ice Age, which connected Siberia, Alaska, and the Yukon, was named Beringia after Vitus Bering, a Danish explorer for the Russian tzar in the 18th century, who explored the waters of the North Pacific between Asia and North America.

Berlin Wall A barrier of barbed wire and, later, of concrete and minefields, the Berlin Wall was built in 1961 between the eastern (communist-controlled) sector of the city of Berlin and the western sector. The wall was built at the direction of the Soviet Union to prevent migration from east to west and to minimize cultural contact between East and West Berlin. With the uprising against communism in East Germany in 1989, the East German government was forced to declare free rights of emigration for all citizens, and in December of 1989 the wall was opened for free passage. Soon after, Germany was reunited and the eastern part integrated into the Federal Republic of Germany. The divided Germany became a site for criminologists to test theories about the criminogenic character of capitalism and of socialism. It was often argued that East Germany (socialism) produced lower crime rates. *See also* **Cold War**.

Bernardo, Paul, & Karla Homolka Convicted in 1995 of the first-degree murder of teenagers Leslie Mahaffy and Kristen French, Paul Bernardo and his wife Karla Homolka had abducted, raped, tortured, and murdered the two teenagers in separate incidents. The two had also raped Homolka's sister, who subsequently died, perhaps of the drug used to render her unconscious. The couple had videotaped their crimes and while these tapes were not found in time to be used as evidence and Bernardo's lawyer did not immediately turn them over to the police, a great controversy ensued about the right to show these tapes. Bernardo was also charged with 18 other rapes that occurred over a period of six years. Bernardo received a sentence of life imprisonment. Homolka received a 12-year sentence because she gave evidence about Bernardo's involvement in the murders and she was portrayed as being forced into the activities by her husband. When the evidence of the videotapes became available, it was less clear whether she had been the unwilling accomplice she claimed to be. On July 4, 2005, Homolka was released from prison, having served her sentence until almost the last hour. Prior to her release, the Crown, using a seldom-used section of the *Criminal Code* (810.02), was able to obtain a court decision placing strict conditions on Homolka after her release. A few months later, however, the Quebec Superior Court struck down these conditions. Reference: Williams, S. (1997). *Invisible Darkness: The Strange Case of Paul Bernardo and Karla Homolka.* Toronto: Little Brown.

bicameral legislature A bicameral legislature has two houses: upper and lower. This is a common feature of federal systems like those of Canada, Australia, Germany, the United States, and India, in which there is a lower house, where representation is based on population, and an upper house, where representation is based on an allocation of seats to regions and provinces or states. Generally, the houses have similar powers, although it is customary, as it is in Canada, that financial legislation must be initiated in the population-based lower house. While Canada's House of Commons is elected, the Senate consists of members chosen by the prime minister and appointed by the governor general to serve until age 75. A long-term prime minister may therefore have lasting influence on the party composition of the Senate. Britain also has a bicameral legislature, although it is a unitary state: The lower House of Commons is elected on a population basis and the upper House of Lords combines members appointed for life on the recommendation of the prime minister, members who hold inherited seats as representatives of Britain's landed aristocracy, senior appeal court judges, and the bishops and archbishops of Britain's Anglican Church.

bicultural This term was coined in 1963, when Prime Minister Lester Pearson established the Royal Commission on Bilingualism and Biculturalism. *Bicultural* implied that Canada was composed of two cultures reflecting the two dominant language groups and two nations struggling for accommodation within Canada. Within a very few years, the concept of multiculturalism gained dominance, as Prime Minister Pierre Trudeau attempted to present a vision of one Canada united by tolerance and support for diversity. The equality of French and English was enshrined in an official policy of bilingualism, guaranteeing equality of access to federal government services and institutions in either official language throughout Canada. Later, the *Canadian Charter of Rights and Freedoms* contained in the *Constitution Act, 1982* added further support to bilingualism. It guarantees that individuals resident anywhere in Canada, who have French or English as their first language or who were educated in either French or English, have the right, if there are sufficient students in this category, to a primary and secondary education in that language.

bilineal descent A system of family descent where blood links and rights of inheritance through both male and female ancestors are of equal importance is called a *bilineal descent* system.

Bilingualism and Biculturalism (Royal Commission on) Established by the Canadian government in 1963 and active until 1969, the Royal Commission on Bilingualism and Biculturalism was charged with the responsibility of examining the status and role of French in Canadian government and other public institutions and in the social life of Canada. Headed jointly by André Laurendeau and A. Davidson Dutton, the commission also included the celebrated constitutional lawyer and mentor of Pierre Trudeau, Frank Scott. Later, the commission also examined the place of other ethnic cultures in Canadian society. The most important outcome of the commission's work was the federal government's adoption of official bilingualism enshrined in the *Official Languages Act, 1969.*

Bill In parliamentary procedure, all proposals submitted to Parliament to be passed into law are called *Bills.* Once a Bill is passed by both the House of Commons and the Senate and has received royal assent, it becomes a statutory Act of Parliament.

Bill 101 Passed by the Parti Québécois government of Quebec in 1977 and creating a charter for the

French language, Bill 101 was a further development of Bill 22, which was enacted by the Quebec Liberal government of Robert Bourassa in 1974. The Bill had first been introduced by the newly elected Parti Québécois government as Bill 1, to symbolically express the reclamation of the province and the French language from the English. The draft of Bill 1 was withdrawn under pressure, but substantially reintroduced as Bill 101. This Bill declares French to be the language of government, work, and instruction in the province of Quebec, and forces immigrants to attend school in French (with limited exceptions). The law was found to conflict with the *Canadian Charter of Rights and Freedoms* in the *Constitution Act* of 1982, and was struck down by Quebec's Superior Court and the Supreme Court of Canada. Quebec responded by restoring the law, using the "notwithstanding" provision of the *Constitution* that allows Parliament and provincial legislatures to override certain *Charter* provisions. The event intensified Quebec's deep resentment of the adoption of Canada's 1982 *Constitution* without the agreement of Quebec's legislature. *See also* **Parti Québécois**.

Bill of Rights *See Canadian Bill of Rights.*

bin Laden, Osama Born in Saudi Arabia in 1957, bin Laden became known as the most wanted man in the Western world due to his direction and financing of terrorist attacks, primarily on the United States. When the Soviet Union invaded Afghanistan in 1979, bin Laden went to Afghanistan to respond to what he saw as an attack on Islam. The resistance movement he was part of eventually gained sufficient support from the United States to drive the Soviet Union out of Afghanistan. The resistance movement then began to struggle to create an Islamic state within Afghanistan and to export this revolution to other Islamic nations. Osama bin Laden was in Saudi Arabia during the Persian Gulf War, a war in which Saudi Arabia surrendered a great deal of sovereignty for United States protection. Again, bin Laden demonstrated his outrage at this treatment of Muslims and was placed under house arrest. He subsequently returned to Afghanistan and used his wealth to organize the dispossessed and disenfranchised of the Muslim world. He appeared to survive the United States invasion of Afghanistan and continues to communicate with followers. Reference: Anonymous. 2003. *Through Our Enemies' Eyes:*

Osama bin Laden, Radical Islam and the Future of America. Dulles, VA: Brassey's Inc. *See also* **terrorism; World Trade Center, New York**.

biosphere The total inhabitable area of land, air, and water is called the *biosphere*. Within the biosphere, the basic unit of analysis or study is the ecosystem.

birth rate The birth rate is calculated as the number of births in a given population during a particular year, divided by the actual population, and then multiplied by 1,000, to give a birth rate per 1,000 of the population. The resulting figure is known as the *crude birth rate*. Generally, to observe trends and predict population growth, demographers (statistical analysts of population) use *fertility rates*, which relate the number of births not to total population but to the population of women in their child-bearing years (usually defined as from 15 to 49 years of age). Birth rates are of interest in predicting crime trends, since crime and age are closely correlated. *See also* **baby boom; fertility rate**.

Black Panthers A Black militant party, the Black Panthers were founded (1966) in Oakland, California, by Huey P. Newton and Bobby Seale. Originally encouraging violent revolution as the means of achieving Black liberation, the Black Panthers called on all Blacks to arm themselves for the liberation struggle. The Black Panthers were involved in many violent confrontations, and several people were killed. Many of the Black Panthers brought to trial were eventually acquitted, and the killing by the police of two Black Panthers while in their beds confirmed that this group had been subjected to extreme police harassment.

Black, Davidson (1885–1934) A Canadian anatomist and amateur paleoanthropologist, Davidson Black was involved in the discovery and naming of "Peking Man." *See also* **Peking Man**.

Blishen scale Based on the Pineo–Porter index, Canadian sociologist Bernard Blishen developed the Blishen scale, an index of occupational prestige, educational requirements, and income for a list of occupations. Knowing a person's occupation then can be used as an indicator of their socioeconomic status, and the researcher never has to ask a person about his or her income. Reference: Blishen, Bernard R. (1967). A socioeconomic index of occupations in Canada. *Canadian Review of Sociology and Anthropology*, 4, 41–53.

Bloc Québécois This political party was formed in 1991 after the failure of the *Meech Lake Accord*, which had proposed extensive constitutional changes. The Accord would have created increased powers for the provinces and a unique status for Quebec within Confederation. Federal Cabinet Minister Lucien Bouchard left the Progressive Conservative government in protest at the failure and founded the Bloc Québécois with the main goal of promoting the agenda of a sovereign Quebec at the federal level of politics. The founding of the Bloc contributed to the electoral destruction of the Progressive Conservatives in the 1993 election, when they were reduced to two seats in the House of Commons. In that and subsequent elections, the Bloc has won a large majority of the parliamentary seats in Quebec.

Bluefish Caves This archaeological site, located about 54 kilometres from the community of Old Crow in the Yukon, has yielded evidence of possibly the earliest human presence in North America. Bones and small tools have been found that date back to between 15,000 and 12,000 years ago, and there are claims of evidence of human habitation as far back as 23,500 years ago.

BNA Act *See **British North America Act**.*

Boas, Franz (1858–1942) German cultural anthropologist Franz Boas was born in Germany and began his career there, but a trip to Baffin Island in 1883–1884 and then to British Columbia in 1886 shaped his interest in studying culture and he remained in North America for the rest of his life. Having a background in science, Boas quickly saw the importance of the new field of anthropology being established on a solid foundation of evidence and he also saw the need to gather this evidence quickly, as European exploration and development threatened the way of life of many native peoples. His field methods continue to influence anthropology and his record of native languages and observations of many aspects of culture continue to be important. Perhaps his greatest legacy is the number of anthropologists he trained and sent into the field. In his writing, Boas challenged the conventional academic wisdom that tried to build explanations on the back of race or ideas of the primitive mind. Reference: Stocking, George (Ed.). (1974). *The shaping of American anthropology, 1883–1911: A Franz Boas reader*. New York: Basic.

Bomarc missiles *See **Lament for a Nation**.*

Bountiful A town of between 600 and 1,000 people in the southern interior of British Columbia, Bountiful is home to one of five breakaway Mormon sects in North America that still practise polygamy. While the Mormons banned this practice in 1890, there have always been some holdouts. In Canada, the Bountiful religious leader argues that the *Charter of Rights and Freedoms* protects this aspect of the religion, and perhaps the Canadian government is reluctant to actually test this provision. Some legal actions have been taken against groups in the United States, and in Canada there is growing pressure on governments to respond to concerns about early "marriages" of children and the coercion of women.

Bourdieu, Pierre *See **cultural capital**.*

bourgeois From the French, *bourgeois* means *middle class*. In feudal time, the cities had become the place of business and residence for a growing class of merchants, professionals, and craftspersons. They were seen as having a social status between the peasant class and the land-owning or aristocratic class—hence the idea that they were the middle class. This new middle class came to feel oppressed by the traditions and restrictions of feudalism and aristocratic rule, and eventually were able to grasp power and transform social values. They are associated with the Bloodless Revolution of Great Britain in 1688 and the French Revolution in 1789. The term *bourgeois class*, or *bourgeoisie*, was used by Marx to refer to the corporate or capitalist class in modern societies that is thought, particularly in socialist perspectives, to be also a ruling class.

BP It is customary when using radiocarbon dating, and other dating methods, to give the age of objects using the initials "BP," which stand for "Before the Present," rather than using the Christian calendar.

bracketing A term derived from German philosopher Edmund Husserl (1859–1938), *bracketing* describes a method used by phenomenological sociologists and ethnomethodologists. This approach focuses on revealing the beliefs, ideas, and values that are simply taken for granted in the social world. By suspending belief in the naturalness and normality of the social world (placing what are normally automatic assumptions in brackets), it reveals the underlying thinking and values that people bring to bear in understanding the world and engaging in social action. This analysis then gives the researcher the information necessary to investigate the ordinary methods that social members use to comprehend the social world and give it reality and concreteness.

branch plants Subsidiaries of a parent corporation headquartered in another country, branch plants, usually of United States corporations, are a prominent feature of the Canadian economy. There is great controversy about the role of branch plants: Some analysts view them as an important engine of Canadian economic development, while others claim that they have helped to obstruct the autonomous development of the Canadian economy and maintain a state of national technological and economic dependency.

Brave New World In his 1932 book *Brave New World*, British futurist and social critic Aldous L. Huxley (1894–1963) imagines that the authorities of society use new technologies, drugs, and instruments of propaganda like subliminal advertising to keep people happy and unaware or unconcerned about what is actually happening to them and their communities.

Bretton Woods Conference Against the backdrop of the great depression and World War II, the United States, having emerged as the new global military and economic power, initiated a conference held at Bretton Woods, New Hampshire, in July 1944. The purpose of this conference was to forge a set of international institutions designed to bring about world economic stability through international cooperation on economic matters and to serve as a vehicle for reconstruction of nations ravaged by war. The International Monetary Fund and the World Bank were developed at this time, and the World Bank made its first loan (to France) in October 1946. The International Trade Organization that was also discussed at this historical meeting did not materialize until the World Trade Organization was created in 1994. Note that the charter for the United Nations was drafted in 1945.

Bre-X A mining company whose stocks soared on claims of an enormous gold find, Bre-X went bankrupt in November of 1997 when it was found that the core samples taken from the area had been "salted" (gold was added to the samples after extraction) and the "gold deposit" was worthless. While billions of dollars were lost by investors, many people, including Bre-X company executives, made millions on stock deals. Reference: Goold, D., & Willis, A. (1997). *The Bre-X Fraud*. Toronto: McClelland and Stewart.

bride price The transfer of wealth or possessions by the prospective groom's family to the prospective bride's family before marriage, the bride price is considered by some to be similar to the engagement ring.

British Commonwealth *See* **Commonwealth**.

British North America Act (BNA Act) Passed by the British Parliament in 1867, the *British North America Act* created the nation of Canada. The *BNA Act* was the *Constitution* of Canada, as it provided the legal framework in which the political relations of the peoples of the nation were to be carried out. The most distinctive feature of the *BNA Act* was its division of powers between the federal and provincial governments. This Act provided no means for its own amendment; this could be done only by Britain's Parliament at Canada's request. In 1982, Canada adopted a new *Constitution* that established complete constitutional autonomy from Britain; the *BNA Act* was then renamed the *Constitution Act, 1867. See also* **constitution**.

brokerage party A political party that is not driven by ideology but by a pragmatic desire to gain and retain political power, a brokerage party, although usually allied to business interests, generally pursues centrist policies and attempts to command the middle ground in public debate. Patronage is an important incentive to party membership and for mobilizing financial support.

Brown vs. Topeka Board of Education The U.S. Supreme Court 1954 ruling in the *Brown vs. Topeka Board of Education* case set aside a Kansas statute that permitted cities of over 15,000 to maintain separate schools for Blacks and Whites. The court ruled that all segregation in public schools was inherently unequal. This ruling began the desegregation of schooling and eventually of other public places and programs. Prior to this, the U. S. Supreme Court had found that segregation did not breach civil rights and was constitutional, and America became increasingly racially divided. *See also* **White Paper (1969)**.

bulimia A mental disorder associated with food and body image, bulimia is sometimes life-threatening. A person with this disorder will engage in binge eating followed by periods of vomiting or laxative use. The late Princess Diana was a celebrity sufferer of this condition.

bureaucracy A formal organization with defined objectives, a bureaucracy is a hierarchy of specialized roles and systematic processes of direction and administration. Bureaucracy was found in earlier times in history (for example, in administration of agricultural irrigation systems, the Roman army, and the Catholic Church), but it became most prominent in the large-scale administration of agencies of the modern state and modern business corporations. German sociologist Max Weber (1864–1920) gave particular attention to bureaucracy and saw this form of social organization becoming dominant in modern society due to the commitment to the value of rationalization—the organization of social activity so as to most efficiently achieve goals. *See also* **rationalization**.

Business Council on National Issues Now called the Canadian Council of Chief Executives, the Business Council on National Issues was formed in 1976, largely in response to the nationalist policies of the Trudeau (Liberal) government. Its members represent 150 leading Canadian corporations (many foreign-owned or foreign-controlled) dedicated to shaping economic and social policy so as to achieve a quite specific agenda. The group supports free trade (and may have initiated the early discussion of this topic), and it has been speculated that it provided much of the policy for the Conservative government elected in 1984. For sociologists, the group is of interest as a visible demonstration of the social and political linking of corporations.

Butler case The debate around pornography and obscenity reached the Canadian Supreme Court with the *R. vs. Butler* case (1992), and the outcome was historic. The court used the opportunity to examine and clarify the underlying rationale for the regulation of sexual expression. The *Criminal Code* states that obscenity is "the undue exploitation of sex or of sex and one or more of the following subjects; namely, crime, horror, cruelty and violence." The Supreme Court said that the meaning of "undue" must be determined by a community standard of tolerance and then added that "this determination must be made on the basis of the degree of harm that may flow from such exposure, harm of the type which predisposes persons to act in an anti-social manner." In explicitly finding pornography to be harmful, the court said it harms women's rights to be equal, their sense of self-worth, and their physical safety. This ruling made it clear that obscenity is not about the explicitness of sex nor is it about one morality versus another; rather, it is about harm. Reference: *R. v. Butler* [1992] 1 S.C.R. 452.

bystander problem In 1964, Kitty Genovese was attacked and murdered on a New York street—over a period of half an hour—while 38 bystanders watched. After this horrific event, the question was asked: Why did no one call the police or go to her assistance? Many assumed this incident was a sign of the anonymity of modern urban life, but when social scientists began to research the problem, they found that responsibility became dispersed, allowing each person to assume that the other must have taken responsibility. Reference: Darley, J., & Latane, B. (1968). Bystander intervention in emergencies: Diffusion of responsibility. *Journal of Personality and Social Psychology, 8,* 377–383.

C

C-31 Indian A 1985 amendment to the *Indian Act*, Bill C-31 led to the term "C-31 Indian" being used as a reference to a new category of Status Indian. In the past, native women were discriminated against if they married a non-Status Indian or a non-Indian. In these circumstances, they lost their Indian status and could not confer status on their children. Similarly, natives who had chosen to be enfranchised had been required to give up their Indian status. Bill C-31 attempted to rectify this discrimination in order to conform to the equality provisions of the 1982 *Canadian Charter of Rights and Freedoms*. Children born out of wedlock could have their Indian status acknowledged if either parent was a registered Indian. Further, Indian status was open to those who had lost it due to discrimination or enfranchisement. The Bill also prevented people from losing or gaining status through marriage. The Bill also gave native bands control over their membership list. In effect, a band could refuse membership to the new category of Status Indians created through this Bill. This Bill has resulted in a great deal of conflict, as it swells the numbers of registered Indians and leads to the possibility of some people being registered and yet not being accepted as members of any bands, thus affecting their rights under the *Indian Act*.

Calder case *Calder v. Attorney General of British Columbia* (1973) involved a request by the Nisga'a peoples of British Columbia for a declaration that legal title to their land had not been lawfully extinguished. The Supreme Court of Canada's decision in favour of the Nisga'a considerably advanced the position of aboriginal peoples in their claims that aboriginal ownership of land had been continuous and had survived European colonization. Six of the seven judges agreed that aboriginal legal ownership of the land had existed prior to the arrival of Europeans. In deciding whether this legal ownership still existed, three judges stated that the aboriginal peoples did still own the land, while the other three judges argued that they had ceded effective control to the Crown and implicit extinguishment had taken place (the seventh judge ruled on a technical matter, so did not address the question of legal ownership). In 1974, largely in response to this decision, the federal government established an office to deal with native land claims. In April 2000, after long and complex negotiations and intense public debate, the Canadian Parliament passed the *Nisga'a Final Agreement Act*, which settled land claims and established a limited sphere of self-government. Reference: *Calder v. Attorney General of British Columbia* (1973) 34 D.L.R. (3d) 145; Tennant, Paul. (1990). *Aboriginal Peoples and Politics: The Indian Land Question of British Columbia, 1849–1989*. Vancouver: University of British Columbia Press.

call girl A call girl is a type of prostitute who waits to be called by a client rather than one who stands on a street corner or looks for clients in bars or other locations. Call girls tend to be more "up-market" and expensive than street prostitutes.

Calvinism A Christian doctrine associated with French reformer and theologian John Calvin (1509–1564), Calvinism was seen by German sociologist Max Weber (1864–1920) as a component of the Protestant ethic, a set of social and religious ideas he considered to be favourable to the development of capitalism. *See also* **Protestant ethic**.

Canada Assistance Plan (CAP) Federal legislation passed in 1966, the Canada Assistance Plan (CAP) was considered by many to be a keystone of the Canadian welfare state. The legislation required the federal government to shoulder half of the cost of social programs undertaken by the provinces, chiefly social assistance (welfare programs). This policy enabled the federal government to set national standards for social programs and, backed by its right to withhold payments to provinces whose policies did not conform to federal standards, it was able to impose some consistency across the country. In 1991, the federal government imposed a limit on the funds it would pay out for social programs to more affluent provinces, and this led to the situation where the federal government was paying only approximately one-third of the actual costs. In 1996, CAP was replaced by the Canada Health and Social Transfer program, which combines federal funding for health, postsecondary education, and welfare, and transfers a designated amount of money to each province rather than transferring a percentage of actual costs. The replacement of the CAP was seen as the end of an era by many Canadians since it reduces the ability of the federal government to impose national standards and will encourage many provinces to reduce their social spending to fit within the transferred funds. Social programs that soften the impact of the free market on individuals are of interest to social scientists since research suggests that crime rates can be reduced by such programs.

Canada Health and Social Transfer Program *See* Canada Assistance Plan.

Canadian Bill of Rights The *Canadian Bill of Rights* was adopted by the Conservative government of John Diefenbaker in 1960 and was a significant, but not extremely useful, step in the evolution of human rights legislation in Canada. The Bill was not part of the nation's highest law (the *Constitution*), so it could be amended like any other piece of legislation and covered only federal legislation. *See also* *Canadian Charter of Rights and Freedoms*.

Canadian Charter of Rights and Freedoms Part of the *Constitution Act, 1982,* the *Charter* came into effect in April 1982. The *Charter* provides protection for a wide range of individual rights typical of liberal democracies but until this time not constitutionally protected in Canada. As a part of the *Constitution* of Canada, the *Charter* cannot be changed without the consent of both Parliament and the provincial legislatures. The *Charter* includes provisions to protect mobility rights and minority language rights. The provincial legislature of Quebec did not support the *Constitution Act* of 1982, and its adoption without this consent increased nationalist support for sovereignty in Quebec. Several efforts have subsequently been made to make constitutional changes and achieve consensus with Quebec. *See also* **Canadian Bill of Rights; Charlottetown Accord; constitution; Meech Lake Accord.**

Canadian Citizenship Act (1947) This Act changed the status of a Canadian from that of a British subject to a Canadian citizen. It was an important milestone in the process of eliminating colonial ties and creating a sense of distinctive Canadian identity.

Canadian Council of Chief Executives *See* **Business Council on National Issues.**

Canadian Press Begun in 1917, Canadian Press is a cooperative operated by 98 member newspapers and 500 broadcast partners. The agency supplies Canadian newspapers and broadcast media with the majority of their domestic and world news. In 1996, there was concern that the continuing concentration of ownership of newspapers would result in the breakdown of the cooperative and lead to fewer sources of news.

cannabis Also known as *marijuana, Mary Jane, dope, pot, grass, ganja*, and a wide variety of other terms, cannabis is a drug derived from the leaves of the *cannabis sativa*, a member of the hemp plant family. Ingestion of this drug is known to decrease physical activity, change estimations of space and time, increase appetite, and frequently lead to euphoria. It is not known to be addictive, and in recent years its medicinal effects have been noted and are now being scientifically studied. Canada has passed regulations making the medical use of cannabis legal; the government has contracted with a company to produce the plant. The general use of cannabis remains forbidden under the *Controlled Drugs and Substances Act* and is a criminal offence, although there have been several attempts to decriminalize possession and use of the drug. In September 2002, a Senate committee recommended that marijuana possession and cultivation be made legal (not just noncriminal), and that only behaviour causing demonstrable harm to others— illegal trafficking, selling to minors, and impaired driving—should be prohibited. The report also calls on the government to declare an amnesty for any person convicted of possession of cannabis under current or past legislation. Reference: Special Committee of the Senate of Canada. (September 2002). *Cannabis: Our Position for a Canadian Public Policy*. Ottawa: Government of Canada; Alexander, Bruce K. (1990). *Peaceful Measures: Canada's Way Out of the "War on Drugs."* Toronto: University of Toronto Press. *See also* **Le Dain Commission.**

cannibalism This term was first used by Christopher Columbus and his explorers, who had brought a Carib Indian (after whose tribe the Caribbean Sea was named) back to Spain for exhibition. The Spanish misheard the name of the island people as "Canib," which over time was changed to "canibales," meaning thirsty and cruel in Spanish; this version soon became changed further into "cannibal." Chroniclers of that time reported that the Carib people engaged in eating of human flesh. It is now agreed that various people throughout the world have engaged in this practice, although it was often associated with mysticism and ritual. In archaeology and anthropology, the term used for this practice is *anthropophagy*.

capital Central to a capitalist economic system, capital is an accumulation of goods or wealth used for the production of other goods and services, rather than for immediate or personal use. If one just plays games on a computer, the computer cannot be considered capital. However, if the computer is used to produce reports or graphs that are then sold, the computer can be considered as capital. *See also* **capitalism.**

capital accumulation The process of accumulating resources for use in the production of goods and services is called *capital accumulation*. Private capital accumulation takes place when productive capacity exceeds immediate consumption needs. For example, a farmer can accumulate capital (stored grains, improved equipment, etc.) during years of good harvests and good farm revenues. Generally, accumulation is directly linked to profitability: The resources used to make commodities can be replaced and augmented when the commodity is sold for a profit. Capital accumulation can also take place in the public sector, where, from a structuralist approach within a conflict perspective, the state is seen as performing the function of aiding in the accumulation of private capital. This function may be performed by the state providing an educated work force (human capital), building rail lines into resource areas, maintaining a legal system to resolve contract disputes, and providing tax incentives or tax breaks. *See also* **structuralist approach.**

capitalism Capitalism is an economic system in which economic activity is primarily directed toward the production of commodities for sale in the marketplace. The capital to carry out production (the goods or wealth used to produce other goods for profit) is privately owned, and profit is reinvested so as to accumulate capital. Since the system is competitive, constant reinvestment and development of the means of production are required to maintain a producer's market position and this leads to an unending process of technological development and transformation. *See also* **capital; labour theory of value**.

capital punishment Punishment of crime by execution of the offender is termed *capital punishment*. The word *capital* is from Latin, referring to the head, the locus of life. While capital punishment is still widely imposed in world societies, it has been abolished in the countries of Western Europe and in Canada. The last hanging in Canada took place in 1962, after which the Canadian government routinely advised the governor general to commute all death sentences. Capital punishment was formally abolished by changes to the law in 1976. A free vote was held in the House of Commons in 1987, and the majority supported the continued abolition of the death penalty. Reference: Archer, Dana, Gartner, Rosemary, & Ceittel, Marc. (1983). Homicide and the Death Penalty: A Cross-National Test of the Deterrence Hypothesis. *Journal of Criminal Law and Criminology, 74*, 991–1014.

career In common usage, *career* refers to the sequence of stages through which people in a particular occupational sector move during the course of their employment. It has also been applied to analyzing the various stages of an individual's involvement with criminal activity.

cargo cult A form of millenarian movement (a belief in what is to come), cargo cults are found in the islands of Melanesia in the South Pacific. These cults believe that ritual activities and observances will lead to the arrival of free cargoes of goods. It appears that the cults developed from the indigenous belief that necessary goods and animals for food and supplies are released by the gods or guardian spirits when the people have completed proper ritual observances. The influence of the modern world is evidenced today in that the cargoes are expected to arrive by boat or plane, as do the goods and supplies used by White immigrants and colonizers. These cults have proved to be enduring even when cargo does not materialize,

since this is seen as a sign that ritual observation and activity has been inadequate or inappropriate. *See also* **revitalization movement**.

carrying capacity A term from ecology, *carrying capacity* refers to the level of land or resource use—by humans or animals—that can be sustained over the long term by the natural regenerative power of the environment.

Cashel, Mount (Orphanage abuse) *See* **Mount Cashel Orphanage abuse**.

caste A status group, within a system of hierarchical social stratification, in which membership is hereditary is called a *caste*. Caste differentiations are usually based on religious and mythical traditions, and caste membership determines occupational roles, place of residence, and legal and customary rights and duties. Caste is maintained from generation to generation by the practice of within-caste marriage (endogamy) and strict formality in social interaction with other castes. *See also* **class**.

caucus Each party in a legislature forms an organized group—a caucus—to support or oppose a government. When a party is in office, the main role of the caucus is to organize support for the government, contribute to party discipline through peer pressure, and maintain party morale. An Opposition party caucus allocates roles as government critics among its members, corresponding to the roles of government ministers.

causality In order to establish causality (a relationship between two variables such that one [the independent variable] can be claimed to have caused the other [the dependent variable]), three conditions must be met: (1) there must be a correlation or association between variables, (2) the independent variable (the cause) must occur before the dependent variable (the effect), and (3) the relationship must not be spurious. *See also* **spuriousness; variables**.

cause Those features or characteristics that produce a particular effect (e.g., characteristics that might cause an individual to commit a crime) are examples of *cause*. Causal analysis is a positivist approach to social science. In order for something to be a cause, it must meet four criteria: (1) the cause must happen before the effect, (2) there must be a correlation between the causal variable and the effect variable, (3) all other possible reasons for the correlation must be examined and discarded, and

(4) a theory should be available that links the cause to the effect. *See also* **theory**.

CCF *See* **Co-operative Commonwealth Federation**.

Chambliss, William Professor of sociology at George Washington University, William Chambliss is associated with the development of conflict perspectives within criminology. He argues that people's social experiences as individuals and their interactions with groups shape individual values and norms. In a complex society, there are many groups in a wide variety of social and economic situations and, consequently, there is normative conflict between these groups and their members. Those groups that have more social and political power are able to have their norms and values enshrined within the law and reflected in the application of law. Consequently, the law reflects the norms and values of dominant classes and opposes the norms and values associated with the poor, criminalizing the behaviour of many poor and powerless citizens. Chambliss grounded this general theoretical approach in historical analysis of the law and policing, and in participant observation work that led to a controversial exposure of political corruption, racketeering, and organized crime in Seattle. Reference: Chambliss, William. (1978). *On the Take: From Petty Crooks to Presidents.* Bloomington, IN: Indiana University Press.

Chantek *See* **language among nonhuman primates**.

Charlottetown Accord An agreement between the federal government of Canada and the 10 provincial governments, the *Charlottetown Accord* proposed amendments to the Canadian *Constitution* established by the *Constitution Act, 1982*. Major aspects of the Accord were the entrenchment of a right to aboriginal self-government and decentralization of power from the federal to provincial governments, as well as clauses recognizing the distinct character of Quebec society and culture. The Accord provided for a national referendum to be called before legislative change was made. The Accord was defeated in a national referendum in 1992. Reference: McRoberts, K., & Monahan, P. (1993). *The Charlottetown Accord, the Referendum and the Future of Canada.* Toronto: University of Toronto Press. *See also* **referendum**.

Charter decisions In 1982, Canada adopted a new *Constitution Act* that, for the first time, included a *Charter of Rights and Freedoms* providing constitutional guarantees of civil rights. Included are fundamental freedoms of thought, belief, and opinion; democratic rights; mobility rights; legal rights (including the right to due legal process); equality and language rights; and aboriginal rights. All laws passed before or subsequently to 1982, by Parliament or a legislature, must be in conformity with these *Charter* guarantees. After the passing of the *Constitution Act, 1982*, and the *Charter*, Canada's courts began to deal with a stream of cases based on the *Charter*. These have included important cases on aboriginal rights, the abortion law (this was struck down as discriminatory against women and as offending provisions for the security of the person), language rights, and access to medical use of marijuana. In some cases, Parliament or a legislature may enact that a law shall be valid notwithstanding provisions of the *Charter*. When this takes place, the law must be renewed by additional legislation every five years. Reference: Greene, Ian. (1989). *The Charter of Rights*. Toronto: Lorimer. *See also* **notwithstanding clause; Supreme Court of Canada**.

charter groups Usually distinguished by ethnic identity, charter groups have played a pioneering role in the opening and development of new territories and immigrant societies. In Canada, these groups have customarily been identified as the British and the French.

Charter of Rights and Freedoms *See* **Canadian Charter of Rights and Freedoms**.

Chicago School Research and social theory that emerged in the first half of the 20th century from the world's first school of sociology at the University of Chicago is referred to as belonging to the Chicago School. Due to its phenomenally rapid growth, the city of Chicago was seen as a laboratory for sociological research into the effects of urbanism on culture and social relationships. In criminology, it focused on the sociocultural causes of urban crime and on crime prevention. Among the Chicago School's major researchers were Robert Park (1864–1944), Ernest Burgess (1866–1966), Louis Wirth (1897–1952), and Frederick Thrasher (1892–1962). Canadian sociology was influenced by the Chicago School through the work of Carl Dawson (1887–1964), who studied at the University of Chicago and brought the perspective of urban studies and social disorganization to McGill University in 1922. Canadian sociologist Everett Hughes (1897–1983), who also trained at the University of Chicago, joined Dawson at McGill. Reference: Shore, Marlene. (1987). *The Science of Social Redemption: McGill, the Chicago School, and the Origins of Social Research in Canada*. Toronto: University of Toronto Press.

chiefdom A chiefdom is a form of political organization in which two or more groups are organized under a single ruling leader (the chief). This office is usually hereditary and occurs in societies that are relatively stratified, so that individual status is shaped by relationship to the chief. Reference: Kurtz, D.V. (2001). *Political anthropology: Paradigms and power*. Boulder: Westview Press.

child pornography *See* **Badgley report; online pornography; Sharpe decision**.

child sex tourism A worldwide effort is being made to curb the part of the multibillion-dollar sex-tourism industry that targets children. Child sex tourism, the practice of travelling to another country for the purpose of sexually exploiting children, is an offence under Canada's *Criminal Code*. In 2005, Donald Bakker of Vancouver became the first person convicted of offences under this legislation. Among other things, he was convicted of sexual offences against 16 young girls in Asia.

chronometric dating Used in archeology to provide, or estimate, a fairly absolute age of items, chronometic dating allows for dating on the modern calendar. The three most frequently used methods are radio-carbon analysis, potassium-argon analysis, and amino acid racemization. *See also* **relative dating**.

church An institution composed of members sharing some common religious and ethical views and joining them together in religious celebration and social activities is defined as a church. Churches, as distinct from sects or cults, tend to be established, culturally accepted, and broadly supportive of the surrounding institutions of society; to be hierarchical; and to have a priesthood or set of authorized office holders. *See also* **cult; sect**.

citizen Originally, citizenship was a status possessed by individuals in ancient Roman society, distinguishing them as free individuals with full legal rights from those, like slaves, who were in servitude and lacked civil rights. *Citizen* is used generally to refer to an individual as an active member of a democratic political community. It was not until the *Canadian Citizenship Act* of 1947 that the people of Canada became "Canadian citizens."

Prior to that date, immigrants and native-born people alike were simply British subjects.

Citizenship Act (1947) *See* **Canadian Citizenship Act**.

civilization Archaeologists and anthropologists use the term *civilization* to describe societies that exhibit complex culture and social organization. Characteristics of complexity can include the presence of cities, occupational specialization, intensive agricultural production, social stratification, long-distance trade and commerce, monumental public architecture, and writing and other intellectual achievements. Using these characteristics, it is possible to identify many ancient societies, such as the Babylonians, Egyptians, Chinese, Greeks, Romans, and the Maya of Mesoamerica, as civilizations. Social scientists often prefer to avoid the term because it was used in a moral sense by Europeans during the 19th and early 20th centuries to suggest a contrast between civilized societies and uncivilized less-complex societies and became part of an ideology upholding colonial domination.

civil society The concept of civil society captures that sphere of social life between the intimate bonds of the family and friends, the formal organizations of the state, and the restraining forces of the economy. As such, it includes voluntary organizations, community groups, and organizations such as unions and churches. If the role of the state is to shrink, then family life and civil society may come to play a larger role in society. The reverse may hold, as well. Marxists see history as being made from the dynamics of civil society.

clan A noncorporate kin group with unilineal descent, a clan unites a number of lineages originating with a common ancestor (this may be more imagined than real). Clan members may share a common name.

Clarity Act The near-victory for Quebec sovereigntist forces in the 1995 referendum forced Canadian politicians to address a question they had tried to avoid: If Quebec was to separate from Canada, under what conditions could this legally be done? In 1998, the federal government referred the issue to the Supreme Court in the *Reference re Secession of Quebec*. In its ruling, the Supreme Court concluded that any referendum question posed to the Quebec public must be "clear" and also that a "clear majority" would be required before negotiations on sovereignty could take place with Canada. Both of these requirements were embodied in a Bill presented to the House of Commons in December 1999. The Bill was passed in 2000 and the resulting Act of Parliament has become generally known as the *Clarity Act*. Reference: Cameron, B. (Ed.). (Not yet published). *The Supreme Court, democracy and Quebec secession.*

Clark, S.D. (1910–2003) Born in Lloydminster, Alberta, sociologist Samuel Delbert Clark studied at the London School of Economics, where he met Canadian political economist Harold Innis (1894–1952). Both were influenced by the British tradition of political economy. On his return to Canada, he taught at the University of Toronto (where he received his Ph.D.) and in 1962 became the first chair of the sociology department. Until then, sociology had been a branch of the Department of Political Economy. Clark worked with Innis to establish a distinctively Canadian approach to sociology, and his publications and research identified the importance of this discipline. He developed a tradition of looking at Canadian social development and focused on the facts of Canada as a hinterland and a colony. Reference: Magill, D.W., et al. (Eds.). (1999). *Images of Change.* Toronto: Canadian Scholars' Press. *See also* **Innis, Harold.**

class The term *class* is used in various ways in sociology. It usually implies a group of individuals sharing a common situation within a social structure, usually their shared place in the structure of ownership and control of the means of production. Karl Marx (1818–1883), German philosopher, social scientist, historian, and revolutionary, for example, distinguished four classes in capitalist societies, a bourgeois class that owned and controlled the means of production, a petite bourgeoisie of small business owners and professionals, a proletariat of wage workers, and a *lumpenproletariat* of people in poverty and social disorganization who are excluded from the wage-earning economy. In land-based economies, class structures are based on an individual's relationship to the ownership and control of land. *Class* can also refer to groups of individuals with a shared characteristic relevant in some socioeconomic measurement or ranking (for example, all individuals earning over $50,000 a year): It then has a statistical meaning rather than being defined by social relationships. While *class* is extensively used in discussing social structure, sociologists also rely on the concept of status, which offers a more complex portrait in which individuals within a class can be seen as having quite differentiated social situations. *See also* **lumpenproletariat; petite bourgeoisie; proletariat; status.**

class consciousness The awareness of individuals in a particular social class that they share common interests and a common social situation, class consciousness is associated with the development of a "class-for-itself," where individuals within the class unite to pursue their shared interests. *See also* **class-for-itself.**

class consciousness, false When members of a social class absorb and become committed to values and beliefs that serve and support the interests of other classes rather than their own, false class consciousness is said to exist. The concept assumes that there is an objective "class interest" of which its members are unaware.

class crystallization It is difficult for individuals to change their social class, because their whole life situation—income, wealth, education, status—is shaped by their class location. *Class crystallization* describes where the divisions between social classes become obvious and somewhat fixed.

class-for-itself A class of individuals conscious of sharing a common social and economic situation, a class-for-itself unites to pursue common interests. *See also* **class consciousness.**

class fraction Usually used by political economy theorists in discussions of the corporate class to acknowledge significant segmentation of this class, class fraction is commonly linked to such distinctions as that between finance-based capital and industrial-based capital, each viewed as having different interests and perspectives. This is a useful concept in avoiding the simplistic view that the "corporate class" is a necessarily unified group.

classical conditioning A basic form of learning whereby a neutral stimulus is paired with another stimulus that naturally elicits a certain response is referred to as *classical conditioning*. The neutral stimulus comes to elicit the same response as the stimulus that automatically elicits the response.

classical criminology Considered to be the first formal school of criminology, classical criminology is associated with 18th- and early 19th-century reforms to the administration of justice and the prison system. Associated with authors such as Cesare Beccaria (1738–1794), Jeremy Bentham (1748–1832), Samuel Romilly (1757–1818), and others, this school brought the emerging philosophy of liberalism and utilitarianism to the justice system, advocating principles of rights, fairness, and due process in place of retribution, arbitrariness, and brutality. Critical criminologists see in these reforms a tool by which the new industrial order of capitalism was able to maintain class rule by appearing to apply objective and neutral rules of justice rather than obvious and direct class domination through coercion. Criminal law is stated in terms of moral universals, rather than being seen as rules that simply protect the interests of property holders. The claims to fairness in the justice system provide a sense of legitimation for the state and the order it represents. Reference: Mannheim, Hermann. (Ed.). (1972). *Pioneers in Criminology* (2nd ed.). Montclair, NJ: Patterson Smith Publishing. *See also* **Positivist School**.

classical economic theory Known also as *laissez faire*, classical economic theory claims that leaving individuals to make free choices in a free market results in the best allocation of scarce resources within an economy and the optimal level of satisfaction for individuals—"the greatest happiness for the greatest number," according to utilitarianism adherents. *See also* **classical liberalism**.

classical liberalism A political and economic philosophy emerging along with the growth of capitalism, classical liberalism's central beliefs are that unregulated free markets are the best means to allocate productive resources and distribute goods and services, and that government intervention should be minimal. Behind this is an assumption about individuals being rational, self-interested, and methodical in the pursuit of their goals. By the end of the 19th century, the belief in free markets became moderated in some versions of liberalism to acknowledge the growing conviction that liberty or freedom for the individual was a hollow promise if the social conditions of society made liberty meaningless. It was believed that the state must become more involved in managing the economy in order to soften the negative effects of market economies and maximize the well-being of each individual. This new direction for liberalism is often referred to as "progressive liberalism." This newer philosophy supported the growth of the welfare state, but has come under attack in the past two decades. Reference: Girvetz, Harry K. (1963). *The Evolution of Liberalism*. New York: Collier. *See also* **classical economic theory; neoconservatism**.

classification of living things In the early days of exploration and observation, a great need arose for a way to bring some order to information being accumulated. The method used in the classification of living things today is a variant of that developed in the 18th century by Carl Linnaeus (1707–1778) (he was also known as Carl von Linné, and he was a Swedish medical doctor whose passion was botany). This scheme organizes everything into a kingdom, phylum, class, order, superfamily, family, subfamily, genus, and species. Humans, for example, fit into the *animalia* kingdom, the mammalian class, the *hominoidea* superfamily, the *genus homo*, and the species *sapiens*. Since it is tradition to use two terms to describe every organism, humans are referred to as *Homo sapiens*.

class-in-itself A social class composed of individuals who objectively share class membership—they share a common social and economic situation—yet who are unconscious of their class membership or of shared interests that unite them are termed a *class-in-itself*.

classless society A society that does not have a hierarchy of different social classes and in which individuals have similar resources of wealth, status, and power is a classless society. Found in simple hunter–gatherer societies (like that of the pygmies of the Congo), a classless society is also a socialist vision of a future society founded on collective ownership of the means of production.

claustrophobia This is an anxiety disorder exhibited by the fear of being in confined spaces.

claw back *Claw back* is a term used to describe Canadian government policy toward what were once considered universal benefits of the welfare state. While all senior citizens receive Old Age Security payments from the government, if an individual's total income exceeds a certain amount, a portion (or all) of this benefit is taxed back (clawed back) through annual individual income taxation. In the future, Old Age Security payments will be made to individuals based on their income (or household income for couples). *See also* **means test; universality**.

Clayoquot Sound protest Located on Vancouver Island and the site of one of the largest stands of old-growth temperate rain forest in the world, Clayoquot Sound became the site of a prolonged battle between protesters, owners, loggers, and the government during the early 1990s. Before the conflict was resolved, 800 criminal convictions were achieved for acts of civil disobedience, the largest criminal prosecution for civil disobedience in Canada. In the end, the protesters partly won, as large sections of the forest were saved from logging.

clitoridectomy *See* **female genital mutilation**.

closed-class society The opposite of social mobility, the term *closed-class society* refers to a society in which it is improbable that individuals will be able to change their social class location, usually because class location is ascribed. *See also* **class crystallization**; **status, ascribed**.

closure A procedural motion to end a debate in a meeting or assembly is called a *closure*. Opposition parties usually accept reasonable limits on debate, but occasionally they will use all possible methods of delaying the legislative process. Closure is then used to terminate the debate and take an immediate vote on the legislation. In 1956, in a controversial use of closure, the federal Liberal government pushed through legislation to authorize construction of a natural gas pipeline from Alberta to central Canada over Opposition objections to what appeared to be American financial control of the project. The Liberals lost the subsequent election partly because of public distaste for what seemed to be dictatorial actions. *See also* **pipeline debate**.

Clovis culture Stone spear points were found at a site near Clovis, New Mexico, in the 1930s and dated to 11,200 years ago, leading many archaeologists to believe that the Clovis people were the first human inhabitants of the Americas. The dating of the spear points is consistent with the theory that the first humans arrived on the American continent by way of a land-and-ice bridge across the Bering Strait. During the 1990s, however, growing evidence emerged that the Clovis culture may not represent the first inhabitants of this continent and that some peoples may have arrived farther south, by sea crossing, in separate migrations up to 10,000 years earlier. It has also become evident that the technology of the Clovis culture most closely resembles that of the Upper Paleolithic Period (Later Stone Age) in France and Spain rather than that of Siberia. Reference: Dewar, E. (2001). *Bones: Discovering the First Americans*. Toronto: Random House Canada.

Cloward, Richard, & Lloyd Ohlin American sociologists Richard Cloward (1926–2001) and Lloyd Ohlin (1919–) developed differential opportunity theory, a further development of U.S. sociologist Robert Merton's theory of anomie. Differential opportunity theory argues that for an individual to become involved in criminal acts, that person must not only be denied access to legitimate means of attaining goals, but must also have access to illegitimate means of attaining them. The theory focuses on delinquent gangs and argues that three types of gang subculture emerge: criminal, where the gang is organized effectively to pursue criminal activity; conflict, where the gang is less organized and the emphasis is on violence and destructiveness; and retreatist, where there is minimal organization and the gang is successful in neither legitimate nor illegitimate activities and retreats into a world of alcohol and drugs. Cloward is perhaps better known for his work on welfare reform in the United States. Reference: Cloward, Richard, & Ohlin, Lloyd. (1960). *Delinquency and Opportunity: A Theory of Delinquent Gangs*. Glencoe, IL: The Free Press.

cluttered nest A recent term, *cluttered nest* captures the phenomenon of young adults returning to live with their parents or choosing to remain at home past the customary age for leaving home. This practice is connected to deterioration of employment opportunities for young adults and to later age at first marriage.

coalition government A government formed by two or more parties, a coalition government usually occurs when no party has a majority in Parliament or a legislature. Coalition governments are common in electoral systems based on proportional representation, which tend to sustain a more fragmented party system. In Canada, coalition is less common than the formation of a minority government, which must bargain with Opposition parties for support without giving them official government status.

cocaine First isolated in 1860, cocaine is an alkaloid derivative of the coca leaf. It was used in many popular medicines and, in 1886, was added to a new soft drink called Coca-Cola. This ingredient was removed from Coke in 1906. As a powerful natural stimulant, cocaine produces euphoria, laughter, restlessness, and excitement. *See also* **crack**.

Code of Hammurabi The first body of law that has survived for scholars to study, the *Code of Hammurabi* was named after Hammurabi, the king of Babylon in approximately 2000 B.C. Hammurabi prepared a legal system defending varying rights and based on a philosophy of retribution

coercion Coercion is the use of force or commands to gain obedience without the willing consent of the individual.

cognatic descent Also referred to as *bilineal descent*, cognatic descent is a system in which descent is traced through both paternal and maternal links.

cognitive anthropology Also known as *ethnoscience*, cognitive anthropology examines the ways that peoples of different cultures classify or categorize items of the everyday world. This field of study has some connection to ethnomethodology.

Cohen, Albert (1918–) American sociologist Albert Cohen is known for his study of the origins and dynamics of male juvenile gangs. Combining the differential association theory of U.S. criminologist Edwin Sutherland (1893–1950) with the strain or anomie theory of U.S. sociologist Robert Merton (1910–2003), he argues that delinquent subcultures emerge that have norms and values opposed to those of the outer community and that juveniles attach themselves to these subcultures as a result of class and status differentials and parental and school socialization. Boys from less favourable backgrounds experience status frustration within the wider community and gravitate to gangs to gain feelings of enhanced status within a subculture. Their criminal acts become principally motivated not by gain, but by a desire to achieve and maintain high status within the gang peer group. Reference: Cohen, Albert. (1955). *Delinquent Boys.* Chicago: University of Chicago Press.

cohort People sharing a similar experience or event at a particular time are called *cohorts* (e.g., all children born in Toronto in 1963 or all students graduating from high school in 1980). Cohorts are frequently used in longitudinal research. Marvin Wolfgang, for example, established a research project to follow all male children born in Philadelphia in 1940 in order to determine their encounters with the police. *See also* **longitudinal studies**.

Cold War The mutually hostile relations after the end of World War II in 1945 between the now fallen communist systems of Eastern Europe, the Soviet Union, and Asia, and the world's capitalist societies and their allies led by the United States were called the *Cold War*. While this was a war of propaganda, spying, sabotage, and political and economic sub-

version on both sides, it avoided the "hot war" of direct conflict between the world's dominant military powers. The Cold War reflected the new realities of the nuclear age and the catastrophic consequences of armed superpower conflict. The economic and political collapse of communism has now ended this era in international relations.

collapsed societies For most of the modern era, social scientists have been concerned with understanding economic and social development: How did we get to this point? However, there is now a growing interest in understanding how societies collapse or fall apart. There is of course a long list of such societies, including the Sumerians, the Maya, the Anasazi, and the people of Easter Island. This new interest arises of course from worries about our own demise as a civilization. Reference: Wright, Ronald. (2004). *A short history of progress.* Toronto: Anansi Press.

collective solidarity Similar in meaning to French sociologist Émile Durkheim's (1858–1917) term *mechanical solidarity*, collective solidarity refers to a state of social bonding or interdependency that rests on similarity of beliefs and values, shared activities, and ties of kinship and cooperation among members of a community.

colonialism Political domination of one nation over another that is institutionalized in direct political administration by the colonial power, control of all economic relationships, and a systematic attempt to transform the culture of the subject nation is known as *colonialism*. It usually involves extensive immigration from the colonial power into the colony, with the immigrants taking on roles as landowners, businesspeople, and professionals. Colonialism is a form of imperialism. Canadian society can itself be seen as a colonized nation with regard to Britain and the United States, but can also be seen as a colonizing nation in relation to First Nations peoples. *See also* **dependent development**; **Fanon, Franz**; **imperialism**.

Columbine High School In April 1999, two students of this U.S. high school, using firearms from their homes, killed 12 students and a teacher by sniping at them from the area around the schoolyard. All of North America was shocked by this event and Canadians were doubly shocked when a copycat shooting occurred a week later in a Taber, Alberta, school, resulting in the death of one student and the critical wounding of another. Reference: Fox,

J.A., & Levin, J. (2001). *The Will to Kill: Making Sense of Senseless Murder*. Boston: Allyn & Bacon. *See also* **Taber, Alberta**.

command economy Directed by state authorities rather than market forces, command economies can be identified as existing in some ancient and some more recent societies. In the ancient world, command was found in agricultural economies, especially those dependent on large-scale systems of irrigation requiring extensive regional planning and coordination. The power to control water resources gave central authorities immense social and economic dominance. Mesopotamia (modern Iraq) and Egypt are examples. Large sectors of the economy were also commanded in other ancient and medieval societies like Rome, China, and among the Inca. In modern times, command economies were dominant in the Soviet-style communist societies, where state central planning agencies allocated capital and resources, established production targets, and fixed the levels of prices. Command economies, because they rely on centralized bureaucratic administration, appear to be inherently less efficient than market mechanisms in allocating resources and stimulating economic growth. Soviet-style central planning has now been generally abandoned as a method of economic management. *See also* **state capitalism**.

Commission on Systemic Racism in the Ontario Criminal Justice System Growing tension between the police and the Black community of Toronto and a destructive riot in the summer of 1991 led to the 1992 report by the Commission on Systemic Racism in the Ontario Criminal Justice System to the premier of Ontario. This led to the creation of a commission of inquiry and to several published reports from the commission. Reference: Commission on Systemic Racism in the Ontario Criminal Justice System. (1994). *Racism Behind Bars: The Treatment of Black and Other Racial Minority Prisoners in Ontario Prisons*. (Interim report). Toronto: Queen's Printer of Ontario. *See also* **racial profiling**.

commitment The degree to which an individual pursues conventional goals is described as *commitment*. Reference: Hirschi, Travis. (1969). Aspects of the Social Bond. *Causes of Delinquency*. Berkeley, CA: University of California Press.

commodity A good or service that is exchanged or sold in the marketplace is called a *commodity*.

common law The common law tradition found in English Canada derives from feudal England, where it had become the practice for the king to resolve disputes in accordance with local custom. Customs that were recognized throughout the country were called *common custom*, and decisions made by the king and by subsequent courts set up to settle disputes became known as *common law*. Common law is considered to be a source of law, which means that the cases settled over the past 600 years themselves become part of the law, and these precedents become binding on present and future judges. Statutes are another source of law. *See also* **stare decisis; statutes**.

commons (the) *The commons* refers to the social and environmental spaces and resources that are or have been held by a community in common, and may include such things as common grazing lands, water wells, hunting grounds, or city streets. Liberal economics frequently claims that there is and has long been a "tragedy of the commons" where the fact of collective ownership has led to collective neglect or overexploitation of land, water, and plant and animal resources. In this view, privatization, rather than collective ownership, is required to create the proprietorial interest that will lead to the best care of resources. Others see the commons as under siege by private interests that wish to convert citizens into isolated consumers unable to express any common community purpose. Reference: Hardin, Garrett. (1968). The tragedy of the commons. *Science, 162,* 1243–1248.

common-sense reasoning A term used by ethnomethodologists, *common-sense reasoning* is derived from the work of Austrian philosopher Alfred Schutz (1899–1959), and refers to the practical or everyday reasoning used by members of society to create and sustain a sense of social reality as being objective, factual, predictable, and external to themselves. Since the objectivity of the world as a practical accomplishment is the focus of ethnomethodology, this kind of reasoning is a primary topic of investigation. Also referred to as *mundane reasoning*. Reference: Pollner, M. (1987). *Mundane Reason: Reality in Everyday and Sociological Discourse*. Cambridge: Cambridge University Press. *See also* **ethnomethodology**.

Commonwealth An organization of 53 nations, most of which were previously colonies of Britain, the Commonwealth has the broad objectives of promoting democracy, good government, and human rights. The term *British Commonwealth* was first used in 1884 as a substitute for the phrase *British Empire*. The formal organization of the Commonwealth had its origins in the Imperial Conferences of the 1920s and the *Balfour Declaration* of 1926, which clearly articulated the idea that the United Kingdom and its dominions were equal in status. In 1946, the term *British* was dropped from *British Commonwealth* to create the Commonwealth. The modern Commonwealth emerged in 1950 when the prime minister of Canada, Louis St. Laurent, proposed that India be allowed to remain as part of the Commonwealth even though it had chosen to be a republic after gaining independence.

communism A political theory that advocates collective ownership of the means of production (resources, land, and capital), abolition of private property, and equalization of incomes, communism differs from socialism because it contemplates revolutionary social change rather than just electoral politics. The first modern communist society was established in Russia after the revolution of 1917, and this political system was imposed by the Soviet Union on many countries of Eastern Europe after World War II. In Asia, a successful communist-led revolution in China in 1949 led to the growth of communist regimes and political movements in other areas, including Korea, Vietnam, and Malaysia. These centralized and dictatorial communist systems were far from the model societies envisaged by Karl Marx and Friedrich Engels, who believed that a communist revolution would create cooperative collective ownership, a true community-based democracy, and a weakening of the role of the state. *See also* **socialism**.

communitarianism A philosophy or belief system that places priority on the community or on social values, communitarianism is often contrasted to individualism or libertarianism. It claims that meaning in individual life and individual liberty are possible only within a strong and vital community, so government policies and individual choices should be responsive to social values. *See also* **community; libertarianism**.

community A society where people's relations with each other are direct and personal and where a complex web of ties links people in mutual bonds of emotion and obligation is a community. In the social sciences, especially sociology, the idea of community has provided a model to contrast to the emergence of more modern, less personal societies where cultural, economic, and technological transformation has uprooted tradition, and where complexity has created a less personal and more rationalized and goal-directed social life. *See also* ***Gemeinschaft; Gesellschaft***.

community of anxiety British novelist Ian McEwan uses the community of anxiety concept to capture the growing unease of modern society. This unease is created by a shared feeling that the world is getting worse and bad things are about to happen to people, one's self included. This shared feeling is escalated by international terrorism, environmental degradation, and a growing dependence on technology. Reference: McEwan, Ian. (2005). *Saturday*. New York: Random House.

community psychology A perspective that analyzes social problems, including crime, as largely a product of organizational and institutional characteristics of society, community psychology is closely related to sociology.

compensation model In contrast to the similarity model, the compensation model argues that for women to succeed in a world dominated by men, women must surpass the standards set for men.

comprador elite The term *comprador elite* is used in critical theories of the sociology of development to imply that a foreign-allied national business class tends to encourage local economic development that benefits other nations rather than its own. The members of a comprador elite belong to a national business class of senior corporate managers who derive their position and status from connection to foreign corporations of developed nations. *See also* **metropolis–hinterland theory**.

comprehensive land claims Claims to land made by native peoples not covered by a treaty with Canada or the British Crown, comprehensive land claims are most significant in Canada's North and in British Columbia, two regions with few treaties. Since the establishment of the land claims process in 1974, some claims have been resolved in the North, and the principles of a treaty with the Nisga'a in British Columbia were signed in 1996 and passed into law in April 2000. *See also* **Calder case**.

compulsive disorder People with a compulsive disorder, a form of mental illness, exhibit the recurrent need to perform certain actions. They may repeatedly wash their hands, wipe doorknobs, repeat certain words, or rearrange objects to put them into a certain order.

Comte, Auguste (1798–1857) French philosopher Auguste Comte invented the term *sociology* and was chiefly responsible for it becoming thought of as a social science, rather than a branch of philosophy. In Comte's view, human society and culture could be seen as progressing through three stages: theological, metaphysical, and positive. In the first stage, phenomena were explained by an appeal to supernatural forces invested in animals, objects, or religious deities. The second stage, metaphysical thought, also explains phenomena as a result of external forces, but these are conceived of as abstract energies rather than the will of gods. Both modes of thought contrast with the positive, which is empirical, experimental, and grounded in the principles of scientific method. During the positive stage, the foundations of the natural sciences, astronomy, physics, chemistry, and biology are developed and these, in Comte's view, pave the way for the development of positive sociology, the culmination of the development of science. Today, to call a sociologist a *positivist* has become a criticism, yet few sociologists are prepared to deny their discipline the title of a "social science," and this is Comte's enduring legacy. *See also* **Martineau, Harriet; positivism.**

conduct norms Specifications of proper and appropriate behaviour generally supported and shared in by members of a group are conduct norms. Societies contain different groups whose conduct norms are to some extent divergent.

confederation Confederation is the joining together of territories with separate political systems into a political union that establishes a federal government. The federal government is constitutionally permitted to exercise specific powers, while other powers are reserved for the exclusive jurisdiction of provincial, territorial, or state governments. Canadian Confederation was established by the *Constitution Act, 1867* (originally the *British North America Act, 1867*), which joined Ontario and Quebec (the "Province of Canada") with Nova Scotia and New Brunswick. Six other provinces later joined Confederation: Manitoba (1870), British Columbia (1871), Prince Edward Island (1873), Alberta and Saskatchewan (1905), and Newfoundland (1949). The Yukon, Northwest Territories, and Nunavut do not have provincial status and exercise limited powers of government under the authority of the Government of Canada. Within Confederation can be found three distinct visions of the nation of Canada. One sees Canada with a strong federal or central government and weaker provincial governments; the second sees Canada with a weak federal government and strong provincial governments; and the third sees Canada as the federation of a French-speaking nation and an English-speaking nation. These three visions have created tensions within Canada that continue to influence Canadian politics. Reference: Moore, Christopher. (1997). *1867: How the Fathers Made a Deal.* Toronto: McClelland and Stewart. *See also* **British North America Act; national policy.**

confidence vote In parliamentary systems such as Canada's, governments receive legal authority from their majority support in elected parliaments. They are appointed from those parliaments and responsible to them. If a government loses an important parliamentary vote, it is therefore considered to have lost the confidence of its parliament and must resign from office. Canadian governments have been defeated on matters of confidence on a number of occasions, the last in 2005, when Paul Martin's minority Liberal government was defeated in a confidence vote and lost the subsequent election. *See also* **King–Byng Crisis; responsible government.**

conflict perspectives Conflict perspectives are sociological perspectives that focus on the inherent divisions of societies with social inequality and the way these social divisions give rise to different and competing interests. The central assumption is that social structures and cultural ideas tend to reflect the interests of only some members of society, rather than society as a whole. This contrasts with consensus or functionalist perspectives, which assume a foundation of common interest among all members of society. Marxism and feminism are examples of conflict perspectives. *See also* **critical perspectives; feminism; Marx, Karl.**

conglomerate A corporate organization in which divergent enterprises retain separate organizational and legal structures but are joined together by the controlling ownership of a corporate holding company is called a *conglomerate.* For example, companies B, C, and D may all be owned by company A. This whole structure is a conglomerate.

conscience, collective A concept associated with French sociologist Émile Durkheim (1858–1917), *collective conscience* refers to the common norms, values, and beliefs shared in by members of a community. It consists of beliefs and ideas that shape the structure and direction of community life, rather than just the personal interactions of individuals.

conscription crisis During World War I (1914–1918), the use of conscription was generally supported in English-speaking Canada, but there was widespread opposition to it in Quebec. In the late 1930s, when a new European war seemed increasingly likely, Canada's prime minister, Mackenzie King, promised that if Canada became involved in war, there would be no conscription of individuals for service overseas. When World War II (1939–1945) began, it became obvious that Canada could not avoid conscription if there was to be major involvement in the war against Germany. Conscription for service in Canada was introduced in 1940, and in 1942, the government asked the Canadian people to release it from the pledge not to introduce conscription for service overseas. In a national vote—a plebiscite—English-speaking Canada strongly supported a change in policy, but Quebec was strongly against. As a result of this split in opinion (the conscription crisis), the government adopted a cautious policy and not until November 1944 did it finally send conscripted armed forces to Europe. By that time there was a more supportive opinion in Quebec. Reference: Granatstein, J.L., & Hitsman, J.M. (1977). *Broken Promises.* Toronto: Oxford University Press.

consensus perspective Also known as *functionalism*, the foundation of consensus perspective is the assumption that societies have an inherent tendency to maintain themselves in a state of relative equilibrium through the mutually adjustive and supportive interaction of their principal institutions. The approach also assumes that effective maintenance of a particular form of society is in the common interest of all its members. This perspective has its roots in the work of French sociologist Émile Durkheim (1858–1917). *See also* **Durkheim, Émile; functionalist explanation; structural functionalism.**

conservatism It is important to think of conservatism as a set of ideas that are not necessarily the same as those upheld by political parties calling themselves "Conservative." Some modern Conservative parties are strongly associated with the idea of a reduced role for government (privatization, reduced social programs) and promotion of free markets. This perspective, however, is based on classical liberalism rather than conservatism. Conservative ideas do not welcome the unrestricted operations of a free market, but value social stability and the maintenance of traditional community bonds and social hierarchies. Conservatives assume that institutions and values that have lasted a long time embody the collective experience of the community. They have persisted because they have played a valuable and positive role in society. *See also* **classical liberalism; neoconservatism.**

Conservative Party of Canada The December 2003 union of the Progressive Conservative Party and the Canadian Alliance Party (successor to the Reform Party) produced the Conservative Party of Canada. The joining of the two parties was seen as a way to end the division of the political right in Canada and to create a more nationwide support base than either of the individual parties was able to achieve in previous elections. The new party achieved minority government status in the January 2006 election.

conspicuous consumption Denoting the public display of individual possessions and consumption of expensive goods and services, the term *conspicuous consumption* was first used by U. S. economist Thorsten Veblen (1857–1929) to convey the idea of a society where social status is earned and displayed by patterns of consumption, rather than by what an individual does or makes. Reference: Veblen, Thorsten. (1899). *The Theory of the Leisure Class.* New York: Mentor [1933].

constitution The set of arrangements by which a nation governs itself is called a *constitution.* In Canada, the core of the *Constitution* is the *BNA Act* and its amendments (now called the *Constitution Act, 1867*) and the *Constitution Act, 1982.* Most of what we take to be the *Constitution,* however, is not contained in these documents: Things like the principles of constitutional monarchy, responsible government, and the collective responsibility of the Cabinet are not mentioned and are provided for by unwritten constitutional conventions. In Canada, constitutional convention, embodying political traditions and practices, is unusually important and the system of government cannot be understood simply from the written laws. For example, it is constitutional convention, but not law, that ministers must be members of the House of Commons or the Senate, or that the governor general must appoint the leader of the largest party in the House of Commons as prime minister. It is appropriate to also include court judgments interpreting constitutional Acts and formal agreements between federal and provincial governments as parts of Canada's constitutional arrangements. *See also* **constitutional convention**.

Constitutional Act, 1791 Passed by the Parliament of Britain under pressure from the United Empire Loyalists who had arrived in Canada (many into the old province of Quebec) and wished to continue to live under British institutions, the *Constitutional Act, 1791*, divided the old province of Quebec into Upper Canada (now Ontario) and Lower Canada (Quebec). A powerful British minority remained in Lower Canada and these people were given significant representation in the legislative assembly (30% of the seats for 10% of the population). Upper Canada elected to develop British institutions, while Lower Canada chose to retain the arrangements it had been granted under the *Quebec Act, 1774*. *See also* **United Empire Loyalists**.

constitutional convention Constitutional conventions are those parts of a constitution that have been established by political practice and are not written down as formal provisions. Britain is unique internationally in having a constitution that is almost entirely unwritten, and many aspects of this unwritten constitutional tradition were exported to Canada and form part of its system of government. For example, new students of Canadian politics are often puzzled to read in a written part of the *Constitution*, the *Constitution Act, 1867*, that Section 3.9 states: "The Executive Government and Authority of and over Canada is hereby declared to continue and be vested in the Queen." What the *Constitution Act* does *not* say, however, is that it would be profoundly unconstitutional for the monarch, or the governor general acting on her behalf, to exercise this authority without the advice and consent of the prime minister and Cabinet, who are responsible to an elected House of Commons. An unwritten constitutional convention has developed called "responsible government," meaning that the government must be answerable to the House of Commons and depend

on it for support. And, in turn, the formal power of the monarch to exercise authority is used constitutionally only as advised by the prime minister and Cabinet. *See also* **constitution**.

constitutional monarchy *See* **monarchy, constitutional**.

consumer culture A consumer culture is one in which the attainment of ownership and possession of goods and services is presented as the primary aim of individual endeavour and the key source of social status and prestige. *See also* **audience**; **popular culture**.

content analysis A research method, content analysis involves the gathering of data capturing one or more variables descriptive of the content of a cultural expression, such as movies, newspaper stories, speeches, cartoons, or advertisements. A researcher may, for example, analyze stories about sexual assaults to determine how blame is allocated in such stories, or may examine the covers of popular magazines such as *Time* or *Maclean's* to see which sex or racial group is typically depicted, or to observe differences in the depiction of men and women. Reference: Voumvakis, S.E., & Ericson, R.V. (1984). *News Accounts of Attacks on Women*. Toronto: Centre of Criminology.

contest mobility A British term, *contest mobility* refers to what North Americans would call *social mobility* through equality of opportunity. Recruitment for positions in society is seen as a contest in which the contestants are competing freely.

continentalism Originally associated with the American vision of a "manifest destiny" of the United States to occupy the whole North American continent, *continentalism* now refers specifically to social and economic policies that encourage and advance economic and political integration of the countries of North America. The term is also used generally to refer to processes of economic and political integration of continental nations. The *North American Free Trade Agreement* is an example of continentalism at work. *See also* **Lament for a Nation**.

contradictions of capitalism The term *contradictions of capitalism* is associated with Karl Marx (1818–1883), German philosopher, social scientist, historian, and revolutionary, who claimed that capitalist societies suffered from two irresolvable problems that would prevent both social harmony and a stable economy. First, Marx assumed that the competitive processes of a capitalist market society would lead to a concentration of capital ownership in fewer and fewer hands. Marx built this claim on the assumption, which he held in common with *laissez-faire* economics, that a competitive economy must lead inevitably to the elimination of some producers by others; there must be winners and losers and the winners would grow increasingly large. Capitalism, Marx argued, contrary to the general assumption of *laissez-faire* economics, had an inherent tendency toward concentration of capital in oligopolies and monopolies. The concentration of capital involved, first of all, the displacement of the handworker and the craftsworker and increasing domination of factory-based technology. An industrial proletariat of wage workers emerged, and grew larger, as independent producers were eliminated by factory-based competition. As capitalist corporations grew more concentrated and larger, the number of individuals owning the means of production became fewer. The class structure became polarized, and the economic and social conditions of the two opposed main classes became more strongly contrasted, leading to political activation of the working class and prolonged conflict with the dominant bourgeois class through political and industrial organization. It is this development of social polarization that provides the unsolvable social or relational contradiction of a capitalist society. The social organization of a capitalist society also presented an inherent structural contradiction in the economic dynamics of capitalism. While capitalism revolutionized the means of production by promoting the greatest economic development in human history, its class structure focused the capacity to consume in a tiny minority of the population. The mass social scale of production could not remain compatible with the concentration of wealth in fewer and fewer hands. As a result, there must be inherent instability, or anarchy, in the whole capitalist system of production. The social effects of such instability in turn must intensify the political struggle of social classes, hastening the event of socialist revolution. *See also* **communism; dialectical materialism; dialectical philosophy; monopoly; oligopoly.**

control variable In causal analysis, in order to test for spuriousness, researchers use one or more control variables, which may be related to the independent variable or to the dependent variable. To avoid con-fusing results, the researcher holds the control variables constant (they do not vary), allowing the investigator to determine if the original relationship between the independent variable and dependent variable still holds. For example, to investigate the relationship between race and sentence severity in court, it would be necessary to hold prior criminal record constant, since prior record may be related to both sentence severity and to race. *See also* **variables.**

conversational analysis Also known as *sequential analysis*, conversational analysis is one of three central themes that are the focus of ethnomethodology, the other two being mundane reasoning and membership categorization. Sociologists typically examine talk or conversation to learn something of people's attitudes, the ways in which people's lives are structured, and how people differ from each other in their values and assumptions. The ethnomethodologist, on the other hand, treats talk or conversation as a topic to learn how ordinary members of society use properties of talk (e.g., its sequential properties) in order to do things with words. A great deal of research has been done on the structure of turn-taking, story-telling, and openings.

Co-operative Commonwealth Federation (CCF) Founded in 1932 in Calgary, the CCF adopted a radical socialist political program at its first convention in Regina, Saskatchewan, in 1933. At the federal level, the party built popularity during World War II and briefly led in public opinion polls in 1943. In 1945, 28 members of Parliament were elected. Although the party had limited success in federal politics, it gained power in Saskatchewan in 1944 to become North America's first social democratic government. The main support for the party came from farmers' movements and labour unions, and from socialists in many spheres of society, especially the churches. In 1961, the party was dissolved and was reestablished as the New Democratic Party. Reference: Lipset, S. (1950). *Agrarian Socialism: The Co-operative Commonwealth Federation in Saskatchewan.* Berkeley, CA: University of California. *See also* **New Democratic Party.**

core-periphery nations *See* **metropolis–hinterland theory.**

corespective behaviour Behaviour by a company that avoids cutthroat competition in favour of a live-and-let-live attitude toward competitors, corespective behaviour is a strategy to reduce corporate risk and is in direct conflict with the values of liberal ideology, which emphasizes competition.

corporate crime A crime committed by corporate employees or owners to financially advantage a corporation, corporate crime may involve acts such as fraud, environmental pollution, creation of unsafe products, and dangerous work environments. *See also* **white-collar crime**.

corporate elite The owners, directors, and senior executives of the largest and most important of a nation's business corporations are called the *corporate elite*. They can be variously defined according to the criteria of corporate size and type of enterprise. *See also* **comprador elite**.

corporate kin A kinship group that has control over property and other rights, corporate kin can act as legal individuals and have authority over kin members, in contrast to noncorporate kin, such as clans.

corporatism A political ideology, corporatism is historically associated with fascism. It upheld strong political leadership and strict social hierarchy, and attacked the democratic system as inefficient, indecisive, and disorganized. The main idea was that the major sectors of industry, organized in groups called *syndicates*, should have direct political representation in the political system as a part of legislatures. In theory, labour as well as capital has representation, but labour's voice is controlled because free unions are suppressed. As a political doctrine, corporatism has had only a marginal influence in Canada, but the idea of giving corporations a direct role in shaping public economic policy is evident in the modern globalization process, where corporations acquire rights to sue governments and where international bureaucratic organizations set trading and investment rules that strictly limit the actions of elected governments of nation–states.

correlate Any variable that is correlated (the relationship between the two variables is one of correlation) with another variable is a correlate. Age and sex are the two strongest correlates of crime. *See also* **correlation**.

correlation From an empiricist perspective, criminologists tend to look at the social world in terms of variables (anything that varies within a population or group rather than being constant). Everyone in your class is a student, so that is a constant; however, there is a great deal of variation by factors like sex, age, income, program, GPA, religion, and ethnic heritage. If you gathered information from the whole class on these variables, you might begin to see that some variables vary in patterned ways. People with a particular ethnic heritage may tend to be more religious than those with other heritages, which would suggest a correlation: As one variable varies, so does the other. If there were more students of that particular ethnic heritage in the class, then religiosity for the group would also increase. As one goes up, so does the other. This is referred to as a *positive correlation* or *positive relationship*. If one variable goes up as the other goes down, this is called a *negative relationship*. For example, as age goes up, the crime rate goes down: This is a negative (or inverse) correlation. A correlation does not mean that one variable causes the other. For example, research done for the Marshall inquiry attempted to determine if there was a correlation between being Black and receiving a harsh sentence (*see* **Marshall inquiry**). A causal relationship has to be determined by further research.

correlation, zero-order A correlation between two variables that does not include a control variable is a zero-order correlation. A first-order correlation, then, would include one control variable as well as the independent and dependent variables.

correspondence principle Based on the concept that aspects of a society's culture and social structure have a complementary fit or integration, the correspondence principle has been used extensively in the sociology of education to analyze and describe the way that schools and other institutions socialize and educate individuals to take places in a structure of social inequality.

counterculture A set of cultural ideas that, to some extent, differ from and conflict with those generally upheld in the society, a counterculture develops when members of a group identify common values that distinguish their group from others. These types of groups may be based on common appearance, ethnicity, sexuality, status, or social behaviour. The term is close in meaning to *subculture*, but the concept of counterculture stresses the idea of an open and active opposition to dominant cultural values.

court of last resort The court of last resort is the last court to which an offender can appeal his or her case, usually the Supreme Court of Canada. It is often suggested as well that the "public" may be the court of last resort, suggesting that citizens themselves have to decide the morality of an issue. *See also* **Supreme Court of Canada**.

crack Crack is a form of cocaine produced by using ammonia or baking soda to remove the hydrochlorides from street cocaine, in order to create a crystalline form of cocaine that can be smoked. This is not a pure form of cocaine, however, as it contains residues from the baking soda and hydrochlorides. Crack provides a powerful high, and users become addicted quite quickly. Also known as *rock, gravel,* and *roxanne. See also* **cocaine**.

craft union A labour union that brings together skilled workers in the same area of craft or skill (typographical unions, carpenters, stoneworkers, iron moulders, boilermakers, railway engineers, etc.) is called a *craft union*. Historically, these unions had considerable influence in the workplace because their members possessed crucial knowledge and physical and conceptual skills, and struggled to maintain control of their work process and standards of training and apprenticeship. Craft unions became uneasy about the rise of industrial unions, which brought together all workers in a single industry regardless of their craft or level of skill. In this way, craft unions were somewhat elitist and perhaps cautious. Elizabeth Comack, professor of sociology at the University of Manitoba, argues that 19th-century Canadian industrialists, with the assistance of the federal government, exploited this tension within the union movement and used craft union fears of the threat of competition from Asian immigrants to transform concern about labour problems into a race issue. The government introduced legislation to control narcotics, which they linked to the Asian community, and this encouraged suspicion of Asians from other workers, thus splitting and weakening the union movement. It took many decades for some of the rifts within the union movement to be healed. *See also* **syndicalism**.

Creole A complex pidgin language, Creole has become the mother tongue of a population. *See also* **pidgin**.

Cressey, Donald R. (1919–1987) Professor of sociology at the University of California, Santa Barbara, Donald R. Cressey was known for his investigations and analysis of organized crime and financial crime. One of his most recognized books, *Theft of a Nation*, was only slightly facetious in its conclusion that since the Cosa Nostra was so powerful, the authorities should negotiate with them and agree to legalize their gambling rackets, provided they paid taxes on the profits and gave up involvement in politics and political funding. Reference: Cressey, Donald R. (1969). *Theft of the Nation: The Structure and Operations of Organized Crime in America*. New York: Harper and Row.

crime Any form of human behaviour that is designated by law as criminal and subject to a penal sanction is considered to be a crime. While crime is the central focus of criminology and a major topic of the sociology of deviance, there is no consensus on how to define the term. While the everyday use of the term seems to refer to intentional violations of criminal law or public law in general, many sociologists consider crime to be a social construction, or a label, and look at crime as being created through the passing of laws and the application of those laws. *See also* **classical criminology; criminology; critical criminology; deviance; labelling theory**.

criminogenic Those conditions or structures that themselves seem to create crime are criminogenic. Just as, for example, hospitals create disease (e.g., infections), it is possible that prisons or even courts or youth correction centres are criminogenic.

criminology A social science studying crime and related phenomena such as law-making, criminal behaviour, victimization, and punishment, criminology emerged from sociology in North America, while in Europe it is more related to law. There is some debate as to whether it is an independent social science or if it is a field of interdisciplinary study. As with many social sciences, it contains many competing perspectives. Reference: Siegel, Larry, & McCormick, Chris. (2003). *Criminology in Canada* (2nd ed.). Toronto: Nelson. *See also* **classical criminology; Positivist School**.

critical criminology A form of criminology (the study of crime), critical criminology uses a conflict perspective of some kind: Marxism, feminism, political economy theory, or critical theory. In all of these, the focus is on locating the genesis of crime and the interpretation of what is "justice" within a structure of class and status inequalities. Law and the definition and punishment of crime are then seen as connected to a system of social inequality and as tools for the reproduction of this inequality. Reference: Fleming, T. (Ed.). (1985). *The New Criminologies in Canada: State, Crime, and Control*. Toronto: Oxford University Press.

critical perspectives This term refers to perspectives within sociology that uncover and analyze the sources of social inequality and advocate social change. Two examples are Marxism and feminism. Marxism examines class inequality and advocates collective ownership of the means of production as a foundation for establishing social equality. Feminism examines gender inequality and advocates a transformation of gender roles in society and a systematic uprooting of cultural attitudes that support and encourage the social subordination of women. The term is closely associated with conflict perspectives. Reference: Taylor, Ian, Walton, Paul, & Young, Jock. (1975). *Critical Criminology*. London: Routledge. *See also* **conflict perspectives; feminism**.

critical theory A sociology developed by the Frankfurt School, critical theory is influenced by divergent intellectual ideas, including Marxism and psychoanalysis. It starts from two principles: opposition to the status quo and the idea that history can be potentially progressive. Together, these principles imply a position from which to make judgments of human activity (rather than just describing) and provide the tools for criticism. Sometimes associated with highlighting the "dark side" of modernity, critical theory attacks social ideas and practices that stand in the way of social justice and human emancipation (the rational organization of society as an association of free people). Critical theory is opposed to "bourgeois liberalism." *See also* **Frankfurt School**.

Cro-Magnon Appearing approximately 36,000 years ago, Cro-Magnon (an early form of *Homo sapiens*) showed signs of the anatomically modern human. While coexisting with Neandertal, Cro-Magnon is seen somewhat stereotypically as smarter, more refined, and more capable. While there are clear physical differences, it is difficult to interpret these without being biased by our contemporary physical ideals. Strong evidence exists for a rich symbolic life as seen in carvings and in paintings like those in the Lascaux Cave in France. Their extinction is unexplained: Did they die out because they failed to adapt to climate change? Or did they interbreed to create modern humans?

cross cousins Offspring of siblings of the opposite sex are cross cousins. Some societies prefer that a person marry a cross cousin: A man may marry his father's sister's daughter or a woman her father's sister's son. *See also* **parallel cousins**.

cross-cultural analysis Also known as *comparative analysis*, cross-cultural analysis is a method central to many social sciences involving the comparative examination of differing cultures. This method is crucial for distinguishing universal aspects of human culture and social organization from those that are particular to individual societies. By observing the range of variation in culture and organization between societies, a deeper understanding of individual development, family, gender, crime control, social inequality, etc., can be developed.

cross-sectional research Research that makes observations at only one period in time (for example, conducting a survey or opinion poll), cross-sectional research is analogous to taking a still picture of the population or group being investigated. Longitudinal research, on the other hand, makes more than one set of observations and can be compared to a simple moving picture. *See also* **longitudinal studies**.

Crow kinship system The mirror of the patrilineal Omaha kinship system, the Crow kinship system is associated with matrilineal descent. *See also* **Omaha kinship system**.

Crown corporation A corporate organization established by government, but having a separate legal and organizational identity from the government itself, Crown corporations have been established in a wide variety of social and economic sectors, including transportation, mining and manufacture, communications, and financial services. Canada has relied heavily on Crown corporations, especially as a means of stimulating economic development and meeting communications and cultural objectives.

crystal meth *See* **methadrine**.

cult The cult concept was originally developed as one component of a typology: churches, denominations, sects, and cults. Churches and denominations are seen as established forms of religious organization, while sects are groups that have broken away from established groups in order to preserve what they thought were central traditions or orthodoxy. Cults, on the other hand, are religious forms and expressions that are unacceptable or outside cultural norms, and thus are seen as the first stage of forming a new religion. However, the term now has a rather negative meaning, suggesting strange beliefs, charismatic leadership, manipulation of members, strong emotional bonding, and slavish devotion to the group. *See also* **church**; **sect**.

cult of domesticity The belief that family and individual life are most fulfilling when experienced in a private household where a woman is the chief homemaker and caregiver, the term *cult of domesticity* is also associated with the idea that women have moral and temperamental qualities that are best expressed in the personal and domestic sphere of life. The cult of domesticity has been given emphasis at various times in Canadian history, most recently in the period from 1945 to approximately 1960. *See also* **baby boom**.

cultural capital As used by French sociologist Pierre Bourdieu (1930–2002) in the sociological analysis of education, *cultural capital* refers to the way that schools reflect standards of cultural expression and definitions of valued abilities that are characteristic of the socially and economically dominant class in society. Students who bring this cultural capital (a form of human capital) to school are apt to be most successful in meeting criteria set by the schools; the result is that the school system supports and justifies the privileges of children of the wealthy and powerful. The school can alternatively be seen as bestowing cultural capital on students, improving the equality of opportunity for those groups not already in possession of this capital essential for maintaining an open-class society. Reference: Bourdieu, P. (1973). Cultural Reproduction and Social Reproduction. In R. Brown (Ed.), *Knowledge, Education and Cultural Change.* London: Tavistock.

cultural construction A perspective on a subject that is shaped by cultural assumptions, rather than having a natural or objective basis is called a *cultural construction.* For example, marriage is a cultural construction: It is not biologically necessary for men and women to marry. Another example is gender: We have concepts of masculine and feminine that suggest to us how men and women should behave, but few of these gender differences are determined by biological sex.

cultural ecology In the study of the interaction between culture and environment, cultural ecology, culture is viewed in the context of the surrounding social and physical environment, and the effects of culture on environment and of environment on culture can then be studied. A central assumption of this perspective is the idea that cultures in similar environments share many characteristics.

cultural explanation A cultural explanation for a phenomenon (such as homicide) is phrased in terms of the culture of the offender's nation or subgroup. For example, John Hagen, professor of psychology at the University of Michigan, has argued that Canada has a lower homicide rate than does the United States because Canada's culture (its values) is more traditional than that of the United States. Canada's culture, he argues, tends to focus on respect for authority and communitarianism, and is more elitist than American culture. Reference: Hagan, John. (1977). *The Disreputable Pleasures: Crime and Deviance in Canada.* Toronto: McGraw-Hill [1984].

cultural genocide Derived from the word *gens*, meaning a clan or community of people related by common descent, the idea of cultural genocide implies the process of undermining, suppressing, and ultimately eliminating cultures. In Canada, the term has been used to refer to the government policy of using residential schools to separate native children from connection with their own cultures and languages and to impose European culture on them. *See also* **genocide**; **potlatch**; **residential schools**.

cultural imperialism The practice of systematically spreading the influence of one culture over others by means of physical and economic domination, cultural imperialism usually involves an assumption of cultural superiority (ethnocentrism). In Canada, the term is associated with the concern that the power of the United States' entertainment and communications media tends to marginalize Canadian stories and Canadian experiences and to reduce Canadians' ability to communicate with each other. With the spread of satellite television, cultural imperialism is seen as a global problem. *See also* **ethnocentrism**; **imperialism**.

cultural lag Used by U.S. sociologist William Ogburn (1886–1959), the term *cultural lag* captures the notion that technology (or what we might call *material culture*) often changes faster than the cultural institutions (including law) of the society.

culturally prescribed aspirations A rejection of the notion that aspirations are entirely a matter of self-creation, culturally prescribed aspirations are defined by culture and transmitted by other members of the society. U.S. sociologist Robert Merton (1910–2003) assumes that everyone within a culture shares the same cultural goals or aspirations and that the primary goal in modern capitalist society is wealth. It should be noted that Merton wrote during the Great Depression, and his ideas may be appropriate only for an age of scarcity. Do they apply to an age of prosperity? Other sociologists have argued, and demonstrated, that groups of people may have quite different aspirations or goals.

cultural studies The term *cultural studies* is associated with work at the Frankfurt School in the early decades of the 20th century and the writings of the Birmingham Centre for Cultural Studies (begun in 1964). Both of these groups began to look at culture as a force shaping actual human experience, rather than at the level of abstract generalization. Their focus was on examining the function of culture in everyday life and its role in a system of social hierarchy and domination. These studies eventually began to build on Antonio Gramsci's (1891–1937) concept of hegemony to demonstrate how class or patriarchal rule is supported not only by overt mechanisms of law and the exercise of power, but is also pervasively dispersed throughout society in institutional structures and cultural beliefs and values. Cultural studies now include a substantial portion of sociological work and are associated with the Birmingham School in the United Kingdom and the work of Stuart Hall (1932–). Reference: Davis, Helen. 2004. *Understanding Stuart Hall*. London: Sage Publishing. *See also* **hegemony**.

culture The generally shared knowledge, beliefs, and values of members of society, culture is conveyed from generation to generation through the process of socialization. While culture is made up of ideas, some sociologists also argue that it is not exclusively ideational but can be found in human-made material objects. They define a separate material culture. This distinction appears weak, since human-made material objects must embody human ideas. Culture and social structure are considered as the two key components of society and are therefore the foundation concepts of sociology. Reference: Gamst, F.C., & Norbeck, E. (1976) *Ideas of culture: Sources and uses*. New York: Holt, Rinehart and Winston.

culture-bound Theories, interpretations, or claims of various sorts based on the assumptions and values of one's own culture are considered to be culture-bound. This term is used in criticism of some anthropological work.

culture of poverty thesis The theory that certain groups and individuals tend to persist in a state of poverty because they have distinct beliefs, values, and ways of behaving that are incompatible with economic success, the culture of poverty thesis is controversial and is opposed by situational theory, which locates the genesis of poverty in economic and social structures of society rather than in the value orientations of individuals or groups. Reference: Lewis, Oscar. (1966). The Culture of Poverty. *Scientific American, 215*, 19–25.

culture shock When individuals encounter a new and different culture and experience a major disruption of their normal assumptions about social values and behaviour, culture shock is said to have occurred. Their old values seem unable to provide guidance in the new situation, yet the new culture seems strange and unacceptable. It is experienced by individuals who travel to a very different society and discover cultural ideas and practices that differ very much from their own. Culture shock is common among immigrant groups and can sometimes affect whole societies if they are swept up in rapid social change. The concept has been applied to the experiences of aboriginal peoples following colonial contact.

D

Dalkon Shield An intrauterine device (IUD) used by women as a form of birth control, the Dalkon Shield was produced by the A.H. Robbins Co. During the 1970s, women began to suffer health problems as a result of the use of this device; investigation determined there was a design fault that could have been corrected by the maker. In June 1974, Robbins suspended domestic sale of the Dalkon Shield (foreign distribution continued for another 10 months) but stopped short of recalling it, defending its safety and effectiveness "when properly used." Eleven years later, the company declared bankruptcy in the face of claims filed against it as a result of the defective IUD.

dark figure of crime The total amount of crime in a community consists of crimes that are known or recorded and the dark figure of crime, the amount of crime that is unreported or unknown. Criminologists have used differing methods (like victimization surveys) to try to decrease the amount of unknown or unrecorded crime. The notion of a dark figure of crime is based on a positivist approach to criminology and assumes that crime is real or objective.

date rape drug Rohypnol is a drug used in the short-term treatment of some sleep disorders that came to be used by those attending nightclub "raves," as it causes euphoria rather quickly (it may also cause drowsiness). Since this state of euphoria also reduces inhibition and causes memory loss, Rohypnol also has been used to dope the drinks of women in order to get them to have sex. The drug is also known as *ropies, ruffies, R-2, rib*, and *rope*.

dating in archaeology Archaeologists use two main methods to date objects and remains: absolute (or chronometric) dating and relative dating. *See also* **chronometric dating; relative dating**.

Davis Inlet A Mushuau Innu population of approximately 535 living in Davis Inlet of Labrador gained international attention in 1993 when video pictures spread across the nation showing young people openly sniffing gasoline and talking to the interviewer about their hopelessness and the suicides of many of their friends. The community became a symbol of the plight of many aboriginal nations in Canada. While government aid was provided, problems continued for many years. The community has now been relocated to a more accessible area (now called Natuashish) with richer resources to support traditional occupations of fishing and hunting.

Dawson, Charles A. (1887–1964) Charles A. Dawson trained at the University of Chicago and established the first sociology program at McGill University, Montreal, in 1922. Being shaped by the Chicago School, he educated students in the areas of urban studies, social reform, and the development of crime and deviance in the urban community. He was joined in 1929 by Canadian sociologist Everett Hughes (1897–1983), who also trained at the University of Chicago. *See also* **Chicago School; McGill School**.

Debert site An archaeological site in central Nova Scotia, the Debert site was first found in 1948 but studied much later to reveal evidence of Paleo-Indian habitation 10,600 years ago, the earliest most northeasterly evidence of Paleo-Indians. Reference: MacDonald, G.F. (1968). *Debert: A Paleo-Indian site in central Nova Scotia*. Ottawa: National Museum of Man.

decarceration *See* **deinstitutionalization**.

deconstruction A concept central to postmodernism, deconstruction is a process of rigorously analyzing and making apparent the assumptions, judgments, and values that underlie social arrangements and intellectual ideas. Authors such as J. Derrida (1930–2004) reject the idea that texts (e.g., the writings of Marx or Plato) have an objective link to external events and represent truth. Rather, they suggest that texts contain material that undermines the claims or arguments that the text itself is presenting. This being so, these texts cannot be used to learn about the external events of the social world or to evaluate those events; rather, they can be examined internally only to search for the hidden assumptions or subtext that give them meaning. Reference: Caputo, John, & Derrida, J. (1997). *Deconstruction in a nutshell: Conversation with Jacques Derrida*. New York: Fordham University Press. *See also* **postmodernism**.

decriminalization Removing a prohibited activity from the *Criminal Code*, thus making it noncriminal, is termed *decriminalization*. The activity may continue to be regulated or controlled through other legal mechanisms. Today, demands for decriminalization are mostly associated with drug use and possession. Critics of these laws argue that they create social problems and promote crime by defining victimless activity, engaged in by millions of Canadians, as criminal. They claim that drugs like marijuana are harmless and argue that even use of hard drugs is a health and social issue and should not be a focus of criminal law.

deep ecology A set of ideas within the environmental movement, deep ecology stresses the belief that modern societies have become anthropocentric—placing the human species and its interests at the top of the agenda. Supporters of deep ecology argue that society must become biocentric—seeing all biological organisms, including humans, as having value in and of themselves. This suggests that the human relationship with the natural environment should not be based on its value for the human species; rather, things should be valued for themselves and, consequently, we should return as much of the environment to its natural state as possible.

defining the situation This term refers to the process through which humans go when trying to comprehend the social situations in which they find themselves and deciding on what values and norms are relevant in guiding social interaction. If you contrast macrostructural studies and symbolic interactionism, this concept is associated with the latter. The structural view tends to focus on the situation individuals are in, not on their definition of the situation. The term was first used by U.S. sociologist W.I. Thomas (1863–1947).

definition of the situation In symbolic interactionism, sociologists reject the notion of objective social structures existing independently of the actor; it is assumed that actors behave in accordance with how they have defined the situation. Definitions of the situation can be negotiated by two or more actors. For example, when a 911 operator receives a call, the operator and the caller interact in negotiating the definition of the caller's situation. This definition then determines how the caller will be received, what message may go out over the radio, and what action may be taken. If a situation is defined as real, it *is* real; this is a subjective approach to the study of social phenomena. *See also* **symbolic interactionism**.

deinstitutionalization A reduction in the size of populations held in institutions of involuntary confinement, primarily mental hospitals and prisons, deinstitutionalization began in the 1970s. It was very successful in reducing the population of mental hospitals, where the program was based on the premise that patients would be better off in the community, and that community care would be cheaper than institutional care. Many Canadian communities found that support resources were inadequate, however, leaving uncared-for and confused former patients to wander the streets of Canada's towns and cities. In the United States, the program was applied to prisons, and for a short time, prison populations appeared to decrease but, since the 1980s, there has been a dramatic increase in rates of incarceration and prison populations. Reference: Chan, J.B.L., & Ericson, R.V. (1981). *Decarceration and the Economy of Penal Reform*. Toronto: Centre of Criminology, University of Toronto; Scull, A.T. (1977). *Decarceration: Community Treatment and the Deviant: A Radical View*. Cambridge: Polity Press.

Delgamuukw A major case on aboriginal rights, *Delgamuukw v. British Columbia was* decided by the Supreme Court of Canada in 1997. The court held that aboriginal title to land was not extinguished by the establishment of sovereignty by the Crown. It also stated that Crown ownership of lands was a separate issue from jurisdiction over those lands. Where aboriginal title to land was established by long-term exclusive and continuous occupation, the Crown may still infringe on aboriginal title for valid legislative objectives, such as settling foreign populations or for economic development. The court specified that groups with aboriginal title should be involved in the decision-making process regarding their lands. Depending on the nature of any proposed infringement, fair compensation would normally be required. Reference: Persky, Stan. (1998). *Delgamuukw*. Vancouver: Douglas and McIntyre.

demand characteristic As used in experimental psychology, *demand characteristic* refers to unintended features of an experiment that affect the results, thus compromising the internal validity of the study. The term is also used in the sociology of deviance to refer to those organizational features of work settings, other than the formal goals of the organizations or principles such as due process or fairness, that shape arrest decisions, plea bargaining, or jury deliberations. Examples of demand characteristics that police officers may attend to in making decisions on the street are the informal expectations of police culture, their workload, their need to accumulate overtime, or organizational rules. Reference: Blumberg, A. (1967). The Practice of Law as a Confidence Game. *Law and Society Review*, 1(1), 15–39.

demand mobility A form of social mobility that takes place over time, demand mobility is not caused by individuals ascending or descending in class or status, but rather by changes in the occupational structure of the economy. It results from there being greater demand for some kinds of labour and a shrinking demand for others, and not from the openness of the society. In a situation of high-demand mobility with little openness, one might find that workers occupy the same relative positions in social and economic position as their parents, although performing quite different kinds of work. *See also* **equality of opportunity; social mobility**.

democracy In the original Greek, *democracy* literally meant "rule by the people." In the Greek world, political organization was usually centred around "city–states," and male citizens had equal rights to participate in government. The Greek concept of citizenship implied that citizens must become actively involved in government, not just vote for representatives. In modern usage, the term has become narrowed to mean a system of government where citizens have equal legal rights to vote in free elections. *See also* **autocracy**; **meritocracy**; **plutocracy**.

democratic deficit The gap between the principle of democratic control exercised by citizens of a nation and the actual amount of democratic control available to them, the democratic deficit may be increased by government's executive domination over elected assemblies because of the system of strict party discipline or from the transfer of decision making to nonelected agencies. Many social scientists believe that this deficit has increased substantially because of free trade agreements; the deregulation of corporate activity; the growth of multinational corporations, which are now beyond the ability of any one nation to control; and the growth of superbureaucracies designed to coordinate cross-border activities.

demographic transition The transformation of the structure of a population accompanying the change from an agrarian economy to an industrial economy is called *demographic transition*. The former society is characterized by high birth rates and high death rates, providing some stability to population size. The transition period typically involves declining death rates while birth rates remain high, leading to population growth. Stability is found in mature industrial societies with low death rates and low birth rates, a situation that creates a rising average age of the population. *See also* **demography**.

demography Demography is the study of populations, including their size, structure, and transformations. Studying the structure of a population provides some predictive power about crime rates. For example, a community with a high ratio of young males will have more crime than a community with a high retirement population.

dependency ratio The proportion of the population that is outside the labour force and thus dependent on the economic activity of those working, the dependency ratio is typically calculated as the proportion of the population between the ages of 0 to 16 and those over 65 to those between the ages of 16 to 65. As industrial societies have matured, and particularly in those with a large baby boom such as Canada, the dependency ratio has increased significantly (for example, from 1 dependant to 20 workers to 1 dependant for 3 workers). Concerns over the dependency ratio have already begun to shape social policies in many parts of Europe. *See also* **baby boom**; **demographic transition**.

dependent development A central concept of dependency theory, rather than seeing the world's nations dividing economic labour and interacting as equal partners, dependent development suggests that some nations are able to impose unequal exchanges on others, and thus retard the economic development of these nations or make their development dependent on stronger or more economically advanced nations. Dependent development has typically involved the exporting of primary resources. *See also* **colonialism**; **imperialism**; **metropolis–hinterland theory**.

dependent variable In a causal analysis, the dependent variable is that variable considered to be the effect; it depends on the independent variable. For example, if examining the relationship between race and sentence length, sentence length would be the dependent variable. *See also* **independent variable**.

Derrida, Jacques *See* **deconstruction**.

descriptive statistics Descriptive statistics are statistical tools or techniques used to describe a sample or a population. For example, a mean, median, or mode is a descriptive statistic. *See also* **inferential statistics**.

deskilling The process by which division of labour and technological development have led to the reduction of the scope of an individual's work to one, or a few, specialized tasks is called *deskilling*. Work is fragmented, and individuals lose the integrated skills and comprehensive knowledge of the craftspersons.

determinism The determinism theory holds that examination of one or more definable factors allows for a complete explanation and prediction of the characteristics of society or the individual. For example, to argue that societies gain all their central characteristics from the psychological drives of human beings is a form of psychological determinism; to explain the social roles and behaviour of men and women by reference chiefly to their sex is biological determinism. *See also* **economic determinism; methodological individualism; psychological reductionism**.

deterrence The attempt to control crime by creating a threat of punishment, deterrence is directed to specific individuals (individual deterrence) or other potential offenders (general deterrence). The sentencing system attempts to prevent crime through the fear of punishment. Reference: Gibbs, Jack. (1968). Crime, Punishment and Deterrence. *Social Science Quarterly, 48*, 515–530. *See also* **general deterrence; specific deterrence**.

deviance This term commonly refers to violations of social norms (including legal norms), but many sociologists reject this behavioural or normative definition of deviance and see deviance instead as simply a label. Deviance in this view is that to which we react, through social control responses, as deviance. *See also* **labelling theory**.

deviance amplification *See* **amplification of deviance**.

deviance, primary In primary deviance, the individual commits deviant acts that do not emanate from a deviant or criminal sense of self. U. S. anthropologist Edwin Lemert (1912–1996) postulated that a person may commit many deviant or criminal acts in this manner, but if caught and labelled by agents of control, the "offender" may come to see herself or himself in a different manner and become a secondary deviant. Reference: Lemert, Edwin. (1951). *Social Pathology*. New York: McGraw-Hill. *See also* **deviance, secondary**.

deviance, secondary In secondary deviance, the individual commits deviant acts after being identified and perhaps labelled by agents of social control. Although recognizing that these acts are socially defined as deviant, the individual remains committed to continuing them. The deviant acts flow from the adoption of a deviant self-identity that confirms and stabilizes the deviant lifestyle.

dialectical materialism Although dialectical materialism is a concept linked to Marx's ideas, Marx never actually used the expression in his writing. In general, this concept suggests that the process of social change is not attributable to changes in culture or ideas, but arises within the material conditions of people's lives, in the way they are organized around economic activity. *See also* **contradictions of capitalism; dialectical philosophy**.

dialectical philosophy Dialectical philosophy is the belief that social organization, culture, and intellec-

tual ideas change because of the development of contradictions that create challenges to the existing state of affairs and lead to the emergence of something new from this tension. Georg Hegel (1770–1831) developed this idea in Western philosophy when he claimed that every existing social arrangement or intellectual belief system represents a "thesis"—a way of doing or thinking about things—that gives rise to a contradictory, or opposing, "antithesis." From the contest between "thesis" and "antithesis" emerges something new and unique: a "synthesis." There is some element of this conception in the writing of Karl Marx (1818–1883), German philosopher, social scientist, historian, and revolutionary, when he claims that contradictions arise in capitalism and the resolution of these contradictions produces a new type of social and economic system. This suggests that the seeds of capitalism's demise or transformation are located within capitalism and are not generated from outside. *See also* **contradictions of capitalism; dialectical materialism**.

diaspora Diaspora is a wide geographic dispersion of a people or ethnic groups seeking refuge from war, famine, or persecution. The best-known example is the dispersion of Jews from the Middle East, which occurred over a period of more than 2,000 years and resulted in Jews living in many countries around the world. In 1948, the new State of Israel's founding declaration symbolically reversed the diaspora by proclaiming that all the world's Jews could acquire citizenship in Israel just by arriving on its shores. A more modern example is the international dispersion of the citizens of Somalia as their country experiences political conflict and famine. Approximately 200,000 Somalis have arrived in Canada.

differential association Developed by Edwin Sutherland (1883–1950) in the 1930s, differential association is a radical explanation for criminal behaviour, since it argues that crime, like any social behaviour, is learned in association with others. The phrase *differential association* simply means that people have different social situations and thus learn different things. What is learned is cultural material. If an individual regularly associates with criminals and is relatively isolated from law-abiding citizens, then that individual is more likely to engage in crime. First, the individual learns some specific skills needed to commit crime (how to open a locked vault), and, second, learns ideas that justify and normalize crime. This concept leads directly to a subcultural theory of crime that asserts that not all groups in society uphold the same values or norms and that, for some groups, crime is normative. Reference: Sutherland, Edwin. (1939). *Principles of Criminology*. Philadelphia: Lippincott.

direct investment One of two large categories of foreign investment, *direct investment* refers to financial investments in a company in order to gain control or ownership, while *portfolio investment* refers to financial investment for the purpose of interest or dividends.

discourse analysis An important theme in postmodernism, especially for writers like French historian and philosopher Michel Foucault (1926–1984) for whom it is important to analyze how people talk about the world around them, the central idea of discourse analysis is that the way people talk about the world does not reflect some objective truth about that world, but instead reflects the success of particular ways of thinking and seeing. These ways of thinking and seeing tend to become invisible, because they are simply assumed to be truthful and right, and in this way people's thought processes themselves can come to represent and reinforce particular regimes of power and coercion. *See also* **Foucault, Michel**.

discrimination The unequal treatment of individuals on the basis of their personal characteristics, discrimination may be predicated on age, sex, sexual orientation, ethnicity, or physical identity. Discrimination usually refers to negative treatment, but discrimination in favour of particular groups can also occur. *See also* **prejudice**.

disenchantment of the world *See* **rationalization**.

disenfranchised Literally, this terms means to be without the right to vote (e.g., Ukrainian Canadians were disenfranchised in 1917). More commonly, however, the term is used to describe groups that have little power or representation in the political process. Young people could be described as disenfranchised, since they have a low rate of voting and, more importantly, they have little representation in the political process or institutions that concern them. *See also* **enfranchisement**; **suffrage**; **Ukrainian Canadians**.

dissociation *Dissociation* can be used in a psychological way or in a sociological way. In psychology, it refers to the tendency for people in crisis to dissociate their experiences from aspects of their personality or identity. This can lead to multiple personalities. For the sociologist, it refers more to social isolation from others for a variety of reasons.

distributive justice One of two key categories of justice or fairness (the other being retributive justice), *distributive justice* refers to fairness in the allocation of the rewards or benefits of society or of an institution within society. For example, it is seen as fair that those student essays that best meet the criteria of academia should receive the best grades. When Karl Marx asserted that workers produced value in a commodity that they did not receive and were thus exploited, he was concerned about distributive injustice. Retributive justice, on the other hand, refers to fairness in the administration and imposition of punishment on those who have brought harm or negative consequences to individuals or society. It is seen as fair, for example, that those who violate the law should receive punishment. The criminal justice system can be thought of as the institutionalization of this type of justice. *See also* **retribution**.

division of powers A specification in a federal constitution of the respective powers and jurisdictional areas of federal and provincial levels of government is defined as *division of powers*. Canada's division of powers is specified in the *Constitution Act, 1867*. Typically, the federal level is accorded a paramount power that can be activated in emergency situations or those involving a crucial national interest. The division of powers in Canada makes it one of the most decentralized nations in the world.

Divorce Act Until the *Divorce Act* of 1968, divorce was difficult to obtain in Canada, and in Quebec and Newfoundland, where no legislation existed, divorce could be obtained only through a private Act of Parliament. The 1968 Act created two grounds for divorce: fault (adultery, mental and physical cruelty, homosexuality, imprisonment, or addiction) and marriage breakdown (which required separation of the parties for at least three years). The divorce rate jumped considerably after the passage of this Act. The 1985 *Divorce Act* removed the fault grounds and provided that divorce could be obtained when marriage breakdown could be proven by a separation of one year. *See also* **annulment**.

dizygotic twins Commonly known as *fraternal twins*, dizygotic twins are from two separate fertilized eggs; consequently, they share no more genetic material than any other siblings and may be of different sexes. Studies of twins have been a valuable research tool for sorting out the effects of heredity and environment. *See also* **monozygotic twins**.

documentary method of interpretation Although used by Karl Mannheim (1893–1947) and Alfred Schutz (1899–1959), the current meaning of *documentary method of interpretation* derives from the work of Harold Garfinkel, (1917–), the founder of ethnomethodology. He asserts that the documentary method is used by laypersons and sociologists alike in common-sense reasoning about the world. The method consists of treating an actual appearance as the document of, or as pointing to, a presupposed underlying pattern. A child's choice of toys (a boy choosing a truck or a girl choosing a doll) is seen as an indication of an underlying pattern of biological preferences (or for the sociologist, of gender socialization). Further, there is a reciprocal relationship between the "document" and the underlying pattern: The underlying pattern is now given some legitimacy because of the observation of the individual "document"—the child's choice of toys. *See also* **ethnomethodology**.

"doing gender" A concept derived from a theory to explain crimes by men, "doing gender" postulates that all cultures have an ideal of manliness and that failure to meet this is perceived as effeminate. This being so, men need opportunities to "do gender"— to make their manliness apparent. Abuse of women and crime itself may be seen as ways to assert manliness. Reference: Messerschmidt, James. (1993). *Masculinities and Crime*. Lanham, MD: Rowman and Littlefield.

dominant ideology thesis Associated with Karl Marx (1818–1883), German philosopher, social scientist, historian, and revolutionary, the dominant ideology thesis holds that each historical era is dominated by the intellectual ideas of its economically and politically ruling class. The institutions and culture of a society are widely permeated by this ideology, which provides the key institutions and values of the society with an appearance of naturalness and inevitability. It is not claimed that only one ideology is present within a society, or that this ideology is without challenge. Marx envisaged a process of class conflict in society that develops the contest between dominant ideology and the ideas

or counterideologies that challenge them. *See also* **class consciousness, false; ideology**.

domination *See* **authority**.

double-blind procedure A method of enhancing internal validity in an experiment, in a double-blind procedure, neither the researcher nor the subjects know which group is the experimental group and which is the control group. This prevents the researcher from communicating expectations and the subjects from acting in ways they think are expected of them.

double burden *Double burden* is used to describe the situation of women who perform paid work outside the domestic sphere as well as homemaking and child-care work inside the home. Since domestic work is private and outside the cash economy, it is not remunerated; this causes it to appear as something less than real work and as part of the natural gender role of women. Canadian studies have consistently demonstrated that women perform by far the largest share of this domestic work. Men, however, spend considerably more hours at paid work; recent data suggest that total hours worked by men and women are roughly comparable. However, the demands of providing and arranging child care, which fall primarily on women, lead to many women being subjected to demands greater than those imposed on male workers. Some feminists have advocated wages for housework to gain recognition for this work that women do in the private world of family and household.

double marginality A theory used to explain why women tend to commit fewer crimes than do men, double marginality argues that women are isolated within the family and are denied access to male-dominated street crime. Hence, they are doubly marginalized, and this leaves only avenues toward less serious crimes and victimless crimes like drug abuse. Reference: Messerschmidt, James. (1986). *Capitalism, Patriarchy and Crime*. Totowa, NY: Rowman and Littlefield.

double standard A cultural practice that accords less freedom and choice to one sex than the other, *double standard* is usually used to refer to different norms of sexual morality for women than for men. Men's sexual activity is viewed positively as natural, right, and normal, whereas women are seen as diminished in status if they engage in sexual relationships outside marriage. This double standard of conduct was once severely oppressive to women (and still is in many non-Western societies), but has reduced relevance in Western societies today, where premarital sexual activity is normative for both sexes. *See also* **status offence**.

Douglas, Tommy (1904–1986) Leader of the first socialist government elected in North America when his Co-operative Commonwealth Federation Party won the 1944 Saskatchewan election, Tommy Douglas left the premiership in 1961 to become the first leader of the federal New Democratic Party. His greatest achievement was the establishment of a medicare system in Saskatchewan in 1961, which was successfully launched despite a strike by most of the province's doctors. By 1972, encouraged by federal government financial participation, all of the provinces had adopted the medicare program. Reference: Stewart, W. (2003). *The life and political times of Tommy Douglas*. Toronto: McArthur and Company. *See also* **Co-operative Commonwealth Federation**.

Doukhobors Of Russian origin, the Doukhobors are a pacifist sect, rejecting both the orthodoxy of established religion (they believe that God dwells in each person and not in the church) and secular governments. After many years of persecution, a group of 7,400 sailed to Canada in 1898–1899 and settled in Saskatchewan. When it became clear that they would have to take an oath of allegiance in order to homestead the land, most objected and moved to British Columbia in 1908. Here the group established a complex pattern of communal living. Extremists among the group (the Sons of Freedom) continued to reject government regulation and were in conflict for several decades with the government over compulsory schooling, registration of births, and taxes. Many were arrested, a special prison was established, and many children taken into care. Some stability returned to the community in the 1970s, and the Sons of Freedom and the more orthodox Doukhobors live in the interior of British Columbia in relative harmony. In 1996, the government of British Columbia made it possible for Doukhobor communities to hold land without paying taxes. In place of taxes, they would pay a fee for government services. Reference: Woodcock, George, & Avakumovic, Ivan. (1968). *The Doukhobors*. Toronto: McClelland and Stewart [1977].

dowry The wealth or possessions that a bride brings into the marriage, a dowry is typically a transfer of wealth from the bride's family to the husband.

Dragon Bone Hill *See* **Peking Man**.

dramaturgical model As used by Erving Goffman (1922–1982) and symbolic interactionists since, the dramaturgical model is a metaphor for understanding human interaction and how humans present their self in society. All of the world is conceived as a stage, and individuals are seen as actors who present a show of their self by putting their "best foot forward." The metaphor is extended by Goffman through concepts such as "front stage," "back stage," and "presentation of self." Reference: Goffman, Erving. (1959). *Presentation of Self in Everyday Life*. New York: Doubleday Anchor. *See also* **Goffman, Erving**.

drift A psychological state of weak normative attachment to either deviant or conventional ways, the idea of drift was developed by David Matza (1930–) to demonstrate that delinquents are not fundamentally different from nondelinquents, but they drift in and out of delinquency and may become committed to this way of life. Reference: Matza, David. (1969). *Delinquency and Drift*. Englewoods Cliff, NJ: Prentice-Hall.

dual labour market In this theory, the market for labour is divided between a primary labour market and a secondary labour market. The first consists of jobs that are more highly paid, have good benefits, are secure, and offer some prospect of advancement. These jobs are usually found in the least competitive areas of the economy (e.g., those requiring a great deal of capital to begin). The secondary labour market consists of jobs that are less well-paid, have little security, and are seldom unionized. It has been noted that, for various reasons, women tend to be concentrated in the secondary labour market.

Durham Report Lord Durham (John G. Lambton) was sent from Britain following the Rebellion of 1837 in what was then referred to as Lower Canada. He arrived thinking the dispute was over responsible government, only to find what he called "two nations warring in the bosom of a single state." A follower of the great liberal thinker, British philosopher and economist John Stuart Mill, he brought what he thought to be good liberal principles to this dispute and saw the answer in the forcible assimilation of the French. This response was seen as the reconquest of the Québécois and led to resistance and growing nationalism. In the 19th century, liberal thought held that self-rule was possible only if people are indeed a people or a nation. They must share a sense of political allegiance and common nationality. With this in mind, the assimilation of minorities was seen as essential to the development of the nation–state. This of course led to administrators being sent from Britain to the colonies who were ill-equipped to deal with the many issues of minority rights, and they proceeded to impose what was good for Britain on many areas of the world. Today, Canada is at the forefront in developing ways to incorporate minority rights and national rights into liberal theory. Reference: Kymlicka, Will. (1995). *Multicultural citizenship.* Toronto: Oxford University Press.

Durkheim, Émile (1858–1917) French sociologist Émile Durkheim is associated with the Positivist School and functionalism. In sociology, Durkheim's principal influence has been for his concepts of anomie, or normlessness, and of mechanical and organic solidarity. In Durkheim's sociology, high levels of suicide reflect weakness in society's integrative mechanisms. This line of thinking suggests that, if normative regulation and structural integration can be strengthened, rates of crime will be correspondingly reduced. Reference: Giddens, A. (1979). *Émile Durkheim.* New York: Viking. *See also* **anomic division of labour; anomie; mechanical solidarity, organic solidarity**.

dyslexia A form of cognitive impairment associated with learning difficulties in school, dyslexia has been shown to correlate with elevated levels of criminal offending, but it is unclear if this is a direct result of dyslexia or a result of the economic and social marginalization that may occur as a result of school failure. This cognitive impairment is often associated with a person reversing letters or an inability to grasp a number sequence.

E

echo generation Children born to the baby boomers, or those Canadians born between 1980 and 1995, belong to the echo generation. Reference: Foot, David. (2001). *Boom, Bust & Echo: Profiting from the Demographic Shift in the 21st Century.* Toronto: Stoddart. *See also* **baby boom**.

ecofeminism A set of ideas within the environmental movement, ecofeminism's basic assumption is that patriarchal societies tend to associate women with nature and debase, or rape, both. Thus, it is necessary for the environmental movement to overthrow patriarchal structures and ideologies in order to protect or enhance the natural environment.

ecological fallacy Generally, an error made in reasoning about differing units of analysis, ecological fallacy is specifically the error of using data generated from groups as the unit of analysis and attempting to draw conclusions about individuals. For example, if neighbourhoods with high rates of unemployment also have high crime rates, it is an error to conclude that it is necessarily the unemployed people in these neighbourhoods who commit crime. *See also* **units of analysis**.

ecological footprint The amount of the earth's surface required to sustain the consumption of an individual, the ecological footprint of a North American is many times higher than for people in the less-developed world. If the typical North American patterns of automobile use and mass consumption, centred on shopping, spread around the world, could the earth survive?

ecological studies Developed by criminologists in the early part of the 20th century, ecological studies look at the relationships of various areas of a community to each other and the ways in which particular forms of behaviour may flourish in some communities and not in others. *See also* **Chicago School**.

ecology Ecology is the study of the interdependence of living beings, of their relationships to the world around them, including to other living beings.

economic anthropology The study of the economic systems of various cultures or subgroups of society is called *economic anthropology*. Reference: Plattner, S. (Ed.). (1989). *Economic anthropology.* Menlo Park, CA: Stanford University Press.

economic determinism Economic determinism is a form of determinism that explains social structure and culture as a product of the social and technical organization of economic life. German philosopher, social scientist, historian, and revolutionary, Karl Marx (1818–1883) has been described—many claim incorrectly—as an economic determinist. *See also* **determinism**.

egalitarian A shortening of the word *equalitarian*, *egalitarian* suggests a commitment to, or a state of, equality. Egalitarian societies or groups are contrasted to hierarchical or class-based societies or groups.

ego In anthropology, *ego* refers to the individual from whom the networks of kinship and family relationship and descent are reckoned and traced. In psychology, the term is used to refer to the self of the individual, and the way that individual has constructed a personality and identity in society. In Freud's psychoanalytic theory, the ego is the outcome of the individual's struggle to adapt basic drives (the *id*) to the imperative control of society and culture (the *superego*). Between drives and the coercive influence of social expectation, an individual creates a sphere of unique personality.

Eichler, Margrit (1942–) Born in Germany, Margrit Eichler completed her final degree in sociology at Duke University, North Carolina. She came to Canada in 1981 and has developed an international reputation for her work on feminist methods and family policy.

electoral college The United States *Constitution* provides for the election of the president and vice president by an indirect process known as an *electoral college*. It requires that each state must hold an electoral college at which the state's presidential electors cast their votes for a presidential candidate. The number of each state's presidential electors is determined by the state's population. The successful candidates must receive an absolute majority of the total votes of the electoral colleges. Although the constitution permits the state legislatures to determine how their presidential electors are to be chosen, in practice they all now hold a popular vote to choose the electors, each of whom is pledged to support a particular candidate in the electoral college. Although almost all states now list only the names of the principal candidates on the ballot, in some states, the names of only the college candidates appear on the ballot or the names of the presidential and vice presidential candidates predominate, with the electoral college candidates listed beneath. This indirect method of election leaves the electoral colleges to decide between candidates who have not received an absolute majority of the total college votes, which has occurred in the past. The system can also produce a distorted result when college votes and total national popular vote diverge, as in the election of George W. Bush in 2000 when he received more college votes but fewer popular votes than his Democratic opponent.

embourgeoisement thesis The argument that, contrary to the class conflict theory of German philosopher, social scientist, historian, and revolutionary Karl Marx (1818–1883), increasing numbers of the working class will come to assume the lifestyle and individualistic values of the middle class and will reject commitment to collective social and economic goals is called the *embourgeoisement thesis*. The opposite would be *class consciousness*.

emigration *Emigration* refers to people who leave their home country: emigrants.

emotional labour As used by Arlie Russell Hochschild, *emotional labour* refers to paid work requiring the worker to maintain observable facial and bodily displays with the intention of creating particular emotional feelings in clients. Among workers performing emotional labour are flight attendants (who continue to smile as the plane crashes), bill collectors, funeral directors, doctors, and nurses.

empire Deriving from the Latin term *imperium* and first used to describe the Roman empire (31 B.C. to A.D. 476), the term *empire* has lost a clear sense of application but generally refers to a group of countries (usually unified by force) coming under a single political authority (sometimes called the *emperor*). There may be forms of local government, but the local area is directed by the central nation and may come to adopt the cultural and political practices of the dominating nation. Usually associated with colonialism, the term should not to be confused with the term *federation*, which implies that groups of people, perhaps even nations, have reached a mutual agreement to create a unifying political structure. *Empire* is also different from *superpower*, which refers to a nation that has the power to impose its will on other parts of the world but may not have political authority over those nations. Examples of empire include the British Empire (1583–1960?), the Spanish Empire (1492–1975), the Holy Roman Empire (843–1806) and the Austro-Hungarian empire (1867–1918). In order to make sense of the current power of the United States, the term *empire lite* has been used. *See also* **empire lite**.

empire lite This is a term used by Michael Ignatieff to capture the exceptional empire of the United States—exceptional in that it does not conform to the usual concept of an empire: It has no colonies and it does not conquer territory to obtain markets. Instead, it is an empire that does not believe itself to be an empire, has a global sphere of influence without local administration, and achieves hegemony without colonies. Reference: Ignatieff, M. (2003). *Empire lite*. Toronto: Penguin Canada. *See also* **Ignatieff, Michael**.

empirical evidence Evidence that can be observed through the senses, empirical evidence must, as a minimum, be sensed by at least one faculty of sight, hearing, touch, smell, or taste and, to some extent, be measurable. This is the only form of evidence acceptable to positivism, which describes social science as the study of a social world deemed to be external to the observer and proceeding with the researcher being a neutral "observer" of that external world.

empiricism Empiricism is the philosophical belief that sensory input (seeing, touching, hearing, etc.) is the sole source and test of knowledge. *See also* **empirical evidence; epistemology; positivism**.

employment equity Equity can be thought of as a state of being equal or fair, and fairness in dealing with people. Employment equity has come to have several dimensions. First, it suggests equal pay for equal work or equal pay for work of equal value. The goal of both of these principles is to establish equality between men and women, or able-bodied and physically challenged persons, or Whites and people of colour. The term has also come to imply proportionate hiring of various minority groups. In addition to requiring equal pay for equal work and equal pay for work of equal value, employment equity also requires measures to ensure employment access by inclusive hiring practices that may involve provision of special services for certain types of employee, from those who need child care to those who require accommodation of physical limitations.

empty nesters Parents who have seen their children mature and establish residences of their own are called *empty nesters*. Sociologists have noted a number of changes related to this stage of the family life cycle: movement to smaller homes, women returning to paid work, changes in attitudes, changes in relationships with children, increased social involvement in community matters, and the potential for psychological feelings of rolelessness.

enculturation Enculturation is the process of transmitting a society's culture from generation to generation. *See also* **socialization**.

endogamy People who tend to marry within their own status or class, religion, or ethnic group are practising endogamy—seeking a mate or marriage partner from within a group defined by social status, ethnic identity, family relationship, area of residence, or some other distinct social characteristic. Some societies have rules of endogamy that specify marriage to a particular kinship-related partner. A low rate of endogamy suggests that a group is being assimilated into the surrounding society. The opposite of endogamy is *exogamy*. Both practices are defined by values and norms that vary cross-culturally.

enfranchisement The right to vote in the elections of a nation, called *enfranchisement*, is now constitutionally guaranteed in Canada. Women, for example, were federally enfranchised in 1918. The last large adult group to achieve this right was the federal prison population (although this still remains controversial). *See also* **suffrage**.

Engels, Frederick (1820–1895) A lifelong intellectual collaborator with German philosopher, social scientist, historian, and revolutionary Karl Marx (1818–1883) and co-author of the foundational text of Marxism, *The Manifesto of the Communist Party* (1848), Frederick Engels also wrote extensively as a journalist and political commentator and completed a number of philosophical and historical works. It is generally agreed, however, that Marx's work was more original and revealing, although Engels' famous work, *Origins of the Family, Private Property and the State* (1884) enjoyed considerable popularity among feminists in the early 1960s. One reason for this popularity was the book's claim that human society was originally matriarchal but became patriarchal when private property emerged and men seized control of it. Later feminists find this perspective too narrowly materialist and emphasize the cultural dimension of the inequality experienced by women.

Enlightenment Project In order to understand what postmodernism is about, it is essential to understand what modernity means for the social sciences. This is linked to what is deemed to be the Enlightenment Project. The age of enlightenment ushered in human rationality as the source of knowledge, thus encouraging the rejection of previous authorities such as the church or custom. This new acceptance of human rationality became linked to science as the key to understanding the natural and social worlds, and led to a search to understand causality and to the belief that human rationality would lead to a more enlightened, progressive age characterized by human liberation. These beliefs shape social sciences by giving science a privileged position in the pursuit of truth, encouraging the search for sets of concepts to provide a framework for understanding social life, regardless of particular social situations or time and the acceptance of metanarratives (large and abstract social theory, including sociology) as superior to other narrative accounts about society. Much of this is apparent in some of the works of Karl Marx. Marxian theory is a large metanarrative about the historical development of Western societies, and because of its claim to be based on scientific observation and its use of a conceptual framework (modes of production, relations of production), it claims a privileged position and a universal nature (it is intended to apply to all capitalist societies). Further, it is claimed that by using the metanarrative, the consciousness of workers can be enhanced (corrected) and an age of liberation will follow. Modernity or the Enlightenment Project is reflected in positivism, the importance of the scientific method, the belief that social science can be used to better society (French sociologist Émile Durkheim is very explicit about this), and the sweeping away of the subjective beliefs of "ordinary actors." *See also* **deconstruction**; **metanarrative**; **positivism**; **postmodernism**.

Eoanthropus dawsoni *See* **Piltdown Man**.

epidemiology A term used largely in medical sociology, *epidemiology* describes the study of the occurrence and distribution of diseases. Such investigations look for changes in the frequency of occurrence (or incidence) and association of diseases with particular physical or social locations. Epidemiological research can be conducted on crime—viewed as analogous to a disease of society—and a host of social problems. For example, a researcher may map the distribution of youth crime in relation to race, social class, school success, or family structure in the hope of finding those factors that appear to be associated with delinquency.

epistemology The study of what is meant by *knowledge* and of what it means to *know* something is called *epistemology*. All science, since it is concerned with verification and proving or disproving, must make assumptions about how we know things to be true or false. All science then adopts an epistemology. In sociology, there has been a long debate about the sources of knowledge and this can be seen in the differences between positivism and postmodernism, or between positivism and phenomenology. For sociologists, this debate is most frequently engaged over the methods to be used for learning about the world: the survey or experimental method of positivism on one side versus participant observation or using one's own "member's" understanding to analyze conversations. *See also* **empiricism**; **ethnographic research**; **member**; **positivism**; **verstehen**.

equality of condition Where there is very little difference in individuals' possession of wealth, status, and power, equality of condition exists. This condition cannot be found in any complex society.

equality of opportunity Where differences in individual's wealth, status, and power are not so great as to create advantage and disadvantage in the pursuit of personal achievement, equality of opportunity is said to exist. Liberal ideology and consensus theory claim that broad equality of opportunity exists in modern societies. Sociologists since Durkheim have been interested in inequality of opportunity, since it is believed that people's commitment to the norms and rules of society are diminished as inequality rises.

equalization payments Funds transferred from the Government of Canada to some of the provinces to compensate them for having a smaller per capita tax base than other provinces are called *equalization payments*. The intent of the payments is to support a comparable level of provincial government services across all of Canada. Historically, Ontario has been the chief net contributor, via federal taxation, and Quebec the chief net beneficiary. The Atlantic provinces, Manitoba, and Saskatchewan have also been recipients, while Alberta and British Columbia have been net contributors.

Eskimo kinship system Anthropologists distinguish among many kinship systems. The Eskimo system—the kinship system followed by most North Americans—is one where there is bilineal descent and an emphasis on the nuclear family, and it does not distinguish proximity of relationship to cousins or uncles and aunts. Other kinship systems are the

Hawaiian, Iroquois, Crow, Omaha, and Sudanese. Reference: Schusky, E.L. (1975). *Variations in kinship.* New York: Holt, Rinehart and Winston.

essentialism *See* **feminism, difference**.

esteem Referring to honour or positive evaluation within a group or community, esteem has been thought of by some sociologists as a form of status that can operate independently of income, wealth, or power. *See also* **class crystallization; status**.

ethnic cleansing The physical expulsion or killing of one ethnic group by another in order to gain control of land and resources, ethnic cleansing is usually linked to an ideology supporting ethnic hatred. The term became widely used to describe what occurred when the former state of Yugoslavia divided along ethnic lines and there was wholesale violence against ethnic minorities, particularly between Serbs and Bosnian Muslims. Serbian President Slobodan Milosevic of Serbia was later tried for war crimes before the International Criminal Tribunal for the Former Yugoslavia. Reference: Ignatieff, M. (1998). *The warrior's honor: Ethnic war and the modern conscience.* Toronto: Penguin Books. *See also* **Rwandan genocide**.

ethnic group A group of individuals having a distinct culture in common, the idea of *ethnic group* differs from that of *race* because it implies that values, norms, behaviour, and language, not necessarily physical appearance, are the important distinguishing characteristics. Usually, ethnic groups are thought of as minority groups—subcultures within another culture.

ethnic identity An individual's awareness of membership in a distinct group and of commitment to the group's cultural values establishes that individual's ethnic identity. This is the subjective aspect of ethnicity, but for many people their ethnic heritage has little subjective meaning, although it can be objectively determined.

ethnocentrism The assumption that the culture of one's own group is moral, right, and rational, and that other cultures are inferior is ethnocentrism. When confronted with a different culture, individuals judge it with reference to their own standards and make no attempt to understand and evaluate it from the perspective of its members. Sometimes ethnocentrism is combined with racism—the belief that individuals can be classified into distinct racial groups and that that there is a biologically based hierarchy of these races. In principle, however, one

can reject a different culture without in any way assuming the inherent inferiority of its members. *See also* **racism; xenophobia**.

ethnographic present The custom in anthropology of writing about cultures in the present tense, even if the description is a reconstruction of a culture long distant in time, represents the ethnographic present. This style is adopted to indicate a belief in the accuracy of this representation at a particular moment in time.

ethnographic research Ethnographic research uses participant observation as a tool for gathering information and is a form of what is termed *qualitative research*, in contrast to *quantitative research*, which focuses on measurement and formal analysis. As participant observer, the researcher becomes actively immersed in the chosen setting in order to gain understanding by experiencing aspects of the life of an individual or group. Ethnographic research is the foundation of anthropology, which has been principally concerned with the descriptive recording and analysis of the group life of traditional, generally preliterate, societies. Until the 1950s, anthropologists would often resist close involvement in community life and maintain quite formal and narrow relations with the host society in order to do better "objective science," but today anthropologists generally seek active involvement as a source of understanding. Ethnographic research is also central to symbolic interactionism, phenomenological sociology, labelling theory, and ethnomethodology, where the goal is to comprehend the subjective perspectives of individuals. Ethnographic research is linked to a reaction to positivism that distrusts subjectivity in research and attempts to treat human subjects as objects that can be scientifically investigated. Reference: Le Compte, M.D., & Schensul, Jean J. (1999). *Designing and Conducting Ethnographic Research.* Lanham, MD: Rowman & Littlefield Pub. *See also* **epistemology; positivism; qualitative research; quantitative research**.

ethnolinguistics The study of the relationship between language and culture is called *ethnolinguistics*.

ethnomethodology A sociological theory developed by Harold Garfinkel (1917–), building on the influence of phenomenologists such as Edmund Husserl and Alfred Schutz and more recent linguistic philosophers, roughly translated, *ethnomethodology* means the study of people's practices or methods.

There are three central strands to ethnomethodology: mundane reason analysis, membership categorization, and conversational (or sequential) analysis. This is a microperspective; it does not see the social world as an objective reality, but as something that people must build and rebuild constantly in their thoughts and actions. Rather than treating ordinary members of society as "cultural dopes" driven by society, it tries to uncover the methods and practices that are used by people as they create the taken-for-granted world. Reference: Garfinkel, Harold. (1967). *Studies in Ethnomethodology*. Englewood Cliffs, NJ: Prentice-Hall. *See also* **common-sense reasoning; sequential analysis**.

etiological factors Factors that encourage or cause a particular outcome are called *etiological factors*; for example, addiction to hard drugs is a factor that can lead people into prostitution or criminal behaviour. Being raised in a violent home is a factor that can lead to violent behaviour or being victimized by violence.

etiology The study of the origins or causes of things, etiology is typically used in medical research to describe the study of the causes of disease. The term is also used in the social sciences, however, in reference to social problems such as crime and deviance.

eugenics Roughly translated as *good genes*, the eugenics movement, active in many parts of the Western world, was driven by the belief that social intervention should occur in order to protect the best gene pool. This was achieved by encouraging people who were considered to represent "good" genes to breed and, more importantly, to support interventions by the state to prevent those considered to have "bad" genes from breeding. In Alberta, for example, the *Sexual Sterilization Act*, in force from 1928 to 1972, allowed the state to sterilize 2,832 people—most, or all, without their consent. Reference: McLaren, Angus. (1990). *Our Own Master Race: Eugenics in Canada, 1885–1945*. Toronto: McClelland and Stewart.

European Union (EU) The EU developed from the original European Economic Community established by the *Treaty of Rome* in 1957. At that time, six nations joined together in a free trade association and agreed to the free movement of persons and mobility of employment and political rights within the European Community. They also made a commitment to develop common standards in social and economic policy. Political cooperation increased over time, as the new supranational European institutions, like the European Commission and the European Parliament, promoted the establishment of new European-wide policies. The European Community now includes most other Western European nations and has expanded its membership to much of the former communist-controlled Eastern Europe and Greece. In October 2005, the EU and Turkey began membership talks. There is little consensus in Europe about the ultimate destination of the EU, some seeing it as a framework for a future federal state of Europe, while others resist its incursions on separate national sovereignties and want to roll back its mandate to the macroregulation of trade and other aspects of economic policy. The federal vision of Europe has suffered setbacks in more recent times, as new treaties intended to promote further integration have been rejected in referendums by national electorates.

euthanasia Literally translated as *a good death*, euthanasia is the painless killing of a person, at that person's request, to escape from the indignity and suffering of an incurable medical condition. Some societies make legal provision for such deaths; Canada does not. *See also* **Latimer, Robert**.

evolutionary psychology A relatively new paradigm for understanding human social behaviour, evolutionary psychology argues that attributes such as altruism, romantic love, protection of children, pair-bonding, coyness in females, sexual aggression, sexual attraction, and conscience have a genetic basis. Applying Darwinian principles to the understanding of human behaviour, it is claimed, provides insights into things such as human kinship structures, male–female relationships, family formation, sibling rivalry, and domestic violence. Reference: Evans, Dylan. (2000). *Introducing Evolutionary Psychology*. New York: Totem Books.

exceptional state Exceptional state arises when a liberal democratic society adopts government policies that rely on the coercive power of the state, rather than trying to maintain compromises that balance conflicting interests. This is a departure from the usual role of democratic states and is therefore exceptional. British cultural theorist Stuart Hall used the term to describe what happened in Britain in the 1980s, when economic failure led to mass unemployment, a government fiscal crisis, and a loss of support among important groups; there was a crisis of legitimacy. The British government fostered a sense of an enemy within the society and claimed that social instability was caused by rampant crime and militant unionists. This "threat" then justified giving the state coercive powers that it used to control the crisis. *See also* **fiscal crisis; legitimation crisis**.

exchange theory A theory associated with the work of U.S. sociologist George Homans (1910–1989) and Austrian sociologist Peter Blau (1918–2002), exchange theory is built on the assumption that all human relationships can be understood in terms of an exchange of roughly equivalent values. These exchanges are seldom monetary; rather, they are frequently intangibles like intimacy, status, and connections.

exchange value In Marxian analysis, the theoretical value of any commodity exchanged or sold in the marketplace is the amount of socially necessary labour time embodied in it. In actual market conditions, the money or equivalent paid for a commodity (the price) may differ from the value of the commodity, although in a perfectly working market, price and value would be identical. It is the unique characteristic of capitalism that the great majority of goods and services are produced to be sold, rather than for their immediate-use value to the producer. In less modern economies, the production of commodities took place only in limited sectors and most production was for use values. *See also* **labour theory of value**.

executive disengagement The detachment of senior executives of large corporations or other institutions from the day-to-day work and work situation of lower-level employees, executive disengagement develops both because lower-level employees will customarily assume that executives are best left uninformed of certain decisions and actions of employees, and because of the assumption that executives cannot be legally expected to have complete control over their individual staff members. This concept of separation from daily responsibility has been challenged in Canada, and executives can be found liable, for example, for sexual harassment committed in their institutions. A legal responsibility has been established to create an environment in which harassment is not tolerated and where, if it occurs, the perpetrator is promptly disciplined and fired.

exogamy The custom of seeking a mate or marriage partner outside of one's own kinship group or class, religion, ethnic group, or area of residence, exogamy is often seen as a measure of integration.

experiment The favoured research method for testing causal relationships among variables, although not always possible in some social sciences, is experiment. The classical model of the experiment has the following general structure: Research subjects are assigned in a random manner to the control group and to the experimental condition group. The first group does not receive the factor or variable thought to be the causal one, while the second group does receive this factor or variable. After the passage of time, both groups are measured to determine the level of the predicted effect. For example, if someone believes that taking pill X reduces cancer, that person might recruit a number of subjects and randomly assign them to two groups. The first group takes a placebo, while the second group takes pill X. After some time (in this case perhaps 20 years), the rate of cancer in both groups is determined. Since ethical questions are raised when using this method to test for harmful relationship, researchers often have to rely on less powerful experimental designs. *See also* **preexperimental design; quasi-experiment; randomization**.

explanation (scientific) All science aims to provide explanation of phenomena or behaviours. Two ways of providing a useful explanation are: (1) a causal explanation can be offered if research can clearly establish that one variable is caused by another, and (2)—and more powerful—a theoretical explanation locates the phenomenon or behaviour in question within a theory, a conceptual model of how some aspect of the world works. It should be noted that explanation in history in particular is somewhat different from other explanations. *See also* **theory**.

exponential growth Exponential growth follows a geometric progression (e.g., 1, 2, 4, 8, 16, 32) rather than a linear progression (e.g., 1, 2, 3, 4, 5, 6).

external validity This term refers to the accuracy of scientific results when generalized beyond the laboratory or survey situation to the real world. If it is thought that the researcher could expect to find confirmation of research results in the ordinary life of the community, the results would be said to be externally valid. *See also* **internal validity**.

extraversion Extraversion is a personality characteristic associated with sociability, impulsiveness, and aggression.

Exxon Valdez A tanker carrying oil for Exxon (the oil company), the *Exxon Valdez* hit a reef near the Alaskan city of Valdez on March 24, 1989, on its way to California. Some 40 million litres of oil spilled into pristine Prince William Sound. This incident drew worldwide attention to the tremendous actual and potential harm from the movement of oil around the world. Reference: Keeble, John, & Fobes, N. (1999). *Out of the Channel: The* Exxon Valdez *Oil Spill*. Washington: University of Washington Press.

F

failed state A term gaining currency in the 21st century, *failed state* is used to describe societies where coherent state organization has broken down, there is no legitimate authority or rule of law, and the population is subject to control by warring factions all competing for control. The modern example of greatest concern to the world is Somalia, which has been locked in civil war since 1991. After failed interventions by the United Nations and the United States, in an attempt to impose coherent government, the international community has retreated to just providing food and medical aid. Meanwhile, much of Somalia's population disperses around the world in an exodus of refugees from the conflict. The term is increasingly associated with efforts to intervene in a state in the name of humanitarian relief or security. The notion of "failed" has been added to undercut the premise of the *Treaty of Westphalia* (1648), which contained the idea that nation–states were the highest level of power.

Fair Deal During the 1948 presidential election in the United States, President Harry S. Truman ran on a platform of human rights, which he presented under the name *The Fair Deal*. When elected he was able to get a great deal of liberal legislation passed that extended aspects of the welfare state first introduced as part of the "New Deal" of Franklin D. Roosevelt. His proposal to introduce a national health insurance plan, however, was blocked by the American Medical Association.

false consciousness *See* **class consciousness, false**.

false positives When trying to identify dangerous offenders (and other things as well), researchers often make mistakes. One of these mistakes is known as a *false positive*; for example, identifying someone as dangerous (and possibly keeping that person incarcerated or denying parole) when the person is not dangerous. The other type of error would be a false negative: Identifying someone as nondangerous when that person in fact goes on to commit a dangerous act.

falsifiability (or refutability) A central tenet of science, falsifiability (or refutability) demands that all claims or assertions investigated by science must be open to being proven false. If a researcher cannot define what would count as empirical or experimental disproof of a claim, then the claim itself must fall outside the domain of science. This tenet is consistent with the belief that, in science, it is possible to prove something to be false but not to prove something to be true. In fact, it is assumed that we can never prove something to be true—we can only fail to disprove something and therefore accept its truth for the time being. Science does not try simply to illustrate or demonstrate its theories or hypotheses; rather, it actively tries to disprove them. This approach to science comes from Karl Popper (1902–1994). Reference: Popper, K. (1963). *Conjectures and refutations: The growth of scientific knowledge*. London: Routledge [1992].

familism Referring to core values of a family type, familism emphasizes commitment to the family as a unit (e.g., staying together for the sake of the children). This value is found in the "bourgeois family," which reflects the cultural belief that the family is the foundation of society and the source of human identification and moral discipline. The modern conjugal family, by contrast, is typically described as having a central value of individualism that de-emphasizes the importance of the family unit. *See also* **family**, **bourgeois; individualism**.

family allowance Introduced in 1945, the family allowance was a monthly payment given to the mother of every child under age 16 (changed to age 18 in 1973) who, if of school age, was attending school. Beginning in 1978, a merging of social security programs and income tax provisions introduced the notion of a child tax credit as a way to target families in need of government assistance. This eventually led to the elimination of the family allowance and, many argued, to the end of universality as a principle of Canadian social security. The family allowance was also known as the *baby bonus*.

While the government once fulfilled an obligation to every child, we now have a system in which the government makes no tax or social security allowance for many children.

family, bourgeois A family system based on private family life, the bourgeois family assigns women to the domestic sphere, with men acting as family heads in the social and economic spheres.

family class immigrant *See* **sponsored immigrant**.

family, conjugal A nuclear family of adult partners and their children (by birth or adoption), the family relationship in a conjugal family is principally focused inwardly, and ties to extended kin are voluntary and based on emotional bonds, rather than strict duties and obligations. *See also* **family, nuclear**.

family, consanguineal A family system of nuclear families linked through shared descent from a common ancestor is called a *consanguineal family*. The individual nuclear families are bound into complex ties of obligation and daily activity with each other. Consanguineal families can be linked either matrilineally or patrilineally.

Family Court A provincial court with jurisdiction over some aspects of family law, the Family Court is usually involved in child custody matters and support payments. At some times, the Family Court has also served as a Youth Court.

family, egalitarian A family system based on the equality of the participants and in direct contrast to the patriarchal family, an egalitarian family usually features an equal relationship between the adult partners, although it can mean permissive, rather than authoritarian, parent–child relationships. In North American families, this family form is most likely to be found among young, well-educated couples. The term *symmetrical family* is sometimes used as an equivalent. The concept is in many respects an ideal, rather than descriptive of typical or usual family relationships. *See also* **double burden**.

family, nuclear The nuclear family has the same composition as the conjugal family, but the term *nuclear* does not imply that the family is inwardly focused and relatively autonomous from extended kin, as in the case of the conjugal family. Extended, or consanguineal (based on shared blood descent), families can be thought of as composed of linked nuclear families. *See also* **family, conjugal**.

Fanon, Franz (1925–1961) Born in Algeria, a colony of France until gaining independence in 1962, psychoanalyst and social philosopher Franz Fanon articulated the moral and psychological damage resulting from colonization. His writings have become a source of understanding for many of the colonized peoples of the world. Reference: Fanon, Franz. (1961). *The wretched of the earth*. New York: Grove Press [1963]. *See also* **colonialism**.

fascism A key principle of fascism, a political doctrine opposed to democracy and demanding submission to political leadership and authority, is the belief that the whole society has a shared destiny and purpose that can be achieved only by iron discipline, obedience to leadership, and an all-powerful state. Fascism first developed in Italy under the leadership of Benito Mussolini (dictator of Italy from 1922 to 1943), and later influenced the development of German fascism in the Nazi movement led by Adolf Hitler (dictator of Germany from 1933 to 1945). While fascism increases the power and role of the state in society and suppresses free trade unions and political opposition, it preserves private ownership and private property.

fatalistic suicide Identified by French sociologist Émile Durkheim (1858–1917), fatalistic suicide occurs in social conditions where the individual experiences pervasive oppression. For example, the condition of slavery may make an individual feel that suicide is the only way to escape.

fecundity *Fecundity* refers to the potential number of children a woman can have. *Fertility rate*, on the other hand, refers to the actual number of children a woman has.

federalism, asymmetrical When a federal system of government does not accord precisely the same legal powers and areas of jurisdiction to all of its constituent states or provinces, asymmetrical federalism is said to exist. In Canada, this form of federalism has been advocated as a way to reconcile Quebec to the federal system by awarding the province specific additional powers connected to the protection and promotion of the French language and culture.

federalism, centripetal A federal system where there is a strong federal government and weaker provincial governments, centripetal federalism is the opposite of centrifugal federalism, where power would be dispersed from the centre to the provincial governments. In Canada, the debate over these visions of federalism has continued since before Confederation and is still unresolved. *See also* **confederation**.

female circumcision A general term used to refer to various practices now referred to as *female genital mutilation*, *female circumcision* implies a comparison to male circumcision, but it is argued that there is no real comparison between the two. *See also* **female genital mutilation**.

female genital mutilation Comprising traditional and ritualistic practices found in many patriarchal cultures of the world, female genital mutilation involves the cutting or removal of the genitals of females. A clitoridectomy may involve removal of the hood of the clitoris; complete removal of the clitoris; or infibulation, suturing of the vaginal opening. Since many immigrants to Canada arrive from countries in which these practices are found, there has been concern about the health issues and the gender-based rights issues arising from this tradition. Prevention programs and legal measures have been taken to eliminate the practice. Reference; Boddy, Janice. (1989). *Wombs and alien spirits*. Madison: University of Wisconsin.

femicide Since technically the term *homicide* refers to the killing of a man, the term *femicide* has been used to refer to the killing of a woman.

feminism A diverse political and intellectual movement chiefly developed by women but experiencing increasing influence with both sexes, feminism seeks to criticize, re-evaluate, and transform the place of women in social organization and in culture. Common to feminists is the assumption that social organization and culture have been dominated by men to the exclusion of women and that this exclusion has been accompanied by a diverse pattern of devaluation and disadvantagement that have marginalized women's status in most known societies. Consequently, a major area of concern to feminism is the recovery and articulation of women's experience in history and in contemporary societies, and a wholesale reconstruction of the fundamental intellectual assumptions of social practices and of many areas of study, including especially sociology, psychology, history, and other social and humanistic disciplines. *See also* **ecofeminism; liberal feminism; patriarchy; radical feminism**.

feminism, cultural A feminist perspective that reverses the assumption that men exhibit the normative form of behaviour and that women are different and, thus, the "other," cultural feminism makes female cultural characteristics the norm. The characteristics of women are positively evaluated and those of men, as the "other," are seen as bad or evil. For example, women are characterized as cooperative (and that is good), while men are characterized as aggressive and competitive (and that is bad).

feminism, difference Difference feminism rejects the belief that the differences between men and women are socially constructed or are established through socialization. Rather, it believes that men and women are different in essence, and that these differences arise from differing human natures. Cooperation and competition, therefore, are not just values that have been socially assigned to women and men, respectively, but are values that arise from the fundamentally different character of the two sexes. This is a form of essentialism.

feminism, standpoint Standpoint feminism is influenced by the sociology of knowledge, which claims that less-powerful members of society are able to achieve a more complete view of social reality than are others. Less-powerful groups, like women and minorities, may be less incorporated into the reward system of society and more clear-sighted and critical about its inequalities and deficiencies. The sociology of knowledge assumption behind this is the idea that knowledge is socially constructed and shaped by the social position occupied by the "knower." It follows then that the researcher's point of view is also shaped by his or her position in society, and standpoint feminism acknowledges this and claims for women a positive role in contributing to a rounded understanding of the character of the society. This acknowledgment is a rejection of traditional notions of objectivity. *See also* **sociology of knowledge**.

feminist criminology While there has always been a criminological interest in the criminal behaviour of women, it was not until the early 1970s that a plethora of literature appeared that clearly revealed the sexist assumptions behind most criminological theory and called for a reorientation of criminology. By including women in the academic study of crime and developing a realistic understanding of women, the whole field of criminology would need to rethink much of its theory about men and women. Reference: Smart, Carol. (1976). *Women, Crime and Criminology: A Feminist Critique*. London: Routledge and Kegan Paul.

feminist movement The feminist movement is a social movement whose goal has been, and continues to be, the elimination of the patriarchal nature of society. Two large waves of feminist organization can be identified: The first followed the French Revolution and extended the principles of liberty and freedom to women. This period is associated with English writer Mary Wollstonecraft (1759–1797). The second can be identified with French writer Simone de Beauvoir (1908–1986) and her book *The Second Sex* in 1952 and, in North America, with the publication in 1963 of *The Feminine Mystique* by U.S. writer Betty Friedan (1921– 2006). *See also* **social movement**.

feminist theory While there is not a single feminist theory, central to all such theories is an attempt to understand the social, economic, and political position of women in society, with a view to liberation. Feminist theory has challenged the claims to objectivity of previous social science and, by examining society from women's position, has called much social science into question as being male-centred and a component of the hegemonic rule of patriarchy. *See also* **ecofeminism; liberal feminism; Marxist feminism; radical feminism**.

feminization of poverty The incidence of poverty among women becomes much higher than among men in the feminization of poverty, a social process. Changes in social policy, the structure of the family and the workplace, social security provisions, life expectancy, and other aspects of society have had the unintended result of increasing the female proportion of the population with low incomes or in poverty. In Canada, poverty rates are particularly high among female single parents and among elderly women. The feminization of poverty is often cited as an explanation for an increase in women's involvement in crime and contrasted to a "liberation" explanation.

feral child A child who, in legend or in fact, has been raised and protected from infancy by animals is called a *feral child*. The most famous example is the "Wild Boy of Aveyron" who was discovered in 1800 at the age of 11 or 12 after having apparently been raised by animals. Although considerable effort was made to "civilize" the child, there was little success and he was able to master only a few words. The case is offered in the social sciences to emphasize the importance of socialization and the social nature of the human species. A more recent example of a child growing up in isolation from human contact is found in the story of Genie (Curtiss 1977). References: Shattuck, Roger. (1980). *The Forbidden Experiment: The Story of the Wild Boy of Aveyron.* New York: Washington Square Press; Curtiss, Susan. (1977). *Genie: A Psycholinguistic Study of a Modern-Day "Wild Child."* New York: Academic Press. *See also* **socialization**.

fertility rate The number of children born to women in their fertile years within a given population, the fertility rate is usually expressed as the average number of children born to women over a lifetime. Not to be confused with the birth rate. *See also* **birth rate**.

fetal alcohol syndrome This term was first used in 1973, when two scientists noticed similar deformities in the infants of six mothers with a history of alcohol abuse. The consumption of alcohol during pregnancy is now known to result in brain abnormalities and other deformities in some children. It is believed that this syndrome may account for the criminal behaviour of many offenders.

fetishism Fetishism is a disorder in which the person becomes sexually aroused by inanimate objects such as someone's underwear, a piece of fur, or a rubber doll, or is fixated on nonsexual parts of the body such as the feet or knees.

feudalism A system of economic and social organization, feudalism has historically been found in several areas of the world, including Japan, China, other parts of Asia, the Americas, and many countries of Eastern and Western Europe. In Western Europe, feudalism was at its height between about 1000 and 1500. The system was founded on a web of military obligations between powerful overlords and their vassals. Vassals, who were usually landlords of knightly rank, owed duties of military service in return for grants of land (fiefs) from the overlord. The land and the military obligations were usually passed from father to son. The usual economic foundation of the system was the feudal manor, an agricultural organization that included a central farm owned by the landlord and small land holdings for a class of bonded farm labourers (serfs). The serfs were required to work the central manorial farm and to provide the lord with produce and money payments in return for their own rights to land use. The system gradually declined as cities and towns grew, money became the basis for economic transactions, and power became centralized in nation–states under monarchies. Loss of rural population from plague also hastened the end of this system of economic organization, especially in England.

fictive kinship The custom of considering nonbiologically related individuals (e.g., friends) as part of a kin group is called *fictive kinship*.

fiduciary relationship A relationship of guardianship and trust, a fiduciary relationship is based on the maintenance of the utmost good faith and truthful service. In Canada, the original relationship between the federal government and First Nations was established on the principle that the government would act as trustee of the aboriginal peoples until they were at a stage of economic and social development that would lead to limited self-government and greater social integration with other Canadians. Today, there is much soul-searching among Canadians about the treatment of aboriginal peoples by successive governments and by agencies such as the churches acting on their behalf. Many see this history as a profound breach of the fiduciary duty of government to act solely in the best interests of the people.

filibuster Prolonging debate in a legislature in order to prevent the passage of legislation or other government business, filibustering is sometimes used by Opposition parties to highlight their opposition to government policies and to obstruct the government's program. In Canada and other parliamentary systems, the filibuster is not a very powerful weapon because the government is able to curtail debate by introducing "closure motions" that can be passed by a simple majority. In the United States, it is a more useful device for the Opposition, since closure of debate requires special majorities varying between three-fifths and two-thirds of all Senate members.

First Nations This term emerged in the mid-1980s to describe Canadian aboriginal individuals and communities. The traditional term "Indian" has fallen into disfavour, as it is both mistaken (it was applied only because European explorers had expected to find India across the Atlantic Ocean) and ignores the great variety of history and culture among First Nations societies. The name *First Nations* is also politically significant, since it implies possession of rights arising from the original historical occupation of Canadian territory. Canada's principal national organization of aboriginal people (but not including the Inuit) is the Assembly of First Nations.

first reading In parliamentary procedure, a Bill (a request to the Crown that a matter become law) has three readings. The first reading usually just introduces the Bill and is not debatable. Agreement at this stage just gets the Bill into the process, and it is sent to committee. When the Bill appears for second reading, it is debatable and can be defeated, amended, or approved. If it is approved, it goes to third reading, which is normally a vote of formal approval to send it to the Senate and not a time for extended debate.

Firth, Raymond (1901–2002) Raymond Firth was born in New Zealand, where he obtained a degree in economics. After meeting and studying with Polish anthropologist Bronislaw Malinowski in London, he changed fields and went on to teach at the London School of Economics for many years. He was a prolific writer, but his classic work was done on the people of Tikopia in the Solomon Islands (1936). Like Malinowski, he was a functionalist and developed the distinction (now not seen as important) between social organization and social structure. Firth developed the field of economic anthropology. Reference: Firth, Raymond. (1936). *We, the Tikopia: A Sociological Study of Kinship in Primitive Polynesia.* (With a preface by Bronislaw Malinowski). London: Allen and Unwin.

fiscal crisis This term refers broadly to a long-term situation in which government expenditures exceed government revenues. Within modern Marxist theory (neo-Marxism), the term has been used more specifically to refer to a situation in which governments have increased their role in society in serving the needs of private capital, but have not been able to adequately tax private capital to support the expenditures. For example, technical employment training has now largely become a preserve of the state (rather than the private employer), leaving the state with additional expenditures, but without corresponding revenues. According to neo-Marxism, this tendency is linked to the development of economic concentration and monopoly, and is built into the capitalist economic system. The fiscal crisis of the state is thought to drive much contemporary government policy on social programs. Reference: O'Connor, James. (1973). *The Fiscal Crisis of the State.* New York: St. Martin's Press.

fiscal policy Fiscal policies are government economic policies that rely on economic regulation and control exercised through government taxation and budgetary policy "to regulate the economy." Fiscal policies are in contrast to monetary policies, which seek to influence the direction of the economy by controlling both the rate of interest (the cost of borrowing money) and the amount of money available within an economy (the money supply). *See also* **monetary policy**.

flag debate After what was commonly known as "the great Canadian flag debate," Canada officially adopted its Maple Leaf flag in 1965 only after prolonged and unusually emotional public discussion. The flag flown by Canada after Confederation was the Red Ensign, a red-background flag with the British Union Jack in the top left-hand corner and the Canadian coat of arms centred in the remaining right-hand area. Over time, there was increasing disquiet that the flag, with its explicit connection to Britain, suggested a semicolonial status for Canada, and by 1925, Prime Minister Mackenzie King had tried and failed to have a distinctly national flag adopted. In 1946, he tried and failed again. In 1964, Prime Minister Lester Pearson, a brilliant diplomat, assigned the issue to a 15-member, all-party committee of the House of Commons. This committee, after considerable discussion, returned to the House recommending today's Maple Leaf flag. A long debate then ensued, since the new design was ferociously opposed by many MPs, especially Conservative leader John Diefenbaker, who railed against a flag that failed to acknowledge the "founding races" of the country by displaying the Union Jack. Eventually, at the suggestion of a Quebec Conservative, a motion was adopted to limit speeches to 20 minutes, and after 250 of them, a vote of 163 to 78 brought the Maple Leaf flag to Canada on December 15, 1964. The flag was officially proclaimed in January 1965 and first flown on Parliament Hill on February 15, 1965. At the ceremony, to the shock of many Canadians, John Diefenbaker was seen to bow his head in sorrow and cry.

flapper Adolescent girls and young women who rebelled against the rigid Victorian sexual standards for women were called *flappers*. While the age of consent had been raised to 18 in many North American jurisdictions in the latter half of the 19th century, the open expression of sexual interest by women in the early 20th century set off alarm bells. The Juvenile Court movement of the early 20th century could be seen as one aspect of a strategy to control the sexuality of young women by using courts and penalties to regulate their sexual behaviour. Through the 1950s and 1960s, Canadian juvenile courts punished young females much more frequently for promiscuity than it did young males.

flat tax Currently gaining significant public support in North America, imposition of a flat tax would mean that all citizens would pay the same percentage of taxation on their income. This would simplify tax law and the completion of tax returns, but would make income tax regressive. *See also* **regressive taxation**.

fluorine test A method of relative dating in archaeology, the fluorine test builds on the assumption that fluorine in bones increases with age.

folklore A term once used in contrast to the literate culture of the modern, *folklore* is now used to refer to the oral traditions and verbal arts of a culture.

folk society A society of primary communal relationships with little complexity, minimal division of labour, and largely insulated from contact with other societies is called a *folk society*. The term is an ideal type associated with American anthropologist/sociologist Robert Redfield (1897–1958) and is closely related to German sociologist F. Tonnies' (1855–1936) concept of *Gemeinschaft*. *See also* ***Gemeinschaft***.

forces of production In Marxian terms, forces of production are the essential component of the economic system of society. This term refers to the materials used in the production of goods as well as the tools, knowledge, and techniques used to transform these materials. Not included are the class structure or relations of society, which are known as the *relations of production*. *See also* **mode of production**; **social relations of production**.

Fordism This term refers to the system of mass production (e.g., the assembly line) pioneered by Henry Ford to meet the needs of a mass market.

Ford Pinto After the 1973 world oil crisis, American carmakers rushed to design compact cars with greater fuel efficiency. Ford manufactured the Pinto and, wanting to retain a large trunk, they repositioned the gas tank. Their crash tests showed that the tank was apt to explode; however, the car was marketed, and approximately 500 people died in fires caused in crashes. It was later learned that Ford had done a cost analysis: The company compared the cost of recalling and redesigning the car with the cost of lawsuits for death and injury. It was determined that paying for lawsuits was the cheapest option. Ford became the first corporation charged with murder, a charge of which the company was acquitted.

Fossey, Dian (1932–1985) Zoologist Dian Fossey, born in California, became part of a group of three women (British primatologist Jane Goodall and Canadian orangutan expert Biruté Galdikas being the other two) encouraged by British/Kenyan archaeologist and anthropologist Louis Leakey to follow their interests in studying primates in the wild. Fossey began studying mountain gorillas in Zaire and later in Rwanda, where she was murdered in 1985. She had grown increasingly worried about the poaching of gorillas in the area and had begun a campaign to limit this activity. A foundation has been established to continue her work in conservation. Reference: Mowat, Farley. (1987). *Woman in the mists: The story of Dian Fossey and the mountain gorillas of Africa.* New York: Warner Books. *See also* **Galdikas, Biruté; Goodall, Jane; Leakey, Louis and Mary.**

Foucault, Michel (1926–1984) French historian and philosopher Michel Foucault represents French intellectual tradition and, through his studies of the prison system, has had an influence on criminology, although his entire output has influenced all social sciences. In his book on incarceration, he studied the new body of knowledge represented by penology and criminology, the new architecture of the penitentiary, and the new form of regulation of the body that these two combined. In each of these, he sees new forms of power and it is this idea of power being encoded in all aspects of our talk and writing that has influenced social science. Reference: Foucault, M. (1975). *Discipline and Punish: The Birth of the Prison.* New York: Vintage. *See also* **discourse analysis; postmodernism.**

four pillars A coordinated strategy to reduce negative impacts on society from the trading and use of addictive drugs, the four pillars are prevention, treatment, harm reduction, and enforcement. Prevention involves interventions with individuals and families. Treatment helps people to emerge from the drug lifestyle and regain integration into society. Harm reduction involves programs like safe injection sites, supplies of clean needles, and rapid health care responses to overdose crises. Enforcement focuses on police action to reduce the role of organized crime and maintain safety in neighbourhoods.

fourth estate The print news and journalistic media— newspapers, magazines—are called the *fourth estate.* Today, the electronic news media of radio, television, and the Internet have created a fifth estate. The terms suggest that the media represents a powerful force within a society and can shape political events and opinions, as well as being watchdogs over the use of authority by political and corporate authorities. The intimate connection between media and corporate capital is pointed out by skeptics. The origin of the term *fourth estate* is from medieval France where, on rare occasions, the Crown consulted a constituent assembly representing the French people. The assemblies were composed of representatives of the three "estates" of French society: the clergy composed the first estate; the aristocracy composed the second estate; and the middle-class merchants, professionals, state administrators, and wealthier farmers composed the third estate.

fragment theory Associated with Harvard political science professor and author Louis Hartz (1919– 1986), fragment theory holds that European immigrants to the New World brought particular elements or "fragments" of their heritage cultures and these then tended to set lasting historical patterns in the political cultures that developed. For Canada, Hartz saw two main fragments: the feudal values and attitudes brought by immigrant peasants and the Catholic clergy from France in the 1600s and 1700s, and the more liberal attitudes of the English, Scottish, and Irish. Fragment theory is considered by many social scientists as quite weak in its explanatory value for the Canadian political culture, which has also been shaped by both conservatism and socialism, as well as by geography, climate, and patterns of initial population settlement. Reference: Hartz, L. (1964). *The founding of new societies.* Fort Washington, PA: Harvest Books (imprint of Harcourt, Brace).

Frankenstein Written by Mary Wollstonecraft Shelley (1797–1851), the daughter of English writer Mary Wollstonecraft (1759–1797), Frankenstein, published in 1818, depicts the creation of a man through the application of science, who subsequently gets out of control and kills his creator.

Taken as a metaphor of the limited vision but overwhelming arrogance of scientific "man" or rational "man," the book is now seen as an indictment of the new society that was emerging in the 18th and 19th centuries.

Frankfurt School A group of chiefly German social theorists associated with the Frankfurt Institute of Social Research, the Frankfurt School was founded in 1923. Authors associated with the school are T.W. Adorno, Max Horkheimer, Herbert Marcuse, and Friedrich Pollock. The underlying philosophy of this group can also be found in the more recent work of Jurgen Habermas, a student of Adorno. The school developed critical theory, an extension and development of the ideas of Karl Marx and Sigmund Freud. Much important work flowed from this school, which examined culture as a lived experience and its role in modern societies. Reference: Wiggerhaus, R. (1995). *The Frankfurt School: Its History, Theories and Political Significance*. Boston: MIT Press. *See also* **critical theory; cultural studies**.

Frazer, Sir James (1854–1941) Often referred to as the father of anthropology, Sir James Frazer, born in Scotland, spent most of his life at Cambridge University. His great work *The Golden Bough* is a study of religious beliefs and rituals around the world. His interest in religion probably stemmed from his own agnosticism and his evolutionary belief that all human minds were the same but simply developed at different rates according to culture. The study of religious rituals then would reveal the stops made by all humankind along the way to modernity. This belief was soon rejected by the academic world but Frazer became very popular and his work has never been out of print. Reference: Fraser, Robert. (1990). *The Making of "The Golden Bough": The Origins and Growth of an Argument*. New York: St. Martin's Press.

free trade Free trade between nations is conducted without tariffs, import quotas, or other restrictive regulations. Free trade, especially with the United States, has been controversial throughout post-Confederation Canadian history and has been widely distrusted as likely to lead to Canada playing the role of resource provider to a more advanced U.S. manufacturing and service economy. Since 1989, when a free trade agreement with the United States was introduced (*see* **Free Trade Agreement** [**Canada–U.S., 1989: FTA**]), Canadian opinion has tended to become more supportive of this policy, especially in light of the general globalization of trade and international communication. Since the initial free trade agreement, growing consensus is that there has been an economic (and to some extent social) integration of the two nations. In 1994, Canada, the United States, and Mexico entered into a trilateral free trade agreement: the *North American Free Trade Agreement* (*see* **Free Trade Agreement** [**Canada–U.S.–Mexico, 1994: NAFTA**]). *See also* **dependent development; metropolis–hinterland theory; staples trap**.

Free Trade Agreement (Canada–U.S., 1989: FTA) The *Canada–U.S. Free Trade Agreement* signed in 1989 provides for elimination of Customs duties on all goods originating in either country. It also includes a mechanism for dispute settlement. The section of the FTA about energy gives Canada free access to the U.S. energy markets; it also establishes rules for prorationing, which requires that, regardless of any energy shortage, Canada continue to export the same proportion of its total energy output as the United States currently receives. *See also* **Free Trade Agreement (Canada–U.S.–Mexico, 1994: NAFTA)**.

Free Trade Agreement (Canada–U.S.–Mexico, 1994: NAFTA) The *North American Free Trade Agreement* expanded the Customs-free area and dispute resolution mechanisms in the FTA to include Mexico. It was implemented in 1994. *See also* **free trade**.

Free Trade Agreement of the Americas (FTAA) The FTAA is a projected agreement that would expand the framework of the *North American Free Trade Agreement* (NAFTA) to cover the whole of the Americas (excluding Cuba). *See also* **Free Trade Agreement (Canada–U.S.–Mexico, 1994)**.

free trade election The Canadian federal election of 1988 was contested largely on the issue of entering into a free trade agreement with the United States. The Progressive Conservative governing party and corporate Canada were in favour of such an agreement, while many groups organized in opposition. The Conservatives won the election and the *Canada–U.S. Free Trade Agreement* was entered into in 1989.

free trade zones Specially designated geographical areas within a nation that are exempt from the regulations and taxation normally imposed on business, free trade zones are intended to facilitate cross-border production and trade. Unsavoury examples of these zones are found along the United States–Mexico border—industrial factory belts in Mexico referred to as "maquiladoras," where workers are paid low wages and work long hours, with no benefits and no occupational health or safety provisions.

free vote An unusual event in parliamentary systems of government, a free vote situation occurs when members are not given party directions on how they should cast their votes. In parliamentary systems, governments are required to maintain the confidence of Parliament, so governing parties usually impose strict discipline on the voting behaviour of their members. Free votes are not on topics that involve major policy issues; they are more likely to be on matters of personal judgment or conscience that do not have major consequences for government. Examples are the flag debate of 1964 and the issues of capital punishment in 1976 and abortion in 1990. The Liberals and Conservatives supported free votes on these issues, but the New Democratic Party imposed party discipline.

free will In the criminological debate over the causes of criminal behaviour, the philosophy of free will argues that all individuals are conscious, willful, rational, and goal-directed, rejecting the idea that individuals' behaviours are caused (or determined) by factors outside of their consciousness. To treat individuals as though their behaviour is determined is to treat them as objects, but if we accept the philosophy of free will, we must treat individuals as subjects and attempt to understand how they make the social world meaningful. The criminal justice system, of course, is built on the philosophy of free will, since it adjudicates individual responsibility.

French Revolution The French Revolution brought the ideas of liberty, equality, and democracy to continental Europe and set off a profound and irreversible historical transformation. The revolution began in 1789, and some historians have traced the end of the revolution to the overthrow of Robespierre, its most radical leader, in 1794, others to the seizure of power by Napoleon Bonaparte in 1799, and yet others to the final defeat of Napoleon Bonaparte at the Battle of Waterloo in 1815. From 1789 to 1815, France was transformed by revolution. It began with the overthrowing of the monarchy, introducing a reign of revolutionary

terror. The king and queen and many of the aristocracy were executed, and there were mass executions of political opponents. Attempts were made to export the revolution to the rest of Europe, as the French armies moved east and forced monarchs to give up power, granted freedom and land to the serfs, and recruited thousands of the ordinary people into the French army to help carry forward the message of equality and liberation. This initiated a period of international wars with Britain and the old powers of Europe, leading to the ultimate defeat of French forces at the Battle of Waterloo in 1815. For the social sciences, the French Revolution is important because it represents the triumph of the liberal claim that all humans are essentially equal and all have a right to liberty and freedom of choice. Along with England's Bloodless Revolution in 1688 (sometimes called the *Glorious Revolution)*, which irreversibly established the principle of a limited constitutional monarchy; the Industrial Revolution, which gained momentum in the mid-1700s; and the American Revolution of 1776, the French Revolution ushered in the social, economic, and political transformation of Western societies and helped create the age of modernity, democracy, economic development, and legal equality for all citizens. The history of the French Revolution has fascinated social scientists since the early 19th century and continues to shape modern culture and intellectual ideas.

Freud, Sigmund (1856–1939) Born in Frieberg, Moravia, which is now part of the Czech Republic, Sigmund Freud was the founder of psychoanalysis, the theory that adult personality is shaped in early infancy and is especially influenced by an individual's experiences in sexual exploration and development. Reference: Freud, S. (1930). *Civilization and its discontents.* New York: W.W. Norton [1989].

Freudian slip Psychoanalyst Sigmund Freud argued that our hidden or suppressed thoughts have a tendency to emerge unexpectedly in what appear to be ordinary mistakes of language or errors of memory—Freudian slips. These errors supposedly reveal our hidden wishes and desires.

Front de libération du Québec (FLQ) The English translation of this term is *Front for the Liberation of Quebec.* The FLQ was founded in 1963 and inspired by the terrorist war being waged against French colonial domination of Algeria. The FLQ was dedicated to the use of terrorism and violence to promote the establishment of a separate and socialist Quebec state. In 1963, FLQ groups set off bombs in mailboxes and other locations in Quebec; in 1964, they conducted a holdup that resulted in the theft of military equipment and some $50,000 in cash. Between 1963 and 1970, the FLQ carried out more than 200 bombings, including one at the Montreal Stock Exchange that injured 27 people. The terrorist activities of the group ceased after the October Crisis of 1970, during which two prominent politicians were kidnapped by the FLQ and one was murdered. *See also* **October Crisis**.

FTA *See Free Trade Agreement* (**Canada–U.S., 1989**).

FTAA *See Free Trade Agreement of the Americas.*

functionalist explanation The explanations offered by functionalists or structural functionalists have a property referred to as *teleology*—explaining things in terms of their end results or purposes. Functionalists tend to explain features of social life in terms of their function (the part they play) in social life. These kinds of explanations are found in biology as well, and it is not surprising that functionalists like Durkheim adopted an organic metaphor. The lungs, for example, are explained in terms of what they do in and for the human body. The classic example of this reasoning is found in Durkheim's discussion of the functions of crime in any society. He argues that as darkness needs light, a moral society needs immorality as a way to make morality visible. Others have argued that crime or deviance also help society by clarifying the moral boundaries of the group. Many would argue that these are not explanations at all, but are logically circular. *See also* **structural functionalism**.

G

Galdikas, Birutė Canadian Birutė Galdikas is the world's foremost authority on wild orangutans. In 1971, she began living in the rain forests of Borneo, where she studied the orangutans, developed conservation programs, and campaigned for a large wildlife reserve. She now teaches at Simon Fraser University. Reference: Galdikas, Birutė. (1995). *Reflections on Eden: My Years with the Orangutans in Borneo. See also* **Fossey, Dian.**

Garden of Eden theory *See* **out-of-Africa hypothesis**.

Garfinkel, Harold (1917–) For information about the work of Harold Garfinkel, now professor emeritus at Harvard University, *see* **ethnomethodology**.

GATS *See General Agreement on Trade in Services.*

GATT *See General Agreement on Tariffs and Trade.*

Gemeinschaft A German word, translated as "community," *Gemeinschaft* was used by sociologist Ferdinand Tonnies (1855–1936) to define an "ideal type" or model society where social bonds are personal and direct and there are strong shared values and beliefs. Characteristic of small-scale, localized societies, it is in contrast to *Gesellschaft*, which refers to complex, impersonal societies. American sociologist Talcott Parsons (1902–1979) amplified the contrasts of *Gemeinschaft* and *Gesellschaft* with his "pattern variables" value alternatives. *See also* **Gesellschaft; pattern variables**.

gender gap The gap between the political party preferences of men and women, the gender gap became significant during the 1990s, with women in most Western societies more likely to support liberal or socialist parties favouring public welfare programs, and men more likely to support conservative or right-of-centre parties. All political parties now give some attention to positioning their policies and advertising to appeal to both women and men.

gender roles Gender roles are social roles ascribed to individuals on the basis of their sex. The term *gender* differs from the term *sex* because the former refers specifically to the cultural definition of the roles and behaviour appropriate to members of each sex, rather than to those aspects of human behaviour that are determined by biology. Thus, giving birth is a female sex role, while the role of infant nurturer and caregiver (which could be performed by a male) is a gender role usually ascribed to females. *See also* **sex**.

General Agreement on Trade in Services (GATS) As the nature of capitalism changed and corporations provided more than trade goods such as automobiles or steel, the *General Agreement on Tariffs and Trade* (GATT) was changed to include the trade in services (health care, accounting, management). This set of rules is the *General Agreement on Trade in Services. See also* **General Agreement on Tariffs and Trade**.

General Agreement on Tariffs and Trade (GATT) When the United States blocked the development of an international trade organization in 1944, nations gradually negotiated a set of rules to govern international trade. These rules form the *General Agreement on Tariffs and Trade.*

general deterrence As used in criminal justice, *general deterrence* refers to crime prevention achieved through instilling fear in the general population by the punishment of offenders. *See also* **specific deterrence**.

generalized other This is a term used by U.S. social psychologist George Herbert Mead (1863–1931) to refer to an individual's recognition that other members of that person's society hold specific values and expectations about behaviour. In their behaviour and social interaction, individuals react to the expectations of others, thus orienting themselves to the norms and values of their community or group.

generalized reciprocity Examples of generalized reciprocity, a mode of exchange in which the value of the good or service is not calculated nor is repayment specified, include food-sharing among hunting–gathering societies and the giving of gifts in modern societies.

Generation X Born approximately between the years 1960 and 1970, at the end of the baby boom, Generation X was caught in the forces of economic restructuring and globalization. Also referred to as "thirty-somethings," they will all, of course, soon become "forty-somethings." The term was coined by Canadian author Douglas Coupland (1991) as the title of a novel exploring the experience of growing up in the shadow of the baby boom generation. Reference: Coupland, Douglas. (1991). *Generation X: Tales for an Accelerated Culture.* New York: St. Martin's Press.

Geneva Conventions A number of international treaty agreements signed in Geneva, the Geneva Conventions were intended to regulate the conduct of opposing armed forces in wartime. The first was signed in 1864, after a Red Cross campaign, and it established rules of conduct toward the sick and wounded, both on the battlefield and during imprisonment. More treaties were later added, including the 1925 gas protocol that prohibited the use of poison gases and biological weapons, and the 1929 treaty on the treatment of prisoners of war.

genocide Genocide is the systematic killing of an entire ethnic community. In Canadian history, the physical elimination of the Beothuk aboriginals of Newfoundland as a result of disease and deliberate killing is perhaps an example. The term was first used in a 1944 book by Raphael Lemkin (*Axis Rule in Occupied Europe*) and by 1946, there was a United Nations resolution condemning genocide. *See also* **Armenian genocide**; **cultural genocide**; **Holocaust**; **Rwandan genocide**.

Genovese, Kitty *See* **bystander problem**.

gentrification A process of change in the social and economic condition of urban neighbourhoods, gentrification results in poorer original residents being replaced by newcomers from the middle-class and professional groups.

geological time scale A set of standard terms have evolved to refer to time in the history of the geological world: eons, eras, periods, epochs. The times that are of most relevance in the history of human development are located in the Phanerozoic Eon, the Cenozoic Era, and the Neogene Period. The Neogene Period is subdivided into four epochs: Miocene, Pliocene, Pleistocene, and Holocene. These epochs cover from the current age to 23 million years ago. The Stone Age for example is located in the Pleistocene and Holocene epochs, covering from the present to 1.8 million years ago.

geopolitics This term refers to both an academic form of analysis as well as an ideology behind political actors. As academic study, geopolitics is similar to what was called *international relations* in the past, and includes an analysis of the relationship between political power and geographic space. Such study may look at conflict between powerful nations in terms of their attempts to control territory, resources, ports, rivers, and sources of wealth. For example, many people try to analyze the United States invasion of Iraq in these terms. Geopolitics is also embedded in the thinking of political players. For example, it is clear that the United States under the presidency of T. Roosevelt chose to turn itself into an empire through the Spanish American war (1898) and "occupation" of Panama in 1903. The terms *heartland–hinterland* (preferred by geographers) and *metropolis–hinterland* (preferred by sociologists) derive from this form of analysis. Reference: Zimmerman, W. (2002). *First great triumph.* New York: Farrar, Straus and Giroux.

George, Dudley In 1995, the Chipewyan peoples of Kettle Point and Stony Point in Ontario protested against the tardy return of land taken from them many years previously for a military base. During a confrontation, a member of the Ontario Provincial Police shot an unarmed protester, Dudley George. A commission of inquiry was established, and rumours circulated about the possible involvement of the provincial government in directing the activities of the police. Reference: Edwards, Peter. (2001). *One Dead Indian: The Premier, the Police and the Ipperwash Crisis.* Toronto: Stoddart. *See also* **Gustafsen Lake; Oka Crisis**.

gerontocracy Ruled by elders, a gerontocracy is a society in which power, wealth, and prestige flow upward within an age pyramid. While historically authority or power was in the hands of elders in many small-scale societies and great reverence was paid to these elders, in modern society, wealth may flow toward the elders, but there is little positive evaluation or prestige bestowed on the elderly and they are seen as having little authority.

gerrymander Meaning to draw constituency or electoral district boundaries to favour the election of particular parties, an example of gerrymandering could involve defining the boundaries of an electoral district to include a prosperous area of town and exclude a poorer area, thus enhancing the chances of a Conservative candidate. The term is said to have arisen in Massachusetts in 1812, when an artist added wings, claws, and teeth to an electoral district map and suggested it be called a "salamander." Since the state governor at the time was Elbridge Gerry, the name was soon modified to "gerrymander."

Gesellschaft A German word translated as "society-association," *Gesellschaft* was used by German sociologist Ferdinand Tonnies (1855–1936) to refer to an "ideal type" or model of a society where social bonds are primarily impersonal, instrumental, and narrow. Characteristic of large-scale, complex societies, with a strict division between private and public spheres of life, it contrasts to the community-oriented life of the *Gemeinschaft*. American sociologist Talcott Parsons (1902–1979) amplified the contrast of *Gemeinschaft* and *Gesellschaft* with his "pattern variables" value alternatives. *See also* ***Gemeinschaft*; ideal type; pattern variables**.

Ghost Dance In 1889, Wovoka, a Paiute Native American had a vision in which he saw the second coming of Christ and received a warning about the evils of the colonizers of native lands. This vision led to a great revitalization movement among natives as they struggled to deal with the consequences of their poverty and disruption. Belief in this vision spread quickly, and people were encouraged to engage in the Ghost Dance in order to hasten the arrival of the new age. Part of the vision was that the world was going to be destroyed and that the Indians would once again arise and be free. United States government agents became concerned over the spread of this movement and the dance was outlawed. Reference: Kehoe, A. (1989). *The ghost dance: Ethnohistory and revitalization.* Fort Worth: Holt, Rinehart and Winston.

Giddens, Anthony (1938–) British sociologist Anthony Giddens has become the most quoted social science author of his time and at the forefront of many debates about contemporary sociology. He is also associated with the development of a new political philosophy referred to as the "Third Way," which is a blend of social democratic theory and neoliberal theory. This philosophy was taken up by British prime minister Tony Blair in his reform of the British Labour Party and in his subsequent victory for the Labour Party in Britain. This philosophy when put into practice is what is often meant by the "new left." *See also* **structuration; Third Way**.

Gift (The) This 1925 essay by French sociologist and anthropologist Marcel Mauss (1872–1950) explores the way in which gift-giving among tribal societies is a moral exchange, driven by obligation, and how the giving away of one's possessions as gifts creates individual wealth and status by expanding and cementing a complex network of personal and family obligations to the giver. Mauss was the son of Émile Durkheim's sister. *See also* **reciprocity**.

Gini coefficient Developed by Italian statistician Corrodo Gini (1884–1965), the Gini coefficient provides a mathematical expression of the degree of concentration of wealth or income. While it has been criticized over the years, it continues to be used by social scientists in describing inequality or comparing inequality among nations. A Gini coefficient of approximately 0.400 is normal for most developed economies. For a fuller grasp of how the coefficient is determined, *see also* **Lorenz curve**.

Gladue case A precedent-setting case regarding aboriginal offenders, in the Gladue case, the court determined that in passing sentence in cases where a term of incarceration would normally be imposed, judges must consider the unique circumstances of aboriginal people and are under an obligation to consider alternatives to prison. Reference: *R. v. Gladue* [1999] 1 S.C.R. 688.

glass ceiling In the analysis of women in the workplace, the glass ceiling concept is useful for describing the invisible barriers that block the promotion of women. It refers to barriers that are not explicit, but are inherent in the social organization and social relationships of the workplace. For example, women may find their corporate careers obstructed because they are excluded from the recreational and social associations created by male co-workers and lack the social contacts that are important in gaining status and recognition.

global commons *Global commons* refers to the international dimension of the commons, which on a local level relates to the social and environmental spaces and resources that are or have been held by a community in common. *See also* **commons (the).**

Global Compact In January 1999, Kofi Annan, Secretary General of the United Nations, spoke to the economic leaders of the world assembled at Davos, Switzerland, to unveil a plan for international corporations to voluntarily agree to meet global standards for human rights, labour rights, and environmental protection. The immediate goal was to convince 1,000 corporations to join this compact.

globalization A comprehensive worldwide process, globalization is the internationalization of communication, trade, and economic organization. In the economic sphere, globalization can be seen in international trade agreements, vast increases in the volume of international trade, and the growing economic interdependency of nations. It is also marked by the expansion in size and power of multinational corporations and the development of the American entertainment industry's domination of international cultural communication. Generally, the process is seen as being driven by the growth of international capitalism and involving the transformation of the cultural and social structures of noncapitalist and pre-industrial societies. Reference: Giddens, Anthony. (2000). *Runaway World: How Globalization Is Reshaping Our Lives.* New York: Routledge. *See also* **free trade.**

Goffman, Erving (1922–1982) Canadian-born sociologist Erving Goffman was associated with the Chicago School of symbolic interactionism and later was a professor of anthropology and sociology at the University of Pennsylvania. Perhaps his most important book, *The Presentation of Self in Everyday Life* developed a "dramaturgical" model of people's interactions with society. In private, "back

stage," they express their spontaneous identity, but in public, "front stage," they manage their social presentation to create an impression that will cause their audience to define them in the desired way. They behave as actors as they manage the impression they are creating. Another of his important works is *Asylums,* which examines the transformation of identity that takes place when individuals enter total institutions like mental hospitals or prisons, where their previous sense of self is stripped away and they are resocialized to a new identity. This transformation can be so powerful that inmates become incapable of recovering their previous sense of self. Reference: Goffman, Erving. (1959). *The Presentation of Self in Everyday Life.* New York: Doubleday; Goffman, Erving (1961). *Asylums: Essays on the Social Situation of Mental Patients and Other Inmates.* New York: Anchor/ Doubleday.

Goodall, Jane British zoologist Jane Goodall (1934–) is the world's foremost authority on chimpanzees, having studied their behaviour through observation in the wild for 35 years. A meeting with British/Kenyan archaeologist and anthropologist Louis Leakey in 1957 started her on this research path, and she arrived in Tanzania in 1960 to begin her observations. Over the years, her publications have changed the way many people think about chimpanzees. Reference: Goodall, Jane. (1990). *Through a window: My thirty years with the chimpanzees of Gome.* Boston: Houghton Mifflin. *See also* **Leakey, Louis and Mary**

goods-producing economy An economy whose central method of capital accumulation is the manufacture of goods for consumers (televisions), for public consumption (trains), or for private economic use (robots for building cars) is a goods-producing economy. It has been claimed for several years that Western societies have passed through this goods-producing, or industrial, stage and have now entered a new economy founded on the delivery of services and the production and dissemination of knowledge. *See also* **service economy.**

Goodwin, Ginger A coal miner originally from England, Ginger Goodwin (1887–1918) became a union organizer in British Columbia. While fighting for better conditions for mine workers (including an eight-hour day), Goodwin organized strikes at the Cominco and Trail mines. In 1918, his earlier exemption from conscription due to poor health was reversed, some speculated in retaliation for his strike activities against coal baron Robert Dunsmuir. Goodwin went into hiding, and when an order went out to arrest those who did not show up for their conscription duties, he was hunted down and shot by a local police officer in a wooded area near Cumberland, BC. Reference: Stonebanks, Roger. (2004). *Fighting for Dignity: The Ginger Goodwin Story*. St. John's: Canadian Committee on Labour History.

Gouzenko case Igor Gouzenko (1919–1987) was a Soviet citizen who worked as a clerk in the Soviet embassy in Ottawa from 1943 to 1945. When he discovered that he and his family were to be returned to the Soviet Union, he defected and reported to Canadian authorities that a Soviet spy ring was operating in Canada. This was the first of several "spy scares" to emerge in the West after World War II. After much controversy, the Canadian government acknowledged that such a spy ring was operating, and Gouzenko was given protection and a new identity; he and his family remained in Canada. As a result of this case, there was an escalation of repressive measures against potential dissidents in Canada. Reference: Whitaker, R., & Marcuse, G. (1994). *Cold War Canada: The Making of a National Insecurity State, 1945–1957*. Toronto: University of Toronto Press. For American equivalents, *see* **McCarthyism**.

government In modern states like Canada, *government* can be defined as the complex of institutions that exercise the state's authority to establish rules and direction for the community and make binding authoritative decisions. All formal governments—federal, provincial, municipal, and their agents—possess authority derived from the state, and each government has the right to exercise this authority within its jurisdictional areas. Government has not always been a specialized formal process, and most small-scale societies have governed themselves with chiefs or councils of elders. Today, the democratic framework of elected governments is dominant internationally, but its history is brief since even complex societies tended to be governed by traditional rule of monarchs and their counsellors until the 18th and 19th centuries. *See also* **state**.

governor general The head of state, the Queen, is represented by a governor general who holds by delegation most of the monarch's formal legal authority within Canada. By constitutional convention, the governor general acts only with the advice and consent of ministers who are responsible to the House of Commons. After 1931, when the complete governmental autonomy of Canada from Britain was formally recognized, the governor general ceased to have any kind of responsibility to British ministers and became the personal representative of the Crown in Canada. The governor general is selected by the prime minister and Cabinet and is appointed by the Queen for a period of five years. Since 1952, when Vincent Massey became the first Canadian-born governor general, only Canadian citizens have been appointed to the office. The duties of the office are largely formal and ceremonial but can become politically important in situations where no party has a clear majority in the House of Commons. In this situation, the governor general might decide who will form a government or when the House should be dissolved for a general election.

governor general, first woman Canada's first woman governor general was Saskatchewan-born Jeanne Sauvé (1922–1993), who served from 1984 to 1989. She had previously been a minister in Pierre Trudeau's government and in the early 1980s achieved wide respect for her role as Speaker of the House of Commons.

Grant, George *See Lament for a Nation*.

Green Party Internationally, the name *Green Party* is adopted by political parties whose main policies are promotion of environmental sustainability and opposition to uncontrolled development and economic growth. The most successful Green Party is in Germany, which first elected Green members of the Bundestag (the German parliament) in 1983 under its system of proportional representation. In recent times, the Green Party has joined the German Social Democratic Party in coalition governments. Green Parties have gained support at both the federal and provincial levels in Canada but have failed to elect members to either Parliament or a legislature. This has added to growing support for the adoption of proportional representation in our electoral system.

greenhouse effect A term from environmental science, *greenhouse effect* refers to an increase in the average temperature of the earth brought about by the effects of atmospheric pollution. The pollutants are suspended in the lower atmosphere above the earth and retard the loss of heat by convection from the earth's surface.

Green Revolution This term refers to the great rise in agricultural productivity brought about by new plant hybrids, fertilizers, and agricultural chemicals in the 1950s and 1960s. Advocated by developed nations as a way to help developing nations produce sufficient food, there is now a concern that this enforced transformation of agricultural methods has harmed the environment, diminished local control, and erased local methods of production.

Grits A name used to refer to members of the Liberal Party of Canada, *Grits* derives from the mid-1800s when it was first applied to members of a radical farmers' movement in southwestern Ontario. In the early 1870s, this and other movements joined together to establish the Liberal Party, which then inherited the nickname.

gross domestic product Gross domestic product is the value of all the goods and services, including the value of dividend, interest, and other payments made to overseas investors, produced by a nation over a one-year period.

grounded theory A grounded theory is one that has been derived through inductive reasoning, thus giving it a firm grounding in data or observations of the world. Much sociological theory, on the other hand, is overly abstract and its references to the real world are unclear. Such abstract theory would be simply a logical construction deduced from assumptions and propositions.

group A group is an aggregate of individuals having some characteristic in common. The distinguishing characteristic might be the group members' appearance, language, socioeconomic status, or shared cultural values and practices. A group is often characterized by a sense of common identity and shared interests and goals among its members, but a group may exist simply because its members share some objective characteristic and are defined as a group by others.

Group of 8 (G8) Summit Founded in 1975 as an annual economic conference between leaders of the six largest free market economies, today's G8 Summit brings together leaders of the world's richest nations—France, the United States, Britain, Germany, Japan, Italy, and Canada (Canada joined in 1976), and Russia. Russia had been in attendance (although not a full member) since 1994 and recently attained full member status in 2002, when it was announced that the 2006 conference would be held in Russia. The annual leaders' conference is supported by ongoing contacts at the ministerial level and by the work of an extensive official secretariat. While initially focused on macroeconomic issues, like world trade and investment, the G8 has expanded its areas of concern to include microeconomics, environmental issues, human rights, and international security.

group, primary A circle of individuals with whom a person is extensively involved is a primary group. The group's members have bonds of common activity and emotional commitment. People interact in primary groups as whole person to whole person: Relationships are comprehensive and emotionally charged. Examples include the family and small traditional communities. The term was developed by U.S. sociologist C.H. Cooley (1864–1929) and contains echoes of *Gemeinschaft*. *See also* **Gemeinschaft**.

group, secondary The members of a secondary group, individuals who are jointly linked by some common, instrumentally related characteristic, have some specialized and specific relationship to each other. Examples include a professional association, colleagues in the workplace, a political party, or a tennis club. The term was developed by U.S. sociologist C.H. Cooley (1864-1929) and contains echoes of *Gesellschaft*. *See also* **Gesellschaft**.

group size Social scientists have long wondered why humans have such large brains. It has been speculated that the reason for this—and, more specifically, the ratio of the neocortex to the total brain—is to allow humans to participate in larger groups. Indeed, when this ratio is calculated for a range of primates, this appears to be the case. There is a correlation between the neocortex ratio and the average size of the "community group." Further, using this knowledge, it is speculated that the effective size of a human community is about 150. Beyond this, humans do not appear to be able to fully grasp their social place in the community, and divisions and hierarchies emerge. The number of 150 is approximately the size of most hunter–gatherer societies. Reference: Dunbar, R.I.M. (1992). Neocortex size as a constraint on group size in primates. *Journal of Human Evolution*, 20, 469–493.

groupthink The term *groupthink* was developed by U.S. social psychologist Irving Janis (1918–1990) to describe the process by which a group of individuals (e.g., a committee) arrives at a decision that many of its members privately think is unwise.

Gustafsen Lake Located about 450 kilometres northeast of Vancouver, the remote setting of Gustafsen Lake became the scene of a violent standoff between a small native group and the RCMP and Canadian Army. In 1989, a local property owner gave natives permission to use a small piece of land for sun dances, but in 1993, he withdrew this permission. The native group threatened to initiate a land claim to the area and continued to use the land until August of 1995, when the RCMP were called and told that firearms were located on the property. With the arrival of the RCMP and the Canadian Army, a 31-day standoff began, during which several shots were fired, although no one was killed. One of the native leaders was charged with endangering life and sentenced to three years in prison. While on day parole, he fled to the United States. He was successful in challenging the extradition order and became the first Canadian to be granted political asylum in the United States. Reference: Dacajewiah "Splitting the Sky" (Hill, John Boncore) with "She Keeps the Door" (Bruderer, Sandra). (2002). *From Attica to Gustafsen Lake*. Chase, BC: John Pasquale Boncore. *See also* **Ipperwash; Oka crisis.**

H

hallucinogens Chemicals that cause the apparent perception of objects not really present are hallucinogens.

Harper, John Joseph A Manitoba native leader, John Joseph Harper was mistaken for a car thief and shot by the Winnipeg Police on March 9, 1988. His death was one among many instances of alleged mistreatment of aboriginal peoples in the province and led to the *Report of the Aboriginal Justice Inquiry of Manitoba: The Deaths of Helen Betty Osborne and John Joseph Harper* (1991). Reference: Sinclair, Gordon, Jr. (1999). *Cowboys and Indians: The Shooting of J.J. Harper*. Toronto: McClelland and Stewart.

Harris, Marvin (1927–2001) U.S. anthropologist Marvin Harris made an important contribution to the social sciences through the development of a theory of cultural materialism. Harris combined elements of Marxist historical materialism with cultural ecology and applied this to helping non-anthropologists understand what he called *cultural riddles*, such as why the Jews and Muslims do not eat pork, or why the Hindus ban the eating of cows. All of this is seen as a reasonable adaptation to the practical problems facing these groups at the time these taboos emerged. Reference: Harris, M. (1985). *Good to eat: Riddles of food and culture*. New York: Simon and Schuster.

hashish A concentrated form of cannabis made from the resin of the female plant. *See also* **cannabis.**

hate crime There is no such thing as a *hate crime*, but a 1995 amendment to Canada's *Criminal Code* made *motivation by hatred for a designated group* an aggravating factor to be considered in sentencing. Sexual orientation has been added as a designated group. *See also* **hate propaganda**.

hate propaganda In 1970, it became a criminal offence to promote hate against identifiable groups. There have been few convictions under this provision, among them Jim Keegstra and Ernst Zundel. Both cases involved anti-Semitism and denial of the Holocaust. Reference: *R. v. Zundel* [1992] 2 S.C.R. 731.

Hawaiian kinship system The least differentiated of kinship systems, the Hawaiian kinship system puts many relatives into a small number of categories. There is no term for uncle, so your father and your father's brother and mother's brother are placed in the same category. This system is thought to be associated with ambilineal descent systems, where individuals may choose to join either their matrilineage or patrilineage group but not both.

Hawthorne effect An increase in worker productivity observed at the Chicago Hawthorne plant of General Electric in the 1920s and 1930s, attributed to improvements in worker–management communication and increased involvement of workers with each other, is known as the *Hawthorne effect*. The term is now used more generally to refer to improvement of worker productivity that does not result from any objective change in working conditions or work organization, but rather seems to arise from workers having more positive psychological feelings about the workplace.

Head-Smashed-In Buffalo Jump A UNESCO World Heritage Site located 18 kilometres from Fort Macleod, Alberta, Head-Smashed-In Buffalo Jump reveals aboriginal occupation for almost 5,500 years, and is the site of an ingenious method of killing buffalo for use by the community. The buffalo were herded through a series of coulees and rock walls, to eventually plunge over a precipice to their death. Archaeological investigation of the articles the aboriginals left behind has helped in the understanding of the technology of the time and the way of life of the native peoples of the area.

head tax When it appeared that the Canadian Pacific Railway could not be completed on time, the federal government was lobbied to have an open immigration policy. (It is not without interest that Canadian Pacific also had a steamship line bringing these immigrants to Canada.) As a result, between 1881–1885, 10,000 Chinese immigrant labourers arrived in British Columbia. These new arrivals to the province created a wave of opposition, and in 1885, the federal government imposed a head tax of $50 on every Chinese immigrant entering Canada. This fee was raised to $100 in 1900 and to $500 in 1903. The tax was removed in 1923 when the *Chinese Exclusion Act* was passed, stopping all immigration of Chinese until 1947. It is estimated that the Government of Canada collected $24 million from this head tax, an entry fee not imposed on any other group. Since 1984, Chinese Canadians have been seeking redress for this injustice. In November 2005, the federal government accepted that the tax was discriminatory and agreed to contribute $12.5 million to a new foundation for a program of education in race and ethnic relations. The agreement has met with a very divided response in the Canadian Chinese community.

hegemony A concept of Italian Marxist Antonio Gramsci (1891–1937), the term *hegemony* refers to the way in which the political and social domination of the bourgeois class in capitalist society is pervasively expressed not only in ideologies, but in all realms of culture and social organization. The comprehensive expression of the values of a class-divided society in social life lends this form of society an appearance of naturalness and inevitability that removes it from examination, criticism, and challenge. While arising in the analysis of a class-divided society, the term is also used in discussion of a patriarchal society or a colonial society.

heritability The extent to which a characteristic of a living organism is genetically determined, rather than shaped by the surrounding environment, is known as *heritablity*. In the social sciences, this term is chiefly associated with debate about the heritability of characteristics such as intelligence,

criminality, gender behaviour, and aggressiveness: Are each of these (however measured) shaped most by biological (genetic) inheritance or by the influence of environmental factors like culture, socialization, and physical nutrition?

heroin First produced from morphine in 1875, heroin was found to have powerful painkilling abilities. It was used to replace morphine, because heroin was thought to be nonaddictive.

heuristic device An abstract concept or model useful for thinking about social and physical phenomena is known as a *heuristic device*. For example, sociologists use the concept of social structure to help them to define and analyze aspects of society that create patterns and regularity in the everyday roles and activities of individuals. Sociologists do not imagine that individuals mechanically and automatically act in precisely prescribed ways within social structures, or that social structures are unchanging or fixed, but the concept of structure and regularity is an essential tool for understanding how social life itself is possible.

hidden curriculum The hidden curriculum comprises the norms, values, and social expectations indirectly conveyed to students by the styles of teaching, unarticulated assumptions in teaching materials, and the organizational characteristics of educational institutions. Social scientists find that the influence of the hidden curriculum on educational outcomes is equal to or greater than the overt or intended curriculum.

hierarchy A structuring of social statuses and roles within an organization or society, a hierarchy is ranked according to differentiations of power, authority, wealth, income, etc. Related terms are *ranking* or *stratification*.

hinterland *See* **metropolis--hinterland theory**.

Hirschi, Travis (1935–) A professor of sociology at the University of Arizona, Travis Hirschi is associated with the development of social control theory, which focuses on the strength of social bonds, rather than on the idea of individual pathology. According to this theory, delinquency arises when there are weak bonds of social attachment, since commitment to others reduces the chance of deviant behaviours. He later elaborated a theory with a different emphasis that focused on self-control and the idea that effective internalization of control must occur at an early stage of individual social development. In this theory, the quality and orientation of early parental socialization is crucial. Thus, observed differences in crime rates between groups based on race, sex, and ethnicity are reflective of contrasted early socialization patterns, rather than of later differential associations, etc. He thus advocates a focus of public policy on strengthening families and improving child-rearing practices. Reference: Hirschi, Travis, & Gottfredson, Michael R. (1990). *A General Theory of Crime.* Menlo Park, CA: Stanford University Press.

historical materialism The central concept of social analysis in the work of Karl Marx (1818–1883) and Friedrich Engels (1820–1895), the core idea of historical materialism is that the political and intellectual history of human societies is shaped most importantly by the social and technical organization of economic production and exchange. This view suggests that it is not principally intellectual ideas and knowledge that shape the structure and cultural values of social life, but rather it is the shape of social life, especially in the social organization of economic production, that chiefly shapes intellectual ideas and knowledge. *See also* **dialectical materialism**.

Hobbes, Thomas (1588–1679) The most famous work, *Leviathan*, of English political philosopher Thomas Hobbes was founded on the argument that rebellion against established rulers was morally wrong and always disastrous in its consequences. He argued that without an ordered state, life for humans in the "state of nature" was violent and short, since without a constraining framework of law and authority, human passions would lead to a war of all against all. To prevent this catastrophe, citizens must come to accept a constituted political authority that must become the sole power defining what is moral and just and right and wrong. Rebellion against a ruler could be justified only when the ruler failed to protect or became a threat to the lives of citizens. For individuals to substitute their own judgment of right and wrong for that of the sovereign authority in a community would invite all others to do the same, with the consequence that these conflicting visions would lead to political chaos and even civil war. Therefore, humans cannot avoid the necessity of a sovereign political authority to establish and enforce a framework of law and morality that governs all.

Holocaust Originally a term from ancient Greek, *holocaust* refers to a human sacrifice by burning the victim. In modern times, however, it has come to refer to the attempted genocide of Jews by the German Nazi regime during World War II and the resulting systematic murder of 6 million Jews between 1941 and 1945. *See also* **genocide**; **rape of Nanking**.

homicide While the killing of a person by another person is known as a homicide, not all homicides are classified as murder or manslaughter. *See also* **murder**.

hominids Members of the Hominoid family, to which humans and African great apes belong, are called *hominids*.

hominine Hominines are members of the subfamily of hominids to which humans belong.

hominoid From the Latin word *homo* meaning human being and the suffix *oides* meaning resembling, hominoids are creatures that resemble humans.

Homo In the Linnaean classification of living things, *Homo* is the name for a genus with the following characteristics: a brain size of at least 600 cubic centimetres, possession of a language, precision grip and an opposable thumb, and the ability to make tools. Modern humans belong to this genus, as do some earlier species. The genus *Homo* includes the species of *sapiens* as well as now-extinct species (*habilis*).

Homo erectus A descendant of the early members of the genus *Homo* and an ancestor of *Homo sapiens*, *Homo erectus* dates back 1.8 million to 400,000 years ago. Early evidence of this extinct species has been found in Africa, Europe, and Asia. *Homo erectus* displayed a larger brain than its predecessors and appeared to have had more sophisticated tools than other early humans. Reference: Rightmire, G.P. (1990). *The evolution of Homo erectus*. Cambridge: Cambridge University Press.

homogamy *Homogamy* is the term for a marriage between individuals who are, in some culturally important way, similar to each other. The similarity may be based on ethnicity, religion, or socioeconomic status. Canadians, for example, tend to be homogamous, with marriage partners usually having quite similar social and economic status and ethnic affiliation. This is a descriptive concept only and does not refer to rules or customs about mate selection.

Homo habilis First discovered in the Olduvai Gorge by Louis and Mary Leakey in 1960, *Homo habilis* fossils suggest a hominine with a brain larger than that of apes and perhaps with a structure that supported speech and tool-making. Dating back 2.4 million to 1.6 million years ago, *habilis* is the first representative of the genus *Homo*. *See also* **Leakey, Louis, and Mary.**

Homolka, Karla *See* **Bernado, Paul, & Karla Homolka**.

homophobia Literally an uncontrollable fear of homosexuals and of homosexuality, *homophobia* is also the term generally used to describe a negative and contemptuous attitude toward same-sex sexual relationships and those who participate in them.

Homo sapiens Modern humans belong to the *Homo sapiens* species, and present evidence suggests this species emerged about 150,000 years ago. Archaic forms of this species are the Neandertals (or *Neanderthals*, the accepted spelling by some since 1904, when German spelling became regularized to be more consistent with pronunciation).

homosexuality Homosexuality has long been tangled in the law, but only when involving sexual relations between men. Lesbian sex has rarely been given legal attention, and there has been no law against it in Canadian history, either before or after Confederation. Male homosexuality has a quite different history. The term *homosexual* was first used in 1869, and by the beginning of the 20th century, although there was a consensus developing among intellectuals that homosexuality was best understood simply as sexual variation, there were clear indications of growing official hostility toward it. Under the Nazi regime, some 100,000 to 400,000 male homosexuals were murdered in the concentration camps. In Canada, male homosexuality remained punishable by up to 14 years in prison until legal reform in 1969. In 1974, the American Psychological Association removed homosexuality from its catalogue of illnesses, and, in 1996, protection against discrimination based on sexual orientation was added to Canada's human rights legislation. The *Canadian Charter of Rights and Freedoms* has also been expanded by courts to include protection against discrimination. In February 2000, federal legislation was introduced to amend dozens of laws to ensure that same-sex couples receive the same benefits as heterosexuals in common-law relationships, and in July 2005, same-sex marriage became legal under federal legislation. *See also* **same-sex marriage**.

horizontal integration The expansion of a corporation to include other previously competitive enterprises within the same sector of goods or service production represents horizontal integration. For example, one candy maker may take over another candy maker. This process is characteristic of capitalist economies, which have a marked tendency to sectorial concentration into fewer and fewer enterprises and business conglomerates.

household In anthropology, *household* is used to discuss domestic organization and to distinguish the domestic unit from the family unit, since they do not always coincide. For example, among the Nayar, married men and women were members of separate households. The household unit is the basic unit of residence where economic activity, consumption, shelter, and child-rearing are organized.

Hudson's Bay Company The Hudson's Bay Company was incorporated in 1670 by royal charter of King Charles II of England to exercise political and economic control over all the lands and the sea around Hudson Bay and the entire area that drained its lakes and rivers into Hudson Bay. The Bay's main interest was to monopolize the extraordinarily profitable fur trade, particularly in the beaver pelts that were prized by European hat makers. The extent of the Bay's territory ran from Edmonton in the west to north of Ottawa in the east, and from areas south of the present border with the United States to Baffin Island in the north. Over this vast territory, the Bay wielded unchallengeable political and economic power and was, for almost 200 years, the effective government of this area. After Confederation, the new federal government of Canada determined immediately that the Bay must be shorn of its monopoly domination of trade and resources and of its quasi-governmental powers. In 1869, under pressure from the British government, Canada and the Bay reached an agreement by which the Bay surrendered almost all its territory. The company retained great tracts of land, however, and for another hundred years exercised extensive powers and influence in Canada's remote northern communities. In 1987, this role in the north was ended when the Bay sold its northern stores, and the company then became similar to any large corporate retail organization.

Hughes, Everett C. *See* **McGill School**.

human capital Human capital comprises the talents and capabilities that individuals contribute to the process of production. Companies, governments, and individuals can invest in this "capital," just as they can invest in technology and buildings.

humanism An ethical doctrine that asserts the central importance of human life and experience on earth, humanism also implies the right and duty of each individual to explore and develop his or her potential. Humanism is, to some extent, in opposition to religious doctrines, such as Christianity, that diminish the importance of earthly life and assert that human existence is merely a stage of preparation for heavenly life after death. In the social sciences, humanism is evident in those groups who argue that social theory must conceive of the human actor as a subject, rather than as an object.

human rights *See Canadian Bill of Rights; Canadian Charter of Rights and Freedoms; rights, human; Universal Declaration of Human Rights.*

hunter–gatherer society The earliest form of human society, hunter–gatherer societies still exist to some extent in remote regions of the world. These societies have an economic base that rests on the use of the naturally occurring animal and plant resources of the environment. They do not practise agriculture or raise and herd animals. Social structure is usually egalitarian, with little economic and gender inequality. Private property ownership is minimal. In Canada, the Inuit and the First Nations communities were primarily hunter–gatherer societies prior to European contact. This aboriginal lifestyle had experienced major disruption by the second half of this century, but many communities are now attempting to recover traditional ways. Reference: Brody, H. (2000). *The other side of Eden: Hunters, farmers and the shaping of the world.* Vancouver: Douglas and McIntyre.

Hutterites An Anabaptist (opposed to infant baptism) group, Hutterites emerged in central Europe in 1528 under the leadership of Joseph Hutter. The basic components of their religious beliefs are communal ownership of property, communal living, nonviolence, and commitment to adult baptism. A large number of Hutterites emigrated to Canada in 1918, and the majority now live in the Prairie provinces and retain traditional styles of dress and custom. Mennonites originated at approximately the same time as the Hutterites, but arrived in Canada from the United States in 1786. *See also* **sect.**

hydraulic theory Used to explain the emergence of civilization, hydraulic theory sees this development as a result of building elaborate farming irrigation systems requiring managers and administrators.

hypothesis A testable statement (i.e., it may be true or false) of a specific relationship between or among variables. In the classic model of science, this testable statement is deduced from a theory. *See also* **hypothetico-deductive model of science.**

hypothetico-deductive model of science Using this classical or traditional model of how science operates, scientists are assumed to begin with a theory, deduce a hypothesis from the theory, and then gather evidence to test the hypothesis. If the hypothesis is confirmed, the theory is assumed to be correct or useful. *See also* **hypothesis; theory.**

I

I The concept of *I* was used by U.S. social psychologist George Herbert Mead (1863–1931) to refer to the aspect of identity, or self, that reacts in social interaction to the expectations of others. In social interaction, individuals are aware of the expectations of others, but they do not necessarily conform to these expectations in their reactions. This spontaneous, never entirely predictable element of individual personality makes each individual a unique social actor. *See also* **me.**

Ice Age The earth's temperatures have fluctuated greatly over time and have on occasion created what are referred to as *Ice Ages*, periods during which portions of the globe were covered in ice as the northern glaciers expand. The most recent Ice Age was at its maximum about 18,000 to 15,000 years ago and ended about 10,000 years ago. During this time, according to the Bering Strait theory, human settlement of the Americas occurred. However, recent evidence now suggests that humans would have had to circumnavigate a vast glacier barrier to have settled in this region so early. For many years, it was assumed that there was an ice-free corridor in the western Arctic, roughly along the Mackenzie River Valley, allowing the new arrivals to walk south and survive on local vegetation and animals. It now seems clear, however, that the two primary ice sheets moving from the east and the west had indeed met, thus blocking access to the south. *See also* **Bering Strait theory.**

id This concept of Sigmund Freud (1856–1939), the founder of psychoanalysis, defines the id as the unconscious drives and psychic energies of humans as biological organisms. As such, it is untouched by culture and social learning, and encompasses all that is primitive, natural, and precivilized in human passions and energies. Freud seems to have assumed that the human struggle to achieve self-consciousness against the ungoverned and unconstrained passions of the id remained deeply buried in the unconscious minds of all human beings. *See also* **ego; superego**.

idealism A perspective that asserts the independent causal influence of intellectual ideas on social organization and culture, idealism is contrasted to materialism, which focuses on concrete aspects of social organization as causative of particular intellectual ideas and values. German sociologist Max Weber (1864–1920) can be said to have given an idealistic explanation of the growth of capitalism by linking it to the emergence of a "Protestant ethic." *See also* **Calvinism; historical materialism**.

ideal type An abstract model of a classic, pure form of social phenomenon, the ideal type is a model concept and does not necessarily exist in exact form in reality. An example is German sociologist Ferdinand Tonnies's dichotomy of *Gemeinschaft* and *Gesellschaft* (*see* **Gemeinschaft** and **Gesellschaft**). Tonnies (1855–1936) described two opposite, or polar, types of social association: one personal and committed (community association), and one impersonal and unemotional (society association). These two formal types then provide a benchmark for the analysis and comparison of societies that actually exist. German sociologist Max Weber (1864–1920) also used this method of analysis with his ideal types of bureaucracy, authority, and social action. *See also* **action theory; authority; bureaucracy**.

identity politics Identity politics is thought to be a central aspect of postmodern politics and communities in which the legitimacy of a unitary public identity or an overarching sense of self has diminished; in its place, the previously private identities of citizens (based on their race, ethnicity, sexual preference, physical state, or victimization) compete for public recognition and legitimation. Some theorists fear that this will lead to private values and identities taking precedence over public involvement as citizens. Reference: Elshtain, J.B. (1993). *Democracy on Trial*. Toronto: Anansi Press. *See also* **citizen**.

identity theft Theft of one or more pieces of personal identification (e.g., social insurance number, passport, bank card, or birth certificate), identity theft can facilitate access to another person's financial resources.

ideographic explanations Explanations of specific events, phenomena, or behaviours that are sought in the careful examination of specific preceding events are said to be *ideographic explanations*. For example, why did Mary murder the butler? Or, what caused World War I? For the most part, clinical psychologists and historians are interested in ideographic explanations. Other disciplines, like sociology, are interested in explanations of classes of events or behaviours and seek these in a careful examination of a few general categories or classes of preceding events. For example, why do men murder their partners? Or, what are the causes of international violence? These explanations are known as *nomothetic explanations*.

ideological hegemony In an ideological hegemony, a particular ideology is pervasively reflected throughout a society in all principal social institutions and permeates cultural ideas and social relationships. *See also* **hegemony; ideology**.

ideology A linked set of ideas and beliefs that act to uphold and justify an existing or desired arrangement of power, authority, wealth, and status in a society is an ideology. For example, a socialist ideology advocates the transformation of society from capitalism to collective ownership and economic equality. In contrast, a liberal ideology associated with capitalist societies upholds that system as the best, most moral, most desirable form of social arrangement. Patriarchal ideology also has this characteristic of asserting claims and beliefs that justify a social arrangement—in this case, male social domination of women. Another example is a racist ideology, claiming that people can be classified into distinct races and that some races are inferior to others. Racist ideologies are used as justification for systems of slavery or colonial exploitation. Although there is often a dominant ideology in a society, there can also be counterideologies that advocate transformation of social relationships. *See also* **dominant ideology thesis; hegemony**.

Ignatieff, Michael (1947–) Canadian historian Michael Ignatieff, in his 1978 publication *A Just Measure of Pain*, provides a complex analysis of the rise of the penitentiary, claiming that this development is the result of more complicated factors than the rational conspiracy of the ruling class. Subsequently, Ignatieff has become an important commentator on human rights, nationalism, and international conflict. After periods in Britain and the United States, Ignatieff returned to Canada in 2005.

IMF *See* **International Monetary Fund**.

immigration The movement of peoples into a country or territory (movement of people within countries is referred to as *migration*), immigration has played the central role in the development of Canada from the first permanent European settlements in the mid-1600s to the 1990s, when 16% of Canadian residents were born outside Canada. The birth rate of Canada's population—the number of children born to a woman in her fertile years—is about 1.6, much lower than the 2.1 that would be needed to maintain a stable population. The prospect of a declining and aging population has led to some calls for increased immigration to Canada. Economic recession, the demands on public services resulting from the concentrated patterns of immigrant settlement, and concern about interethnic tensions have more recently led to controversy about levels of immigration. A special mention should be made of Quebec, where, until the 1960s, the population increased, mostly because of a high birth rate. Historically, Quebec has had one of the highest birth rates in any known world society. Although there has been immigration of Francophones to Quebec, chiefly from old French colonial territories, the great majority of the Francophone population has descended from the approximately 60,000 people who remained there when the French domination of Quebec ended in 1759. Reference: Avery, Donald. (1995). *Reluctant Host: Canada's Response to Immigrant Workers, 1896–1994*. Toronto: McClelland and Stewart.

imperialism Domination by one or more countries over others for political and economic objectives, imperialism can be effected by military force or through the economic and political power exercised by state and corporate agencies. Imperialism is sometimes organized in a formal empire, with a ruling nation and colonized territories, but it can also exist where one nation or region exercises dominant influence over international trade and investment, patterns of economic development, and mass communication. *See also* **colonialism**; **empire**; **metropolis–hinterland theory**.

incest Sexual intercourse between individuals who are culturally regarded as too closely related for sexual intimacy to be legitimate or moral is known as *incest*. Incest rules vary cross-culturally, but generally all cultures forbid intercourse between parents and children, between siblings, and between grandparents and grandchildren. Rare historical exceptions to the rules existed in ancient Egypt and traditional Hawaii, where siblings were favoured marriage partners among the royal family and probably other members of the aristocracy and the wealthy. Many cultures have mythical or religious stories that warn of the terrible consequences of violating incest rules.

incidence A contrasting term to *prevalence*, *incidence* tells us the frequency of occurrence of some event during a particular time period. For example, there were 582 criminal homicides in 2005 in a particular area, or the country's rate of crime for one year was higher than for the previous year.

independent immigrant One of three classes of immigrants to Canada (the other two being family class and refugees), independent immigrants do not require sponsorship—they apply on their own—but they are rated on a point system, which tends to give points to education and training, labour market demands, age, and the presence of family already in Canada. *See also* **sponsored immigrant**.

independent variable Causal research examines the world in terms of variables (those things that reveal variation within a population). An independent variable is typically the cause, while a dependent variable is the effect. In experimental research, the independent variable (the cause) is the one that the investigator manipulates. The effect (the dependent variable) is dependent on the causal variable. If unemployment is thought to cause crime rates to increase, unemployment is the independent variable (it can vary between high and low) and crime rates comprise the dependent variable. Something that is an independent variable at one time can be a dependent variable at another.

index Many of the concepts that social scientists study are quite complex and cannot adequately be measured by a single indicator. In these cases, researchers develop several indicators and, in some cases, will give a different weight to each indicator. This combination of indicators and weights is an index. Socioeconomic status is difficult to measure, so the indicators of income, occupation, and education are typically used. If occupation is seen as more central, it may be given more weight. *See also* **Blishen scale**.

indexicality As used by ethnomethodologists, *indexicality* refers to the contextual nature of behaviour and talk. Talk, for example, is indexical in the sense that it has no meaning without a context or can take on various meanings dependent on the context. As we construct talk or listen to talk, we all must engage in the interpretive process of constructing a context. With this context, we give the talk a sense of concreteness or definiteness. There is no way to avoid indexicality, however, nor a way to remove it, since talk about context itself is also indexical. For this reason, constructing a sense of reality is an ongoing accomplishment of social members. *See also* **thick description**.

Indian Act The *British North America Act* (1867), which created the nation of Canada, gave responsibility to the federal government for the native peoples of the new nation. Federal legislation governing native peoples was first passed in 1868, and in 1876, the first *Indian Act* was passed. This Act provides a legal definition of *Indian* and, for those covered by the designation, provides a framework within which their activities are governed. From the outset, the Act espoused the goal of assimilation and, in the name of this end, authorized many repressive actions by the state. The Inuit (until recently referred to as *Eskimos*) of the north were not included in the *Indian Act*, and a court decision in 1939 was required to declare them a federal responsibility. The Act has been described as a "total institution" since the lives of native peoples covered by it are lived out entirely within its rule. The Act has been a powerful instrument for the colonization of native lands and peoples. Since 1970, there have been suggestions that the *Indian Act* be removed and that native peoples become similar to other citizens in Canada. *See also* **C-31 Indian; institution, total; potlatch; reserves; White Paper (1969)**.

indigenous peoples Those people inhabiting a land prior to colonization by another nation are considered to be indigenous. In Canada, this would include the Indians and Inuit, but would probably not include the Métis, who are of mixed European and aboriginal descent. *See also* **aboriginal peoples**.

individualism A value system, central to classical liberalism and capitalism, individualism upholds choice, personal freedom, and self-orientation. *See also* **classical liberalism**.

individualistic theory This type of theory focuses on explaining the behaviour of individuals based on factors or features of the individual. An alternative to this approach would be to explain the behaviour of a group (the crime rate of Canada) in terms of characteristics of this group.

individual pathology This term is used to refer to biological or psychological explanations of criminal or deviant behaviour by individuals. The assumption is that the deviant behaviour of individuals can be at least partly explained by some physical or psychological trait that makes them different from normal, law-abiding citizens.

individuation Unlike *individualism*, which refers to an individualistic value system, *individuation* refers to the process by which individualism is accomplished, the breaking down of obligatory ties and responsibilities to other people or institutions, so that the individual is freed from social bonds. Such a process must also lead to the adoption of the value of individualism. *See also* **individualism**.

inductive reasoning Developing a theory or reaching a conclusion after consideration of several empirical observations is inductive reasoning. *See also* **grounded theory**.

industrialization The process of developing an economy founded on the mass-manufacturing of goods, industrialization is associated with the urbanization of society, an extensive division of labour, a wage economy, the differentiation of institutions, and the growth of mass communication and mass markets. Many Western societies are now described as *postindustrial*, since much economic activity is based on the production of services, knowledge, or symbols.

industrial relations A general term referring to workplace relationships between workers and management, industrial relations has become an important professional and academic discipline, since successful management of industrial relations is closely linked to workplace productivity and product quality. There have been many different approaches to the management of industrial relations in modern capitalist societies, but these approaches generally share the characteristic that they seek to discipline, motivate, and engage workers in processes of production or administration without making any fundamental change to the structure of ownership or direction of the workplace. At the end of the 19th century, scientific management became increasingly popular as a means of workplace direction, and this approach relied on close and systematic control of the work process and of the work methods used. Beginning in the 1920s and 1930s, a new movement in industrial relations began to focus instead on the management of human relations in the workplace, after it was demonstrated that creation of a positive communicative atmosphere at work was capable of stimulating worker productivity. In more recent years, the idea of quality control circles, where workers take direct responsibility as work groups for productivity and work quality, has become popular, following successful use of this approach in Japan. There have also been numerous other schemes to increase worker participation in the workplace, either through enhanced workplace communication, consultation, and cooperative worker–management planning, or through worker representation and participation directly in management. *See also* **alienation; scientific management**.

Industrial Revolution The term is used to describe the profound technological changes that began in England in the mid-18th century, when machines were introduced for the production of goods for trade and profit and to enhance the productivity of labour. Before the 18th century, there was very little power machinery except windmills and watermills, and production was carried out with hand tools and hard human labour. The Industrial Revolution introduced technologies that could employ power from water, steam, gas, coal, electricity, and oil to replace or enhance human labour. This made possible a level of economic productivity that had never before been achieved, and it initiated a process of unending technological transformation and social change. In addition, the wealth from the Industrial Revolution made possible the building of asylums and prisons, and the new economy necessitated changes in policing and the administration of justice. Socially, the Industrial Revolution is associated with the rational organization of work, a transformation from a society of self-sufficient producers to a society of employed wage workers and the spread of a market-driven system of allocation of resources. In Canada, these changes occurred in the 19th century. Social scientists continue to be interested in how this technological transformation affected social relations, politics, community life, family structure, and women's role

in society. Many people argue that the computerization of society is bringing with it a set of changes equal in importance to the Industrial Revolution. It was against the staggering changes brought about by the Industrial Revolution that sociology emerged, as well as an interest in social problems, including crime. Karl Marx, Émile Durkheim, and Max Weber, among other social scientists, were among those responding to these changes. Reference: Hobsbawm, E. (1969). *Industry and Empire.* London: Pelican Books.

inequality of condition Inequality of condition, where individuals have very different amounts of wealth, status, and power, is a characteristic of all complex modern societies; however, equality of condition is often present in small-scale, hunter–gatherer societies. *See also* **class**.

inequality of opportunity When differences in individual possession of wealth, status, and power result in definite advantages and disadvantages in the pursuit of personal success, inequality of opportunity exists.

infanticide An offence under Canada's *Criminal Code* (introduced in 1948), infanticide involves the killing of a child (either willfully or by omission) under the age of one year by the mother who has not fully recovered from the effects of childbirth. A father committing such an act would be charged with murder. This is an unusual category of crime in that it appears to recognize that the psychological and physical condition of the offender may have contributed to the commission of the offence.

inference The logical process of moving from an indicator or observation to a conclusion or general rule is called *inference*.

inferential statistics Statistical tools or techniques used to draw inference about a population on the basis of research evidence from a sample, inferential statistics can be used, for example, to estimate the frequency or value for a particular variable within a population. This is found commonly in reports of public opinion polls when it is noted that "a sample of this size is accurate to within +/− 3.2% [or some other percentage], 19 times out of 20 [i.e., 95%]." *See also* **descriptive statistics; statistics**.

inferiorization This term refers to the process of imposing a stigmatized or inferiorized identity on a group of people. The people stigmatized tend to adopt a sense of inferiority that leads to a sapping of confidence and ability, inhibits political organization, and results in a host of personal and collective social problems. This concept can be linked to the theory of a culture of poverty. *See also* **culture of poverty thesis.**

infibulation *See* **female genital mutilation**.

informal economy Also known as the *underground economy*, or the *hidden economy*, *informal economy* refers to economic activities that are carried on outside the institutionalized structures of the economy. For most purposes, this means they are transactions not reported to the Canada Revenue Agency or to the government departments responsible for Employment Insurance and Worker's Compensation, or to municipal governments. Usually these transactions are based on cash exchanges, but they may be bartered for goods or services.

infrastructure In Marxist theory or political economy theory, *infrastructure* refers to the base or economic foundation of society upon which the cultural and social institutions of society are built. The concept of infrastructure is similar to mode of production and would include the forces of production and the relations of production. *See also* **base (or infrastructure); mode of production.**

inherent right to self-government The declaration that self-government is an inherent right (claimed particularly by native peoples in Canada) rejects the notion that the right is bestowed by the Government of Canada. Rather, the right existed prior to Canada becoming a nation and therefore acknowledges that native peoples were, and perhaps still are, nations with the right to fully make decisions for themselves. *See also* **nation**.

initiative A process long established and very common at state level in the United States, voters are asked to approve specific ballot proposals (initiatives) that have been put forward by voter petition. Initiatives may be on any subject within the jurisdiction of the state. In California, for example, proposals supported by 5% of the number of voters who voted in the previous election for governor are required to mount the initiative. If the proposal is adopted in a subsequent ballot, it is then implemented by the state government, although the legislature may amend or reject it. Any changes to the initiative must however be supported by the public in a further vote on the initiative.

Innis, Harold (1894–1952) One of the most important figures in the development of Canadian political economy and communication studies, Harold Innis graduated from McMaster University, served in World War I, and then went on to study at the University of Chicago, where he completed a doctorate in economics. In political economy, his major contribution was the development of the staples thesis that saw Canada's economy and political history as being shaped by its role as the provider of raw resources to more advanced economies. Production of staples was also seen as shaping Canadian regionalism and communications. Later, he became interested in the impact of media, and his book *The Bias of Communication* set out the foundations of modern communication theory, grounding it in history, sociology, and economics. Reference: Innis, Harold. (1951). *The Bias of Communication.* Toronto: University of Toronto Press [1991].

institutional completeness This term describes the condition of a group within a larger society where the major institutions—the economy, politics, family, and schooling—are reproduced, thus enabling the smaller group to have little social connection with the larger group.

institutionalization In a state of institutionalization, social interaction is predictably patterned within relatively stable structures regulated by norms. For example, seeking a diagnosis for a physical illness or obtaining advice or a cure is institutionalized within the health care institution, conflict over values or interests is institutionalized within the political system, and sexual access and raising children is institutionalized within the family structure.

institution, social A social institution is a relatively stable structure with a pattern of social interaction that persists over time. Institutions have structural properties—they are organized—and they are shaped by cultural values. Thus, for example, the institution of marriage in Western societies is structurally located in a cohabiting couple and regulated by norms about sexual exclusiveness, love, sharing, etc. There is not full agreement about the number or designation of social institutions in a society, but the following would typically be included: family, the economy, politics, education, health care, and the media.

institution, total A social institution that encompasses individuals, cutting them off from significant social interaction outside its bounds, is a total institution.

These institutions are frequently involved in the process of resocialization, whereby individuals are detached from their previous sense of identity and reshaped to accept and absorb new values and behaviour. Examples include religious orders, prisons, and army training camps. Reference: Goffman, Erving. (1961). On the Characteristics of Total Institutions. In Donald Cressey (Ed.), *The Prison*. New York: Holt, Rinehart and Winston.

instrumentalist Marxism In instrumentalist Marxism, the role of the state is seen from a conflict or Marxist perspective as an instrument of the dominant class of the society and is assumed to operate at its behest. This approach stresses the importance of the intimate connection of the capitalist class to the state power apparatus and argues that it is this interconnection that explains political and economic policies in capitalist societies. This view has now been largely displaced by a structurally focused analysis. *See also* **relative autonomy; structuralist approach**.

integration, social This term has two common definitions: (1) The joining of different ethnic groups within a society into a common social life regulated by generally accepted norms and values. This process need not involve the obliteration of distinct ethnic identity, which would be assimilation, but it implies that ethnic identity does not limit or constrain commitment to the common activities, values, and goals of the society. Canada's official policy of multiculturalism assumes that social integration can be achieved without the elimination of the cultural distinctiveness of ethnic groups. (2) In the work of French sociologist Émile Durkheim (1858–1917), *social integration* refers to the density of connection between individuals and social institutions. He assumes that a society requires intense individual participation in a wide range of institutions for it to maintain social integration and provide individuals with a sense of meaning and belonging.

internal validity Internal validity is a standard or criteria against which research results are judged. To be internally valid, the results of an experiment or survey must be accurate indications of the results of manipulating independent variables in experiments or must reflect the attitudes or knowledge of respondents in the case of a survey. For example, if evaluation of a drug claimed to prevent colds was conducted by giving it to people unlikely to encounter other infected persons (e.g., lighthouse keepers), the results can be seen as having been produced by the way the experiment or survey was conducted, and the results would be considered internally invalid. Something internal to the research process produced the results, so researchers are no longer measuring what they claim to be measuring. Selection bias in the allocation of subjects to the experimental and control groups may contaminate the results, as can questions in a survey that elicit socially desirable answers. Placebos and double-blind procedures in experiments are used to enhance internal validity. The random assignment of subjects to the control and experimental groups is also essential for establishing internal validity. *See also* **double-blind procedure; external validity; validity**.

International Bill of Rights This term commonly refers to the collection of three international legally binding documents: *The Universal Declaration of Human Rights* (1948); *The International Covenant on Civil and Political Rights* (1966); and *The International Covenant on Economic, Social and Cultural Rights* (1966). These documents were drafted by the UN Commission on Human Rights and adopted by the UN General Assembly. *See also* ***Universal Declaration of Human Rights***.

International Criminal Court The International Criminal Court was established on July 1, 2002, when sufficient nations (60) ratified the agreement to create the court to prosecute those who engage in crimes against humanity, genocide, or war crimes. The court serves as an independent criminal court, overseen by the signatories, to which cases can be referred by the security council of the UN for violations of laws set out in the founding agreement. The United States has not supported this court and in fact has engaged in several actions to undermine or weaken the court, perhaps feeling that it will be brought before the court itself.

International Monetary Fund (IMF) Like the World Bank, the International Monetary Fund (IMF) emerged from the 1944 United Nations Bretton Woods Conference with a mandate to promote international monetary cooperation, facilitate the expansion and balanced growth of international trade, promote exchange stability, assist in the elimination of foreign exchange restrictions, shorten the duration of recessions, and lessen the degree of disequilibrium in the international balance of payments. The IMF is less involved than the World Bank in solving the problems of poverty, but is highly involved in monitoring the trade patterns of the world and in managing the world's financial stability. Reference: Blustein, P. (2003). *The chastening: Inside the crisis that rocked the global financial system and humbled the IMF.* New York: Public Affairs. *See also* **Bretton Woods Conference**.

Internet luring The practice of communicating through the Internet with an underage person for the purpose of committing a sexual offence, Internet luring usually involves an adult "meeting" a child in a chat room and then, over time, encouraging the child to meet the adult in person. This offence was created through changes to Canada's *Criminal Code* in 2002.

internment Internment camps that segregated and confined "suspicious persons" were used in Canada during both World Wars. During World War I (1914–1918), German, Austro-Hungarian (including Ukrainian), and Turkish nationals were interned. During World War II, German, Italian, and Japanese nationals, even naturalized and native-born Canadians of these nationalities, were interned. A total of 720 Japanese Canadian citizens were interned, while another 20,000 were removed from their homes and relocated away from the Pacific coast for "national security" reasons until 1949, when they were allowed to return. *See also* **redress agreement; Ukrainian Canadians; *War Measures Act*.**

interpretive theory A general category of theory including symbolic interactionism, labelling, ethnomethodology, phenomenology, and social constructionism, interpretive theory is typically contrasted with structural theories, which claim to remove the subjectivity of the actor and the researcher and assume that human behaviour can best be understood as determined by the pushes and pulls of structural forces. Interpretive theory is more accepting of free will and sees human behaviour as the outcome of the subjective interpretation of the environment. Structural theory focuses on the situation in which people act, while interpretive theory focuses on the actors' definition of the situation in which they act. *See also* **definition of the situation**.

intersubjectivity Sociologists who reject the assumption of the objective nature of social reality and focus on the subjective experience of actors have to avoid the fallacy of reducing the world to only personal experience. The concept of intersubjectivity achieves this: Ordinary people as well as sociologists assume that if another stood in their shoes they would see the same things. We all constantly make our subjective experience available and understandable by others as well.

interval measures *See* **level of measurement**.

invisible hand of the market A phrase associated with the great Scottish classical economist and philosopher Adam Smith (1723–1790), *invisible hand of the market* refers to the self-regulating capacity of free markets. Free markets, through the mechanism of supply and demand, are assumed to provide the optimal allocation of scarce economic resources to alternative uses without the need for any conscious direction or control. *See also* **market economy**.

in vitro fertilization In in vitro fertilization, a human egg is fertilized outside of the womb (usually in a laboratory dish). The fertilized egg is then implanted into the womb, where normal development of an infant occurs.

involvement The degree to which an individual is active in conventional activities is called *involvement*. Reference: Hirschi, Travis. (1969). Aspects of the Social Bond. *Causes of Delinquency*. Berkeley, CA: University of California Press.

Ipperwash *See* **George, Dudley**.

iron cage This phrase is associated with German sociologist Max Weber (1864–1920), who wrote that the new emphasis on materialism and worldly success that arose with capitalism and Protestantism had imprisoned human society in an iron cage of self-perpetuating rationalization and depersonalization.

iron law of oligarchy First defined by German sociologist Robert Michels (1876–1936), this term refers to the inherent tendency of all complex organizations, including radical or socialist political parties and labour unions, to develop a ruling clique of leaders with interests in the organization itself rather than in its official aims. These leaders, Michels argued, came to desire leadership and its status and rewards more than any commitment to goals. Inevitably, their influence was conservative, seeking to preserve and enhance the organization and not to endanger it by any radical action. Michels based his argument on the simple observation that day-to-day running of a complex organization by its mass membership was impossible; therefore, professional full-time leadership and direction was required. In theory, the leaders of the organization were subject to control by the mass membership, through delegate conferences and membership voting, but, in reality, the leaders were in the dominant position. They possessed the experience and expertise in running the organization, they came to control the means of communication within the organization, and they monopolized the public status of representing the organization. It became difficult for the mass membership to provide any effective counterweight to this professional, entrenched leadership. Michels also argued that these inherent organizational tendencies were strengthened by a mass psychology of leadership dependency; he felt that people had a basic psychological need to be led. *See also* **oligarchy**.

Iroquois kinship system This is a bifurcated system in which you would distinguish relatives on your father's side from those on your mother's side. This system is associated with unilineal descent.

J

James Bay and Northern Quebec Agreement* and the *Northeastern Quebec Agreement Signed in 1975 and 1978, respectively, these were the first modern treaties signed with native peoples in Canada, arising from Quebec's need to develop hydroelectric power on traditional native homelands. The agreements entitled the James Bay Cree and the Inuit of Northern Quebec to millions of dollars in compensation, defined native rights, and established regimes for future relations between natives and nonnatives in the region and among local, regional, provincial, and federal governments.

Jekyll and Hyde In Robert Louis Stevenson's 1886 classic *The Strange Case of Dr. Jekyll and Mr. Hyde*, Dr. Jekyll is a stereotypical member of the middle class—repressed and moralistic. Through the ingestion of a drug, Dr. Jekyll becomes his mirror opposite—Mr. Hyde, vital, egocentric, ferocious, and a sexual predator. While expressing a Christian dichotomy between good and evil, the two characters are also seen as expressing the conflict within the self between ego and id, as well as the conflict between culture and nature.

Jenness, Diamond (1886–1969) Born in New Zealand, anthropologist Diamond Jenness came to Canada in 1913, immediately travelling to Canada's North to study native peoples. In 1926, he was appointed chief anthropologist with the National Museum of Canada in Ottawa (replacing Edward Sapir) and from this position exerted great influence over the development of Canadian archaeology and anthropology.

Judeo-Christian ethic This term refers to broad moral precepts associated with the Jewish and Christian religions. Among these are the idea of responsibility for one's own actions and of redemption of the criminal or sinner through just punishment and repentance.

judge-made law Another expression for *common law*, in judge-made law, the cases decided by courts form the precedents on which subsequent decisions are based. It has also come to refer to the way that the *Canadian Charter of Rights and Freedoms* has expanded the powers of judges to declare laws unconstitutional or to direct changes in the law and in government policies. While based on the *Constitution*, these decisions are often seen as undermining the role of electoral democracy and the sovereignty of Parliament.

judicial activism When judges, through their interpretations of constitutional texts, strike down or invalidate laws passed by Parliament, the term *judicial activism* applies. In Canada, judicial activism has developed since adoption of the *Canadian Charter of Rights and Freedoms* (1982). Activist judgments tend to seek out the broad principles of constitutional laws, like the *Charter*, and apply these principles, rather than explicit wording. For example, Canada's judges have decided that *Charter* rights to nondiscrimination extend to gays and lesbians, although sexual orientation is not explicitly cited in the *Charter*. They have "read in" this provision. In contrast, judges rendering deferent judgments tend to stay closely with the explicit wording of constitutional law in reaching their decisions and take direction from Acts of Parliament whenever this is judicially tenable. For example, in 2002, the Supreme Court accepted Parliament's legislative judgment that the harm caused by marijuana is sufficient to justify criminalization of its possession, trade, and cultivation.

judicial deference *See* **judicial activism**.

Jukes and Kallikaks These names were pseudonyms for two families whose offspring were traced by social scientists over many generations to determine the number of "social degenerates" in each family. The study of the Juke lineage was published in 1877 and of the Kallikaks in 1912. These studies

were used to argue that criminal behaviour is inherited and that it begins with "bad genetic material." The Kallikak family, for example, had two branches: the first the result of a liaison with a feeble-minded barmaid (producing a large number of "degenerates"), and the second from a marriage to a virtuous Quaker girl, which produced only three "degenerates." These studies became part of a widespread eugenics movement and the forced sterilization of many individuals thought to have "bad genetic material." Reference: Gould, Stephen Jay. (1981). *The Mismeasure of Man.* New York: W.W. Norton.

Jung, Carl (1875–1961) Originally associated with Sigmund Freud, Swiss psychologist Carl Jung developed a distinctive tradition within psychoanalysis, known as *analytical psychology*, that focused on the idea that all humans share in a collective unconscious mind that is exhibited in the classic forms—or archetypes—of different cultures and in the thoughts, experiences, and behaviour of individuals.

just desserts A philosophy of punishment usually contrasted with utilitarianism, the concept of *just desserts* justifies punishment solely in terms of what the offender did, rather than justifying punishment in terms of its utility (the good it will produce). The offender is thought to get what he or she deserves—that person's just desserts. An example of this type of reasoning would be as follows: If people are to be treated as rational and moral, they have a right to be punished when they have done wrong. To not punish them would be to deny them their moral agency. Reference: Von Hirsch, A. (1993). *Censure and Sanctions.* New York: Oxford University Press.

K

Kennewick Man The ancient human skeletal remains that are referred to as the *Kennewick Man* were found in July 1996 beside the Columbia River near Kennewick in Washington state in 1996. Examination of sedimentary layers, skeletal measurement, and carbon dating established that the remains were about 9,000 years old. Scientists had conflicting opinions, however, about the racial group to which Kennewick Man belonged. United States law directs that ancient human remains are to be handed to the aboriginal tribes of whom they are assumed to be

ancestors, and Kennewick Man was claimed as an "Ancient One" by the local tribes. Some scientists, however, argued that the skeleton appeared to be of a non-Mongoloid race and of either European or South Asian origin. If true, this would provide strong evidence that the Americas were originally populated by multiple migrations from different areas of Asia and might have included early travellers from Europe. The findings and their interpretations have stimulated great legal and academic controversy. Does the desire to see the bones as having European origin reflect a deep-seated racism in academia? Do the bones just reflect the wide variation in skull shapes found among native populations? Who should own the bones? Reference: Thomas, D.H. (2001). *Skull Wars: Kennewick Man and the Battle for Native American Identity.* New York: Basic Books.

Kent State killings Kent State University located in Kent, Ohio, gained international attention in 1970, when National Guardsmen fired on an antiwar demonstration, killing four students.

Keynesian economics The economic theory of British economist John Maynard Keynes (1883–1946), Keynesian economics stresses the necessity of active government intervention in the direction and control of the economy. The most central idea is that the business cycle of capitalist economies, irregular alternations of boom and bust, can be smoothed out by government creation of credit, investment activity, and income transfers during economic contraction, and the raising of revenue surplus during periods of expansion. This approach, in Keynes' theory, offers insurance against the human cost of mass unemployment and the wastage of productive capacity by economic instability. For several decades, beginning in the 1930s, this was the dominant model for the economic policies of Western governments. Since the mid-1970s, monetarism has challenged and, to some extent, displaced Keynesian economics as the framework for public policy and academic work. Keynesian economics is linked to a strong public policy, the welfare state, and active state involvement in the economy, while monetarism supports a noninterventionist state, privatization, and reliance on the self-regulating forces of the market. *See also* **monetarism**.

kinesics A system or method of analyzing postures, facial expressions, and body motions that convey meaning, kinesics was first defined as a field of study by U.S. anthropologist Ray L. Birdwhistell (1918–1994). Reference: Birdwhistell, R.L. (1970). *Kinesics and context: Essays in body motion communication.* Philadelphia: University of Pennsylvania Press.

King–Byng Crisis Also called the *King–Byng Affair*, this was a 1926 constitutional conflict between Prime Minister Mackenzie King and British-appointed Governor General Lord Byng. By constitutional convention, the governor general is expected to accept the advice of the prime minister when dissolution of the House of Commons and a general election is requested. In 1926, King's Liberal minority government was defeated in a House of Commons vote, and King called on the governor general to request dissolution of the House. Byng, however, insisted that since the previous election had been only eight months before and because the Conservatives had more seats than any other party, it was legitimate to call on the Conservative leader first to see if he could form a government that could gain the support of the House of Commons. As a result, a new government was formed by Conservative leader Arthur Meighen; it survived several votes of confidence but was soon defeated. Now a new election became inevitable and the Liberals were victorious in a campaign that stressed the "unconstitutional" behaviour of the governor general. As a result of the conflict, King demanded from Britain the right of the Canadian, rather than British, government to decide who was to be appointed governor general, and the controversy thus led to increased recognition of Canada's sovereign equality with Britain within the British Empire. Reference: Duffy, J. (2002). *Fights of our lives: Elections, leadership and the making of Canada.* Toronto: HarperCollins.

Kinsey Reports This term refers to two volumes by biologist and human sexuality researcher Alfred C. Kinsey (1894–1956): *The Sexual Behavior of the Human Male* (1948) and *The Sexual Behavior of the Human Female* (1953). These books stirred a storm of criticism, as the results about the frequency of sexual activity such as premarital intercourse and masturbation were seen as alarming. Further, the *Kinsey Reports* provided the first scientific enumeration of homosexual activity, and suggested that this sexual preference was very common and must be regarded as normal.

kinship structure *Kinship structure* refers to the way social relationships between individuals related by blood, affinal ties, or socially defined (fictive) connection are organized and normatively regulated. Kinship is the central organizational principle of many traditional societies, since it is through the kinship structure that social placement, cultural transmission, and many functional necessities for life will be met. The extent of relevant kinship connection differs greatly from society to society. Kinship bonds are generally defined more broadly and extensively in traditional societies than in modern capitalist societies. *See also* **Eskimo kinship system**.

kleptomania Not to be confused with shoplifting, which is usually well planned and motivated by need or monetary gain, kleptomania is a compulsive disorder in which the person repeatedly steals things that are not needed.

Koko *See* **language among nonhuman primates**.

Komagata Maru Chartered by a group of Sikhs, *Komagata Maru* was used to sail to Vancouver from Hong Kong in anticipation of immigration privileges being granted to its passengers, 376 Punjabis. At the time of its sailing in 1914, Indians could come to Canada only if they sailed continuously (or directly) from India to Canada, although there were no such regular routes. All others were to be prohibited entry to Canada—a method to restrict immigration of people from the Indian subcontinent. On the *Komagata Maru's* arrival at the port of Vancouver, its passengers were denied entry and were kept on board for two months while negotiations proceeded. These negotiations eventually failed, and the ship sailed to Calcutta, where 20 of the passengers were killed in clashes with authorities who were suspicious of the politics of the travellers. Reference: Johnston, Harry. (1979). *The Voyage of the Komagata Maru.* Delhi, India: Oxford University Press.

Kuhn, Thomas *See* **paradigm**.

kula ring A complex system of visits and exchanges among the Trobriand Islanders of the western Pacific, the kula ring was first described by Polish anthropologist Bronislaw Malinowski (1884–1942) in 1922. Necklaces were exchanged in one direction among the residents of a chain of islands and armbands were exchanged in the opposite direction (hence, the notion of a ring). These exchanges did not serve primarily an economic function but rather served to create social obligations among people whose help might be needed at various times in an individual's life. The person who gave the most gifts would create the most obligations, and in this sense, create the most wealth by forming a relational net that could be depended on.

L

L'Anse aux Meadows Located at the tip of the Great Northern Peninsula of Newfoundland and Labrador, L'Anse aux Meadows is the site of an 11th-century Viking settlement, the oldest known European settlement in North America. It is a UNESCO World Heritage Site.

labelling theory A theory that arose from the study of deviance in the late 1950s and early 1960s, labelling theory was a rejection of consensus theory or structural functionalism. Those approaches to deviance assumed that deviance could be understood as consisting of behaviour that violates social norms. Deviance is therefore something objective: It is a particular form of behaviour. Labelling theory rejected this approach and claimed that deviance is not a way of behaving, but is a name put on something: a label. Law is culturally and historically variable: What is crime today is not necessarily crime tomorrow. For example, in 1890 it was legal to possess marijuana, but illegal to attempt suicide. Today, the law is reversed. This shows that deviance is not something inherent in behaviour, but is an outcome of how individuals and their behaviour are labelled. If deviance is therefore just a label, it makes sense to ask: Where does the label come from? How does the label come to be applied to specific behaviours and to particular individuals? The first question leads to a study of the social origins of law. The second question leads to an examination of the actions of labellers such as psychiatrists, police, coroners, probation officers, judges, and juries. Reference: Becker, Howard. (1963). *The Outsiders.* New York: Macmillan. *See also* **amplification of deviance; moral entrepreneur; secondary deviance**.

labour theory of value A fundamental component of the economic and social theories of Karl Marx (1818–1883), German philosopher, social scientist, historian, and revolutionary, and of his analysis of capitalist exploitation, the labour theory of value argues that the value of any commodity is determined by the socially necessary labour time that

goes into its production. Marx uses the term *socially necessary labour time* because the labour time required to create a commodity depends on the society's levels of technology and craft. In Marx's theory, commodities should in principle be exchanged in the marketplace for prices that exactly correspond to the necessary labour time embodied in them. When a commodity is exchanged—or sold—for more than its labour value, a surplus value is realized. This theory of value provides the foundation of Marx's claim that labour is exploited in a capitalist society: The capitalist, through the power of capital ownership, is able to pay the worker less than the market value of the commodities produced, and the surplus value is captured by capital and largely reinvested to augment the means of production. *See also* **surplus value**.

laissez-faire This term literally means "to leave alone." This economic doctrine states that government should not interfere in the economic or social regulation of society unless absolutely necessary. It assumes that the competitive system of free markets is the best means of allocation of scarce resources between alternative uses. Government intervention in the marketplace to regulate economic activity is seen as illegitimate and inefficient. This doctrine lost popularity in the middle of the 20th century, with the rise of the welfare state and extensive public ownership of parts of the economy, but regained favour in the 1980s and 1990s. *See also* **classical economic theory; invisible hand of the market**.

Lament for a Nation The title of Canadian philosopher George Grant's 1965 prophetic book, *Lament for a Nation: The Defeat of Canadian Nationalism,* presents the argument that Canada's national autonomy was lost to the creeping forces of continentalism. Grant's book was written in response to the 1963 federal election, which saw the Conservative government of John Diefenbaker defeated and the Liberals, under Lester Pearson, come to power. One of the central issues of the election had been nuclear weapons on Canadian soil. Canada had signed the *North American Aerospace Defence* (NORAD) agreement in 1957, which integrated the Canadian and American Air Forces in the defence of the continent under the command of the American government. As part of this agreement, two squadrons of American Bomarc missiles were to be deployed to Canada. What was not made clear immediately was that some of these missiles were to carry nuclear warheads. Diefenbaker was never able to agree to this, and during the Cuban Missile Crisis of 1962, he saw more clearly that Canadian sovereignty had been eroded. The Liberals played on this weakness and, when elected, agreed to the use of nuclear warheads. Grant was responding to this erosion of sovereignty and the clear integration of Canada into the American state. Canadian nationalists have used Grant as a symbol of nationalism because of his clear articulation of the potential for an independent Canadian state, although Grant himself saw the importance of remaining allied to Britain as a way to reduce American influence. Reference: Cayley, David. (1995). *George Grant in conversation*. Toronto: Anansi Press.

land claims *See* **Calder case; comprehensive land claims; specific land claims**.

language among nonhuman primates Several attempts have made to teach primates human language. One of the early attempts was with the chimpanzee known as Viki, but success in getting her to make recognizable sounds was very limited. Attempts were then made to teach American Sign Language; one of the first experiments was with the chimpanzee Washoe. Results were much better with this method—Koko, a lowland gorilla, learned 400 words, and the orangutan Chantek acquired the use of an extensive number of signs and the ability to create "sentences" not used by the researchers, to answer questions, to use language to deceive, and eventually to refer to things apart from their context (a degree of abstract thought). Chantek was able to use language at the level of a two- to three-year-old child. Reference: Miles, H.L.W. (1993). Language and the orangutan. In P. Cavalieri & P. Singer (Eds.), *The great ape project*. New York: St. Martin's Press.

Laporte, Pierre A Cabinet minister in the Liberal government of Robert Bourassa, Pierre Laporte was kidnapped by FLQ terrorists on October 10, 1970, and murdered by them a week later. *See also* **Front de libération du Québec (FLQ); October Crisis**.

latchkey children This term applies to children who spend a part of the day unsupervised, usually the period from the end of the school day until a parent or guardian returns from work.

Latimer, Robert The Latimers, a Saskatchewan farming family, had two children, one with major mental and physical disabilities that kept the child in constant pain. The family was very troubled by their inability to help their child as she suffered. On October 24, 1993, Robert Latimer placed his daughter in the family truck, ran a hose from the tailpipe to the passenger compartment, and took his daughter's life. He was eventually convicted of second-degree murder. The community was greatly divided on the court's decision, and the Supreme Court eventually heard the case to determine if the fact that his daughter was severely disabled and in pain should be taken into account in sentencing. For some, these arguments supported mercy killing. The Supreme Court upheld Latimer's life sentence with no parole for 10 years. Reference: Enns, R. (1999). *A Voice Unheard: The Latimer Case and People with Disabilities*. Halifax: Garamond.

Lavallée case On September 22, 1987, Angélique Lyn Lavallée was acquitted of the murder of her common-law husband. He was shot in the head while leaving a room. After much dispute, the judge allowed the jury to hear and use expert evidence of the abuse the defendant had endured at the hands of her common-law husband, and how this may have led to her murdering him in a form of "self-defence" arising from the "battered wife syndrome." Lavallée's subsequent acquittal was accepted by the Supreme Court in a 1990 judgment, and the criteria for using this defence were clarified. Reference: *R. v. Lavallée* [1990] 1 S.C.R. 852. *See also* **Malott case**.

Laval School The School of Social Sciences founded by Georges-Henri Levesque at Université Laval in Quebec City in 1938 represented the Laval School of thought. Levesque and his many collaborators and students played a major role in the movement for the social and economic modernization of Quebec, which ultimately led to the Quiet Revolution and the rising tide of Quebec nationalism that commenced in the 1960s. Levesque and the Laval School shaped thinking about Canada's history with their argument that the conquest of French Canada by the British had not doomed Quebec to powerlessness and backwardness, but had unleashed dynamic forces that encouraged the emergence of a modern, more liberal, and democratic society. *See also* **Quiet Revolution**.

law A body of rules or norms passed by a legislated authority and enforced by an authorized and specialized body comprises the law. Law clearly identifies the defining characteristic of the state—the ability to establish and legitimately use coercion to enforce a framework of social regulation and direction. The state, by passing laws and having the authority to force compliance, can coerce citizens to act in particular ways (or leave the country). While all large-scale, modern societies have law, some hunter–gatherer, pastoral, or horticultural societies did not. In these societies, social life was regulated primarily by custom and tradition.

Leakey, Louis and Mary Kenyan/British anthropologist and archaeologist Louis Leakey (1903–1972) and his wife Mary Leakey (1913–1996) made an extraordinary contribution to the field of paleoanthropology through their work in the Olduvai Gorge in Tanzania. Although they began their dig in the gorge in 1931 it was not until 1959 that Mary found the first hominine fossil in the area. The area was to become one of the most productive sources of hominine fossils in Africa.

Le Dain Commission Gerald Le Dain (1924–) was the chair of the 1969 Royal Commission on the Non-Medical Use of Drugs, investigating the role that the government and courts should play in prohibiting and regulating drugs used largely for recreational purposes. The commission produced numerous published volumes, which rank among the most thorough and accurate assessments of drugs and drug policy in the world, but none of the recommendations were legislated. The commission stimulated the new sociology of deviance in Canada through its sponsorship of research. Le Dain was later appointed to the Supreme Court of Canada.

left realism A criminological perspective, left realism emerged in Britain in response to the rise of neo-conservatism. The right-wing politics of Prime Minister Margaret Thatcher made it clear that left-leaning criminology had little impact on social policy and was going to have little significance in the future. Some critical criminologists struggled to make their work relevant by focusing on the working class as victims of street crime, state, and corporate crime, and women as victims of male crime. They asserted that official studies of crime underestimated victimization of the working class and women, and supported community-controlled research as a method of getting at the "reality" of their experience. Social policies to reduce victimization of marginal communities, involve communities in crime prevention, return political control to local communities, and increase police account-

ability follow from this beginning point. Left realism can be contrasted with left idealism, which, while also believing that the structure of capitalism is the culprit in crime, tended to see working-class crime as acts of rebellion or political resistance. This can be seen as a somewhat romantic or idealistic view. Reference: Lea, John, & Young, Jock. (1984). *What Is to Be Done about Law and Order?* London: Sage; MacLean, Brian. (1991). The Origins of Left Realism. In B. MacLean and D. Milovanovic (Eds.), *New Directions in Critical Criminology*. Vancouver: Collective Press.

legitimation crisis During a legitimation crisis—a period during which those in authority (a political order, or government) are unable to evoke sufficient commitment or sense of authority to properly govern—the governing party is no longer seen as being legitimate. Low levels of voter turnout in the United States, for example, may be seen as an indicator of a legitimation crisis, as may the massive rejection of the *Charlottetown Accord* in Canada even though acceptance was recommended by most of the established political leaders in the nation. From a political economy perspective, the major source of a legitimation crisis today is the economic transformation of the world in conjunction with what is termed *globalization*. This transformation raises the possibility that citizens will see the economic system with its growing class-polarization and impoverishment as illegitimate, as well as the governments that attempt to regulate this new world economic order. *See also* **globalization**; **exceptional state**.

Leninism This term refers to the ideas of Vladimir Ilich Lenin (1870–1924), leader of the Russian Revolution (1917) and founder of the Soviet Union. Lenin's ideas were mainly derived from Marxism, but he had a distinctive view of the importance of leadership in creating a working-class revolution. He advocated the organization of the working class by a disciplined and centralized communist party, believing, unlike Marx, that class-consciousness could develop only under the guidance and direction of party leadership. Many historians have argued that Lenin's focus on the dominant role of the party and of its central leadership led directly to the establishment of Stalin's dictatorship and to millions of deaths in the attempt to establish Soviet-style communism.

Lepine, Marc *See* **Montreal massacre**.

level of measurement In quantitative social science, concepts are measured in order to provide a frequency count for each value of a variable. Not all measurements have the same qualities, and some statistical tests require particular levels of measurement. There are four levels of measurement: nominal, ordinal, interval, and ratio. Nominal measures allow only for the placing of the subjects into categories (e.g., female and male). Ordinal levels of measurement allow the researcher to rank respondents (e.g., strongly agree and agree). Interval measurements allow the researcher to specify the distance between respondents (e.g., John has 10 fewer units of intelligence than does Mary). A ratio level of measurement allows the researcher to express various scores as ratios, and this requires an absolute zero (e.g., Mary has twice as many siblings as does John). Complex statistical tests require interval or ratio measurements.

levelling mechanism A form of exchange driven by societal obligations, a levelling mechanism requires people to redistribute goods so that no one has more wealth than others.

leveraged buyouts A form of corporate takeover, a leveraged buyout is one in which the purchaser finances the acquisition almost exclusively by incurring debt, rather than from corporate profits and income flows. Typically, the acquiring corporation will issue shares and corporate bonds that are not backed by any significant collateral property or obligation. Bonds issued in these circumstances are popularly called "junk bonds."

levirate marriage A marriage tradition requiring a widow to marry a brother of her dead husband, levirate marriage was practised in some traditional Jewish groups, but marriage was forbidden if the widow had a child with her dead husband. Other examples include groups in India, Mongolia, and Tibet.

Lévi-Strauss, Claude (1908–) Belgian anthropologist Claude Lévi-Strauss exhibited great imagination and gave birth to the form of analysis known as *structuralism*. Lévi-Strauss began his work by looking at kinship patterns and, later, myths. In both fields, he saw deeper structures lying behind the great variety of kinship practices and myths. He came to believe that these deep patterns reflected the structure of the human mind. In this regard, he was influenced by his Russian mentor in linguistics, Roman Jakobson (1896–1982). He was also influenced by French sociologist and anthropologist Marcel Mauss (1872–1950), whose work on establishment of obligation and reciprocity by gift-giving argued that this process was the most effective way to establish the social solidarity seen as essential by Émile Durkheim (1858–1917), French sociologist. Lévi-Strauss then develops from this the claim that kinship rests upon this basis of reciprocity and exchange and specifies the range of people involved in the exchange relationship. *See also* **structuralism**

liberal feminism A form of feminism that argues that the liberal principles of equality, freedom, and equality of opportunity must be fully extended to women, liberal feminism does not call for specific structural changes to society. Neither patriarchy nor capitalism are identified as the enemies of women; rather, the restricted reach of liberalism is identified as the problem. *See also* **feminism**; *Status of Women Report.*

liberalism An ideology that upholds private property, individual rights, legal equality, freedom of choice, and democratic government, liberalism suggests that the essence of freedom is to be free from constraint. It is an ideology that supports capitalism and advocates the principle of free markets left largely undirected by governments. While liberalism upholds free markets, it also places great value on equality of opportunity and is strongly opposed to ascriptive processes in society, since they restrict individual choice and deny equal access to satisfaction. In the 20th century, a more active view of the state's role in creating improved equality of opportunity in society became important within liberalism. (This trend in liberalism was also a reaction to the development of trade unions and of socialist and populist movements.) There was a massive expansion in state-provided education, social programs, etc., from the end of the 19th century until the 1960s and 1970s. In the 1980s and continuing today, a more classical view of liberalism has returned to prominence, one that advocates a much smaller role for the state and increased reliance on the workings of the free market. In making this argument, classical liberals claim that intervention in the market rarely, if ever, promotes choice, but frustrates the market adjustments that ultimately improve efficiency, the wealth of society, and the ability of individuals to make choices. *See also* **classical liberalism**; **neoconservatism**.

Liberal Party of Canada This federal political party was founded in the 1870s, when Reform politicians in Ontario joined with those in Quebec to create a united federal party under a new name. In 1873, the first Liberal government was formed by Alexander Mackenzie. The Liberals have been Canada's most successful political party, occupying the middle ground between the more business-oriented Conservative party and the social democratic welfare-oriented policies of the New Democratic Party. Former Liberal leaders and prime ministers include Wilfrid Laurier, William Lyon Mackenzie King, Louis St. Laurent, Lester Pearson, Pierre Trudeau, Jean Chrétien, and Paul Martin. Reference: McCall, Christina. (1982). *Grits: A Portrait of the Liberal Party.* Toronto: Macmillan Canada.

liberation theology A mixture of Christian belief and political activism usually derived from a Marxist analysis of social inequality, liberation theology encourages priests to assume a political posture in the pulpit and in their activities with the community. This has led to many confrontations between churches and corporate interests, and the religious hierarchy has been urged to restrict the political activity of priests.

liberation thesis As the crime rates for women appeared to increase during the 1960s and 1970s, criminologists talked of the "new female criminal," and some argued that women's growing equality was resulting in a convergence of men's and women's crime rates. This was the liberation thesis and it was hotly contested. Reference: Adler, Freda. (1975). *Sisters in Crime.* New York: McGraw-Hill.

libertarianism A philosophy or belief system that gives priority to the liberty of the individual, libertarianism may be associated with classical liberalism regarding economic matters or the protection of those negative liberties that declare the right of the individual to be free from interference by the state, or the community, unless the actions of the individual constitute harm to others. For example, the individual has the right to freedom of speech, freedom of association, freedom of religious expression, and freedom of contract. Libertarianism is related to individualism and contrasted with communitarianism. *See also* **communitarianism**.

Lilith According to Jewish religious tradition, Lilith was the first wife of Adam; she was replaced by Eve. Some of the writings describe Lilith as a wild creature, the mother of demons, and sexually insatiable. Was Lilith's displacement by Eve because she refused to accept a subordinate gender role as Adam's helpmate? Did she refuse Adam's authority? Was she lesbian? Whatever the answers, Lilith has become an increasingly important character in modern feminist myth. In Jewish tradition, Lilith was a "night demon," but in modern mythology she stands for the independent woman. Canadian singer Sarah McLachlan has made the name popular through the many Lilith Fairs (featuring only female performers) that she has organized across North America.

linguistic divergence This term refers to the development of different languages from a single ancestral language.

linguistics Linguistics is the scientific study of all aspects of language. Reference: Hickerson, N.P. (1980). *Linguistic anthropology.* New York: Rinehart and Winston.

Linnaeus, Carl (or Carl von Linné) *See* **classification of living things**.

Locke, John (1632–1704) A central figure in the development of ideas that contributed to liberalism, John Locke was a British philosopher and medical researcher. His most important political writings are his *Two Treatises of Government*, probably written in 1680. At that time, Catholic influence over England's monarchs, which had in the past led to a civil war, was again increasing, and the heir to the throne who would be crowned James II in 1685 had converted from Protestantism to the Roman Catholic faith. There was a revival of the Catholic doctrine that earthly monarchs governed by divine right and were thus superior to their subjects and not restrained by legal regulation or by Parliament. Against this claim, Locke argued that each person, by that person's own experience, was able to grasp the "law of nature" and thus comprehend what was moral and governed by reason. Since people were endowed with morality and reason, they had the right to liberty and equality; political authority could be justified only as the product of a social contract by which people agreed to allow a government to guarantee the peace and order that were essential to the protection of freedom. If the government exceeded its authority and invaded people's rights, it then lost its legitimate right to govern and the citizen was justified in rising up against it.

Lombroso, Cesare (1835–1909) Italian criminologist and physician Cesare Lombroso's theory of crime proposed that criminals are biologically and developmentally distinct from law-abiding citizens. He identified various physical features or stigmata that allegedly distinguished criminals from noncriminals, such as distinct ear and finger shapes and different slopes of the forehead. *See also* **atavism; Positivist School; stigmata.**

lone-parent family This term is used by Statistics Canada to refer to single-parent families.

longitudinal studies Longitudinal studies measure relationships between variables over a period of time. For example, one might follow a group of males from birth to age 30 to measure their involvement with the criminal justice system over time and relate this information to their parents' socioeconomic status. A series of cross-sectional investigations taken over time will provide a longitudinal study. Reference: West, D.J., & Farrington, David. (1977). *The Delinquent Way of Life*. London: Heinemann.

looking-glass self Developed by U.S. sociologist C.H. Cooley (1864–1929) to describe the social nature of the self and the link between society and individual, in the looking-glass self formulation, social interaction is like a mirror: It allows us to see ourselves as others see us. This was an early formulation of symbolic interactionism, but less influential than that of U.S. social psychologist George Herbert Mead (1863–1931).

Lorenz curve The Lorenz curve was developed by American economist Max O. Lorenz (1880–1962) in order to describe the extent of inequality in a society. Imagine a graph in which the cumulated income (expressed as a percentage) is placed on the vertical axis, and the cumulated number of households (expressed as a percentage) is placed on the horizontal axis. If there were perfect equality (so that the first 10% of the households received 10% of the income, and 20% of the households received 20% of the income, etc.), a diagonal line would be drawn across the graph. When actual income distributions are depicted on this graph, the line (a curve) departs from the line of perfect equality. For example, the bottom 20% of households may receive only 4.5% of the total income. This line is the Lorenz curve and can be expressed mathematically. The Gini coefficient is an expression of the ratio of the amount of the graph located between the line of perfect inequality and the Lorenz curve to the total area of the graph below the line of equality. *See also* **Gini coefficient.**

Love Canal During the 1940s and 1950s, chemical companies were allowed to dispose of chemical waste in an empty canal in the city of Niagara Falls, New York. While the chemicals were sealed in drums, it was only a matter of time until chemicals seeped into a residential development built on top of the filled canal. Great human suffering resulted and, in 1980, a national emergency was declared. A massive cleanup began, accompanied by a compensation process for residents. While industrial pollution had occurred elsewhere prior to this date (and certainly since), the Love Canal site captured the public's imagination and a wariness of industry and its wastes increased.

Lower Canada The *Constitutional Act, 1791*, divided the old province of Quebec into Upper Canada (now Ontario) and Lower Canada (now Quebec). *See also* **Constitutional Act, 1791.**

lower-class culture It has been argued by some that members of the lower class have developed and transmitted to their children a different set of cultural values and expectations. They argue further that this culture is a barrier to its members' success in society. Used in this way, lower-class culture is associated with the culture of poverty thesis. More recently, sociologists have rejected this emphasis on values and argue that structural barriers create the conditions that might generate these values and expectations. If this is so, the solution is to transform the structures, not blame the poor.

Lower Paleolithic The first part of the Old Stone Age, the Lower Paleolithic Period is associated with the appearance of Oldowan tools about 2.6 million years ago.

low-income cutoffs *See* **poverty line.**

LSD A powerful hallucinogen produced by transforming alkaloid compounds, which occur in nature or can be produced into D-lysergic acid diethylamide-25, LSD stimulates the sensory systems so as to produce visual hallucinations.

Lucy Skeletal remains about 3.18 million years old (nicknamed "Lucy") were found in 1974 by U.S. anthropologist Donald Johanson (1943–) in Afar, Ethiopia. The skeleton was of a species now classified as *Australopithecus afarensis* and was about 40% complete. These remains of a distant human ancestor, who walked on two feet, really captured the world's imagination. The name comes from the Beatle's song "Lucy in the Sky with Diamonds," which was playing in the background at the time of discovery. Reference: Johanson, D.C., & Edey, M.A. (1981). *Lucy: The beginnings of humankind.* New York: Simon and Schuster.

Luddites As technology began to transform the early 19th-century workplace, workers in Britain initiated random attacks in which they destroyed the machinery of the developing industrial order and destroyed poorly manufactured and shoddy goods. The workers involved in these actions, Luddites, claimed to be led by Ned Ludd. It was said that Ned Ludd (like Robin Hood) lived in Sherwood Forest; historians assume the name was probably a pseudonym for an individual or group of leaders.

lumpenproletariat A term associated with German philosopher, social scientist, historian, and revolutionary Karl Marx (1818–1883), *lumpenproletariat* refers to the class of individuals in a capitalist society who do not regularly participate in wage labour, but subsist through occasional employment, begging, scavenging, or crime. This class is assumed to expand and contract in number in relation to levels of economic activity in the society.

Lyotard, Jean-Françoise *See* **postmodernism**.

M

Machiavelli, Niccolo (1469–1527) This Italian political thinker's name has contributed a word to the English language—"Machiavellian"—meaning the unprincipled use of intrigue and deceit to gain power or advantage. His most famous work, *Il principe* (*The Prince*), is notorious for its claim that what is prohibited conduct for the individual may still be appropriate conduct for the exercise of statecraft, which at times must employ means, such as violence and aggression, that are immoral for individuals but justified by the goals of the state. This separation of political philosophy from moral or religious considerations made Machiavelli the most radical political thinker of the later Renaissance.

macho/machismo behaviour The public display of characteristically (and usually exaggerated) masculine behaviour is called *macho* or *machismo behaviour. See also* **doing gender**.

Mackenzie Valley Pipeline Inquiry Former Supreme Court judge Thomas Berger began a one-person inquiry in 1974, travelling through Canada's North

to give local peoples a voice in a proposal to build a major gas pipeline from the Beaufort Sea to southern energy markets. Having decided that hunting, fishing, gathering, and trapping continued to be important elements of Dene life, he recommended a delay of 10 years in order to give the native peoples time to prepare for the impact of such a development. In 2004, the question of a pipeline was raised again, and this time, the majority of the northern natives were supportive of the project. Reference: Berger, T. (1988). *Northern frontier, northern homeland: The report of the Mackenzie Valley Pipeline Inquiry.* Vancouver: Douglas and McIntyre.

MacLean, Annie (1870–1934) The first Canadian woman to receive a Ph.D. in sociology, studying at the University of Chicago, Annie MacLean remained in the United States and spent her career teaching in the University of Chicago's Extension Department.

Macpherson, C.B. (1911–1987) Crawford Brough Macpherson was a leading figure in the development of Canadian political economy, which unites political, economic, and historical perspectives in its analysis of society and culture. Macpherson is best known for his book *The Political Theory of Possessive Individualism: Hobbes to Locke* (Oxford University Press, 1962). This book attacks the assumption in liberalism that individuals have the right to freely satisfy their own desires without any responsibility to the community other than the duty not to infringe on the freedoms of others. Instead, Macpherson argued that we are all born into a preexisting society that transmits to us the knowledge, especially the language, that we need to be fully human, and provides us with the personal and economic security that we need to live. This contribution to our lives bonds us to society and, accordingly, individuals are morally obliged to accept responsibility and commitment to others beyond the call of their own self-interest. Reference: Leiss, W. (1989). *C.B. Macpherson: Dilemmas of liberalism and socialism.* New York: St. Martin's Press.

macroeconomics This branch of economics is devoted to the study of economic aggregates at a national or an international level, including gross domestic product, unemployment, size of the labour market, human capital, investment, productivity, and price levels. Economists working for the International Monetary Fund would be specialists in macroeconomic theory. (In contrast to microeconomics, which focuses more on individual economic decisions or corporate behaviour.)

macroperspective A macroperspective analysis focuses on the structure of society and provides a way of seeing society as a unified whole. In this type of perspective, minimal attention is given to the individual or the subjectivity of actors—the structures of society are thought to be primary and responsible for shaping the individual.

magic Magic involves the performance of routines, usually in a fixed or rigid manner, designed to influence the future, persuade the gods, or shape fate. The ballplayer who believes that wearing the same sweater or eating the same meal before a game will determine whether the team wins or not is performing a magic observance. *See also* **witchcraft**.

Magna Carta A document signed, under duress, by King John of England in 1215, the *Magna Carta* is seen as the beginning of English constitutional law, since it redefined and greatly restricted the powers of the king.

majority In sociology, *majority* does not refer to a numerical majority but rather to a group or groups that have power. In South Africa, the Blacks were the majority numerically but a minority in terms of power. This of course began to change with the inclusion of Blacks in the electoral process and the election of Nelson Mandela.

mala prohibita An act that is deemed to be wrong or even criminal only because it is prohibited is called a *mala prohibita*. There is nothing inherent in such an act that makes it criminal: There is no victim and no obvious harm is done. Some would argue that this is the case with laws prohibiting the possession of marijuana: To possess marijuana is not evidently wrong in itself—it is a criminal act only because the law says it is wrong. *See also* ***mal in se***.

Malinowski, Bronislaw (1884–1942) Born in Poland, anthropologist Bronislaw Malinowski was working in Australia when World War I broke out, and although he had studied in Germany (with which Australia was at war) to his surprise he was allowed to conduct fieldwork in the Trobriand Islands rather than being interned. The book resulting from this work, *Argonauts of the Western Pacific*, the first segment of which appeared in 1922, became a classic example of ethnography. Indeed, Malinowski's greatest legacy was the establishment of fieldwork as anthropologists' basic method of gathering data. Malinowski developed functionalism as a tool for explaining aspects of culture, but being influenced by his own training, was inclined to see cultures as serving the needs of individuals, particularly their psychological needs. Reference: Malinowski, B. (1922). *Argonauts of the Western Pacific*. London: Routledge.

mal in se A willful act that is evidently wrong or criminal because it is considered to be inherently unacceptable and immoral and damaging to other people and society as a whole is a *mal in se*. Examples are crimes such as murder, armed robbery, assault, fraud, and larceny, which have victims who are directly harmed. Law reform commissions have recommended that the criminal law be reserved only for these types of acts. Criminal law, however, still punishes a range of acts that are simply *mala prohibita*. *See also* ***mala prohibita***.

Malott case A Supreme Court of Canada decision in the Malott case clarified the approach that courts should take in cases that may involve "battered woman syndrome." The court declared that the battered woman syndrome was not a defence in its own right, but only a psychiatric explanation of the mental state of a woman that might be relevant in understanding a killing and shaping sentencing. Reference: *R. v. Malott* [1998] 1 S.C.R. 123.

Malthusian crisis English political economist Thomas Malthus (1766–1834) argued that while populations grow exponentially, the rate of increase in the food supply is much less. This creates a natural limit on populations and produces miserable conditions for society and inevitable mass starvation. This type of situation is referred to as a *Malthusian crisis*. To avert such a crisis, Malthus advocated that individuals should practise birth control, not by using contraceptives but by reducing sexual intercourse. His ideas caused great public controversy in his time, and still do today. *See also* **demographic transition**; **exponential growth**.

Managerial Revolution Traditionally, manufacturing enterprises were owned and controlled by individuals or families. In the mid-19th century, however, joint-stock companies began to emerge and, over time, increasing numbers of investors held a share of ownership and received a portion of the profits. These companies no longer had a single owner, and managers emerged to control business operations. It was assumed that this new breed of salaried workers would transform the workplace: Values other than profit would enter into business calculations, and there would be greater harmony between workers and executives. Since most managers have become large shareholders (and thus owners), the significance of the Managerial Revolution has been called into question.

manifest destiny A belief found among the early American colonists, manifest destiny held that the destiny of the American colonies was to stretch from the Atlantic to the Pacific and as far south as the Rio Grande River. In the early 19th century, this belief was behind the decision to claim or expand the territories of Texas, Oregon, and California, bringing the country into conflict with Mexico and England. Canadian politicians were concerned that this belief also held that the American state should eventually occupy the territories to the north, and much Canadian policy can be seen as an attempt to cut off American territorial and market expansion.

man in the house rule A regulation in most Canadian provinces, the man in the house rules originally prescribed that any woman who lived with a man could not receive welfare payments in her own right. The assumption was that the man would be supporting her. Revoked in Ontario in the late 1980s, the rule was reimplemented in 1995, but in October 2002, the Ontario Court of Appeal struck down the "spouse in the house" rule for single mothers receiving welfare benefits. Reference: *Falkiner v. Ontario* (Ministry of Community and Social Services), [2002] O.J. No. 1771; 2002, 59 O.R. (3d) 481 33.

manslaughter A culpable homicide other than murder or infanticide, manslaughter is an offence that would otherwise be thought of as murder, except that the killing occurred in the heat of passion caused by sudden provocation or while intoxicated. In legal terms, there must have been no malice aforethought. *See also* **murder**.

maquiladoras *See* **free trade zones**.

Marcuse, Herbert (1898–1979) German-born political philosopher Herbert Marcuse was a member of the Frankfurt School who remained in the United States after World War II. Due to his lifelong commitment to radical politics, he had a great influence on the students of the 1960s and 1970s. He felt that the Marxist prediction that the working class would be the source of opposition to capitalism had failed to come true, and he now looked to marginalized groups (such as students and minorities) to lead the revolution. *See also* **Frankfurt School**.

market economy An economy in which goods and services are freely exchanged without obstruction or regulation is called a *market economy*. In such an economy, decisions about production and consumption are made by many separate individuals, each seeking satisfaction of specific needs and desires. The term is sometimes used interchangeably with *capitalist economy*, but this is an error since a cooperatively based economy could also be operated on market principles. *See also* **invisible hand of the market**.

Marshall inquiry In 1971, Donald Marshall, a teenaged Nova Scotia Mik'maq, was convicted of a stabbing murder. He maintained his innocence, and after he had served 11 years of a life sentence, an official inquiry determined his innocence. In 1987, a Royal Commission of Inquiry examined the case and concluded that the criminal justice system had failed because of police and judicial prejudice and incompetence. Marshall was finally awarded almost a million dollars in compensation. His case, along with others in which justice miscarried, has served to increase Canadians' wariness of any return to a death penalty for murder. Reference: Nova Scotia. (1989). *Royal Commission into the Wrongful Conviction of Donald Marshall Jr.* Halifax: Queen's Printer; Harris, M. (1986). *Justice Denied: The Law versus Donald Marshall.* Toronto: Totem Books. *See also* **wrongful conviction**.

Marsh Report Published in 1943, the *Report on Social Security for Canada,* commonly known as the *Marsh Report,* was written by Leonard Marsh (1906–1982) and resulted from his work as research advisor on the federal government's Committee on Post-War Reconstruction. Although the *Marsh Report* was largely ignored, it does provide the intellectual foundation for much of the welfare state that was developed over the following 25 years. Marsh was born in London, England, and emigrated to Canada in 1930. After the war, he taught at the University of British Columbia. The *Marsh Report* can be compared to Britain's 1942 *Beveridge Report,* which led to the establishment of a system of social security and the National Health Service after the end of World War II.

Martineau, Harriet (1802–1876) British sociologist Harriet Martineau translated and condensed the writings of French sociologist Auguste Comte

(1798–1857) and took a classical sociological perspective in her writings on Britain and the United States. She also brought a feminist perspective to sociology, which remained buried for decades until modern feminist movements resurrected it. Reference: Lengermann, P., & Niebrugge-Brantley, J. (1998). *The Women Founders: Sociology and Social Theory, 1830–1930*. New York: McGraw-Hill.

Marxism This term describes the body of philosophical, political, economic, and sociological ideas associated with Karl Marx and his lifelong collaborator Friedrich Engels. The term is also used more generally to refer to work in the social sciences and humanities that employs key ideas and concepts from Marx and Engels' original writings. *See also* **Marx, Karl**.

Marxist feminism Marxist feminists believe that women's oppression is a symptom of a more fundamental form of oppression: Women are not oppressed by men or by sexism, but by capitalism itself. If all women are to be liberated, capitalism must be replaced with socialism. In Friedrich Engels' (1820–1895) writing, women's oppression originated with the development of private property and of regulated family and marital relationships. Men's control of economic resources developed with a settled society and the development of separate spheres of life for the two sexes. He wrote that, in capitalist societies, women become segregated into the domestic sphere and men into the outer world of paid work. Economic and social inequality between the sexes is increased, and women's subordination in marriage, the family, and society in general is intensified. Engels assumed that socialist revolution, through which the means of production would become common property, would result in the development of equal access to paid work for both men and women and the consequent disappearance of gendered inequality. *See also* **liberal feminism; radical feminism**.

Marx, Karl (1818–1883) German-born social philosopher, political economist, and sociologist Karl Marx, along with his lifelong collaborator Friedrich Engels (1820–1895), was responsible for the development of the social and economic doctrines of communism. The core of Marxist theory is that each historical period has a distinct mode of production that rests on particular forces—or technological organization—of production and distinct ways of organizing social relationships among people in the economy. This mode of production then exerts the primary influence in shaping social relationships within the society in general, as well as its politics, law, and intellectual ideas. This focus on the relationship of law, social control, ideology, and coercion and the economic and social organization of society lies at the heart of critical and left-leaning criminology. *See also* **alienation; class; contradictions of capitalism; historical materialism; Marxism; Marxist feminism; mode of production; reserve army of labour; superstructure**.

masculine female By mixing the notions of gender and sex, the term *masculine female* identifies females who demonstrate features of the masculine gender.

masculinization A term central to the critique of traditional academic discussions of the female offender and of popular depictions of female criminality, *masculinization* refers to the attribution of male characteristics to women in an attempt to understand women's behaviour, rather than locating women's behaviour in female experience or structural location. U.S. criminologist and sociologist Freda Adler (1934–), for example, argued in 1975 that the women's liberation movement would lead to an increase in female crime, because liberation would make women more like men. *See also* **liberation thesis**.

mass culture A set of cultural values and ideas that arise from common exposure of a population to the same cultural activities, communications media, music and art, etc., a mass culture becomes possible only with modern communications and electronic media. A mass culture is transmitted to individuals, rather than arising from people's daily interactions, and therefore lacks the distinctive content of cultures rooted in community and region. A mass culture tends to reproduce the liberal value of individualism and to foster a view of the citizen as consumer. *See also* **mass society**.

Massey Report (Charles) Vincent Massey (1887–1967), the first Canadian-born governor general of Canada, was chairman of the Royal Commission on National Development in the Arts, Letters and Sciences (1949–1951). The commission's 1951 report recommended the creation of the Canada Council and substantial federal government spending on university education, constitutionally a provincial responsibility. Father Georges-Henri Lévesque (1903–2000), founder and dean of the Faculty of Social Sciences, Université Laval, and a commission member, strongly supported this expanded role for federal programs and was denounced by many Quebec nationalists. The commission gave one of the early expressions of the need for Canadians to strengthen their cultural institutions in order to avoid being dominated by American cultural influences.

mass media Sociologically speaking, in modern times the "community" has been replaced by a "mass," a set of autonomous and disconnected individuals, with little sense of community. The mass media (radio, television, newspapers, etc.) then are targeted at the mass rather than at specific groups or communities. *See also* **audience**.

mass murder Multiple murders that can be considered as a single event—for example, "shooting spree" murders—are classified as mass murders.

mass society This term refers to a society with a mass culture and large-scale, impersonal social institutions. Even the most complex and modern societies have lively primary group social relationships, so the concept can be thought of as an "ideal type," since it does not exist in empirical reality. It is intended to draw attention to the way in which life in complex societies, with great specialization and rationalized institutions, can become too anonymous and impersonal and fail to support adequate bonds between the individual and the community. The concept reflects the same concern in sociology—loss of community—that German sociologist F. Tonnies (1855–1936) expressed in his idea of *Gesellschaft*. *See also* **Gesellschaft**; **mass culture**.

master status A status that overrides all others in perceived importance is a master status. Whatever other personal or social qualities an individual possesses, that individual is judged primarily by this one attribute. "Criminal" is an example of a master status that determines the community's identification of an individual. A master status can also arise from other achieved or ascribed roles.

matriarchy A matriarchy is a society or family in which women possess most of the power and authority. While there is some dispute among social scientists, there is no clear evidence of matriarchal societies existing in the world in either the past or the present. Individual families, however, have frequently exhibited a matriarchal structure, with women clearly possessing dominant authority and control. The term must be distinguished from *matrilineal*, which refers to the system of tracing

descent through the bloodlines of women and which exists in a number of world societies. *See also* **matrilineal societies**.

matricide The killing of one's mother is matricide.

matrilineal societies In matrilineal societies, descent is traced through mothers rather than through fathers. In such societies, property is often passed from mothers to daughters and the custom of matrilocal residence may be practised. (*Matrilocal residence* means that a woman remains in her mother's household after reaching maturity and brings her husband to live with her family after marriage.) In such systems, the descendants of men are their sister's children and not their own, who belong to their mother's matrilineage. Matrilineage is sometimes associated with polyandry or group marriage, where women have a variety of sexual partners and the lines of male descent are uncertain.

matrilocal residence *Matrilocal residence* means that a woman remains in her mother's household after reaching maturity and brings her husband to live with her family after marriage.

maturational reform The observation that involvement in crime tends to decrease as people age, maturational reform can be confirmed by a visit to any prison, or by tracking 10-year-olds' crime involvements as they go through adolescence and into adulthood.

Matza, David (1930–) Professor of sociology at the University of California at Berkeley, David Matza developed "neutralization" or "drift" theory to explain why many delinquents tend to drift into and away from deviant behaviour. His theory proposes that the attitudes, values, and norms of delinquents are similar to those of law-abiding citizens, but that delinquents develop techniques of neutralization that provide justification for acts they know to be delinquent. These techniques involve justifications that blame the victim, deny that significant injury was caused, deny responsibility, or claim that acts are justified by the behaviour of the victim. This approach rejects theories such as differential association that locate causes of deviance in the individual's association with deviant subcultures. Reference: Matza, David. (1964). *Delinquency and Drift*. New York: Wiley.

McCarthyism Joseph McCarthy was elected senator for Wisconsin and rose to public attention when in a 1950 speech he claimed to have in his hand the names of 205 individuals who were active members of the Communist Party, many within the government itself. From this point on, he campaigned against communists and others described as subversive to American interests. In 1953, he became chair of the Senate's permanent committee of investigation and turned the committee's attention to the pursuit of communists and subversives (including homosexuals). Although in control of this committee for only a short time, many people were named, many reputations damaged, and public expression of dissent was silenced for a decade. This movement also had an impact on Canada. In an effort to root out communists and potential security risks, tests were developed to identify homosexuals, and several times, Minister of External Affairs Lester Pearson was pressured to fire Herbert Norman, an influential ambassador, but also a homosexual with communist associations in his past. When Pearson repeatedly refused to fire Norman, word was spread—probably by American sources—that Pearson himself may have been a communist sympathizer. Herbert Norman finally committed suicide while stationed as ambassador in Cairo when he realized that this harassment would never end. Reference: Scher, Len. (1992). *The Un-Canadians.* Toronto: Lester Publishing. *See also* **Gouzenko case; Palmer Raids**.

McDonald Report Released in 1981, this was a report by Justice David McDonald of the findings of the Commission of Inquiry Concerning Certain Activities of the RCMP, which investigated allegations of wrongdoing by members of the RCMP. Specific allegations were that violations of the law were committed by the Security Service of the RCMP while gathering information in Quebec regarding the membership and financing of the separatist Parti Québécois led by René Lévesque. The major outcome of this inquiry was the establishment in 1984 of the Canadian Security Intelligence Service (CSIS), thus reducing the mandate of the RCMP. Reference: Canada. (1981). *Commission of Inquiry Concerning Certain Activities of the Royal Canadian Mounted Police.* Ottawa: Queen's Printer.

McGee, Thomas D'Arcy Thomas D'Arcy McGee (1825–1868) was elected to government in 1858 and became a supporter of Canadian federation. Of Irish birth, McGee spent many years defending Irish rights. He gradually alienated his Irish constituency, and when he was assassinated in Ottawa in 1868, it was believed he was the victim of a Fenian conspiracy. Ottawa tailor Patrick James Whelan was hanged for this assassination, although he proclaimed his innocence up until his public execution. Whelan, in fact, probably was not responsible for McGee's death, and his family continues to demand that the family name be cleared.

McGill School A version of the Chicago School of sociology, the McGill School approach began with the establishment of McGill University's first sociology department by Carl Dawson (1887–1964), who obtained his Ph.D. from the University of Chicago. Dawson initiated sociological studies at McGill, with a focus on urban studies, the location of crime in the urban community, and social disorganization. In 1927, Dawson was joined by Canadian sociologist Everett Hughes (1897–1983), who also trained at the University of Chicago. Hughes perhaps had a more lasting record in terms of his publications, which focused on Quebec Francophones. His book *French Canada in Transition* (University of Chicago Press, 1943) is still worth reading. *See also* **Chicago School**.

McIlwraith, Thomas (1899–1964) Appointed in 1925 to teach anthropology at the University of Toronto, Thomas McIlwraith guided expansion of the university's program until it became the first academic department of anthropology in a Canadian university. Reference: University of Toronto. (2001). *A brief history of anthropology at the University of Toronto.* Toronto: University of Toronto Press.

McJob A play on fast-food giant McDonald's name, a McJob is a low-paying, low-status job usually performed on a part-time basis and having no career potential. In the past, such jobs were usually the first work experiences of new entrants into the labour market, but economic changes are now thought to have made them a long-term destination for growing numbers of workers.

McLuhan, Marshall (1911–1980) Born in Edmonton and educated at the University of Manitoba (1934: M.A. in English) and Cambridge University (1942: Ph.D. in English), communications theorist and educator Marshall McLuhan arrived at the University of Toronto in 1946 as an English professor. He was a good friend of anthropologist Edmund S. Carpenter (1922–). Some of his early ideas are reflected in his articles: advertising (1952); comics (1953); Canadian political economist Harold Innis (1953); media as political forms (1954); our electronic culture (1958)). He burst onto the international scene in the 1960s with his writings on communications, which were to build the foundation for the new field of media studies. Through looking at the creation of the alphabet, the development of the telephone, book publication, and the field of television, McLuhan came to the realization that the medium used for communicating information is as important as the message itself—or perhaps more important. From this came one of his most popular phrases: "The medium is the message." He communicated the same idea when he said, "We shape our tools, and then our tools shape us." With the beginning of electronic communication, McLuhan suggested that this new medium would make the world a "global village." His early books include: *The Mechanical Bride*: *Folklore of Industrial Man* (New York: Vanguard Press, 1951); *The Guttenberg Galaxy*: *The Making of Typographic Man* (University of Toronto Press, 1962); *Understanding Media*: *The Extensions of Man* (New York: McGraw-Hill, 1964). Reference: Gordon, W.T. (1997*). Marshall McLuhan*: *Escape into Understanding*: *A Biography*. New York: Basic Books. *See also* **medium is the message**.

me In the concept of U.S. social psychologist George Herbert Mead (1863–1931), *me* refers to the aspect of personal identity or self that is aware of and has internalized the expectations of others. The *me* is guided and shaped by the culture of an individual's society or group, which is internalized and acts to direct and control behaviour. In social interaction, each individual's behaviour is shaped by the interaction of that individual's socially shaped *me* and the more spontaneous and ego-focused *I*. *See also* **I**; **Mead, George Herbert**.

Mead, George Herbert (1863–1931) A founder of the symbolic interactionist approach in sociology and social psychology, George Herbert Mead is best known for his view of personal identity, or self, which he sees as emerging from a dialogue between a unique, ego-driven *I* and a socialized *me* controlled by normative regulation and conscience, similar to Freud's "superego." This model of the self provides an understanding of how individuals can be both socialized for conformity yet preserve personal uniqueness, since their actions and thoughts will be an outcome of this interaction between these two aspects, or phases, of the self. *See also* **I**; **me**.

Mead, Margaret (1901–1978) U.S. anthropologist, author, lecturer, and one of the most influential female thinkers in the social sciences, Margaret Mead did not leave a strong influence on academic anthropology, but she had a great capacity for relating anthropological work to contemporary issues and thus garnered much public attention. Mead was a student of German cultural anthropologist Franz Boas (1858–1942) and adopted the somewhat new idea that nurture was more important than nature in shaping personality and behaviour. With this in mind, Mead set off to do fieldwork in Samoa (the first American woman to do fieldwork outside the continent) to test a simple-sounding hypothesis: If the adolescent behaviour of girls and boys was shaped by nature, then it should be cross-culturally consistent. If however, it is shaped by culture and socialization, then differences would be observed. Her popular book on the subject, *Coming of Age in Samoa* (New York: William Morrow and Company, 1930), claimed very clearly that differences were found and that they were the result of conditioning. It now seems clear that Mead allowed herself to be influenced by her own academic bias and saw what she wanted to see. Derek Freeman reexamined her fieldwork and undertook new research that demonstrated her findings were wrong. This accusation stirred much debate about the ethics of fieldwork and the bias found in much anthropological work, but Mead's reputation remained more or less intact. Reference: Howard, Jane. (1984). *Margaret Mead*: *A Life*. New York: Simon and Schuster.

mean A measure of central tendency for data at the interval or ratio level of measurement, a mean is commonly called an *average*, and is determined by summing the values or scores in a distribution and dividing by the number of values or scores. *See also* **median**; **mode**.

means test A policy for the provision of social assistance or services, a means test determines access by considering whether applicants have the means to provide the service from their own resources. Access to the Legal Aid program in most provinces, for example, is means-tested; legal aid is provided without charge to those unable to pay, while others pay part or all of the cost of the service. A policy of universality is opposed to this; such a program would give all citizens the right to assistance or service without charge. In the past, for example, the "baby bonus" was offered to all mothers of children. Similarly, health care is now offered to all citizens without charge, regardless of income level. There is a growing tendency toward means tests, however. Old age income support is now "clawed back" from seniors with incomes over a certain amount, for example, and in the future will be given only to those with income below a set amount. *See also* **universality**.

mechanical solidarity A term used by French sociologist Émile Durkheim (1858–1917), *mechanical solidarity* refers to a state of community bonding or interdependency that rests on a similarity of beliefs and values, shared activities, and ties of kinship and cooperation. *See also* **ideal type; organic solidarity**.

media Media are the tools and venues of communication via which culture products are assembled, processed, disseminated, and consumed (e.g., printed matter, television, film, radio, theatre, the Internet). Canada has a rich tradition of media studies, beginning with the work of Canadian political economist Harold Innis (1894–1952), Canadian philosopher George Grant (1918–1988), and communications theorist and educator Marshall McLuhan (1911–1980). The singular form of *media* is *medium*.

median The median is the middle of a distribution. When a set of values or scores are arranged in ascending order, it is the value that divides the sequence in half; half of the values or scores are greater than the median and half are less than the median. A median is frequently superior to a mean as a measure of central tendency when there are some scores or values that are significantly higher than all others in the distribution. The median gives these high scores the same emphasis as all other scores, while a mean gives them much greater weight or emphasis. *See also* **mean; mode**.

medical anthropology A form of applied anthropology, medical anthropology focuses on the area of health and illness and health care. Primary questions revolve around: How does culture affect health? How do people conceptualize health and illness? How does social structure shape health and health care outcomes? Reference: Brown, P. (Ed.). (1998). *Understanding and applying medical anthropology.* Mountain View, CA: Mayfield.

medicalization The process of turning what were previously thought to be crimes or sinful behaviour into medical problems is referred to as *medicalization*. Reference: Conrad, Peter. (1975). The Discovery of

Hyperkinesis: Notes on the Medicalization of Deviant Behaviour. *Social Problems, 23*, 12–21.

medical model A model of mental illness or other forms of deviance, a medical model assumes that mental illness is a symptom of some underlying disturbance that can be identified and treated. There is also an assumption that the underlying disturbance is objective, so this model is associated with positivism.

medieval period Also known as the *Middle Ages*, this term was developed in the 18th and 19th centuries to refer to the period of European history between the decline and fall of the Roman Empire and the Renaissance: approximately A.D. 500 to A.D. 1500.

medium is the message "The medium is the message" was the central idea of communications theorist Marshall McLuhan (1911–1980), who demonstrated that each medium (print, broadcast, speech) is connected with a different pattern or arrangement among the senses and thus results in a different awareness or perception. Although the literal message of a radio report of a disaster and the television coverage of the same event may be identical, the event will be perceived differently and take on different meaning because the two media arrange the senses differently. In this sense, the medium (the singular form of the word *media*) is the message; this message is often more important than the literal message. *See also* **McLuhan, Marshall**.

Meech Lake Accord An agreement drafted by the prime minister of Canada and the 10 provincial premiers, signed June 3, 1987, the *Meech Lake Accord* proposed amendments to the *Constitution* of Canada to provide for: explicit recognition of Quebec as a "distinct society"; increased provincial power over immigration; limitation of federal government spending power; recognition of Quebec's right to veto further constitutional change; and provincial participation in the appointments of Supreme Court of Canada judges. The Accord required assent from Parliament and all 10 provincial legislatures, but did not receive final ratification in either Newfoundland or Manitoba before the June 23, 1990, deadline. Principal components of the Accord were later included in the *Charlottetown Accord* (August 28, 1992), a further attempt to amend the *Constitution* of Canada, which was defeated in a national referendum. Reference: Cairns, Alan. (1991). *Disruptions: Constitutional Struggles from the Charter to Meech Lake.* Toronto:

McClelland and Stewart. *See also* **Charlottetown Accord**.

melting pot Canada is often described as a *mosaic* and the United States as a *melting pot*. These terms must be used with caution, as both nations are equally diverse. However, they differ in terms of policy and expectations: In the United States, it is the official policy and the expectation that ethnic minorities will integrate into the society and adopt the dominant culture. This is the melting pot aspect. In Canada, by contrast, there are policies and expectations that ethnic minorities may choose to retain their culture and distinctiveness.

member A central term in ethnomethodological theory, *member* replaces terms such as *status position* or *role* in structural theories. From a structural perspective, an individual actor is examined according to structural characteristics (sex, age, ethnicity, class) and is assumed to behave in accordance with these structural characteristics. The subjectivity of the actor is insignificant. Ethnomethodology, on the other hand, attempts to highlight the subjectivity of the individual actor and thus needs to identify the person in a way that acknowledges that person's knowledge, competence, engagement, commitment, or ability to make sense. The term *member* accomplishes this. Ethnomethodology also refers to membership categories (e.g., teacher, mother, employee) and identifies membership categorization devices and rules of application (e.g., the economy rule and the consistency rule) as a form of ethnomethodological analysis.

memory, recovered It is believed by some that memory has two important characteristics: First, memory records events in an accurate fashion, and second, memories can be repressed and then regained at a much later date and recovered in an accurate state. These ideas were first widely distributed in a 1988 book by Ellen Bass and Laura Davis entitled *The Courage To Heal: A Guide for Women Survivors of Child Sexual Abuse* (New York: HarperCollins [3rd ed., 1994]), which suggested that a person's memory of an earlier victimization may be completely blocked or lost, only to be recovered many years later, often through a process of therapy. This matter raises many questions about the nature of memory itself, and some suggest that memory is not just a form of "photographic record," but is also a social construction. If this is the case, then it may be possible to have "false memories." Recovered

memories have been important in sexual abuse cases. Reference: Johnston, Moira. (1997). *Spectral Evidence: The Ramona Case: Incest, Memory and Truth on Trial in Napa Valley*. Boulder, CO: Westview Press. *See also* **Ramona case**.

mens rea In the context of criminal law, the connotation of this term is *a guilty state of mind*, indicating a blameworthy act committed with criminal intent or an act of gross negligence or recklessness. Canadian courts have traditionally favoured an objective definition of *mens rea* using the test of what a reasonable person would have thought and done in the situation. Recently, a more subjective view has been adopted.

mercantilism Mercantilism is an economic theory that preceded the modern concept of a market economy regulated by the forces of supply and demand. Mercantilist ideas were quite varied, but a common theme was the importance to any nation of maintaining a favourable balance of international trade, ideally leading to net inflows of precious metals. To attain this end, it was appropriate for the state to intervene in the marketplace by vigorous economic regulation backed by state authority. Among classic mercantilist policies were laws requiring colonial territories to trade only with the imperial power, imposition of monopolies in merchant shipping and trading rights, and the establishment of physical quotas to manage and regulate trade. In Canada's early history, trading monopolies of both French and English origin—like the famous Hudson's Bay Company—were an expression of mercantilist policies, and they played a central role in the exploration and economic development of Canada.

meritocracy Meaning rule by those chosen on the principle of merit, meritocracy is consistent with liberal theory and assumes equality of opportunity and occupational advancement based on achievement rather than ascription. The notion of the "spontaneous division of labour" advanced by French sociologist Émile Durkheim (1858–1917), and the 1945 argument of U.S. demographer and sociologist Kingsley Davis (1908–1997) and U.S. sociologist Wilbert Moore (1914–1987) on the function of inequality both depend on the belief that, in a liberal society, people will be rewarded on the basis of talent or merit and that the more talented and thus meritorious will come to occupy the more important positions in society. *See also* **autocracy; democracy; plutocracy**.

Merton, Robert (1910–2003) American sociologist Robert Merton was instrumental in introducing to North America the writings of French sociologist Émile Durkheim (1858–1917). Merton, writing during the Depression and an age of scarcity, developed the idea of "anomie" as an explanation for crime. He also introduced the concepts of the self-fulfilling prophecy and reference group to sociology. Reference: Merton, Robert. (1938). Social Structure and Anomie. *American Sociological Review*, 3, 672–682.

messianic In sociology, *messianic* refers to a movement or belief system that believes a messiah will arrive in the world to relieve messianists of their community troubles.

meta-analysis So much research has been done on specific topics (e.g., the effectiveness of corrections, the effects of divorce on children) that it is possible to do analyses of a collection of research results—this is meta-analysis. One of the more well-known examples of meta-analysis is that done by U.S. criminologist Robert Martinson, who died in 1980, in which he concluded that "nothing works." Martinson did no original research on what works or doesn't work, but reanalyzed all of the available research on the topic.

metanarrative A story, narrative, or theory that claims to be above the ordinary or local accounts of social life is called a *metanarrative*. Postmodernists claim that the majority of the writings of Marx, Durkheim, and Weber are offered as metanarratives, presented as capturing universal properties of social life and thus superior to local or more grounded stories. Postmodernist social theorists argue for a return to the local, the rejection of grand theory and a privileged position for science and its narratives, and an acknowledgment of the inherently political nature of all narratives.

methadone A synthesized narcotic used in the control of heroin addiction, methadone is believed to be less addictive than heroin.

methadrine A powerful amphetamine that stimulates activity in the central nervous system, methadrine was first used by truckers and others required to stay awake for long hours. The drug has now become much more powerful and its use is widespread. In its crystal form (often called *ice*), it is smoked and gives an immediate rush; its use can lead to paranoia, bizarre and aggressive behaviour, and sexual disinhibition. Methadrine is also known as *krank, tweak, speed*. Many Canadian communities are facing an epidemic of its use among young people.

method The tool or instrument one uses to measure social or behavioral matters is defined as a *method*. For example, how can one measure anomie? Anxiety? Political participation? Generally, methods can be divided into two groups: quantitative measures and qualitative measures. In all social sciences, the creativity in research is choosing the best method for a particular topic. German-born Margrit Eichler (1942–), who practises sociology in Canada, has drawn attention to the fact that many of the methods used in the past tended to embed a male perspective, and she has done much to orient the social sciences to methods more amenable to getting at aspects of women's lives.

methodological holism An orientation in research and analysis, the aim of methodological holism is to understand the phenomenon under investigation in its totality as unique and apart from its component parts, rather than to fragment it into known or familiar components. The key idea, in essence, is that the whole differs from the sum of the parts not only in quantity, but also in quality.

methodological individualism The belief that all sociological explanations can be reduced to characteristics of individuals who make up the society, methodological individualism is also known as *psychologism*: explaining social phenomena in terms of the psychological dispositions of members of society. This is a rejection of macrostructuralists working in the tradition of French sociologist Émile Durkheim (1858–1917) or Karl Marx (1818–1883), German-born social philosopher, political economist, and sociologist, who assumed that the characteristics of individuals need not be considered. They argued that social facts (society) had an existence of their own and that it was these in which sociologists were interested. *See also* **psychological reductionism**.

methodology The term *methodology* has two distinct meanings. First, it refers to the study or critique of methods used in a particular field. There are many philosophical issues about the use of particular methods, about positivism, and even about measurement itself. Second, it refers to the body of methods used in a particular field of study. For example, we can talk about the methodology of cognitive psychology.

Métis The term *Métis* refers to people who have a mixed biological and cultural ancestry, particularly those of French and Indian or British/Scottish and Indian heritage. Originally, the term referred to the French Indian people who settled in the Red River area of Manitoba, a group who saw themselves as having a distinct cultural and political position in society, and their history is important in understanding Canada. This group is now represented by the Métis National Council. The Native Council of Canada also acknowledges other people of mixed ancestry as being Métis. *See also* **Red River Rebellion**.

metropolis–hinterland theory A theory of social and economic development, the metropolis–hinterland theory examines how economically advanced societies, through trade and colonialism, distort and retard the economic development of less developed societies and regions. A metropolis is identified as the centre of political and economic power, as having a more advanced labour market, more skilled and educated workers, an abundance of value-added production, a higher standard of living, etc. A hinterland would be less able to withstand the political and economic interference of the metropolis, and would have an abundance of resource-extraction industries, fewer skilled and educated workers, a lower standard of living, and in many ways would emulate the culture of the metropolis. For more than a century, Ontario, or even more narrowly the Toronto region, was seen as the metropolis to a vast Canadian hinterland, and the United States has been seen as the metropolis for a Canadian hinterland. Reference: Davis, Arthur K. (1971). Canadian Society as Hinterland versus Metropolis. In R. Ossenberg (Ed.), *Canadian Society: Pluralism Change and Conflict*. Scarborough: Prentice Hall. *See also* **dependent development; geopolitics; world systems theory**.

microperspective A form of analysis, a microperspective focuses on the individual and his or her subjectivity, rather than focusing on the structures of society thought to be external and constraining on the individual. This perspective is found in symbolic interactionism, ethnomethodology, labelling theory, and interpretive theory.

middle class Three different approaches to defining *middle class* are presented here, although others do exist. (1) In German-born social philosopher, polit-ical economist, and sociologist Karl Marx's (1818–1883) analysis of class, the middle class is the "petite bourgeoisie," who are small-scale independent businessmen or craftsmen or who have special skills that provide an income outside the wage system of employed labour. Marx assumed that this class would diminish in number as capitalist enterprises developed, consolidated into larger units, and eliminated small-scale competition. (2) The term can also be used statistically to define a group of individuals who occupy an intermediate position in a society's income strata: for example, those who earn between 66% and 133% of a society's average family incomes. (3) The two previous definitions are attempts to define the "middle class" objectively, by some standard of measurement, but a more subjective view is possible: The middle class comprises those individuals who orient themselves to the values and expectations that they consider normative for average members of their society. This approach is useful for understanding why most Canadians, irrespective of occupation, wealth, or income, identify themselves as middle class.

middle-class measuring rod This phrase suggests that children and young people from the lower class often find themselves in situations in which they are measured against middle-class standards. Schools, for example, rest on the middle-class values of reading and writing, and the teachers are primarily middle class. Lower-class children often realize they are never going to "measure up" and so anticipate failure, become frustrated, or drop out of school. They may also begin to move toward other marginal students in the school and become engaged in deviant or criminal activity. Reference: Cohen, Albert. (1955). *Delinquent Boys*. New York: Free Press.

Middle Paleolithic Period The middle part of the Old Stone Age, the Middle Paleolithic Period is associated with the emergence of archaic *Homo sapiens*.

millennium Literally, a millennium is a period of 1,000 years, or a one-thousandth anniversary. In Christian tradition, the Millennium refers to the 1,000 years of peace that will accompany the second coming of Christ. Christ's coming is portended by growing strife and conflict (an apocalyptic vision); the term *millenarianism* refers to this belief. These ideas have come together to suggest that the end of those thousand years will be associated with social breakdown, despair, and turmoil, and will be followed by new energy and confidence. The nonreligious beliefs of millenarianism have been associated with the end of 100-year periods (e.g., the end of the 20th century).

Millennium Declaration In September of 2000, the United Nations General Assembly adopted the *Millennium Declaration*, committing all nations to the following general goals by 2015: to reduce extreme poverty by one-half, as well as to provide access to safe drinking water; to achieve universal primary education; to empower women and promote equality between women and men; to cut under-five child mortality by two-thirds; to reduce maternal mortality by three-quarters; to reverse the spread of diseases, especially HIV/AIDS and malaria; to ensure environmental sustainability; and to create a global partnership for development, with targets for aid, trade, and debt relief. Details of these goals and updates on the steps being taken to meet them can be found on the UN website at www.un.org/millenniumgoals.

Mill, John Stuart (1806-1873) English classical economist John Stuart Mill was the most important figure in the development of the doctrine of liberalism. Mill built on the ideas of Scottish classical economist and philosopher Adam Smith (1723–1790) and the utilitarian theory of English philosopher Jeremy Bentham (1748–1832) and his father, James Mill (1773–1836), who was a classical Ricardian economist. John Stuart Mill argued that liberty and democracy were the key to human progress. Democracy provided people with political involvement and purpose, and liberty encouraged human progress through an open and inquiring quest for knowledge. Restraint of the individual was therefore constructive and justified only when necessary to protect the liberty of others. Although Mill was a supporter of *laissez-faire* economics, he encouraged cooperative forms of work organization, and at times seemed to favour collective ownership of land. Consistent with his liberal philosophy, Mill was a passionate opponent of slavery and an early and eloquent supporter of women's right to vote. Reference: Mill, J.S. (2002). *The Basic Writings of John Stuart Mill: On Liberty, the Subjection of Women, and Utilitarianism*. New York: Modern Library.

Mills, C. Wright (1916–1962) C. Wright Mills was an American sociologist who was critical of the pre-vailing paradigm of sociology of his day—functionalism. In his 1956 book, *The Power Elite* (Oxford Press), he draws attention to the linkages among power groups in America and uses the phrase the "military industrial complex." In more recent years, this phrase has been changed to discuss what many see as the "prison industrial complex," a powerful group of corporations with self-interest in maintaining and expanding prisons and privatizing the vast array of services required for prisons to function.

ministerial responsibility Associated with parliamentary systems of government, ministerial responsibility is the convention that a minister is answerable to Parliament for the conduct and actions of his or her ministry's personnel. Originally, the responsibility was quite strictly imposed on a minister, and resignation might be demanded even when the minister did not have, and could not reasonably have been expected to have, knowledge of improper or negligent acts or omissions by officials. In recent times, this idea has been abandoned, and it is rare for a minister to accept responsibility and resign.

Minneapolis Domestic Violence Experiment Conducted from early 1981 to mid-1982, the Minneapolis Domestic Violence Experiment was the first scientific study to investigate the effect of police responses on domestic violence. Police officers were randomly assigned one of three ways to deal with an incident: arrest the suspect, counsel the couple, or remove one member from the home. The results showed that those offenders who were arrested showed a marked reduction in recidivism. Reference: Sherman, Lawrence, & Berk, Richard. (April 1984). Minneapolis Domestic Violence Experiment, *Police Foundation Reports, 1*. Washington, DC: Police Foundation.

minority group A group distinguished by being on the margins of power, status, or the allocation of resources within the society is considered to be a minority group. *Visible minority* refers to those racial or ethnic groups in a society that are marginal from the power and economic structure of society, not to those that are few in number. In South Africa, Blacks are the statistical majority, but for countless decades they constituted a social minority. Women can also be identified as a social minority group.

misandry The hatred of or hostility toward men is called *misandry*.

miscegenation At various times and places (including the American south and South Africa under apartheid), there have been laws prohibiting sexual intercourse, cohabitation, and marriage by racially mixed couples, all of which are known as *miscegenation*. The Supreme Court of the United States struck down miscegenation laws in 1967.

misogyny Misogyny is the hatred of or hostility toward women.

missing women case Over the course of about 10 years, approximately 60 women sex-trade workers disappeared from the streets of Vancouver. It appeared to take a long time for the police to realize that something out of the ordinary was going on, but finally a major investigation was undertaken. Eventually, clues led to a farm in a nearby suburb where prostitutes and drug addicts had been lured with the promise of alcohol and drugs. As of May 2005, one of the owners of the farm (Robert Pickton) had been charged with the deaths of 27 of the missing women as a result of the largest forensic investigation ever undertaken in Canada.

mitochondrial DNA Mitochondria are found in every cell but have useful characteristics. They have their own DNA that can be mapped and they do not recombine, meaning that they are not affected by reproduction; mothers pass this particular DNA code to their offspring. These characteristics allow researchers to determine for a population of humans (rather than for specific individuals) if they have evidence of a specific ancestry. This is useful in settling the debate between the out-of-Africa hypothesis and the multiregional hypothesis. The out-of-Africa hypothesis claims that there was one evolution of humans around 100,000 to 200,000 years ago, so all humans should be able to trace their ancestry back to an original "Eve," so to speak. The multiregional hypothesis argues that while humans emerged from Africa, they evolved from archaic forms of humans (*Homo erectus* or Neandertal) concurrently in different regions. At the moment, the multiregional hypothesis is a minority opinion. This research also makes it possible to begin to understand where the first inhabitants of North America came from. Do they share mitochondria DNA with populations in Siberia, Asia, or Europe? The research on this is still very unsettled, but it is suggesting that the settlement of North America was more complex than once thought.

mobility, social The movement of an individual or group from one class or social status to another is defined as social mobility. Usually, the point of reference is an individual's class or status of social origin, and social mobility occurs when later class or status positions differ from those of origin. Social mobility would be high where individuals have equal opportunity to achieve new statuses and low where there are inequalities of opportunity and processes of status ascription. *See also* **demand mobility; open class ideology.**

mode The most frequently occurring number in a set of scores or values, the mode is a measure of central tendency useful for data at any level of measurement. In a series of numbers, there is frequently more than one mode. Other measures of central tendency are the mean and the median. *See also* **mean; median.**

modelling A form of learning that occurs as a result of watching and imitating others, modelling by parents of the type of behaviour they want their children to develop is central to child development and the process of socialization. Models are also used in research, in which case a model is defined as a schematic description of a system, theory, or phenomenon that accounts for its properties and may be used for further study of its characteristics. *See also* **socialization.**

mode of production Defined as the dominant form of social and technical organization of economic production in a society, historically, a variety of modes of production can be distinguished, based on both technology and the structure of social relationships. Historical modes of production include hunter–gatherer, with very simple technology and common ownership; ancient, with more advanced technology and slavery; feudal, with simple technology and landowning lords and bonded serfs; and capitalist, with sophisticated technology, private ownership of capital, and a wage system. *See also* **state capitalism.**

modernization theory A theory of social and economic development, modernization theory follows functionalist or consensus assumptions that societies need to have harmony among their component parts. This type of assumption leads to the belief that modern (capitalist) economies demand special characteristics in their culture and the structure of social relationships. For example, family systems are assumed to change toward a narrow conjugal form and away from an extended structure, in order to accommodate the individualism and occupational flexibility that is demanded by a modern complex economy undergoing continual transformation.

moiety From the French word meaning *half*, moiety refers to groups created by dividing a society in halves on the basis of descent. Each moiety consists of clans and the large groups are exogamous.

monarchy, constitutional In a constitutional monarchy system of government, the head of state is an individual who usually has acquired the position by hereditary descent. In earlier times in history, monarchs were often absolute in their effective power and were unconstrained by either legal or political limitations. Britain's system of monarchy, from which Canada's is derived, has been subjected to formal constitutional limitation since the *Magna Carta* issued in 1215 by King John of England. The *Magna Carta* was demanded from the king by England's landowning aristocracy, who wanted definite and permanent legal limitations on royal power. Over the centuries, England's monarchical system became gradually transformed into the modern constitutional structure, where the monarch possesses only formal legal power that must, by political convention, be exercised only with the advice and agreement of the monarch's ministers. These ministers are chosen by a prime minister who is appointed by the monarch but who, by political convention, must be the party leader whose party either commands majority support in the elected House of Commons or is likely to be able to form a government supported by other parties. The convention that the monarch will act only with the advice and consent of the prime minister and the Cabinet makes monarchy compatible with a system of parliamentary democracy. Canada's monarchy is similarly structured. The governor general represents the queen (or king) in Canada and possesses the formal legal powers of the monarch but, by political convention, exercises them subject to the advice of the prime minister and other federal ministers. Since 1926, the autonomy of Canada from Britain has been recognized by the requirement that the governor general of Canada be appointed by the monarch only on the advice of the prime minister of Canada. The system of monarchy contrasts with republics, where the head of state is an individual either directly elected by the people (e.g., the

United States, France, Mexico) or appointed by an elected state parliament (e.g., Germany, Israel).

monetarism An economic theory advocating that governments use interest rates and control of the supply of money for the purpose of economic regulation, monetarism is a contrast to Keynesian economics, which advocates taxation and budgetary (fiscal) policy. Use of monetary instruments for economic regulation is said to provide a lever to influence macroeconomic cycles in the economy while avoiding bureaucratic regulation or distortions of market forces. Monetarism has become the dominant framework of theory in both academic economics and public policy. It is closely associated with neoconservatism, a version of liberalism that stresses free markets and individualism rather than the "welfare state" vision that once was dominant in most Western societies. There is controversy over the role of monetarist policies in the current deficit problems of most of the world's largest economies. *See also* **fiscal crisis**; **Keynesian economics**.

monetary policy The use of monetary levers—interest rates, money supply, foreign exchange rate—by governments to achieve some control over the performance of the economy comprises monetary policy. *See also* **fiscal policy**.

monopoly A situation in which one company has gained control of the market for a particular good or service is called a *monopoly*. Monopolies are in direct conflict with the values of liberalism, which emphasize competition among numerous producers.

monozygotic twins Commonly known as *identical twins*, monozygotic twins are from a single egg that has divided after fertilization to create two embryos; consequently, they share exactly the same genetic material and are of the same sex. Monozygotic twins who have been separated in earliest infancy and raised apart have provided a classic research situation for social scientists because their genetic identity, yet different social experience, makes it possible to disentangle the separate effects of heredity and social environment. Reference: Bock, G.R., & Gode, J.A. (1996). *Genetics of Criminal and Antisocial Behaviour*. Chichester: John Wiley & Sons. *See also* **dizygotic twins**.

Monte Verde A paleoanthropological site in southern Chile, Monte Verde has provided evidence that humans occupied the area as long as 12,500 years ago. This has been a controversial site, since these peoples would have predated the Clovis culture, considered the first peoples of North America, which represents a challenge to the Bering Strait theory. Reference: Dillehay, T.D. (2001). *The settlement of the Americas*. New York: Basic Books.

Montreal Forum riot On March 17, 1955, riots erupted in Montreal as hockey fans both inside and outside the Montreal Forum showed their displeasure with National Hockey League president Clarence Campbell. Four days before, Campbell had suspended Montreal Canadiens star Rocket Richard for the rest of the season for fighting. Richard was the best hockey player of his generation—and many others. He was a hero for Montreal fans, and at the first game back at home, their outrage led to street rioting outside the Forum, which was then carried inside, leading to an attack on Campbell, who was watching Montreal play Detroit. (The game was forfeited to Detroit, who was leading 4–1 when the game was abandoned.) The Montreal hockey team was perhaps the most successful team in the league, and during the 1950s and 1960s, evoked the nationalist emotions of the Québécois. When the Parti Québécois was created and won the 1976 election, new political avenues for national expression emerged and hockey lost its national symbolism. Also, in 1967, when the league was expanded and the number of games against its major rival, the Toronto Maple Leafs, was reduced, the team lost much of its drive and became more ordinary.

Montreal massacre On December 6, 1989, Marc Lepine entered the École Polytechnique in Montreal and killed 14 women students before taking his own life. This event has been a rallying point for women's groups, who see the killings as reflective of the generalized devaluation of, and violence against, women in society. December 6 has become a National Day of Remembrance and Action on Violence Against Women. Reference: Rathjen, H., & Monpetit, C. (1999). *December 6: From the Montreal Massacre to Gun Control*. Toronto: McClelland and Stewart.

Montreal School In opposition to the ideas of the Laval School, the social sciences and history faculties at the Université de Montréal argued that the British Conquest of Canada and the resulting *Quebec Act, 1774,* led to the economic and social subordination of Quebec within Canada. They claimed that Quebec was used as a storehouse of resources and as a source of exploitable labour, while most eco-nomic development, senior corporate positions, and political and economic power was concentrated in the rest of Canada and among a narrow, chiefly Anglophone, elite in Montreal.

moral development theory The term *moral development theory* refers generally to theories of individual psychology that investigate how moral reasoning emerges and develops as the individual matures. French psychologist Jean Piaget (1896–1980) is acknowledged as the founder of this approach to human development. American psychologist Lawrence Kohlberg (1927–1987) pioneered an empirical approach to questions of moral development. Reference: Duska, Ronald. (1975). *Moral Development: A Guide to Piaget and Kohlberg*. New York: Paulist Press.

moral economy In a tribal society, exchanges in an economy are driven by moral obligations created by kinship relations, gift-giving, and rituals, rather than by economic exchanges motivated by self-interest, greed, or profit. A hunter or food gatherer might have been obliged to give much of the food to a network of relations, thus accounting for the distribution of food within the community. It was the final collapse of economic exchange as moral obligation that German-born social philosopher, political economist, and sociologist Karl Marx (1818–1883) bemoaned when he described the "cash nexus" that had become the central medium and motivator of exchange in a capitalist society. *See also* **potlatch**.

moral entrepreneur Moral entrepreneurs, whether individuals or groups, are in the business of persuading society to make policy from particular moral viewpoints. In symbolic interactionism (or labelling theory), social policy is not seen as the implementation of a shared consensus about what is best. Rather, the society is viewed as consisting of a plurality of understandings of what is best. In order for social policy to arise, some individual or group has to initiate a social movement tasked with articulating a definition of a social problem so that a desired social policy is consistent with this definition of the problem. Examples of moral entrepreneurs include MADD (Mothers Against Drunk Driving), the pro-life movement, the gun lobby, antipornography groups, the anti-tobacco lobby, and Emily Murphy (a Canadian who became the first woman magistrate in the entire British Empire and was one of the "Famous Five" who gained official recognition of women as "persons"). Reference: Becker, H. (1963). *Outsiders: Studies in the Sociology of Deviance*. New York: Free Press.

moral panic Coined by British sociologist Stanley Cohen in 1972, the term *moral panic* suggests an overreaction to forms of deviance or wrongdoing believed to be threats to the moral order. Moral panics are usually fanned by the media and led by community leaders or groups intent on changing laws or practices. Sociologists are less interested in the validity of the claims made during moral panics than they are in the dynamics of social change and the organizational strategies of moral entrepreneurs. Moral panics gather converts because they touch on people's fears and also because they use specific events or problems as symbols of what many feel to represent "all that is wrong with the nation." The moral panic about youth violence, for example, presents this violence as a symbol of all that is wrong with Canada—it is claimed that the *Canadian Charter of Rights and Freedoms* has undermined authority, the family has fallen apart, immigration has brought many disreputable groups into the country, governments and their agents have become self-serving and out of touch with the reality of social life, and economic transformation has marginalized and demoralized young people. Reference: Cohen, Stanley. (2002). *Folk Devils and Moral Panics* (3rd ed.). London: Routledge.

moral rhetoric In the study of crime, moral rhetoric is the set of claims and assertions that deviants make to normalize and rationalize deviant behaviour. Individuals, businesses, and public institutions may be blamed for unfairness, exploitation, or some moral or biological failing, thus justifying them as targets of crime. The moral rhetoric of a group is an important component of socialization into a deviant identity.

Morgentaler, Henry Born in Lodz, Poland, in 1923, Henry Morgentaler is Jewish but survived the wartime Nazi death camps and in 1950 came to Canada, where he trained as a physician. He began general practice in Montreal in 1955. He soon became interested in family planning and by 1967 appeared before a House of Commons committee to urge repeal of the criminal law against abortion. In 1973, he publicly announced that therapeutic abortion was safe and socially necessary, and that he had successfully carried out 5,000 operations. These operations were illegal, since he had not fol-lowed the procedures for approval set out in an abortion law amendment in 1969. He was soon prosecuted, but in November 1973 was found "not guilty" by a Quebec jury, despite conclusive evidence that he had broken the law. Then, in a highly controversial decision in February 1974, the Quebec Court of Appeal set aside the jury verdict and imposed its own verdict of "guilty," sentencing Morgentaler to 18 months in prison. The Supreme Court upheld the decision. In 1975, while still in jail, Morgentaler was prosecuted again for additional offences and again found "not guilty" by a Quebec jury. Parliament then passed an amendment to the *Criminal Code*, proposed by the minister of Justice, which eliminated the power of appellate courts to set aside acquittals and order imprisonment. The minister of Justice also ordered a new trial for Morgentaler on the original charges. In September 1976, the new trial resulted in another acquittal by a Quebec jury. In November 1976, the newly elected Parti Québécois government of René Lévesque announced that there would no longer be prosecutions of doctors who perform abortions in Quebec. Having made abortion more freely available in Quebec, Morgentaler turned his attention to Ontario and opened a clinic there. He was soon charged and prosecuted for performance of illegal abortions, and in November 1984 was tried and acquitted by an Ontario jury. The Ontario government appealed this acquittal to the Supreme Court, but, with the *Canadian Charter of Rights and Freedoms* by then in place, the Supreme Court in 1988 ruled on appeal that the abortion law be struck down as offending Section 7 of the *Charter*. "Everyone has the right to life, liberty and security of the person and the right not to be deprived thereof except in accordance with the principles of fundamental justice." Since then, abortion has been legal in Canada. Reference: Dunphy, Catherine. (1996). *Morgentaler: A Difficult Hero*. Toronto: Random House of Canada.

Morin, Guy Paul Convicted in 1992 of the murder of nine-year-old Christine Jessop, Guy Paul Morin was acquitted in 1995, after many bizarre twists and turns, by the Ontario Court of Appeal on the basis of DNA evidence. Morin joined a growing list of the wrongfully convicted, and his acquittal led to a lengthy investigation of the justice system. Reference: Makin, K. (1993). *Redrum the Innocent*. Toronto: Penguin. *See also* **wrongful conviction**.

morphemes In linguistics, the smallest units of sound that carry meaning are morphemes. *See also* **phonemes**.

Mount Cashel Orphanage abuse The abuse of children has a long history, much of it marked by silence. This silence was broken in Canada when victims of abuse at the Mount Cashel Orphanage in Newfoundland captured public attention. Between 1989 and 1992, eight Christian Brothers who had worked at the orphanage were convicted on charges involving assault and abuse. This case opened the floodgates of grievance from former residents of residential schools, training schools, and young participants in a variety of youth programs. Reference: Harris, Michael. (1990). *Unholy Orders: Tragedy at Mount Cashel.* Toronto: Penguin.

Mousterian tool tradition A result of the tool-making method of the Neandertals, Mousterian tools were flake tools that were lighter and smaller than those of previous traditions.

multiculturalism This term has two distinct but related meanings: On the one hand, *multiculturalism* refers to a condition of cultural pluralism and the attitudes of tolerance that make this possible. On the other hand, it refers to a set of federal government policies designed to "assist all Canadian cultural groups...to grow and contribute to Canada," as well as to assist members of all cultural groups "to overcome cultural barriers to full participation in Canadian society." While there is little debate about the first of these meanings, there is great debate about the implications of the second. Reference: Kymlicka, Will. (1995). *Multicultural Citizenship.* New York: Oxford University Press. *See also* **melting pot**.

multinational corporation A company that has operations in more than one nation is called a *multinational corporation*. The development of these corporations has challenged the belief of liberal ideology that economic power can be counterbalanced by political power. As corporations have less dependence on a national market and can adopt practices that minimize the effect of national policies, they move outside the reach of any political system.

multiregional hypothesis *See* **out-of-Africa hypothesis**.

multivariate analysis A form of quantitative analysis, *multivariate analysis* examines three or more variables at the same time in order to understand the relationships among them. The simplest form of this analysis is one in which the researcher, interested in the relationship between an independent variable and a dependent variable (e.g., sex and political attitudes), introduces an extraneous variable (e.g., age) to ensure that a correlation between the two main variables is not spurious. Presented in tabular form, this analysis divides the age variable into its constituent values (e.g., young and old) and then subdivides each of these values into the values of female and male. Having done this, it is possible to determine whether there is a correlation, among young people, between the variables of sex and political attitudes. Other forms of multivariate analysis are examined in methodology texts under the heading of the elaboration model, and here one finds conditional variables, intervening variables, and extraneous variables. *See also* **variable**.

mundane reasoning *See* **common-sense reasoning**.

Munsinger affair In 1958, Pierre Sévigny, the minister of Defence in the fresh-faced Conservative federal government, began an affair with Gerda Munsinger, a German immigrant known to the RCMP as a security risk with communist affiliations. By December 1960, the RCMP uncovered rumours of the Defence minister's affair, and placed Munsinger's apartment under surveillance. Sévigny was seen to call—and stay overnight. The RCMP reported to Canada's Justice minister, David Fulton. He passed the news to the prime minister, John Diefenbaker, who called Sévigny to his office to confront him with the allegations. The minister confessed, but denied any breach of security. The prime minister insisted that the affair be stopped immediately, demanding that Munsinger be vigorously encouraged to return to Germany. He also decided to retain Sévigny in the Cabinet and to take no further action. The incident remained the secret of a very small circle. But in December 1964, it became obvious that the circle had widened when the new prime minister, Lester Pearson, whose government was under fire for scandals involving Liberal Cabinet ministers, wrote to Diefenbaker to express his concern about the handling of the Munsinger case by the previous Conservative government. Perceiving the letter as a threat to embarrass the Conservatives, Diefenbaker met Pearson to threaten him in turn with revelations of "his days as a communist." It was not until March 4, 1966, when Diefenbaker, speaking in the House of Commons, attacked the Liberal's handling of a security case involving a Vancouver postal clerk,

George Spencer, that the public began to find out about the affair. Spencer had been dismissed from the post office on suspicion of spying for the Soviet Union. Charges were not laid, but the government directed that he be deprived of his pension and placed under permanent RCMP surveillance. To add pathos to the story, Spencer was dying of cancer. Lester Pearson reviewed the case and upheld the actions taken, but Diefenbaker, incensed by the arbitrary denial of due legal process, implied that the treatment of Spencer was a way to look tough on communism and distract attention from allegations of communist affiliation that had been made about Prime Minister Lester Pearson himself. Responding in kind, Justice Minister Lucienne Cardin divulged to the House that there were badly handled "security cases" during Diefenbaker's government, particularly the "Monseignor [sic] case." The press seized on this hint of wrongdoing and, within days, the *Toronto Star* discovered the story and located Munsinger in Munich. She named not only Sévigny, but also George Hees, minister of Transport in Diefenbaker's government, as her intimates. A public inquiry was established to investigate. The inquiry reported there was no breach of security, but criticized Diefenbaker for retaining Sévigny in the Cabinet and censured the behaviour of David Fulton and George Hees. While the press and the public were riveted by this affair of sex, spying, and political blackmail, there was worry that the Liberal government had used its access to security information to damage its Conservative opponents. The handling of the affair seems more sordid than the affair itself.

murder Murder is the killing of a human being willfully, deliberately, and unlawfully.

Murdoch case In a very controversial decision by the Supreme Court of Canada (1975) in deciding the property entitlement of a farm wife on her divorce, Irene Murdoch claimed an equal share of the family property and produced evidence that she had contributed money toward the down payment on the farm, had carried out farm work and housework for more than 25 years, and had been actively involved in running and administering farm business. The Supreme Court decided that Mrs. Murdoch's work had been no more than typical for a farm wife and did not establish any special entitlement to a share in the farm itself. In so deciding, the court upheld traditional views of the property

rights of women—for a wife to own property, it must be bought in her name or she must make a direct contribution to its purchase. While the court agreed that Mrs. Murdoch was entitled to an equal share of the farmhouse and the land on which it was immediately situated, they ruled that this entitlement did not extend to the farmland and equipment. The resulting controversy, led by Canadian women's groups, resulted in an overhaul of statute law, first in Ontario and then in other provinces, to redefine "family assets"—property divisible between the partners—to include all property used by the partners to the marriage during the course of their relationship. Reference: *Murdoch v. Murdoch* [1975] 1 S.C.R. 423.

mutual conversion This phrase suggests that conversion to deviance (and perhaps to other lifestyles) is not a solitary activity but is achieved interactively. For example, someone might encourage you to do something deviant, and if you then participate in the suggested deviant activity, your involvement further reinforces the behaviour of that person

My Lai massacre A story of bureaucratic intrigue and mass murder dating from the Vietnam War, the My Lai massacre occurred on March 16, 1968, when an American fighting unit entered the village of My Lai and killed 400 unarmed women, children, and old men. Four soldiers were eventually brought to trial and one convicted. Reference: Bilton, M., & Sim, K. (1992). *Four Hours in My Lai*. New York: Penguin Books.

mystification Mystification is the process of masking or covering up central aspects of society or of social relationships. Conflict or critical theorists are interested in the ways in which forms of social domination based on sex, class, or colonialism are camouflaged so that these social structures, and the state that assists in their reproduction, are seen as legitimate. Mystification allows for domination that is not based on evident coercion or force, but is maintained by a wide variety of social institutions and cultural values. *See also* **hegemony; legitimation crisis**.

myth Often used incorrectly to refer to a claim considered to be untrue, more correctly, *myth* refers to a narrative account or story that contains the collective wisdom of a society and articulates beliefs concerning key aspects of individual identity or collective life. All societies, for example, have myths about the origin of human life, some have myths about their origin as a society, and others have myths about the shaping of national identity or the evolution of love. Social scientists are interested in the role that these myths play in society and what they might say about the nature of the human mind.

myth of mental illness Hungarian-born psychiatrist Thomas Szasz (1920–) coined this term in challenging the medical model of mental disorders. Szasz argued that mental disorders unlike physical diseases typically have no objective problems that can be identified: There are no broken bones or infections. If mental illness has no objective signs, then mental illness is just a label typically applied to behaviours that arise from what Szasz calls "ordinary problems of living." Reference: Szasz, Thomas. (1974). *The Myth of Mental Illness*. New York: Harper and Row.

N

NAC *See* **National Action Committee on the Status of Women**.

NAFTA *See* **Free Trade Agreement (Canada–U.S., 1994)**.

nation A word somewhat similar to *society* in that it includes all those persons who share common descent, language, and history and close association with each other, for Canadians, *nation* reflects a major debate about the nature of Canada. In English, the term *nation* implies a community of people who have political autonomy and who occupy a distinct territory. In French, in contrast, the term is closer in meaning to a community of people sharing common origins and ties of interrelationship. Thus, when French speakers refer to Quebec as a "nation," they tend to mean Quebec as an historic community of people, rather than necessarily implying that Quebec is, or ought to be, completely politically autonomous and detached from Canada. It is noteworthy that Quebec refers to its legislative house as the *National Assembly* (officially, *Assemblée national du Québec*), while other provinces use the term *legislature*. There are approximately 190 nation–states in the world, but there are 15,000 nations in the second sense of the word. *See also* **Treaty of Westphalia**.

National Action Committee on the Status of Women (NAC) Founded in 1972, the NAC is an umbrella organization of women's groups in Canada, dedicated to lobbying the federal government to adopt changes to enhance the position and life chances of Canadian women. The NAC replaced the National Ad Hoc Committee on the Status of Women, organized in 1971 to pressure for implementation of the recommendations of the Royal Commission on the Status of Women.

National Anti-Poverty Organization Founded in 1971, the National Anti-Poverty Organization is a non-government advocacy organization that conducts research and engages in advocacy on matters of concern to low-income Canadians.

National Assembly of Quebec (Assemblée national du Québec) The official name *Assemblée national du Québec* was adopted by Quebec's legislature in 1968 after the abolition of its legislative council, which had formed a second chamber alongside the legislative assembly. The new name was symbolic— while the rest of Canada's provinces had mere legislatures, Quebec now had an assembly expressing its status and dignity as a distinct culture and a founding nation of Canada.

national debt The total amount owed by governments to lenders who have bought bonds and Treasury bills sold by the government to cover past deficits and operating expenses is a national debt. A substantial portion of Canadian government debt is now held by investors outside the country. Criminologists are interested in the level of this debt, since some theories claim that as national debt rises, there is pressure to cut social spending, and this may result in an increase in spending on social control.

national deficit The national deficit is the difference between governments' revenues, from taxes and charges, and their expenditures on programs, infrastructure, and debt financing. Canada ran a deficit from the 1970s until approximately 1998, when the Liberal government of Jean Chrétien brought in a balanced budget. This long-term deficit left Canada with a substantial debt that is now being reduced from an emerging budgetary surplus. *See also* **national debt**.

National Deviancy Conference (NDC) Formed in Britain in 1968, the National Deviancy Conference was an academic group that reflected the changing mood of deviance theorists. Its members were critical of the positivism practised in criminology departments and were critical of the close relationship between criminology and the state and its apparatus of social control. The NDC tended to focus on symbolic interactionism rather than Marxist theory.

nationalism The concept of nationalism, like the concept of nation, has two quite distinct meanings. Common to both definitions is the idea that it is the nation that provides people with their primary form of belonging and that these nations should be self-governing. People of the world are thus located within nations and identify with these nation–states, and political activity is organized around these nation–states. Michael Ignatieff distinguishes two forms of nationalism. First, "civic nationalism" means that all citizens within a nation–state are treated as equal and share political values. Within this sense of nationalism, one would find pluralistic communities acting as one and treating citizens with equality. It is this sense of nationalism that many thought was emerging after the religious and ethnic struggles of the 19th and early 20th centuries. The second sense of nationalism revolves around the equation of "people" with the nation–state. In this formulation, the nation (or the people) exists prior to the state and in a sense creates the state. In these communities, then, the nation and sense of national identification flow from a common characteristic (usually ethnic heritage) and thus excludes others. This form of nationalism may be less tolerant of difference and can be found in the German nation–state, where citizenship continues to be defined in terms of ethnicity. The concern that nation–states and thus nationalism are increasingly being organized around ethnic (or other) characteristics is frequently described as the *tribalization* of the modern world. Tension between the two meanings of nationalism can be found in discussions around Quebec's right to self-determination: Is civic nationalism at work or is it "people" nationalism? Reference: Ignatieff, Michael. (1993). *Blood and Belonging: Journeys into the New Nationalism.* Toronto: Viking. *See also* **identity politics; postmodernism; tribalism**.

nationalization The collective or public ownership or management of economic resources, nationalization is in contrast to privatization. Canada has long relied on public (or state) ownership of economic resources. In 1962, the Liberal government of Jean Lesage nationalized the hydroelectric industry in Quebec; this was an important component of the rapid economic growth and emerging sense of

self-confidence that has come to be referred to as the "Quiet Revolution" in the province. *See also* **privatization**.

National Party of Canada A short-lived federal political party started by nationalist publisher Mel Hurtig in 1993, the National Party of Canada advocated repeal of the free trade agreement with the United States, increased public involvement in political decision making, and major reforms to fiscal and taxation policy. In the 1993 federal general election, the party received almost 200,000 votes, but failed to win any parliamentary seats. After the election, the party was dissolved by its council amid allegations of financial mismanagement and other internal problems.

National Policy Associated with the second Conservative government led by Sir John A. Macdonald, elected in 1878, the National Policy imposed tariff protection from foreign manufactures. The policy was intended to promote the development of Canadian manufacturing behind a tariff wall. The term *National Policy* is also used more widely to refer to the nation-building policies pursued by Macdonald's government, including construction of the Canadian Pacific Railway and other transportation infrastructure, and the promotion of immigration as a stimulus to western settlement and development.

Natuashish *See* **Davis Inlet**.

natural attitude As used by Alfred Schutz (1899–1959), *natural attitude* refers to characteristics of the world as it is encountered by people living in it: The world is experienced as being historically organized prior to their arrival; it is intersubjective—experienced similarly by others; people accept the world as it is given through experience; and people address the world pragmatically.

Nazism The political doctrine of the National Socialist Party of Germany led by Adolf Hitler, who became chancellor of Germany in 1933 and who assumed absolute dictatorial power until the defeat of Germany in 1945 at the end of World War II, Nazism is chiefly remembered for its ideology of racial purity and of the superiority of the so-called Aryan race. This ideology resulted in the conquest and destruction of much of Europe and its peoples, and the mass murder of political opponents and those judged inferior or deviant. The greatest Nazi crimes were committed against the Jews of Europe, on whom the Nazis unleashed a holocaust of systematic mass killing, claiming 6 million victims, in the name of "racial purification."

NDP *See* **New Democratic Party**.

Neandertals Members of what are referred to as the archaic *Homo sapiens*, Neandertals are associated with the "caveman" stereotype of being dim-witted, brutish, and incapable of language or abstract thought. Although Neandertals appear to have been perhaps twice as strong as any modern humans and somewhat unfinished anatomically compared to modern humans, there is little support for the caveman stereotype. There is evidence of a symbolic life in burials, the use of pigments, and tentative signs of musical instruments. Burial sites also indicate for the first time recognition of sex differences in burial practices. Reference: Shreeve, J. (1995). *The Neandertal enigma: Solving the mystery of modern human origins*. New York: Morrow.

necessary condition In thinking about or looking for a causal relationship, researchers have to decide if they are dealing with a necessary condition. A necessary condition (or variable) is that which must be present for the effect to occur. To put it another way, if B appears, then A must have been present. Social sciences seldom deal with necessary conditions (other than logical ones); rather, they are happy to find sufficient conditions. *See also* **sufficient condition**.

necrophilia Necrophilia is a form of sexual disorder in which the person has a strong desire to have sex with a corpse.

necrophobia A form of anxiety disorder in which the person has exaggerated fears of dead bodies is called *necrophobia*.

neoconservatism A resurgence of economic and political beliefs associated with classical liberalism of the early 19th century, neoconservatism should correctly be called *neoliberalism*. Aspects of this philosophy include an acceptance of an unregulated market economy, a minimal role for government, a suspicion toward the welfare state, a view of citizens as motivated only by self-interest, and a commitment to the central value of individualism. *See also* **classical liberalism**.

neocortex *See* **group size**.

neoliberalism *See* **neoconservatism**.

neolithic This term applies to the New Stone Age, which began about 11,000 years ago and is associated with the first appearance of domesticated plants and animals.

neolocal residence Neolocal residence rules form the basis of most Western domestic structures, in that a newly married couple sets up a new residence independent of the households of either partner's parents.

net widening In critical criminology, *net widening* is the term used to describe the effects of providing alternatives to incarceration or diversion programs to direct offenders away from court or institutional detention. While all of these programs developed since the late 1960s were intended to reduce the numbers of offenders in prison or reduce the numbers going to court, it has been found instead that the total numbers of offenders under the control of the state have increased, while the population targeted for reduction has not been reduced. In short, the net of social control has been thrown more widely (or, some might say, the mesh has been made smaller). Reference: Roach, Kent. (2000). Changing Punishment at the Turn of the Century: Restorative Justice on the Rise. *Canadian Journal of Criminology and Criminal Justice, 42*(3), 249.

neutralization techniques A set of linguistic techniques, neutralization techniques are used by otherwise conventional people to neutralize the guilt they feel from engaging in deviant behaviour. These techniques allow the conventional person to drift further into deviance. Reference: Matza, David. (1964). *Delinquency and Drift*. New York: John Wiley.

new criminology This is a general term for criminology as it emerged from the attack on positivist criminology during the 1960s and 1970s. This new approach reintroduced symbolic interactionism to criminology as well as Marxist theory. It is also the title of an influential book (see the publication details in the following "Reference"). Reference: Taylor, Ian, Walton, Paul, & Young, Jock. (1973). *New Criminology*. London: Routledge and Kegan Paul.

New Deal When Franklin D. Roosevelt was elected president of the United States in 1932, he said: "I pledge you, I pledge myself, to a new deal for the American people." In this context, *New Deal* refers to the unprecedented government initiatives to stimulate industrial recovery from 1933 to 1939. These new programs and reforms of programs were designed to assist victims of the depression, to guarantee minimal standards of living, to provide financial stability for citizens, and to create employment and economic growth. For example, the U.S. *Social Security Act* of 1935 set up a system of old-age pensions and unemployment insurance. This period can be seen as the beginning of a welfare state in the United States.

New Democratic Party Successor to the Co-operative Commonwealth Federation (CCF), the New Democratic Party was formed in 1961 to widen the appeal and broaden the organization of Canadian social democracy. It combined the old CCF with Canada's labour union movement and various social democratic organizations. Like its predecessor, the new party has had limited success in federal politics, although it has exercised considerable influence, especially over the policies of the Liberal party. The party had its greatest impact on federal politics in the years 1972–1974, when the minority Liberal government was dependent on it for parliamentary support. In provincial politics, the party has been much more successful and has formed governments in Saskatchewan, Manitoba, British Columbia, and Ontario. Reference: Laxer, James (1997). *In search of a new left*. Toronto: Penguin Books.

nominal measures *See* **level of measurement**.

nomothetic *See* **ideographic**.

norm A culturally established rule prescribing appropriate social behaviour, a norm is relatively specific and precise, and elaborates the detailed behavioural requirements that flow from more general and overarching social values. For example, it is a value in Western society that one should respect the dead; it is a norm that one should dress in dark colours for a funeral. *See also* **values**.

normal crime This term has two distinct meanings: (1) French sociologist Émile Durkheim (1858–1917) used the concept to refer to what he took to be an average or acceptable amount of crime in society. Part of his argument was that crime (normal crime) is both inevitable and functionally useful for society. (2) U.S. sociologist David Sudnow uses the term *normal crime* to refer to how prosecutors typify individual crimes as fitting into a normal pattern for that category of crime. He refers to normal burglaries, normal pedophilia. A normal crime is more likely to result in a plea bargain in order to speed up the court process. Reference: Sudnow, David. (1976). Normal Crimes: Sociological Features of the Penal Code in a Public Defender's Office. *Social Problems*, *12*, 255–276.

normal curve *See* **bell curve**.

North American Free Trade Agreement (NAFTA) *See* **Free Trade Agreement (Canada–U.S.–Mexico, 1994: NAFTA)**.

Northwest Rebellion of 1885 Like the Red River Rebellion of 1869–1870, the Northwest Rebellion was led by Louis Riel and the grievances of the settlers and Métis (of what is now Saskatchewan) were much the same. Demands were for democratic control of the region and for the protection of land and religious and language rights. The years between the two rebellions, however, saw the English of Ontario transform the image of Riel into that of a traitor and stiffened their resolve to ensure that the West would not become an extension of the French-speaking province of Quebec. Military and police strength had also been established, and the railroad provided transportation for this colonial enforcement arm. The Métis were quickly suppressed and Riel was hanged in Regina on November 16, 1885. The Métis people prefer to refer to this incident as an act of resistance rather than a rebellion. Reference: Woodcock, George. (1975). *Gabriel Dumont: The Métis Chief and His Lost World*. Edmonton: Hurtig Press. *See also* **Métis**; **Red River Rebellion**.

notwithstanding clause The 1982 *Constitution Act* includes the *Canadian Charter of Rights and Freedoms*, which guarantees numerous civil and linguistic rights to Canadians. The *Charter* is supreme constitutional law and Acts of Parliament or a legislature that conflict with *Charter* provisions are null and void. At the insistence of chiefly the western provinces, the *Charter* also contains a clause that allows Parliament or a legislature to enact that a law will be valid and will operate "notwithstanding" a guaranteed *Charter* right that conflicts with it. Such a law must be renewed every five years. Possible use of the notwithstanding clause does not apply to all *Charter* provisions; some, such as those on aboriginal rights, may be modified only by formal constitutional amendment. Although the clause weakens *Charter* guarantees, its use outside Quebec (which at one time routinely invoked it in legislation) has been very rare, since there is strong public opposition to erosion of *Charter* guarantees. No federal government has ever used this clause.

nuclear family *See* **family, nuclear**.

null hypothesis When testing a research hypothesis that the researcher has good reason to believe is true, it is customary to use a null hypothesis. This is typically a hypothesis of no difference or of no association between variables. If the research hypothesis is that men have a higher rate of suicide than do women, the null hypothesis would be that there is no difference in suicide rates between men and women. Researchers then try to disprove the null hypothesis and if they fail to reject it, they accept the research hypothesis. *See also* **falsifiability (or refutability)**.

numbered treaties Treaties had been signed with many native groups in eastern Canada prior to Confederation. With Confederation in 1867 and the purchase of lands from the Hudson's Bay Company, Canada assumed responsibility for the native peoples of western Canada. Beginning in the 1870s, negotiations were begun with native groups. These negotiations resulted in treaties that were numbered, and are still known by those numbers. The total number eventually reached 11. Also called the *land-cession* or *post-Confederation treaties*, all 11 of the treaties were signed between 1871 and 1921, and granted the federal government large tracts of land throughout the Prairies, the Canadian North, and northwestern Ontario, as well as the northeast corner of British Columbia, for white settlement and industrial use. In return for surrendering all title to the lands covered, the native groups received tracts of land for reserves and, in some cases, annuities, gratuities, schools, hunting and fishing rights, gifts of agricultural implements and cattle, annual cash payments for ammunition and twine, and clothing, flags, and medals.

Nuremberg trials A tribunal established in the German city of Nuremberg in 1945 by Great Britain, France, the Soviet Union, and the United States brought to trial 22 high-ranking Nazis whose actions during World War II were deemed to be international crimes against humanity. Twelve defendants were sentenced to death, seven received long prison terms, and three were acquitted. Another tribunal was established in Japan to try Japanese war criminals. Other nations also brought to trial those thought to be guilty of war crimes against citizens: Israel, for example, brought Adolf Eichmann, a major figure in the organization of the Holocaust, to trial in 1960, found him guilty, and he was hanged. *See also* **International Criminal Court; war crimes**.

O

objectivity The term *objectivity* is used in two distinct but related ways. The first refers to the actions of a social scientist: The scientist assumes a position of disinterestedness or impartiality, or is open-minded in the assessment of evidence. Objectivity is thought to be central to the procedures of the scientific method. The second meaning refers to the nature of the statements people make: A statement can be objective, as opposed to the person being objective. An objective statement is one that can be agreed on by others regardless of their backgrounds or biases.

obscenity *See* **Butler case; pornography**.

obsessive With this form of mental disorder, people have recurrent and unwanted thoughts that they cannot get out of their minds.

occupational crime White-collar crime committed by an individual or group of individuals exclusively for personal gain is called *occupational crime*. The distinction between this type of crime and organizational crime is difficult to maintain. *See also* **organizational crime.**

occupational distance This is the distance between one occupation and another, when occupations are ranked on a hierarchy of status. The concept is central to studies of social mobility because it permits some measurement of the extent of mobility. For example, changing one's occupation from unskilled labour to semiskilled labour involves less occupational distance than moving from unskilled labour to professional accountant. Occupational distance is therefore an important measurement in determining the relevance of social mobility. *See also* **demand mobility; social mobility**.

Ocean Ranger This off-shore oil rig sank off the coast of Newfoundland in 1982, killing 84 workers. Investigation determined that inadequate safety equipment was in place to respond to emergencies. Reference: Royal Commission on the Ocean Ranger Marine Disaster. (1984–1985). Ottawa.

October Crisis On October 5, 1970, the Front de Libération du Québec (FLQ) kidnapped James Cross, the British trade commissioner in Montreal, and on October 10, kidnapped Pierre Laporte, minister of Labour in the government of Quebec.

The federal government, led by Pierre Trudeau, invoked the *War Measures Act*, and armed soldiers entered the province of Quebec. Laporte was murdered the next day. More than 450 persons were detained in Quebec, few of whom were charged. Cross was released in exchange for safe passage to Cuba for the kidnappers. The government's handling of the kidnapping and subsequent events were extremely controversial.

OECD *See* **Organization for Economic Cooperation and Development**.

Oedipus complex A concept of psychoanalyst Sigmund Freud (1856–1939), the Oedipus complex theory holds that infants become erotically fixated on their mothers and must be psychologically conditioned, by fear of punishment and disapproval, into diverting or suppressing their sexual energies.

Oka Crisis On July 11, 1990, a dispute over land in the Quebec town of Oka erupted into violence between Mohawk residents of the Kanesatake Reserve outside Montreal and the Quebec Provincial Police. During a brief gun battle, a police officer was killed. A prolonged standoff and road blockade led the province to request that the military be brought in to bring the confrontation to an end. This is one of the few occasions in Canadian history when the army was used against Canadian citizens. An inquiry failed to determine who killed the police officer, and although the prime minister branded the native residents as "criminals," many Canadians sided with them. Reference: York, Geoffrey, & Pindera, Loreen. (1991). *People of the Pines: The Warriors and the Legacy of Oka*. Toronto: Little Brown and Co. *See also* **Gustafsen Lake; Ipperwash**.

Oldowan tools The earliest identifiable stone tools, Oldowan tools were found in the Olduvai Gorge in northern Tanzania. These tools are made by the direct percussion method, by which flakes are removed by using another stone as a hammer to produce an object with two sharp edges.

Olduvai Gorge Located in northern Tanzania and first explored by Kenyan/British anthropologist and archaeologist Louis Leakey (1903–1972) and his wife Mary Leakey (1913–1996), this area has become the most productive source of hominine fossils in Africa. *See also* **Leakey, Louis and Mary**.

oligarchy A society or social system ruled by a few people is an oligarchy. As societies or organizations become large, it is thought that political power becomes concentrated in the hands of a few individuals. *See also* **iron law of oligarchy; plutocracy**.

oligopoly The term *oligolopy* is used to describe situations where a small number of companies own or control the production of a particular good or provision of services within a market economy. This situation typically arises from a concentration of ownership and provides a challenge to liberal theory that claims benefit from a plurality of producers operating in a very competitive market. *See also* **monopoly**.

Olson, Clifford Clifford Olson is one of Canada's most notorious serial killers, and for many has come to represent the essence of evil. Between the years of 1980 and 1981, Olson murdered at least 11 children and young people in the lower mainland of British Columbia. He was eventually identified and convicted. Prior to conviction, however, he struck a deal with the RCMP involving payment of $100,000 to disclose the location of all of the bodies of the missing persons. These monies went to his wife and child. In addition to this controversy, there was worry about the failure to identify Olson sooner. Two weeks after the first murder, the father of a friend of the murdered girl heard a broadcast stating that Olson was being charged with a rape. He called the police and asked if Olson could also be responsible for the missing child. He was told that the rape victim was a prostitute and her testimony would not be considered reliable. In addition, the police had already checked out Olson and did not think he was the offender. Ten more young people were to die before Olson was caught. Reference: Mulgrew, Ian. (1990). *Final Payoff: The True Cost of Convicting Clifford Olson*. Toronto: Seal Books.

Omaha kinship system Similar to the Iroquois system, the Omaha kinship system differs only in the way in which parallel cousins and cross cousins are identified. Omaha descent groups are characteristically patrilineal, and a somewhat complex set of distinctions is involved.

one-percenter This is a term coined after a gathering of the American Motorcycle "Gypsy Tour" on July 4, 1947, when 3,000 riders descended on Hollister, California, for a "dirt hill climb." When violence broke out, the Motorcycle Association issued a statement saying that 99% of riders were respectable pleasure riders and the other 1% were troublemakers. Since that date, groups like the

Hells Angels have referred to themselves as the "one-percenters." This event was depicted in the Hollywood movie *The Wild One*.

online pornography Given the speed of the Internet and the anonymity of users, it is not surprising that the Internet has become a major distribution site for pornography. Changes to Canada's *Criminal Code* in 2002 gave the courts powers to delete child pornography posted on the Internet and to seize materials used in a child pornography offence.

open class ideology The key claim of open class ideology, a component of liberal ideology, is that an individual has meaningful opportunity to rise (or fall) in social class and status as a result of personal ability, hard work, and individual merit. The concept therefore claims that society's status system is based on achievement and not on ascription. *See also* **liberalism; social mobility**.

operant conditioning Operant conditioning is the basic process by which an individual's behaviour is shaped by reinforcement or by punishment.

operationalization In quantitative research, the act of specifying exactly how a concept will be measured is operationalization. Before measuring the concept of, for example, violent crime, a researcher must decide what are indictors of violent crime and then specify how these indicators will be counted. One might, for example, decide to use official reports of crimes known to the police and count all instances of homicide; manslaughter; attempted murder; assault, levels 1, 2, and 3; and sexual assault, levels 1, 2, and 3. Examining how a researcher has operationalized a concept is the first place to look for weakness in the research design. In the above example, for instance, many would argue that assault, level 1 (the lowest level of assault), contains numerous acts that many people would not see as indicators of the concept of violence. The United States government, for example, does not include this kind of assault in its measures of violent crime.

operationally defined To define some concept of study in such a way that it can be observed and measured is to operationally define it. For example, "well-being" might be measured by asking people to rate their overall satisfaction with their lifestyle, or "antisocial behaviour" might be measured by frequency of arrest or criminal prosecution.

opium A narcotic drug derived from the juice of the opium poppy flower, opium is also the source of both morphine and heroin.

Opium Act With the passage of the *Opium Act* in 1908, Canada became the first Western nation to prohibit, under criminal law, the import, manufacture, and sale of opium. Opium was manufactured and used primarily by the Chinese at this time, which raises the question: Why was there a need for a criminal law? While there is some dispute about the origins of the Act, it can be noted that British Columbia was experiencing increased labour tension due to the rapid process of deskilling labour that was occurring. The craft organization of work was breaking down, as management gained control of the work process and began to hire cheap unskilled labour to do much of the work. The Chinese provided a great deal of this cheap labour and some members of the labour movement saw them as the source of their problems. Others, of course, saw the problem in terms of traditional labour–management conflict and argued for a socialist response (reducing private ownership of the means of production). It is clear that there was anti-Asian sentiment in the province, and federal legislation had attempted to restrict Chinese immigration. When Mackenzie King, the Department of Labour minister, was sent to Vancouver to investigate a 1907 riot, he saw that Chinese businessmen involved in manufacturing opium made claims for compensation; he perhaps also saw the solution to his labour problem: Scapegoat the Chinese and turn what was really a labour problem into a racial problem.

Opium Wars The Opium Wars were fought between England and China from 1839 to 1842 and from 1856 to 1860 over China's refusal to continue importing opium. England had forced China to import opium to offset the cost of Chinese tea exports and so that English boats would not have to arrive in China for tea with no cargo. Much of early English capitalism was thus built on a foundation of opium. China lost both the wars and ceded Hong Kong to Britain as payment of reparations. Hong Kong was returned to China in 1996. Reference: Travis, W., & Sanello, F. (2002). *The Opium Wars: The Addiction of One Empire and the Corruption of Another*. Naperville, IL: Sourcebooks.

opportunity structure A shortened phrase, *opportunity structure* refers to the notion that opportunity—the chance to gain certain rewards or goals—is shaped by the way the society or an institution is organized (or structured). The opportunity for girls to succeed in mathematics, for example, may be structured by the fact that most of the mathematics teachers are men, and that perhaps all teachers tend to discourage such an endeavour or suggest that girls are not good at this subject. There may be a sexist structure in the school that shapes opportunity. Reference: Cloward, Richard, & Ohlin, Lloyd. (1960). *Delinquency and Opportunity*. New York: Free Press.

order in council In the British constitutional system, inherited by Canada, the monarch is head of state, must approve all laws for them to be valid, and is advised by a Privy Council. By constitutional convention, the monarch accepts only the advice of members of the Privy Council who are also Cabinet ministers and who have the support of the House of Commons. Most legislation passed by the House of Commons outlines only the broad principles of law and legal regulation, and the law usually provides for the bureaucracy to develop detailed provisions that are then given legal status by being approved by the governor general (representing the monarch) in council.

ordinal measures *See* **level of measurement**.

organic mental disorders Those forms of mental disorder that have organic or anatomical causes (for example, a brain injury or degenerative brain tissue) are organic mental disorders. This type of disorder is also exemplified by senility and Alzheimer's disease.

organic solidarity A term used by French sociologist Émile Durkheim (1858–1917), *organic solidarity* refers to a state of interdependency created by the specialization of roles, in which individuals and institutions become acutely dependent on others in a complex division of labour. The basis of solidarity is abstract and may be weakened by anomie when people fail to comprehend the ties that bind them to others. *See also* **ideal type; mechanical solidarity**.

organizational crime White-collar crime committed with the support and encouragement of a formal organization and intended at least in part to advance the goals of that organization, organizational crime is usually distinguished from white-collar crime. *See also* **white collar crime**.

Osborne, Helen Betty A 19-year-old aboriginal student living in La Pas, Manitoba, who was murdered on November 13, 1971, Helen Betty Osborne had been stopped on the street by four men who wanted to engage her in sex. When she refused, she was abducted, then raped and brutally murdered. While the whole town seemed to be aware of the men involved in the murder, it was several months before the RCMP concluded that the four men in question had been involved. It was not until December 1987 that one man was convicted of murder. A commission of inquiry reported on these events in 1991 and outlined the many ways in which racism had affected the investigation, charges, and trial. *See also* **Aboriginal Justice Inquiry of Manitoba**.

out-of-Africa hypothesis This hypothesis holds that modern humans are descended from one specific population of *Homo sapiens*, first appearing in Africa, replacing the Neandertals and other archaic *Homo sapiens*. This hypothesis is based on evidence from mitochondrial DNA. Unlike nuclear DNA, mitochondrial DNA is located in a different part of the cell and is not influenced by sperm. Therefore, it is inherited only from one's mother. Using the study of this form of DNA, researchers now claim that all living humans can be traced to a hypothetical "Eve" who lived in Africa some 200,000 years ago. The out-of-Africa hypothesis is also referred to as the *Garden of Eden theory* and contrasted to the theory of multiregional development. Under the multiregional hypothesis, *Homo erectus* emerged in Africa and migrated to various parts of Europe and Asia (e.g., Peking Man) and modern humans evolved independently in each of these regions. Reference: Stringer, C., & McKie, R. (1997). *African Exodus: The Origins of Modern Humanity*. New York: Henry Holt/John McKay.

overrepresentation A group that has a number of its members in some condition in greater numbers than their population would suggest has an overrepresentation. If a group makes up 20% of the population, then a researcher might for example predict, other things being equal, that they would represent 20% of offenders, victims, and those in prison. For example, men are overrepresented in prisons, as are aboriginal people. Aboriginal people constitute between 3% to 5% of the Canadian population but represent approximately 19% of admission to provincial and territorial custody facilities and 17% of those in federal custody. Aboriginal people also represent approximately 24% of homicide suspects. Women are overrepresented as victims in sexual assault offences.

Reference: Hendrick, D., & Farmer, L. (2002). Adult Correctional Services in Canada, 2000–2001. *Juristat, 22*(10), 1–24. *See also* **Gladue case**.

P

Pacific scandal This scandal happened in 1873 in Canada and was a case of high-level political corruption involving the prime minister, Sir John A Macdonald, his close political associates, and a 1872 "contribution" of $360,000 (a massive sum in those days) to the election campaign of Macdonald's Conservative party. In 1873, the Liberal party became aware that the funds had been given to the Conservatives partly by Sir Hugh Allan, a leading promoter of the proposed Canadian Pacific Railway who subsequently received the government contract to build the project. The Liberals publicized the story and, faced with the likelihood of being voted out of office by a hostile and indignant House of Commons, the Macdonald government resigned and lost the subsequent election. By 1878, all was forgiven by the voters, however, and Macdonald went on to win the election and enjoy another 13 years as Canada's prime minister. Reference: Simpson, J. (1988). *The Spoils of Power*. Toronto: Collins.

padlock laws On May 2, 1951, in an event that says much about the political style of "Le Chef" Maurice Duplessis, premier of Quebec, the Quebec Superior Court (all courts in Quebec at this time had a large crucifix placed behind the judge) ordered him to pay damages of $8,000 to a Jehovah's Witness, Frank Roncarelli, whose licence to sell liquor was cancelled by the Quebec Liquor Commission in 1946, on the express order of the premier. The premier's displeasure had been incurred because Roncarelli had stood bail for Jehovah's Witnesses harassed and charged for distributing their religious literature. Roncarelli's business had been essentially "padlocked" (because with no liquor licence he could do little business) under provisions of a law passed by the Quebec legislature giving the state and the premier wide powers. This law came into effect after the federal government removed Section 98 of the *Criminal Code*, a provision first introduced in 1917 to control those seen as troublemakers during the Winnipeg General Strike. The court ruled that the premier's actions were motivated by religious hostility and amounted

to political interference with an independent commission, and that he must be held personally liable for the financial damages Roncarelli had experienced. This decision was appealed, however, and went to the Supreme Court, where constitutional lawyer (and faculty member at McGill University) Frank Scott argued the case against Duplessis. On January 27, 1959, the Supreme Court decided against Duplessis and awarded Roncarelli $33,000 plus interest from the 1951 decision, and awarded him another $20,000 to $30,000 in costs. This was the end of the infamous "padlock laws" in Quebec. This and other victories led to Scott's appointment as dean of McGill's law faculty, a position he had been denied in the past due to his radical and outspoken ideas. Issues like the Roncarelli case renewed the interest of Scott and others in the need for a *Bill of Rights* of sufficient strength to control the abuse of power against citizens. His wish came true in 1982, with the introduction of the *Canadian Charter of Rights and Freedoms*. Reference: Berger, Thomas. (1981). *Fragile Freedoms: Human Rights and Dissent in Canada*. Toronto: Clarke Irwin.

paleoanthropology The study of fossil and skeletal remains with the aim of reconstructing human evolution is called *paleoanthropology*.

paleoethnobotany Involving the study of archaeological plant remains, the major research themes of paleoethnobotany are recovery and identification of plant remains, the use of wild plants, the origins of agriculture and domestication, and the co-evolution of human–plant interactions.

paleo-Indians This term refers to the ancient inhabitants of North America some 10,000 years ago.

Paleolithic Period Literally meaning *old stone*, this term refers to the oldest part of the Stone Age. Near the beginning of this time period, the first stone tools appear (*see also* **Oldowan tools**) and in the middle, the hand axe appeared. *See also* **Mousterian tool tradition**.

paleopathology Paleopathology is the study of skeletal remains to determine age at death, causes of death, illness, health, diet, and lifestyle. Reference: Cohen, M., & Armelagos, G. (1984). *Paleopathology and the Origins of Agriculture*. New Haven: Yale University Press.

Palmer Raids As concern grew about the growing number of communists in North America in the early 1900s, Canada and the United States took quite different courses of action. In the United

States, a number of legal decisions were made during the 1910–1920 period that reduced freedom of speech: An elected congressman, Eugene Debs, was first denied his seat in the House because of his opposition to the *Espionage Act* and then convicted under that Act and, was imprisoned in 1918 for voicing his opposition to World War I. A suicide bomb attack on the house of the Attorney General Mitchell Palmer in 1919 resulted in the attorney general authorizing a series of raids near the end of 1919 and into 1920, which came to be known as the Palmer Raids. These raids against alleged communist conspirators resulted in the death of 100 people, the detention of 5,000, and the deportation of many others, and stifled the development of a radical left movement in the United States. This is perhaps one reason why the United States does not have a viable social democratic party while Canada does. Reference: Murray, R.K. (1955). *Red Scare: A Study in National Hysteria, 1919–1920*. New York: McGraw-Hill.

panel study A form of longitudinal research, a panel study is one in which a panel of respondents or subjects is selected and then followed or interviewed over time. If a panel of first-year university students is selected, the researcher would, for example, be able to learn what their routes are toward an undergraduate degree. Drawing a sample of undergraduates at year one, year two, and year three would not provide the same degree of detail. *See also* **longitudinal studies**.

panhandling With the rise in homelessness and increasing poverty, there has been growing public concern about the number of people begging for money on the streets. Many people report being frightened or intimidated by aggressive panhandling. Politicians have attempted to respond to this in several ways, including the passing of the *Safe Streets Act* in Ontario in 1999. Many argue, however, that legislation of this type interferes with the basic civil liberties of citizens.

pan-Indianism This term has been applied to social movements among both Asian Indians and North American First Nations peoples. In both contexts, it refers to a social movement and a political philosophy that asserts a people's common identity and unity across political or state boundaries and tribal divisions.

paradigm A framework used in thinking about and organizing an understanding of natural or social phenomena is defined as a paradigm. All societies, and the individuals within them, tend to have relatively fixed assumptions about how to understand and interpret the world, but there is great variation in these assumptions from place to place and from time to time. For many centuries, for example, natural phenomena like the eclipse of the sun, thunder, lightning, and floods were explained within a paradigm of religious belief and myth; today, they fall within the paradigm of science. This process of sets of assumptions changing over time can be referred to as a *paradigm shift*: A new way of looking at the world emerges. The term came into the social science vocabulary from the writings of Thomas Kuhn (1922–1996), a U.S. historian of science. He challenged the conventional wisdom of history that claimed that science was a long, slow process of building on previous knowledge. Rejecting this view, Kuhn argued that the history of science can be seen rather as a history of dominant paradigms and paradigm shifts. A paradigm in his presentation was a set of assumptions about the kinds of questions to ask in science and how to go about looking for answers. As a particular body of knowledge builds up, a growing number of anomalies emerge that only with difficulty can be forced into the dominant theory. At some point, people begin to see things differently and to ask different questions in an attempt to explain their observations; they eventually arrive at a new theory that better accounts for the anomalies. Reference: Kuhn, T. (1962). *The Structure of Scientific Revolutions*. Chicago: University of Chicago Press.

parallel cousins Offspring of siblings of the same sex are called *parallel cousins*. Some societies prefer that a person marry a parallel cousin: A man may marry his father's brother's daughter or a woman may marry her father's brother's son. *See also* **cross cousins**.

paramount chieftanship A political system similar to a kingdom, paramount chieftanship brings together a number of partly autonomous villages or communities under the hierarchical rule of a grand chief. *See also* **chiefdom**.

paraphilia A paraphilia is a condition in which a person's sexual urges are directed toward non-human objects, or sexual arousal is attained from the giving or receiving of pain, or sexual urges are directed toward those unable to grant consent.

parental responsibility Legislators have been under pressure to make parents more responsible for the wrongdoings of their children. Both Manitoba (1997) and Ontario (2000) have passed a *Parental Responsibility Act,* allowing victims of youth crime to sue the parents of the offender.

Pareto's principle Italian economist and sociologist Vilfredo Pareto (1884–1923) published much in both of his fields of study, although he is not included in many sociology curriculums today. Among other things, he discovered that income and wealth distributions follow a regular pattern in all societies—80% of property is owned by 20% of citizens. Although he did not use the term himself, others have extended this work and called it *Pareto's principle*—80% of consequences are the result of 20% of the causes. *See also* **80/20 principle.**

parliament A parliament is the highest legislative assembly in many countries, including Canada. Canada's Parliament consists of the House of Commons, the Senate, and the Crown (represented by the governor general). Members of the House of Commons are elected by constituencies across Canada. The maximum term of the House of Commons between elections is five years, although elections may be held at any time prior to that if called by the governor general, acting on the prime minister's advice. The Senate is not elected; its members are appointed until age 75 by the governor general on the advice of the prime minister. Seats in the Senate are regionally distributed as set out in the 1867 *Constitution Act.*

Parsons, Talcott (1902–1979) U.S. sociologist Talcott Parsons dominated the field of sociology from the 1950s until the 1970s. Much modern sociology can be read as a rejection of Parsons. Parsons reintroduced the classic ideas of German sociologist Max Weber (1864–1920) and French sociologist Émile Durkheim (1858–1917) to North America and strove for a grand integrated theory of social behaviour. His work remained theoretical and rather abstruse, and therefore was accessible only to the persistent. In general terms, he developed a form of functionalism that reflected the period of stability and prosperity of his own time. He argued that all social systems had four functional prerequisites: adaptation to their environment; goal attainment; integration as ways of dealing with conflict and disequilibrium; and latency, or what he called *pattern maintenance* or *stability.* Each of these prerequisites was organized around a system—a cultural system, a social system a personality system, and a biological system. Reflecting the ideas of Herbert Spencer (1820–1903), a British biologist and early social philosopher, Parsons believed that all systems evolve from the simple to the more complex—a grandiose theory indeed. By the end of the 1960s, however, there was a growing awareness of the conflicts within society and thus arose a desire for theories that brought more relevance to the new reality of society.

participatory management *See* **industrial relations.**

participatory research Participatory research is distinguished from other research techniques in that the subjects, usually oppressed or exploited groups, are fully involved in the research, from the designing of topics to the analysis of data. While the findings of such research may be useful and indeed emancipatory, the process of community-building or neighbourhood-building during the carrying out of the research is of equal importance.

Parti Québécois Founded in 1968 under the leadership of René Lévesque, the main aim of the Parti Québécois was to achieve political sovereignty for Quebec within the framework of a continued association with Canada. The party first came to power in 1976 and began to prepare a political strategy leading to a referendum vote on "sovereignty-association" in 1980. The referendum proposal was defeated by a majority of 60% to 40% but, under its immensely popular leader, the party was able to comfortably win the 1981 provincial election. After losing the subsequent election under new leadership, the party returned to power in 1994 and immediately prepared for a new referendum on sovereignty-association. The proposal was brought to a referendum in 1995 and defeated once more—but by a very narrow margin, ensuring that the issue of Quebec's relationship with Canada will remain at the centre of Canadian political life in the coming years.

patriarchy Literally "rule by the father," *patriarchy* more generally refers to a social situation in which men are dominant over women in wealth, status, and power. Patriarchy is associated with a set of ideas, a "patriarchal ideology" that acts to explain and justify this dominance and attributes it to inherent natural differences between men and women. Sociologists tend to see patriarchy as a social product and not as an outcome of innate differences between the sexes; they focus attention on the way that gender roles in a society affect power differentials between men and women. *See also* **hegemony; ideology**.

patriation of the *Constitution* The "bringing home" of all legal authority over the laws and *Constitution* of Canada is called the *patriation* of the *Constitution*. The *Constitution Act, 1867* (formerly the *BNA Act*), was British legislation, and it could be changed only by Britain's Parliament (although this was done only on the request of Canada's Parliament). In the *Constitution Act, 1982*, a new and exclusively Canadian amending procedure was established and the Parliament of Great Britain no longer holds any legal authority regarding Canada. Reference: Russell, Peter H. (1993). *Constitutional Odyssey: Can Canadians Become a Sovereign People?* Toronto: University of Toronto Press.

patricide In the psychology of psychoanalyst Sigmund Freud (1856–1939), the urge to commit patricide (the killing of one's father) is present in the infant male, whose intense erotic attachment to his mother creates the desire to kill the father in order to take possession of her. In his speculations about the origins of the incest taboo, Freud imagines that in the earliest times of human groups (the "primal horde"), sons did in fact kill their father to gain possession of their mother, and this led to subsequent quarrelling and murder among the sons. These terrible consequences were then averted by the cultural development of the incest taboo and of the castration complex, which created infantile fear of the father and forced the turning away of erotic attention from the mother toward permitted sexual partners.

patrilineal descent In a patrilineal descent system, in which family descent is reckoned through the blood links of males, names and property typically follow the male line of descent. A man's descendants are his own children, and women are little recognized as ancestors.

patrilocal residence The custom of a newly married couple taking up residence in the groom's family household or village is known as *patrilocal residence.*

patrimony A right, a status, or tangible asset inherited from a father or other ancestor, patrimony may, in principle, be inherited by either sex, although the term is generally associated with patrilineal transmission of status, property, and wealth.

pattern variables Pattern variables are five dichotomies developed by U.S. sociologist Talcott Parsons (1902–1979) to draw out the contrasting values to which individuals orient themselves in social interaction. One side of the dichotomies reflects the value patterns dominant in traditional society (*Gemeinschaft*); the other reflects the dominant values of modern society (*Gesellschaft*). The variables, listed with the traditional side of the dichotomy first, are: affectivity–affective neutrality; diffuseness–specificity; particularism–universalism; ascription–achievement; collectivity-orientation–self-orientation. Social scientists, using the tradition of pattern variables, have argued that signs of Canada being a more traditional society are the lower crime rates and greater deference to authority.

pay equity This term generally refers to laws and public and corporate policies that have as their objective the elimination of pay differentials linked to sex, ethnic identity, or particular minority status. Pay equity is usually concerned with correcting the gender-based labour market inequality experienced by women. (In principle, such policies could apply also to men, but there is little evidence of gendered disadvantage for men in the labour market.) Two issues are addressed. First is the problem of relatively direct discrimination: women being paid less than men for the same or essentially similar work. This practice is now illegal in Canada: The law requires *equal pay for equal work*. Second is a more complex problem of identifying and correcting wage inequality that results from historical undervaluation of the types of work that are dominated by women. For example, day-care workers are among the worst paid in Canada, but day-care work is crucial to the working of Canada's economy. Policymakers have concluded that such examples indicate a need for an active principle of establishment of pay equity: *equal pay for work of equal value*. This principle allows comparison of pay rates between different types of work that are evaluated and weighted according to criteria such as skill, education, effort, and working conditions. Some federal and provincial laws mandate this form of pay equity, but there has been cautious application of them.

pedophilia Pedophilia is a sexual disorder in which a person is sexually aroused by children. *See also* **Badgley report; child sex tourism; Internet luring; online pornography; Sharpe decision**.

Peking Man In the early part of the 20th century, most anthropologists believed that the origins of humankind were going to be found in Asia, not in Africa, and consequently many expeditions arrived in China to search for fossilized skeletal remains. Locals pointed interested parties to a site of many bones in a place called Dragon Bone Hill, near the town of Zhoukoudian, about 45 kilometres from Beijing. On the basis of one molar and a few fragments, Davidson Black (1884–1934), a Canadian anatomist and amateur paleoanthropologist, claimed a new form of early human and attached the name of *Sinanthropus pekinensis* (or Peking Man) to the fossil. His reputation depended on the discovery of an intact fossil, and this was achieved in 1929 when an intact skull was removed from the rock. This is now seen as an Asian representative of *Homo erectus*. The Sino–Japanese conflict swept through the region in the 1930s, bringing work to a close and then World War II made the area unsafe. During this time, there was great concern about the safety of the fossils, and a decision was made to pack them up and attempt to remove them to the United States. The fossils were never to be seen again and their loss remains a great mystery. However, the original researchers had made very good casts of the fossils and had photographed and described everything in great detail. Reference: Boaz, N.T., & Ciochon, R.L. (2004*). Dragon Bone Hill*. New York: Oxford University Press.

Pendejo Cave An archaeological site in southern New Mexico, Pendejo Cave is believed by some to point to human habitation as much as 30,000 years ago. The dating of this find is very controversial, since it would contradict the Bering Strait theory Reference: MacNeish, R., & Libby, J. (Eds.). (2004). *Pendejo Cave*. Albuquerque: University of New Mexico Press.

penology The study of the treatment and punishment of criminal offenders, penology is now included within criminology.

per capita *Capita* comes from a Latin term referring to head. Criminologists and sociologists refer to crimes (or divorce rates, etc.) per capita. For example, if there are only 0.01 crimes per capita, this would mean you have a 1% risk of being victimized. Criminologists usually use the idea of a rate per 100,000, rather than the idea of per capita.

"Persons" case An important Canadian case, the "Persons" case determined that women were indeed "persons" under the *Constitution Act, 1867* (formerly the *BNA Act*). Following women's federal enfranchisement, a debate arose over the eligibility of women to be appointed to the Senate. Requests to the government to make an appointment (the name of Judge Emily Murphy, the first woman magistrate in the entire British Empire, was offered) were rejected in 1919 on the grounds that a reading of the *Constitution* meant that "persons" referred only to men. In 1927, Emily Murphy was able to use a provision of the *Supreme Court Act* of 1875 to request a constitutional interpretation of the *BNA Act*: All five judges who heard the case agreed that "Women are not 'qualified persons' within the meaning of Section 24 of the *BNA Act, 1867*." Judge Murphy took her case to the Privy Council in London, and on October 18, 1929, the Privy Council announced that women were indeed persons. Reference: Baines, Beverly. (1993). Law, Gender, Equality. In Sandra Burt et al. (Eds.). *Changing Patterns*. Toronto: McClelland and Stewart.

petite bourgeoisie A middle class of professionals and small-businesspeople, the petite bourgeoisie work for themselves or own small productive facilities. Marx predicted that this class would be gradually eliminated by the consolidation of large capital under competitive forces.

phenomenological sociology Defined as the study of phenomena, phenomenology has had its primary influence on ethnomethodology. In the early development of phenomenology, a distinction was drawn between *phenomena* (things as they appear in our experience) and *noumena* (things as they are in themselves). German philosopher Immanuel Kant (1724–1804) believed that all we can ever know are the former. Austrian Edmund Husserl (1859–1938), who had studied mathematics, physics, philosophy, and psychology, argued that natural and social environments differ in that social objects appear only as perceived objects (i.e., there is no *noumena*); they depend on human recognition for their existence, and because of this, social reality is in constant flux and ambiguity. Social reality is only an experienced reality rather than a natural reality. The *experience* of objects, events, activities, etc., is all there is. By accepting this claim, ethnomethodology has emerged as the study of the creation of social reality through mundane reasoning, account giving, or the use of the documentary method. The concreteness or factuality of the social world is seen to be an accomplishment of members of society and the methods of this accomplishment are the topic of investigation.

philosopher-king A wise ruler seen by Greek philosopher Plato as the ideal governor of the state, the philosopher-king would be unattached to worldly interests and focused on the achievement of justice in an ideal state, where each person must do what that person is best suited for. The term has a Canadian connection to ex-prime minister Pierre Trudeau, whose writings and speeches on issues of equality, justice, citizenship and nationalism conveyed an unusual philosophical preoccupation, for a practising politician, with the means and ends of politics. *See also* **Plato.**

phonemes In linguistics, the smallest classes of sound that make a difference in meaning are phonemes.

phonetics Phonetics is the study of the production, transmission, and reception of speech sounds.

phrenology A biological theory of criminality developed by Austrian anatomist and physiologist Franz Gall (1758–1828) and German medical doctor Johan Spurzheim (1776–1832), phrenology is built on the assumption that segments of the brain are linked to particular emotions and characteristics. This being so, an examination of the skull shows which of these areas is overdeveloped or underdeveloped. It was believed that criminality could be identified in this way. Although later proved to be without empirical support, for a time, every prisoner had a phrenology chart on file.

Pickton, Robert William By May 2005, Robert Pickton had been charged with first-degree murder in the deaths of 27 women, making him the most notorious serial killer in Canada. Forensic investigation at the British Columbia pig farm owned by his family discovered the remains of 31 women. *See also* **missing women case.**

pidgin language A language that combines and simplifies elements of two or more languages is called a *pidgin language.*

Piltdown Man Human fossil remains were discovered in 1912 on an estate near Piltdown Common in England. Named the Piltdown Man, these bones were claimed to be evidence of the evolutionary transition from hominid to *Homo sapiens* and were thought to be very important. While some doubt was raised about the authenticity of the discovery, it was not until 1953 (after the use of fluorine tests for dating archaeological materials) that the bones were revealed as a hoax. There is still considerable mystery about the perpetrator of this hoax, which stood for so long. Reference: Millar, Ronald. (1972). *The Piltdown Men.* New York: St. Martin's Press.

Pineo–Porter index Developed by Canadian sociologists Peter Pineo and John Porter as a simple way to measure socioeconomic status, the Pineo–Porter index uses a composite measure of education and income for 16 occupational categories, so that a researcher can use occupational classification as an indicator of social standing. This index is often used in health research, as well as in other areas.

pink collar *Pink collar* is a term that denotes jobs and employment sectors dominated by women workers.

pink-collar ghetto Expanding the dichotomy between blue-collar and white-collar occupations, *pink-collar ghetto* captures the particular concentration of women in jobs traditionally thought to be "women's work." In 1991, for example, 57% of female workers (and only 26% of male workers) were in the three occupational categories of clerical, sales, and service; 13.5% of women were in the specific occupations of stenographers, secretaries, and salesclerks. Interestingly, 88% of cashiers were women, as were 98% of secretaries, 93% of receptionists, and 81% of elementary and kindergarten teachers.

Pinto (Ford) *See* **Ford Pinto.**

pipeline debate In 1956, the Liberal government announced that it had decided, in the national interest, to promote a natural gas pipeline from Alberta to eastern Canada. The pipeline was to be run in Canada and deliver to Canadian consumers. With government financial support, a private syndicate was established to build the project, but it appeared to be indirectly dominated by American interests. When the Bill authorizing the pipeline was introduced in the House of Commons in May 1956, it met with intense opposition from the Conservatives, who insisted that effective control must be in Canadian hands, and the Co-operative Commonwealth Federation, who wanted public ownership. Together, the two parties were able to stall the measure, and the summer window for starting on the project began to close. Citing the urgency of the measure, the government forced a closure of debate and was strongly attacked for its dictatorial attitude by the Opposition. The event damaged the Liberal's image and contributed to defeat in the 1957 election. *See also* **closure**.

Plains of Abraham This is the battlefield on the outskirts of Quebec City where, in 1759, British forces led by General Wolfe defeated the French forces led by General Montcalm, thus ending the French empire in Canada and securing control for Britain. Both generals were mortally wounded during the battle and at its end, the dead of both armies were buried together in a mass grave. In 1760, the British took control of Montreal and France conditionally surrendered. In the *Treaty of Paris, 1763*, France formally ceded all of its Canadian territories to Britain, but France's conditions were met with guarantees that Quebec would continue to have freedom of worship in the Catholic religion.

Plato (428–347 B.C.) Ancient Greek political and moral philosopher Plato's most important political work, *The Republic*, claimed that the ideal state must be ruled by philosopher-kings. He denounced all other forms of government, including democracy, because they made possible rule by the ignorant or self-interested. Enlightened government by philosophers, however, would be directed only to ends of justice and a virtuous civic life. *See also* **Aristotle**.

plebiscite A plebiscite is a process similar to a referendum, but a plebiscite is intended to gauge the public's opinion on a topic of major importance, rather than being a vote to accept or reject specific proposals. Canada held a wartime plebiscite in 1942 asking the public to support military conscription, if this was found to be necessary. While the predominantly English-speaking provinces of Canada voted 80% "yes," Quebec voted 73% "no." In late 1944, however, Prime Minister Mackenzie King, after stalling as long as possible on the issue, decided that conscription was essential. While only 13,000 conscripted Canadians were actually sent overseas, the Quebec public was angered that its clearly expressed opinion had been overruled.

pluralism This term has three principal meanings in the social sciences. First, it is a model of politics where power is assumed to be widely dispersed to different individuals and interest groups within a society, thus ensuring that political processes will be relatively open and democratic, and will reflect a spectrum of social interests rather than the domination of particular groups. Second, it describes a society where individual and group differences are present and are celebrated as enriching the social fabric. Canada's policy of multiculturalism reflects pluralist values. Third, it is a view of the causation of social phenomena, especially of social change, that examines the interaction of a variety of factors, rather than relying on a single explanatory cause. For example, German sociologist Max Weber (1864–1920), in stressing the importance of cultural as well as material forces in creating change within a society, offers a more pluralistic framework for explanation than the more exclusively materialist approach of Marx. *See also* **historical materialism; Marxism; Protestant ethic**.

plutocracy Literally meaning "rule by the rich," the term *plutocracy* is used to denote a wide range of situations in which a group of individuals are able to exert disproportionate power and influence in society and social institutions because of their wealth.

Polanyi, Karl (1886–1964) Austrian economist Karl Polanyi taught widely, including in the United States. His wife was not able to gain entry to the United States, so she lived in Canada and her husband visited regularly, making contact with many intellectuals and left-leaning people in this country. His key ideas involved a critique of neoclassical economic theory. For example, he challenged the idea that freedom and justice must be tied to a free market economy and he also argued that the new emphasis on the autonomy of the market was dangerous, and that there must be mechanisms of social control similar to those in previous societies. Reference: Polanyi, K. (1944). *The Great Transformation*. New York: Rinehart.

polarization of classes In Marxian analysis, the class structure of capitalist societies becomes increasingly polarized. Over time, it is argued, the secondary classes of capitalism (the self-employed, the residual aristocracy, etc.) will disappear and be absorbed into either the bourgeois class or the proletariat. The class structure will come to consist only of these two classes. *See also* **class**.

political assassinations Politics is a hazardous occupation and many politicians throughout history have paid with their lives for their involvements. William Shakespeare's play *Julius Caesar* commemorates one of the most famous: the murder of Julius Caesar in the Roman Senate on March 15, 44 B.C. Many other celebrated political figures have also died at the hands of assassins, including Abraham Lincoln (April 14, 1865) and John F. Kennedy

(November 22, 1963); Tsar Alexander II of Russia (March 1, 1881); Archduke Franz Ferdinand (June 28, 1914), an event that contributed to precipitating World War I; Dr. Martin Luther King (April 4, 1968); Indian Prime Minister Indira Gandhi (October 31, 1984); and Swedish Prime Minister Olof Palme (February 28, 1986). The only example we have in Canada is that of D'Arcy McGee in 1868. *See also* **McGee, D'Arcy**.

political culture Political culture comprises the aspects of culture that include the norms, values, and orientations of a people to political issues and institutions. Canada has sometimes been said to have a more "conservative" political culture than the United States because our more developed welfare state displays a greater public reliance on government programs. Some sociologists and political scientists have, however, challenged this characterization of Canada and argue that public policies, like universal health care, reflect an innovative approach to social issues in contrast to the more traditional and less activist reliance on the marketplace.

political economy perspective A major tradition in Canadian history and the social sciences associated with the University of Toronto, the political economy perspective is not a specific theory, but rather is a general approach to social analysis that stresses the interconnection of social, political, and economic processes in society. Classic Canadian writers in this tradition include political economist Harold Innis (1894–1952), sociologist S.D. Clark (1910–2003), and political theorist C.B. Macpherson (1911–1987). This perspective remains central to contemporary Canadian social analysis and academic discourse.

political science The only discipline within the social sciences that claims the title "science" in its own name, political science is concerned with the process of government and the relationship of government, the community, and individuals. It also examines the institutions and policy goals of the political system. Unlike its sister disciplines of sociology and anthropology, the origins of political science are ancient and begin with political philosophy, which had already reached a level of great sophistication in Greece with the writings of Plato and Aristotle more than 2,000 years ago. Both of these thinkers set a tradition that has continued to shape the concerns of political science. These concerns include trying to elucidate the best and most just relationship of citizen and state, specifying the best conditions to promote government for the benefit of the people, and defining the essential requirements for a government to maintain legitimacy in the eyes of the community. Since the mid-20th century, concern to make the study of politics more scientific has led to the development of systems theories and a focus on quantifiable aspects of political behaviour, such as voting and other forms of political participation. Efforts have also been made to theorize politics in terms of models, such as game theories or public choice theory.

political socialization The component of the process of individuals coming to learn and internalize the culture of their society or group, political socialization is directly related to the transmission of political values and behaviours.

politics This can be narrowly defined as all that relates to the way a society is governed. Politics is the process by which the community makes decisions and establishes values that are binding upon its members. This definition comes from the original Greek meaning of *politics*, the government of the city–state. In general speech, *politics* refers much more widely to processes that involve the exercise of power, status, or influence in making decisions or establishing social relationships. This latter meaning is implied by the idea of "office politics" or "sexual politics" (as used by feminist activist Kate Millett, whose attack on patriarchy, romantic love, and monogamous marriage in her book *Sexual Politics* [New York: Doubleday, 1970] fueled feminism's second wave) or the claim that "the personal is political."

polity There is debate about what institutions should be included in a description of the polity, an umbrella term used to refer to the roles and institutions of a society that directly shape the way the society is governed. It involves state institutions of government, the political parties, and interest and advocacy groups. It also includes the media and other institutions directly affecting political values, opinions, and behaviour.

polyandry A marriage structure where a woman has more than one husband at one time, polyandry is rare, but where it is found, there tends also to be fraternal polyandry, in which the husbands are brothers.

polygamy A marriage structure in which there is more than one spouse at a time, the term *polygamy* covers both polygyny and polyandry. While polygamy is a violation of the criminal law, there is at least one polygamous colony in Canada—the colony of Bountiful in British Columbia. Male residents of this colony continue to follow a traditional Mormon practice of having more than one wife, which is now prohibited by the mainstream Mormon Church. The Canadian authorities have decided not to enforce the law in this case, although a civil suit is being initiated by women who have been able to leave the colony. *See also* **Bountiful**.

polygyny A marriage structure where men have more than one wife at a time, polygyny is widely spread in world societies, but is practised by only a minority of those communities because population sex-ratios and a lack of economic resources make it inaccessible for the majority. *See also* **Bountiful**.

Popper, Karl (1902–1994) Austrian-born British philosopher Karl Popper made major contributions to the philosophy of science. *See also* **falsifiability (or refutability)**.

popular culture Intellectual opinions of popular culture, the culture of the masses, have been deeply shaped by critical theory. Since the Frankfurt School, which identified with the "high culture" of the intellectual classes, popular culture has been seen as trivial, demeaning, and commercialized, serving the interests of the capitalist system. Postmodernist theorists, however, no longer accept the belief that there is some objectively superior high culture setting a standard from which to make evaluations of others. They have been more interested in popular culture as representing the voices of the previously silent, and by adopting the methods of film analysis or literary criticism, they examine the way popular culture is produced and the underlying assumptions on which its meaning rests. *See also* **consumer culture; critical theory; postmodernism**.

population All elements or all members of a given class or set that a researcher wants to generalize is referred to as a *population*. For example, adult Canadians, teenagers, Canadian inmates, and criminal offenders can each be thought of as a population. Populations are difficult to study because we cannot find all of the members (heroin addicts or male prostitutes) or because of the expense (surveying all teenagers). Social scientists avoid this problem by gathering a sample from the population and then generalizing from the sample to the population.

pork barrel politics A derogatory term, *pork barrel politics* refers to the practice of public funds or resources (the "pork") being distributed by governments and their agents to party supporters in return for financial and electoral support.

pornography The literal meaning of this term is "to write about the harlot." The terms *pornography* and *obscenity* are often used interchangeably, and the law itself is stated in terms of obscenity. Control of sexual expression has a very long history and it was only with the Butler case that a woman's point of view has shaped the way this regulation is discussed. *See also* **Butler case; Sharpe decision**.

Porter, John (1921–1979) Born in Vancouver, John Porter studied at the London School of Economics, where his interests in power and equality were developed. He returned to Canada to become the first sociologist at Carleton University and to publish his book *The Vertical Mosaic*, which many consider to be the most important book in the history of Canadian sociology. In this book, Porter challenged the idea that Canada was a classless society and went on to show how a small group of rich men shaped and controlled the society. Porter spent the rest of his life researching and writing about education and opportunity. One of his students at Carleton was Wallace Clement, who carried on some aspects of his research on power in Canada and is now with the Department of Sociology and Anthropology at Carleton University. Reference: Porter, John. (1965). *The Vertical Mosaic: An Analysis of Social Class and Power in Canada*. Toronto: University of Toronto Press.

positivism One way to think about the relationship between science and society is called *positivism*, which is found in the early writings of French sociologist Auguste Comte (1798–1857). All of the assumptions that Comte makes are now rejected by postmodernists. Comte begins by imposing meaning on history, arguing that societies evolve through three stages: the theological stage, the metaphysical stage, and the positive (or scientific) stage. Each of these stages is reproduced in the evolution of the human mind. The human mind, and the most privileged among these was the sociologist's, would use the scientific method to arrive at an understanding of the universal laws of social development. Comte argues against democratic discourse in the belief that parties involved in the political process are always committed to a particular viewpoint. Only science can rise above the local and particular and understand impartially. The application of this knowledge to society would enable the liberation of individuals. Positivism, therefore, places science in a privileged position, assumes the possibility of a scientific understanding of human and social behaviour, assumes the separation of knowledge and power, and assumes the possibility of objectivity and impartiality. Positivism shaped sociology for a century following its introduction by Comte. *See also* **Comte, Auguste; postmodernism.**

Positivist School In criminology, this term refers to the first scientific school consisting of the Italian criminologists Cesare Lombroso (1835–1909), Raffaelo Garofalo (1852–1934), and Enrico Ferri (1856–1928). They supported the assumptions of positivism and argued that criminality is determined—the effect in a cause–effect sequence—and that the mandate of criminology should be to search for these causes. It was believed that with the exception of those deemed to be "born criminals," the discovery of the causes of crime would allow for effective treatment. This school therefore adopts a medical model (crime as sickness) and advocates rehabilitation of offenders, indeterminate sentences, and the dominance of professionals in correctional decision making. Reference: Ferri, Enrico. (1913). *The Positive School of Criminology.* Chicago: Charles H. Kerr and Co. *See also* **classical criminology; critical criminology; positivism.**

postcolonial world The world after the demise of the great colonial powers is known as the *postcolonial world.* While the United States removed itself from the British Empire in the late 18th century, much of the world remained tangled in colonial control until well into the 1960s.

postcritical (criminology) This term denotes a time following the period in which a critical or conflict perspective was dominant. This perspective would accept the assumptions central to postmodernism or deconstructionism. Reference: O'Reilly-Fleming, T. (1996). *Post-Critical Criminology.* Toronto: Prentice-Hall. *See also* **postmodernism.**

postindustrial thesis The postindustrial thesis holds that modern economies in the Western world have moved from a focus on goods production (an industrial base) to a new foundation of knowledge and sophisticated services. This new economy is assumed to demand different kinds of workers, to allow for more job satisfaction, and to foster less labour conflict. *See also* **embourgeoisment thesis.**

postmaterialist politics This term refers to a widespread international trend for citizens to become more concerned about "quality of life" issues, especially the environment, and less focused on goals like economic development and expansion of national wealth. One aspect of this trend in Europe and in Canada has been rising levels of support for Green Parties and for environmental causes like the Kyoto Accord.

postmodernism *Postmodernism* is a difficult concept to grasp, and has a somewhat different significance in architecture, literary criticism, and art than in the social sciences. In social theory, it is best seen as a rejection of central assumptions of the modern world or of what has been described as the "Enlightenment Project." This project has at least two core beliefs. First is the assumption that modern society will become more democratic and just because of our growing ability to rationally and objectively understand the community's best interests. Second is the assumption that scientists and social theorists hold a privileged viewpoint since they are supposed to operate outside of local interests or bias. Each of these assumptions suggests the possibility of disinterested knowledge, universal truths, and social progress. The late 20th-century writings of French historian and philosopher Michel Foucault (1926–1984) and French poststructuralist philosopher Jean-François Lyotard (1924-1998) called these assumptions into question. Foucault's work has argued that knowledge and power are always intertwined and that the social sciences, rather than empowering human actors, have made humans into objects of inquiry and have subjected them to knowledge legitimated by the claims of science. Similarly, Lyotard has argued that social theory has always imposed meaning on historical events (think of the writings of Marx) rather than providing for the understanding of the empirical significance of events. This rejection of the idea of social and intellectual progress implies that people must accept the possibility of history having no meaning or purpose, abandon the idea that we can know what is or is not true, and accept that science can never create and test theories according to universal scientific principles because there is no unitary reality from which such principles can be established. We are left living in a fragmented world with multiple realities, a suspicion of science or authoritative claims, and many groups involved in identity politics in order to impose their reality on others. The clearest signs of a postmodern approach to sociology can be found in social constructionism, ethnomethodology, and labelling theory. *See also* **metanarrative; positivism**.

potassium–argon analysis A method for absolute dating of rocks in archaeology, potassium-argon analysis builds on the assumption that intense heating (as from a volcano) drives the argon out of the substance but radioactive potassium in the substance begins to decay at a known rate and creates new argon. So, this method calculates the ratio of radioactive potassium to argon. This method was developed in the 1960s.

potlatch A custom of the First Nations peoples of the Pacific northwest coast, a potlatch is a ceremonial period of feasting accompanied by lavish giving away, and sometimes destruction, of goods and property. Those who gave away or destroyed the most property earned the greatest social prestige. Anthropologists have described the ceremonies as a form of "war with property." The potlatch also had important elements of economic distribution, social bonding, and political processes, all central to the maintenance of a society. The Canadian government considered the practice to be destructive of the stability of communities and it was outlawed (from 1884 until 1951) and rigorously suppressed. When the *Indian Act* was revised in 1951, the section banning potlatch celebrations was deleted, but today's potlatch is a much more peaceful celebration. *See also* **cultural genocide**.

poverty line The poverty line is the division, arbitrarily arrived at and usually based on income, that divides the poor from the non-poor. There is considerable controversy about how this line should be determined, and Statistics Canada uses the term *low income* rather than *poverty* and calculates low-income cutoffs. This line or cutoff can be determined in a variety of ways. One method is to determine the minimum income required to purchase a basket of goods and services thought to be necessary to maintain a minimum standard of living. Another alternative is to look at expenditures on the basic necessities of food, shelter, and clothing. Poverty or a low income may be determined when a family spends 20% more of its income on these necessities than does the average family. This method has been used by Statistics Canada. A third method would be to assert that a family is in poverty if its income is less than 50% of the median family income, adjusted for family size. Changes to Statistics Canada policy in the late 1990s reduced the extent of poverty considerably by redefining the concept.

power The capacity of individuals or institutions to achieve goals even if opposed by others constitutes power. Sociologists and political scientists, among others, have examined the way power is exercised through political parties and institutions of the state or the way that men exercise power within the family or the workplace. Since the work of French historian and philosopher Michel Foucault (1926–1984), however, there has been an interest in the way that "knowledge" itself is an instrument of power. Postmodernists such as Foucault adopt a position of "incredulity toward metanarratives" so they no longer assume the validity of particular ways to look at the world or the truth or objectivity of specific perspectives (such as social science theory). Rather, Foucault drew attention to the ways in which the theories of the human sciences, including sociology and political science, are themselves the outcome of struggles between different competing perspectives, in which one becomes temporarily victorious and then becomes a source of repression and constraint. This perspective has roots in the traditional concerns of the sociology of knowledge.

power-control theory An explanation for differences in criminality, the power-control theory builds on the idea that social control is stratified within the family. Traditionally, for example, girls have been subjected to more social control than have boys. Further, mothers have traditionally been responsible for exercising social control, and their increasing involvement in the workplace may enhance their power within the home, decrease their social control activity, and affect the willingness of girls to violate norms. Reference: Hagan, John. (1985). The Class Structure and Delinquency: Toward a Power-Control Theory of Common Delinquent Behaviour. *American Journal of Sociology*, 90, 1151–1178.

practical reasoning *See* **common-sense reasoning**.

preexperimental design A research design that does not fit the standards of an authentic experiment, preexperimental design is usually undertaken for exploratory purposes. Typical of this type of design is the elimination of a control group; for this reason, it is often called a *single-group experiment*. This design will not allow definitive conclusions about the causes of the effect observed. *See also* **experiment**.

prehensile *Prehensile* means having the ability to grasp objects. Primates have prehensile hands and feet, and some primates (certain monkeys) have prehensile tails.

prejudice To make a judgment about an individual or group of individuals on the basis of their social, physical, or cultural characteristics is to show prejudice. Such judgments are usually negative, but prejudice can also be exercised to give undue favour and advantage to members of particular groups. Prejudice is often seen as the attitudinal component of discrimination.

presentation of self As used by Canadian sociologist Erving Goffman (1922–1982), *presentation of self* refers to the methodical as well as the unintentional practices of presenting or displaying one's self in ways that create a particular definition of the situation. This presentation may include verbal messages, as well as gestures, clothing choices, hairstyle, posture, etc. People may try to present themselves in a particular way by dressing up to go to court or may find themselves the victim of a jury's definition of the situation derived from the accused's appearance. The presentation of self is usually done front stage, while back stage, the actors can let down their guard and "be themselves." Reference: Goffman, Erving. (1959). *The Presentation of Self in Everyday Life*. New York: Doubleday & Co.

presentism A term referring to an error in reasoning when someone uses the standard of present social and moral values to judge events and persons of the past, *presentism* is often applied to the claims of those who want apologies from governments and other institutions for historical wrongs.

pressure group A group of individuals and organizations linked together for the purpose of politically promoting particular values and objectives, a pressure group could be made up of people with issue-specific goals (e.g., opposition to nuclear energy), for example, or by people seeking to regularly defend and advance their goals and objectives (e.g.,

the Canadian Federation of Independent Business, the Canadian Labour Congress). Pluralist theory upholds the view that political process and political decision making is best thought of as consisting of open and competitive pressure group interaction and advocacy within a framework of democracy.

prevalence This term relates to the number of particular events in the community. AIDS, for example, may be very prevalent (the total number with this syndrome), but the incidence (new cases) is going down each year.

price fixing Representing corporate interference in the marketplace, price fixing is conspiring with others to not compete by setting a fixed price for goods or services.

primary group *See* **group, primary**.

primary labour market All research on labour markets has shown them to be divided or fragmented. The term used today is *segmented labour market*, suggesting there are many components to the market. Earlier, it was thought that the market was divided into a primary labour market and a secondary labour market. This was interesting because men dominated the primary market, while women and minorities dominated the secondary market. Primary labour markets tend to offer high salaries or wages, better working conditions, and more job stability. This market tends to be found in those sectors of business that are capital-intensive. The labour that is required tends to be more skilled and the high costs of labour can often be covered by the profit generated from an efficient plant. Workers are more apt to be unionized and to be able to make greater wage demands than workers in a secondary labour market. *See also* **secondary labour market**.

primates An order of living things (using a version of the Linnaeus classification system), the primates order contains humans as well as apes and monkeys. All members of this order have a great number of things in common. There are two sub-orders: haplorhines, to which humans belong, and strepsirhines, the most primitive of living primates (e.g., the lemur). Primates first emerged during the Paleocene Epoch.

primatology Primatology is the study of nonhuman primates.

prime minister, first woman Canada's first woman prime minister was Kim Campbell, who succeeded the extremely unpopular Brian Mulroney and became Conservative party leader and prime minister in June 1993. Her party lost the subsequent fall election, experiencing a political landslide that reduced it to just two seats in the House of Commons. Reference: Campbell, Kim. (1996). *Time and Chance: The Political Memoirs of Canada's First Woman Prime Minister*. Toronto: Doubleday Canada.

prime ministers of Canada As of 2006, 22 people had served as Canada's prime minister since Confederation in 1867. Their terms of office and party affiliations were: Sir John A. Macdonald, Conservative, 1867–1873; Alexander Mackenzie, Liberal, 1873–1878; Sir John A. Macdonald, Conservative, 1878–1891; Sir John Abbott, Conservative, 1891–1892; Sir John Thompson, Conservative, 1892–1894; Sir Mackenzie Bowell, Conservative, 1894–1896; Sir Charles Tupper, Conservative, 1896–1896; Sir Wilfrid Laurier, Liberal, 1896–1911; Sir Robert Borden, Conservative, 1911–1917; Sir Robert Borden, Unionist, 1917–1920; Arthur Meighan, Unionist, 1920–1921; W.L. Mackenzie King, Liberal, 1921–1926; Arthur Meighan, Conservative, 1926–1926; W.L. Mackenzie King, Liberal, 1926–1930; R.B. Bennett, Conservative, 1930–1935; W.L. Mackenzie King, Liberal, 1935–1948; Louis St. Laurent, Liberal, 1948–1957; John G. Diefenbaker, Conservative, 1957–1963; Lester B. Pearson, Liberal, 1963–1968; Pierre E. Trudeau, Liberal, 1968–1979; Joe Clark, Conservative, 1979–1980; Pierre E. Trudeau, Liberal, 1980–1984; John N. Turner, Liberal, 1984–1984; Brian Mulroney, Conservative, 1984–1993; Kim Campbell, Conservative, 1993–1993; Jean Chrétien, Liberal, 1993–2004; Paul Martin, Liberal, 2004–2006; Stephen Harper, Conservative, 2006– .

primitive communism An imagined first society in which all resources were owned in common, primitive communism has a close correspondence with some actual hunting and gathering societies.

primitive society This is the term used to denote simple human societies that are assumed to represent how human beings lived in communities in the earliest times of history. The dictionary defines *primitive society* as "belonging to the beginning or to the first times." The term is now out of favour in both sociology and anthropology because it appears to denigrate these simple societies by suggesting that they are less civilized than modern societies. While *primitive* can be used in its formal sense to describe

simple societies, the favoured term today is *hunter–gatherer society*. *See also* **hunter–gatherer society**.

Prince, The *See* **Machiavelli**.

Prison for Women (P4W) Opened in 1934 in Kingston, Ontario, P4W was a source of regular controversy. As the only federal institution for women inmates, women from all across Canada were housed here, leaving many far away from family and support systems. Given the small number of inmates, there were also charges of inequality, since women received fewer program services than did men. Almost from its opening, there were calls for its closure. Modelled on a 19th-century maximum security prison for men, the institution never met the needs of women. After a controversial incident in the 1990s, a commission of inquiry led by Louise Arbour recommended that the institution be closed; by the end of the century, the P4W was closed.

prisonization The process of being socialized into the culture and social life of prison society to the extent that adjusting to the outside society becomes difficult is known as *prisonization*.

prison subculture The culture of prison society, prison subculture is thought by some to arise from the "pains of imprisonment," while others believe it is imported into the prison. Also known as the *convict code*, some of the features of prison subculture are: Do not inform on other prisoners, do not trust staff, help other residents, show your loyalty to other residents, and share what you have. Reference: Wieder, D.L. (1974). *Language and Social Reality: The Case of Telling the Convict Code*. The Hague: Mouton.

private domain (sphere) The distinction between the public domain (or sphere) and the private domain became an important tool of early feminist analysis, as it helped in describing and understanding women's location in society. The parts of society consisting of politics and paid work are seen as the public domain, and family life as the private domain.

private sector The private sector is the part of the economy that is controlled or owned by private individuals, either directly or through stock ownership. There has been a proliferation of private police in Canada and this has raised several questions about training and citizen rights. *See also* **public sector**.

privatization (1) The process of moving economic resources from the public sector to the private sector is called *privatization*. Publicly owned transportation resources, natural resources, hospitals, etc., may be sold to private individuals or to privately owned corporations. Canada has been unusual in having a large public sector. Classical liberal theory, however, is opposed to government involvement and interference in economic activity, and the recent resurgence of interest in classical liberalism (*see also* **neoconservatism**) has led to pressure to privatize government-owned resources and services. *See also* **classical economic theory**. (2) The term has also been applied to the growth in modern societies of a family life separated from the outer community. In traditional societies, there is little separation of private and public spheres, but privatization appears to take place with urbanization and industrialization. *See also* **family, bourgeois**.

probability sample In social science research, a probability sample is drawn from a population by using methods to ensure random selection; each member of the population must have an equal probability of being drawn.

problematic A term used in ethnomethodology, *problematic* was put to effective use by sociologist Dorothy E. Smith (1926–) to describe as a problem of interest that which is normally not seen as a problem because it is taken for granted. By bracketing one's own membership in the world, a researcher makes the common-sense and taken-for-granted world problematic. By making the everyday and ordinary problematic, a researcher is able to uncover the structure and dynamic of the everyday. *See also* **Smith, Dorothy.**

problem population As capitalism matures and more investment is made in technology than in labour, workers become increasingly surplus to the economic engine. Some of these people become problems in relation to the stability of the society and require increasing social control. Reference: Spitzer, S. (1975). Toward a Marxian Theory of Deviance. *Social Problems*, 22, 638–651.

profession The sociology of work sees a number of occupations evolving over time and becoming professions. All professions are thus occupations, but not all occupations are professions. A profession is an occupational group that is largely self-regulating. Such a group has the legitimate authority (usually delegated from government) to set its own standards for entrance, to admit new members, to establish a code of conduct, and to discipline members. The group claims to have a body of knowledge (achieved through education) that legitimizes its autonomy and distinctiveness. Examples of professions include physicians, lawyers, clinical psychologists, and real estate agents. Other groups, such as nurses and police officers, can be seen as having some of these attributes and can be described as *professionalizing*—in the process of becoming a profession.

progress A relatively new concept in Western thought and somewhat reminiscent of Herbert Spencer's notion of evolution, progress is a Victorian idea and is built on the assumption that a pattern of development can be found in human life and that there is an irresistible movement toward improvement. It is this faith in progress that allows us to sustain policies that might look as though they are going to be disastrous; we always believe that things will get better. Reference: Pollard, Sidney. (1968). *The Idea of Progress: History and Society*. London: C.A. Watts.

Progressive Conservative Party of Canada Canada's longest established political party until its merger with the Canadian Alliance Party in 2003, the Progressive Conservative Party originally developed from a Liberal–Conservative coalition that took office in the Province of Canada in 1854. Conservative John A. Macdonald (later Sir John) was a member of the coalition and led the Liberal–Conservatives at the time of Confederation in 1867. After Macdonald's government fell in 1873 as a result of a financial scandal, the party dropped the "Liberal" part of its name and became simply the Conservative Party. A separate Liberal Party also emerged. In 1942, Manitoba Premier John Bracken, who had led a Progressive Party government, won the leadership of the federal Conservative Party, which, at his insistence, had changed its name to the Progressive Conservative Party of Canada. The Liberals are the only other party to have formed Canada's governments since Confederation. *See also* **Conservative Party of Canada; Liberal Party of Canada.**

Progressive Party A Canadian political party formed in the early part of the 20th century, the Progressive Party came into prominence in the federal election of 1922 and in several provincial elections. The party was a broad coalition of social reform groups, including some farmers' and some women's groups. In 1942, the federal Conservative Party changed its name to the Progressive Conservative Party, because Premier John Bracken, long-time leader of Manitoba's Progressive Party, agreed to become leader of the Conservative Party only if the word *Progressive* was added to its name.

progressive taxation A taxation structure that progressively increases the percentage of a citizen's income (or wealth) that is paid in tax as income (or wealth) increases, progressive taxation should result in the more well-off being taxed at a higher rate than are the less well-off. Canadian income taxation is progressive, although recent changes in taxation regulations have made it somewhat less progressive than before. *See also* **flat tax; regressive taxation**.

progressivism Progressivism was a political philosophy that characterized American society from approximately 1890 to 1920. Set against decades of expansion and growth, progressives became acutely aware of the price paid for this development in terms of inequality and social problems. To address these, they called for policy committed to social justice and social democracy. They found new sympathy for the poor, for minorities, and for women and children. To address the needs of these peoples, it saw a need for a strong central government and increasing regulation of many segments of the business world. These attitudes about the role of the state are sometimes referred to as *progressive liberalism* (in contrast to classical liberalism). *See also* **classical economic theory; classical liberalism**.

proletariat A term associated with German-born social philosopher, political economist, and sociologist Karl Marx (1818–1883), *proletariat* refers to the class of individuals in a capitalist society who have no means of production of their own and must subsist economically by selling wage labour to owners of capital. In Marxist sociology, it is assumed that this working class will engage in economic and political struggles with owners of capital and eventually develop class solidarity and revolutionary class consciousness.

proportional representation An electoral system in which the number of seats won is directly linked to the number of votes cast for each party is proportional representation. Examples include Israel, Germany, and, since 1996, New Zealand. In Germany, each voter casts one ballot to elect a constituency representative and one ballot for a party;

parties must win at least 5% of the vote before receiving an allocation of parliamentary seats. In Canada, a simple plurality system is used—the individual receiving the largest number of votes is elected in each constituency. This system leads to persistent disproportion between seats won by parties and the votes cast for them. For example, in 1993, the Reform Party won 19% of the total vote and more than 50 seats, while the Progressive Conservative Party, with just over 16% of the vote, gained only two seats. It is suggested that in a federal system such as Canada's, proportional representation would further weaken the power of the central government.

prostitution The regulation of the market exchange of sexual services (prostitution) has long been achieved through criminal law. In Canada, prior to 1985, the *Criminal Code* made soliciting illegal, and the prohibition was more specifically aimed at "persistent" behaviour. That is, prostitutes had to make a nuisance of themselves (refusing to take "no" for an answer) before law enforcement could be invoked. After 1985, Canadian law prohibited communicating in a public place for the purposes of prostitution. This infringement of free speech was upheld by the Supreme Court in 1990, and many believe has forced prostitutes into more dangerous parts of the community in order to seek clients. In British Columbia, for example, there were one or two murders of prostitutes a year prior to 1985 and as many as five a year after implementation of the new law. Reference: Boritch, H. (1997). *Fallen Women: Female Crime and Justice in Canada*. Toronto: Nelson. *See also* **vagrancy**.

Protestant ethic The Protestant ethic, or set of ideas, emerged in the 16th century and was cited by German sociologist Max Weber (1864–1920) as an important influence in encouraging the development of capitalist society. For Protestants, particularly those influenced by the ideas of French reformer and theologian John Calvin (1509–1564), obedience to God's will demanded energetic and enterprising work in one's occupation or "calling." Profits were morally justified as the reward for this hard work and, as long as they were not casually squandered on luxuries, the making of profit and the achievement of wealth was a just reward for dutiful and energetic work. Weber argued that the Protestant ethic was so strongly supportive of capitalist development that countries where Protestantism became dominant quickly moved ahead of Catholic countries in their level of economic development. Weber claimed that the Catholic Church, in contrast, promoted ideas and attitudes that tended to obstruct economic development. Catholic doctrine stressed the importance of humility and acceptance of one's position in life; it discouraged pursuit of achievement by suggesting that seeking self-advancement was a distraction from the pursuit of a good and moral life in preparation for eternal life after death. Reference: Weber, M. (1904). *The Protestant Ethic and the Spirit of Capitalism.* New York: Charles Scribner and Sons [1958].

proxemics The term *proxemics*, the study of the human use of space within the context of culture, was coined by U.S. anthropologist Edward T. Hall (1914–).

psychoanalytic theory Associated with its founder, psychoanalyst Sigmund Freud (1856–1939), psychoanalytic theory is essentially the concept that many illnesses and neurotic fixations in adults are caused by traumatic infantile experiences in emotional and sexual development. By using means such as dream analysis and free association of words and symbols to help recall earliest memories and emotions, the process of psychoanalysis takes the adult back in time to confront and hopefully resolve the effects of these early negative experiences.

psychological reductionism The process of reducing all social activity and behaviour to the psychological characteristics of the human actors involved, psychological reductionism eliminates the possibility of sociology, since it denies that there is anything greater than the individual. Society is simply an aggregation of individuals. French sociologist Émile Durkheim (1858–1917) argued against this in his study of suicide and demonstrated that even after providing a psychological explanation for individual acts of suicide, there was something still to account for—the difference in suicide rates between societies. This, he showed, was derived from characteristics of the society and could not be explained as dependent on individual psychological characteristics.

psychologism *See* **methodological individualism; psychological reductionism**.

psychopath Although there is dispute about whether the term *psychopath* describes an authentic psychiatric condition, it is typically classified under "per-sonality disorder." Psychopaths tend to be lacking in what is considered conscience, are unable to form emotional attachments (even with friends and family), are quite impulsive, and are totally self-interested. There is also considerable debate about whether a psychopath can be changed.

psychotherapy A treatment technique for mental disorders or other problems, psychotherapy involves the verbalization of a patient's problem, getting the patient to talk about his or her life, childhood, etc. This form of treatment works best with patients with good verbal skills and thus is used quite frequently with middle-class patients.

public health model Unlike a "crime control model," which focuses on punishment or moralizing with the offender, a public health model looks at particular kinds of crime (often drug abuse, prostitution, and youth violence) as public health issues. A public health officer takes a very different view of crime than does a police constable. The public health model encourages us to think of ways to stop the spread of drug abuse or violence, for example, or how to prevent drug abusers from harming themselves or spreading infection to the community, or on initiating education programs in schools to teach young people how to recognize the possible onset of violence, how to prevent it, who to call if violence is experienced, etc.

public sector The part of the economy that is owned or controlled by the public, usually through government agencies, is the public sector. Most schooling is part of the public sector, as are hospitals, provision of social services, and some transit services. The more substantial portion of the economy consists of the private sector—those economic activities controlled or owned by private individuals, either directly or through stock ownership. *See also* **private sector; privatization**.

punishment Punishment is a negative sanction imposed on the violator of a system of rules by an authorized agent of that system of rules. The criminal courts can punish people for their violations of criminal law, the referee can punish those who violate the rules of a game of hockey, and the principal can punish students who violate rules of the school. Reference: Garland, David. (1990). *Punishment and Modern Society: A Study in Social Theory.* Chicago: University of Chicago Press.

Q

qualitative research Research using methods such as participant observation or case studies that result in a narrative, descriptive account of a setting or practice is qualitative research. Sociologists using these methods typically reject positivism and adopt a form of interpretive sociology. In anthropology, this method is associated with ethnography. Reference: Denizen, N. (1997). *Interpretative Ethnography.* Thousand Oaks, CA: Sage. *See also* **ethnographic research; quantitative research**.

quantitative research Quantitative research uses methods that allow for the measurement of variables within a collection of people or groups and result in numerical data subjected to statistical analysis. By its very nature, this is a form of positivism. Reference: Babbie, E., & Benaquisto, L. (2002). *Fundamentals of Social Research.* Toronto: Nelson. *See also* **qualitative research; variables.**

quasi-experiment A research design having some but not all of the characteristics of a true experiment is a quasi-experiment. The element most frequently missing is random assignment of subjects to the control and experimental conditions. Examples of this research design are the natural experiment (where nature has assigned subjects to the two conditions) or trend analysis.

queer culture The word *queer* was a derogatory term for many years, but has now been appropriated by a radical ("in your face") section of the gay and lesbian community to identify gay and lesbian culture or studies, which are becoming as legitimate in the academic community as women's studies or Black studies. Cultural studies examine gay and lesbian culture as depicted in the writings, films, and artwork of the community, and analyze the public identity of this cultural community. *See also* **cultural studies; identity politics**.

Question Period A daily occurrence in the House of Commons, a 45-minute Question Period is provided for members of Parliament to ask questions of government ministers. Questions are usually directed from the Opposition benches and are intended to highlight criticism of government actions and policies. Attended by the media and televised, Question Period provides the best opportunity for the Opposition parties to exercise their role as critics of the government.

Quiet Revolution A period of rapid social change in Quebec symbolized by the 1960 election defeat of the conservative rural-dominated Union Nationale by Jean Lesage and the Liberals on a policy of modernization and nationalism, the Quiet Revolution resulted in the unleashing of modern liberal ideas and the transformation of social institutions such as schooling, the family, politics, and government to reflect those values. These changes led to a decline in the influence of the church, an increased divorce rate, a decreased birth rate, the creation of modern universities and schools, and expansion of the role of government in society. The dynamic new role of government became a focus for the nationalist aspirations of the Quebec people. In 1976, the Parti Québécois was elected, leading to a 1980 referendum on the issue of changing Quebec's position within Canada from that of a province like the others to some form of sovereignty-association. This referendum was defeated; a second, conducted in 1995 on a question of separation with some form of continued economic association, was also defeated, but by a margin of less than 1%.

Quinney, Richard U.S. social philosopher Richard Quinney is associated with critical criminology and the movement for restorative justice and healing rather than coercion and retribution. Like other critical theorists, he located the genesis of law and the mode of its administration in the conflict of group interests in society. The groups that are socially dominant are then able to use their power to impose their own concepts of law and of crime on others. In this perspective, harsh criminal penalties for property offences and lenient penalties for corporate crime are explained as state coercion to maintain the domination of some social groups and classes over others. Thus, law is about political relations rather than consensual social regulation, and law violation is often best viewed as a political act. Reference: Quinney, Richard. (1977). *Class, State and Crime: On the Theory and Practice of Criminal Justice.* New York: D. McKay Co.; Quinney, Richard, R., & Pepinsky, Harold E. (Eds.). (1991). *Criminology as Peacemaking.* Bloomington: Indiana University Press.

R

Rabe, John *See* **rape of Nanking**.

race *Race* is a classification of human beings into different categories on the basis of their biological characteristics. There have been a variety of schemes for race classification based on physical characteristics such as skin colour, head shape, eye colour and shape, nose size and shape, etc. A common classification system uses four major groups: Caucasoid, Mongoloid, Negroid, and Australoid. The term was once popular in anthropology, but has now fallen into disrepute, because the idea of racial classification has become associated with racism—the claim that there is a hierarchy of races. The idea of race categories also appears to be unscientific, since humans are able to mate across all "races" and have done so throughout history, creating an enormous variety of human genetic inheritance. In addition, the defining characteristics of "race" do not appear in all members of each so-called race, but merely occur with some degree of statistical frequency. If the defining characteristic of each "race" does not appear in all members of each "race," then the entire definition is clearly inadequate. Reference: Graves, J.L. (2001). *The Emperor's New Clothes: Biological Theories of Race at the Millennium.* New Brunswick, NJ: Rutgers University Press.

racial profiling Using race as a search characteristic when looking for offenders is called *racial profiling.* The police, for example, are sometimes accused of assuming that Blacks are more likely to commit crimes than are whites and therefore stop more Blacks while driving or on the street in the hope of catching criminals. Research by the University of Toronto has revealed that this is what in fact happens. "Bad" Black kids and "bad" white kids were equally likely to be stopped by the police; however, "good" Black kids were much more likely to be stopped than were "good" white kids. Racial profiling is a very controversial practice, and the police usually deny that they engage in it. Reference: Ontario Human Rights Commission. (1993). *Paying the Price: The Human Cost of Racial Profiling.* Toronto: Queen's Printer.

racism Racism is a form of discrimination based on race, especially the belief that one race is superior to another. It is based on the idea that humans can be separated into distinct racial groups, and that these groups can be ranked in a hierarchy of intelligence, ability, morality, etc. *See also* **ethnocentrism; race.**

radical feminism Radical feminism is relatively recent and differs from traditional Marxism in arguing that women's oppression is historically primary, harder to transform, causes more harm, and is more widespread than class oppression. Similarly, it is argued that women's oppression provides a model for understanding other forms of oppression, such as racism and class domination. Some radical feminists claim that women's oppression is rooted in biology, and its elimination will require a biological revolution, transforming women's relation to reproduction. Within criminology, they focus on documenting and analyzing ways in which the content of law and practices of law enforcement have served to entrench and strengthen male dominance in society. *See also* **feminism; liberal feminism.**

radiocarbon analysis A method of absolute dating in archaeology, radiocarbon analysis uses the amount of radioactive carbon left in organic materials to indicate the age of an object. Since organic material absorbs radioactive carbon (carbon-14), the more radioactive carbon there is, the older the item is. This method is useful for objects up to 70,000 years old but does not give a specific, absolute age; there is always a margin of error. This method was developed by U.S. physical chemist Willard Libby (1908–1980) in 1955.

Ramona case Napa Valley, California, resident Gary Ramona, charged with the sexual abuse of his daughter, who recovered her memory of these events through therapy, won the opportunity to sue the therapist in 1994 for the harm done to him. For the first time, the issue of "recovered memory" was on trial. After a bitter court battle, Gary Ramona won, and the recovered memory movement suffered a serious setback. Hundred of cases have gone before the courts based on recovered memory, but in general terms, the courts have not been very sympathetic to these claims. Reference: Johnston, Moira. (1997). *Spectral Evidence: The Ramona Case: Incest, Memory and Truth on Trial in Napa Valley.* Boulder, CO: Westview Press.

random In the social sciences, random sampling means that every element in a population has an *equal,* and knowable, chance of being selected for the sample. *See also* **randomization.**

randomization In the classic experiment, randomization (or random assignment) is necessary, requiring that subjects be assigned in a random manner to the control group and the experimental group. This randomization results in all other variables being randomly distributed among the two groups, thus controlling for spurious relationships.

rape The original meaning of the term *rape* was to steal or carry off the belongings of another. As women were considered the property of men (their fathers or their husbands) and virginity was all-important prior to marriage, sexual assault or even sex outside of marriage could be considered a violation of the man's property. The *Statute of Westminster* (1275) formalized this offence and laid the foundation that carried forward into modern times. It made rape an offence against the state, introduced the notion of statutory rape (sexual intercourse with a child with or without consent), declared that unless a woman resisted the attack she was partially responsible, and proclaimed that a husband could not be charged with rape of his wife. Until 1982, rape was a criminal offence in Canada and was defined as the offence of forcible sexual intercourse, involving penetration, with someone who has withheld consent, or, in the case of consent, with someone whose consent has been obtained by threat, impersonation, or misrepresentation of the nature of the act. Feminist critiques of this law and changes to Canada's *Criminal Code* resulted in the offence of rape being replaced with three levels of sexual assault offences: Level 1 involves minor physical injuries or no injuries to the victim. It carries a maximum sentence of 10 years' imprisonment. Level 2 involves sexual assault with a weapon, threats, or causing bodily harm. It carries a maximum sentence of 14 years' imprisonment. Level 3 involves wounding, maiming, disfiguring, or endangering the life of the victim. The maximum sentence for this offence is life imprisonment.

rape of Nanking Japan declared war on China in 1931 as part of what is called the Sino-Japanese War, and remained in China until 1945, occupying up to two-thirds of the country. It is estimated that 10 million to 30 million Chinese were killed during this time. This period of occupation is notorious for the brutality of the occupying forces, with countless examples of atrocities similar to the Nazi treatment of the Jews. In December 1937, Japanese forces entered the city of Nanking, resulting in the death of 200,000 to 300,000 local citizens and the rape of at least 20,000 women. In one of the extraordinary events of the war, the de facto German consul in Nanking, businessman John Rabe (1882–1950), a member of Germany's Nazi party, led the creation of international safety zones for refugees from the violence, which is estimated to have saved the lives of perhaps as many as 200,000 Chinese people. At one time, he sheltered 600 people in his own house, symbolically secured beneath a huge Nazi flag bearing the swastika. The Chinese see in this history the second holocaust of World War II, except there is little international recognition of the events of this period. After decades of denying the truth about the massacre and violence, the Japanese issued an apology in 1995 and offered recompense for surviving prisoners of war. It is claimed that the United States reached agreement with Japan after the war whereby, for the exchange of Japanese knowledge of germ warfare, the international community would ignore the atrocities. The events of this period still poison relations between China and Japan. Reference: Chang, Iris. (1997). *The Rape of Nanking: The Forgotten Holocaust of World War II.* New York: Basic Books. *See also* **Peking Man**.

rate When studying crime, if a researcher wants to compare the amount of crime over time or between communities of different sizes, it is not adequate to do a gross count of the amount of crime because the population bases may be different. To get around the problems involved with this, criminologists calculate crime rates (or incarceration rates, conviction rates, and recidivism rates). This is done by dividing the amount of crime by the population size and multiplying by 100,000. This produces a rate per 100,000, but occasionally it is useful to calculate a rate per million or some other figure.

ratio measures *See* **level of measurement**.

rational choice theory Rational choice theory is a theory of criminal behaviour that is found in the classical school of criminology and was widely accepted during the last quarter of the twentieth century. Rather than seeing some abnormality in offenders that distinguishes them from other citizens, rational choice theory argues that offenders are making a rational choice to commit crime after having examined the likelihood of being caught or convicted. These assumptions about behaviour are the foundation on which deterrence as a philosophy of punishment is built. *See also* **classical criminology; deterrence**.

rationalization This term has two specific meanings in sociology: (1) The concept was developed by

German sociologist Max Weber (1864–1920) who used it in two ways. First, it was the process through which magical, supernatural, and religious ideas lose cultural importance in a society, and ideas based on science and practical calculation become dominant. For example, in modern societies, science has rationalized our understanding of weather patterns. Science explains weather patterns as being a result of interaction between physical elements such as wind speed and direction, air and water temperatures, humidity, etc. In some other cultures, weather is thought to express the pleasure or displeasure of gods or spirits of ancestors. One explanation is rationalized and scientific; the other, mysterious and magical. Rationalization also involves the development of forms of social organization devoted to the achievement of precise goals by efficient means. It is this type of rationalization that we see in the development of modern business corporations and of bureaucracy. These are organizations dedicated to the pursuit of defined goals by calculated, systematically administered means. (2) Within symbolic interactionism, rationalization is used more in the everyday sense of the word to refer to providing justifications or excuses for one's actions. *See also* **accounts**.

reaction formation A psychological mechanism, reaction formation emerges when failure is imminent. U.S. sociologist Albert K. Cohen (1918–), for example, found that lower-class boys often turned middle-class values, the very values causing them to fail, on their head. There was a certain degree of nihilism; rather than taking money to purchase things they needed, they might throw the money away, give it to others, or purchase useless articles. Or, rather than valuing a middle-class sofa, they might defecate on it.

Rebellions of 1837–1838 Rebellions occurred in both Upper and Lower Canada (and in many other parts of the world) in 1837–1838, with the main issue being the rejection of colonial rule and the demand for local, responsible government. In Lower Canada, an additional objective of rebellion was the desire to establish primacy for the Québécois nation within Canada. British troops put down the rebellion, often rather brutally, and this event is seen by many as the reconquest of the Québécois (a repeat of the battle of the Plains of Abraham, 1759), which stimulated the growth of Quebec nationalism. *See also* ***Durham Report***.

recall A petition process that allows voters to demand a new election and force an elected member to give up his or her seat, the recall provision has been adopted in British Columbia. A successful recall requires signatures of 40% of the voters who were on the voters list at the time of the last election. So far, the threshold of signatures required has proven too high for recall to succeed.

reciprocity The exchange of goods or services of approximately the same value between two parties is called *reciprocity*. Anthropologists distinguish between generalized reciprocity, where little attention is paid to the value of the goods given nor to the time frame of repayment, and balanced reciprocity, where giving and future receiving are specific in terms of value and time. We can think of this in terms of the exchange of Christmas or birthday gifts. Austrian economist Karl Polanyi (1886–1964) saw reciprocity as one of three principles structuring all economies.

recovered memory *See* **memory, recovered**.

redress agreement In 1988, the federal government of Canada signed a redress agreement with representatives of the Japanese Canadians who were interned, removed from their homes, or had their property confiscated during World War II. The agreement contained an apology, individual compensation for survivors, and public funds for community development. *See also* **internment**.

Red River Rebellion The Red River Rebellion was a revolt during 1869–1870 of the settlers and Métis of what is now Manitoba. In 1867–1868, the Government of Canada negotiated the purchase of the lands owned by the Hudson's Bay Company without consulting with the residents of the territories involved (the largest group were French-speaking Métis). This annexation led to fears, particularly among the French-speaking and Catholic Métis, that language, religious, and education rights would be lost. The residents declared a provisional government in direct opposition to the federal government's wishes, leading to negotiations that resulted in the creation of the province of Manitoba and established French language rights, acknowledgment of the tenure of existing farms, and the promise of millions of acres of land to settle Métis land claims. Métis peoples prefer to refer to these events as acts of resistance rather than a rebellion. *See also* **Métis**; **Northwest Rebellion of 1885**.

Reefer Madness A film made in 1937, *Reefer Madness* depicted marijuana as a drug that produces madness and therefore was to be avoided and banned. While the film is humorous in hindsight, it was a powerful piece of propaganda at the time.

reference group A term from social psychology, *reference group* identifies that group to which people refer or make reference in evaluating themselves. One may make reference to "social science students" when contemplating what political party to vote for, or one might refer to "feminists" when deciding to change or not to change one's name after marriage.

referendum Used to refer political questions to an electorate for direct decision, referendums do not fit well with a parliamentary system of government. Canada has used them infrequently. The first referendum was in 1898 on a question of prohibition, and in 1942, the similar process of plebiscite was used on the matter of conscription. English-speaking Canada voted in support of allowing the government to use conscription, while French-speaking Canada voted against it, thus creating a crisis for government. A federal referendum was also held in 1992 to seek support for a constitutional change (the *Charlottetown Accord*); this was soundly defeated. Provincial governments have relied on referendums somewhat more often. Newfoundland, for example, held a referendum in 1948 on the question of entry into Confederation with Canada (it took two votes to win agreement, and then by only 52.3%); in 1988, the province of Prince Edward Island held a referendum on the question of whether a fixed link with mainland Canada should be established. In 1980, Quebec held a referendum on permission to negotiate sovereignty-association with the rest of Canada (this was defeated by 60% of voters), and a second referendum was held in Quebec in 1995 on a more direct question of separating from Canada (this was rejected by 51% of the voters).

reflexivity As used by ethnomethodologists, *reflexivity* means that an object or behaviour and its description cannot be separated one from the other; rather, they have a mirror-like relationship. Reflexivity and indexicality are properties of behaviour, settings, and talk that make the ongoing construction of social reality necessary. Both of these properties question the objectivity of accounts, descriptions, explanations, etc. An ethnographic description of a setting is reflexive in that the description seeks to explain features of a particular setting (e.g., village life), but the setting itself is what is employed to make sense of the description. *See also* **indexicality**.

Regina Manifesto The founding political program of the Co-operative Commonwealth Federation, adopted at a convention in Regina in 1933, the *Regina Manifesto* was strongly socialist and called for extensive nationalization and radical measures to promote equalization of wealth and incomes. In subsequent years, the party retreated from the radical goals of the *Manifesto* and, in 1956, this change of policy was made explicit in the *Winnipeg Declaration* and became embodied in the policies followed by the New Democratic Party, which succeeded the CCF in 1961.

Regina Riot During the depression, the federal government established work camps for unemployed men in hope of containing anger and frustration. Early in 1935, relief workers in British Columbia staged a strike in support of better living conditions and higher wages. In an attempt to force the government to take action, union organizers planned an "On-To-Ottawa" march. Prime Minister Richard Bennett ordered the march be brought to an end when it reached Regina. This resulted in a riot on July 1, 1935, in which one policeman was killed and at least 100 people were injured.

regression (analysis or line) A measure of association between two quantitative variables, the analysis or line regression form of statistical test is possible only with interval or ratio data. If an independent variable and a dependent variable are placed on the two axes of a graph with the actual data then scattered on the graph, it is possible to draw a line through the resulting points in a way that minimizes the distance between the points. The resulting line (which may be straight or curved) is a regression line. Any particular value for the dependent variable can then be predicted by multiplying the value of the independent variable by the regression coefficient (a number that determines the slope of the line).

regressive taxation Regressive taxation requires that the more well-off pay a lower percentage of their income (or wealth) in tax than a less well-off citizen. Sales tax and the federal goods and services tax (GST) are of this type, as these taxes remain constant regardless of one's income. The consequence is that the more well-off citizen pays a smaller percentage of income to cover the tax on a new refrigerator than does a less well-off person. *See also* **flat tax; progressive taxation**.

reification To treat as though real that which is just an abstraction or a conceptualization is called *reification*. Sociologists since the time of French sociologist Émile Durkheim (1858–1917) have been accused of reifying society, which critics say is just an abstract concept and does not exist. To act as though society exists and thus can act or make decisions or coerce people is to reify society.

reinforcement A process in which a behaviour is strengthened, reinforcement increases the probability that a response will occur by either presenting a contingent positive event or removing a negative event.

relations of production *See* **social relations of production**.

relative autonomy A theory of state power based on Marxist ideas, the relative autonomy perspective assumes that the state can and does play a limited independent role in the maintenance and stabilization of capitalist society. It differs from pluralism in viewing state power as strongly constrained by the ideological and structural characteristics of capitalist society. *See also* **structuralist approach**.

relative dating Relative dating means to date things only in relationship to others, to place in some kind of rank from oldest to newest. This method is not as useful as chronometric or absolute dating. There are three main methods of relative dating: stratigraphy, seriation, and fluorine test. *See also* **chronometric dating**.

relative deprivation Relative deprivation and absolute deprivation are often contrasted. *Absolute deprivation* refers to the inability to sustain oneself physically and materially. Some right-wing groups suggest that this is how Canada should define and measure poverty. Rather, Canada uses a form of relative deprivation: Deprivation is not judged against some absolute standard of sustainability, but of deprivation in relation to others around you. You may have sufficient money to meet your needs and even meet them adequately, but feel relatively deprived.

reliability One of the standards (another being validity) against which the tools used to measure concepts are judged, *reliability* refers to consistency of results over time. If a bathroom scale is used to measure the concept of weight, one must ask: Is this tool (the bathroom scale) reliable? Does it provide consistent results? To check this, get back on the scale a second time to see if it produces the same results. Notice that the bathroom scale may be reliable and yet be inaccurate. Are IQ tests a reliable measure of intelligence? Are official suicide statistics reliable measures of the suicide rate? Are questions about which political party a person would vote for a reliable measure of political preference? Since in many of these examples it is difficult to assume, as in the case of weight, that the results would remain the same over time, it may be more correct to think of reliability as indicating consistency of results among users of the tool or measurement. *See also* **validity**.

religion Religion is an organized system of beliefs about the supernatural or the spiritual world and the associated ceremonies. There are two primary approaches to religion in anthropology. The first, an intellectualist tradition, argues that people adopt religious beliefs as a way to explain natural events in the world. The other approach, the symbolist, portrayed in the work of French sociologist Émile Durkheim (1858-1917), sees religion making symbolic statements about the world. Durkheim saw religion as being a symbol of aspects of human society, so that worship of God is really worship of society itself. Reference: Wallace, A.F.C. (1966). *Religion: An Anthropological View*. New York: Random House. *See also* **sacred–profane**.

religiosity The degree to which one believes in and is involved in religion is known as *religiosity*; for example, attending church, volunteering for the church, giving donations to the church, and believing in the values, morals, and mythology of the religion.

religious right Found more frequently in the United States than in Canada (where its influence is chiefly located in the Conservative party), the *religious right* refers to groups or individuals who combine the economic conservatism of classical liberalism (beliefs in free market economies, small government, and autonomy of the individual) with the socially conservative views of many fundamentalist religions (e.g., they are against abortion, intolerant of homosexuality, and nonsupportive of single mothers, and they propose censorship of children's reading material and recommend reducing rights of criminal offenders, etc.). Since these groups support an economic doctrine that is gaining wide acceptance, they are able to move into positions of power and influence, and their social views are giving shape to many aspects of life. *See also* **neo-conservatism.**

renewable resource A resource that can be exploited without depletion because it is constantly replenished, examples of renewable resources include forest resources, fisheries, naturally occurring food crops, and the fertility of agricultural land. There is heated debate in Canada about where to set the appropriate levels of resource use to make them compatible with long-term renewal.

republic This term has come to mean a society where there is no hereditary or appointed monarch or emperor as head of state. Originally, it referred to a system of political rule where citizens, through representative institutions, participated in government and exercised political power. This meaning derives from the original Latin *res publica*, which means *the public thing*, those things that are connected to ruling the public realm. In its narrower meaning, the term distinguishes Canada, Britain, Norway, Sweden, Denmark, the Netherlands, Thailand, and other countries formally headed by monarchs from France, Italy, Germany, the United States, and many others where the head of state is a president, either directly elected or appointed by an elected assembly.

reserve army of labour In Marxian analysis, the reserve army of labour is that segment of the labour force that is held in reserve, to be called into the work force when need arises. If there was no reserve labour, it might be difficult for new businesses to open or for temporary or emergency projects to be undertaken in the economy. In addition, labour shortage would create upward pressure on wages and increase union power. This reserve labour, of course, needs to be doing something during the period it is held in reserve, so it may be on welfare or working in the household. The term has been useful for understanding women's relationship to the work force. During the economic boom of the 1960–1970s, women entered the work force in large numbers, and there is fear that they will be the first fired during recessions (although this appears not to have happened in the 1990s recession.) Women, young people, and the elderly may all be thought of as reserve labour, since they have traditionally stayed out of the labour force.

reserves Pieces of land set aside, or reserved, for a designated group are called *reserves*. In Canada, as the Anglo-Europeans colonized the land and occupied territories previously inhabited by native peoples, they designated lands for native groups. Although reserved for native bands, the lands remained the property of the Crown. In Canada, there are 576 native bands recognized by the government and 2,281 reserves (often called *reservations*) as well as some Crown land settlements set aside for these peoples. These figures reveal a distinct Canadian pattern of creating reserves—many small reserves were created and typically distributed among the larger nonnative population. All of the reserve lands in Canada add up to only one-half of the Navajo reserve in Arizona.

residential schools Widely established across Canada during the 19th and 20th centuries, particularly in the north, residential schools were established to bring basic education to native and Inuit children. In effect, as well as in intent, these schools served to isolate the young from their own people and became an instrument of attempted cultural assimilation of aboriginal peoples into white European culture. Forced attendance at these schools, which were largely church-run, broke the cultural continuity of aboriginal communities and led to the loss of traditional knowledge, skills, and languages. Today, they are seen as an example of colonial attitudes toward native peoples, and it has become apparent that they often caused great harm by inflicting psychological and physical isolation and abuse on generations of aboriginal children. Many native groups have struggled to have churches acknowledge the harm done and to institute healing programs, and have pressured the federal government to acknowledge its role in this process. In addition, local programs of healing have been developed, and native communities and the broader society have had to come to terms with the legacy of residential schools.

resocialization Resocialization is a profound change or transformation of personality arising from being placed in a situation or environment no longer conducive to maintaining a previous identity. Some choose this kind of transformation by entering a monastery or nunnery, while others have it forced on them by being sentenced to penitentiary. The new identity is a product of these environments and comes from interacting with others and performing the roles required in these settings. *See also* **institution, total.**

R

responsible government A defining principle of parliamentary systems such as Canada's, responsible government requires that the government must always have the support of the legislature. This principle is behind the convention of a government resigning when it loses a confidence vote in the House of Commons. *See also* **confidence vote**.

restorative justice Beginning from the assumptions that the fabric of personal and social life has been damaged by a crime, restorative justice argues that the criminal justice system should be about mediation and conflict resolution in order to restore the emotional well-being and feelings of security of the victim and to repair the damaged social relationships within the community. Reference: Church Council on Justice and Corrections. (1996). *Satisfying Justice*. Ottawa: Church Council on Justice and Corrections.

restructuring *Restructuring* usually refers to the reorganization and rationalization of administration and production in both public and private sectors. In the public sector, it has been encouraged by periods of growing deficits; in the private sector, cost-cutting and reorganization have been encouraged by high interest rates, recession, and lower corporate profit margins.

retribution Deriving from the notions of *retribute* (to give back or return) or to *receive in recompense* and the Christian sense of *deserved, adequate,* or *fit, retribution* is now used exclusively to refer to punishment deserved because of an offence, which must fit with the severity of the offence. Punishment is justified because it makes the offender give up money, personal freedom, or comfort that is equivalent to the harm or loss done to others. Retribution must be distinguished from revenge and retaliation.

retributive justice *See* **distributive justice**.

reverse discrimination Meaning discrimination against a privileged group in order to correct previous discrimination against a disadvantaged group, the accusation of *reverse discrimination* is often directed against those favouring equity programs or affirmative action programs. *See also* **affirmative action**.

revitalization movement Found throughout history, revitalization movements attempt to re-create a culture based on beliefs about an idealized past. These movements have often grown up in response to European colonization, but other examples can be found (such as Mormonism). *See also* **cargo cult; Ghost Dance**.

Riel, Louis (1844–1885) A Métis leader who was executed for treason on November 16, 1885, in Regina, Riel played a pivotal role in the development of Métis and First Nations politics and was actively involved in the Northwest Rebellion and the Red River Rebellion. His execution continues to haunt the political corridors of Canada and leads to periodic requests for an apology or even a finding of wrongful conviction. Reference: Stanley, George F.G. (1963). *Louis Riel*. Toronto: Ryerson Press.

rights, civil Rights designed to protect citizens of a nation from abuse by their governments, civil rights typically derive from citizenship.

rights, human Human rights are deemed to be inherent for all humans and thus not derived from constitutions, courts, or laws. They may, however, be codified in treaties, such as the United Nations *Universal Declaration of Human Rights*. Reference: Ignatieff, Michael. (2000). *The Rights Revolution*. Toronto: Anansi. *See also* **Universal Declaration of Human Rights**.

rites of passage The ritual or ceremonial acknowledgment of a person's passage from one stage of life to the next, examples of rites of passage include a graduation ceremony or a retirement party. Many cultures provide a ritualized acknowledgment of the passage to adulthood, but sociologists note that this has all but disappeared from modern societies.

ritual An action performed because of its symbolic significance and its ability to evoke the emotions of those engaged in the performance, a ritual is usually clearly specified by the group, and there are additional rules about who can perform the ritual, and when the ritual should be performed. Ritual may be important in maintaining the values of a group or in strengthening group ties. Examples of ritual include communion, aspects of the marriage ceremony, or singing the national anthem before sports events. Reference: Rappaport, R.A. (1999). *Holiness and humanity: Ritual in the making of religious life*. New York: Cambridge University Press.

Rodriguez, Sue Sue Rodriguez, a 42-year-old woman living in British Columbia, was afflicted with amyotrophic lateral sclerosis (ALS), or Lou Gehrig's disease, which was eventually going to take her life. Wanting to maintain control over her life, but because of her disability unable to take action herself, she petitioned the Supreme Court to allow someone to assist her in taking her life without facing criminal charges. In a decision on September 29, 1993, the court denied her request. On February 12, 1994, with assistance, Rodriguez took her own life. Member of Parliament Svend Robinson admitted to being present, along with an unnamed doctor, but police did not further investigate the event.

Roe v. Wade *See* **abortion**.

role A position, or status, within a social structure that is shaped by relatively precise behavioural expectations (norms), a role has been described as the active component of status. The individual, placed within a status in a social structure, performs a role in a way shaped by normative expectations. Individuals have varying ideas about normative standards and their own unique values, so role behaviour is not standardized; however, radical departure from expected role behaviour will usually result in social sanctions.

role convergence One explanation for the rising crime rate among women is that their roles have converged with (become similar to) those of men.

role distancing The act of presenting your "self" as being removed or at a distance from the role you are being required to play is role distancing, a concept from dramaturgical sociology. For example, by keeping your eyes open when asked to pray or say grace, you communicate to the group that you are making no commitment to the role. *See also* **presentation of self**.

role-playing Role-playing, in which an individual plays at or pretends to occupy the role of another, is useful for understanding the socialization of children and in particular that stage during which they play at being mothers, fathers, doctors, nurses, or truck drivers. It is during this playing that they master the ability to engage in reflexive role-taking and thus develop their own sense of self. *See also* **role-taking, reflexive**.

role strain Role strain is said to occur when fulfilling a certain role conflicts with fulfilling another role. For example, carrying the load of housework and child care while holding down a paying job could result in a woman feeling guilty about time spent away from her children (her mother role).

role-taking, reflexive Looking at your own role performance from the perspective of another person is reflexive role-taking. In taking the viewpoint of another, you are able to see yourself as an object, as

if from the outside. When we ask: "Am I talking too much?" or "Am I being responsible?" we are engaging in reflexive role-taking: We are using outside standards—the point of view of another—to look at ourselves.

role theory, gender Gender role theory holds that women's lesser involvement in crime can be attributed to their socialization into traditional roles within the family and in society.

royal assent A Bill passed by a legislature does not become law (a statute) until it has been approved by the governor general (federal) or lieutenant governor (provincial), the royal representatives in Canada, thereby gaining royal assent. This stage of law-making is largely symbolic in nature.

Royal Commission on Aboriginal Peoples A commission of inquiry established by the Conservative government in 1991, the Royal Commission on Aboriginal Peoples was a strategy to obtain First Nations' support for constitutional change after the *Meech Lake Accord* was defeated in 1990 by Elijah Harper, an aboriginal member of the Manitoba legislature. The commission made its report in 1996, having examined a wide range of matters affecting aboriginal peoples. The report has the potential to help Canadians redefine the relationship between First Nations peoples and the government, although few of its recommendations have been implemented. Reference: Royal Commission on Aboriginal Peoples. (1993). *Aboriginal Peoples and the Justice System.* Ottawa: Minister of Supply and Services.

Royal Commission on the Non-Medical Use of Drugs *See* **Le Dain Commission**.

Royal Commission on the Status of Women *See* ***Status of Women Report***.

Royal Proclamation of 1763 This proclamation, signed by King George III, provides the basis of native land rights in North America. Signed at the conclusion of the Seven Years' War, at which time the French signed over much of North America to the British, the document proclaims British rule over the territory. The contents of this proclamation are significant. It acknowledges preexisting ownership of land by native peoples: It stated that Indian land could only be bought or treated for by the British government, it established a procedure for obtaining land, and it used the term "Nations or Tribes of Indians." These provisions provide a powerful legal foundation for current disputes over land rights. This royal proclamation has an entirely different significance for the Québécois, since it was intended to make the colony of Canada with a British mould: British civil and criminal law was imposed on the Québécois and Catholics were virtually prohibited from holding public office.

rule of law One of the cornerstones of democratic society, rule of law means that everyone is subject to the law. It is not just the rule that everyone is covered by the *Criminal Code* and must be charged and convicted if appropriate; it also means that no one in the society, the prime minister, Cabinet, senior civil servants, judges, or police has power except as it is derived from law. Authority can come only from law, namely the *Constitution*, a statute, legal regulations, common law, or municipal bylaw. This is a rule of law rather than rule by individuals.

rule of thumb It is often claimed that in the "bad old days," men had the acknowledged right to beat their wives with a stick, just as long as the stick was no thicker than their thumb. However, there is no evidence that such a rule or understanding ever existed. In common usage, a "rule of thumb" is a term for methods of manufacture or measurement that are based on practical experience rather than theoretical knowledge.

Rwandan genocide In 1994, elements of the Hutu majority in Rwanda encouraged the massacre of the Tutsi minority group. Approximately one million Rwandans lost their lives. United Nations and Canadian peacekeepers under the leadership of Romeo Dallaire were in Rwanda at the time of the massacre and attempted to get greater intervention by the United Nations, but were required to stand by and watch the massacre when no action was taken to intervene in the rising tensions. Reference: Dallaire, Romeo. (2003). *Shake Hands with the Devil.* Toronto: Random House Canada.

S

sacred–profane French sociologist Émile Durkheim (1858–1917) claimed that all religions divide objects or phenomena into the sacred and the profane. Sacred objects are those that are extraordinary and are treated as if set apart from the routine course of events in daily life. The profane are those objects or phenomena seen as ordinary and constituting the reality of everyday living. Durkheim believed that the celebration of religious beliefs and sacred ritual united the community, integrating individuals, and that it enhanced the sharing of collective sentiments and solidarity in profane areas of social life. The secularization and rationalization of Western societies has reduced the realm of the sacred.

same-sex marriage On January 14, 2001, the first legal marriage of a homosexual couple occurred in Ontario, resulting from a lower court decision that the ban on same-sex marriages was a violation of equality rights. In July of 2002, the Ontario Supreme Court upheld the lower court decision and in June of 2003, this was again upheld by the Appeal Court. In May of 2003, the BC Court of Appeal ruled that limiting gay marriage was a violation of equality rights. In December 2004, the Supreme Court of Canada ruled that the federal government had the power to redefine marriage to include same-sex unions, but that religious groups could not be forced to perform such marriages. In 2005, the Government of Canada introduced the *Civil Marriage Act*, which would legalize same-sex marriages, and the Bill was passed in June of 2005. These events marked a rapid change from the June 8, 1999, vote in the House of Commons to preserve the traditional definition of marriage as being between one man and one woman.

sample When it is difficult to conduct a census of an entire population, a researcher will work with a portion of that population—a sample—that is thought to be representative of the population in question. Researchers typically try to ensure that a sample has been drawn in a random fashion. This ensures that the distribution of population characteristics corresponds to the assumptions of probability theory, allowing inferences to be drawn about the population. Many times, however, nonrandom samples are used.

sampling The sampling process—the method of drawing a sample from a population—can be based on random selection such that each member of the population has an equal probability of being selected (e.g., putting all the names into a hat). Many statistical tests assume a process of random selection. However, the method may not be based on random selection. You might, for example, select for convenience the first 100 people you meet or all of the students in an introductory criminology class.

sampling error Any sample is only one of many samples that could have been drawn from a population.

Consequently, a researcher may not get the same results with each sample (e.g., the mean or average might vary). As the sample becomes larger, this variation is less drastic, and the sampling error is smaller. Social scientists have ways of calculating the sampling error; you can see this in the news many times when a reporter says: "A survey of this size is accurate within 3.5%, 19 times out of 20." For example, the 3.5% is the sampling error; 95 times out of 100 times the mean would fall within +/− the mean or average reported.

sampling frame A sampling frame is the actual physical representation of a population (a voters list or a student class list, for example) from which a sample is actually drawn. A population is a somewhat abstract concept, while the sampling frame is the real listing of members of that population in a way that it is similar to placing names in a hat for purposes of random sampling.

sanction A positive or negative response by an individual or group to behaviour, a sanction is designed to encourage or discourage that behaviour. Positive sanction would include rewards, compliments, applause, or smiles, while negative sanctions would include punishments, frowns, avoidance, or gossip. Sanctions can be informal (coming from friends and neighbours) or formal (coming from authorized institutions like the police, the government, and the school), and must be seen as forms of social control.

Sapir, Edward (1884–1939) Edward Sapir was born in Lauenberg, Pomerania (Prussia), in what is now Lebork, Poland, and immigrated to the United States at an early age, where he became interested in anthropology, particularly native languages. In 1910, he went to Ottawa to head the newly established division of anthropology at the Canadian National Museum. Although quite unhappy in this position, he remained until 1925. *See also* **Sapir–Whorf hypothesis**.

Sapir-Whorf hypothesis The Sapir-Whorf hypothesis asserts that the concepts and structure of languages profoundly shape the perception and worldview of speakers. Rather than just being a means of expressing thought, language is claimed to form thought. Thus, people of different language communities will see and understand in different ways. Developed in the 1930s by German-born anthropologist Edward Sapir (1884–1939) and U.S. chemical engineer, linguist, and anthropologist

Benjamin Lee Whorf (1897–1941), one of Sapir's students, this hypothesis grew out of contact with the native languages of North America. Most sociologists regard the theory as too deterministic and stress the dynamic way in which language responds to social and technical transformation of society. *See also* **Sapir, Edward**.

scientific management A method of work organization, scientific management involves a specialized division of labour and sets out detailed instructions for the performance of work. The concept of scientific management is associated with the innovative methods introduced by U.S. engineer Frederick Taylor (1856–1915) to separate workers from their knowledge of the work process, to divide labour so as to pay only for the specific skill required to perform a narrow function, and to establish management as the controller of work and the work process. *See also* **industrial relations**; **Taylorism**.

scientific method The methods and techniques of investigation and analysis used in the sciences to develop theories and design experiments, scientific methods usually attempt to discover the causes of things and the relationships between variables. The key assumption of scientific method is that a claim or theory can be tested by discoverable and measurable evidence. Scientific experiment and research have led to the development of many laws: mechanics, electrical energy, light, transfer of heat, relativity, etc. The idea of scientific method has been influential in sociology, but scientific methods cannot be applied to many of the topics that interest sociologists, nor can they be strictly applied where they do have relevance. Generally, scientific method involves the steps of gathering of data, by observation and research; formulation of hypotheses; testing by experiment; replication of tests to ensure consistent results; and avoidance of personal bias and prejudgment. A theory or hypothesis must be stated in a testable form to have scientific status: It must be clear enough that it can be disproven. Early sociologists like French sociologist Auguste Comte (1798–1857) assumed that sociology would develop into a science of society equivalent to the natural sciences of physics and chemistry, and this view continued to be influential in the sociology of French sociologist Émile Durkheim (1858–1917). Modern sociologists tend to reject the idea that sociology can be scientific, but they do employ aspects of scientific method in trying to arrive at a rigorous and systematic understanding of aspects of society. *See also* **sociology of knowledge**.

Scott, Frank (Francis) While some may know Frank Scott (1899–1985) as having been a poet, he was also Canada's preeminent constitutional lawyer from 1940 through the 1960s. He argued important cases before the Supreme Court, assisted the newly elected Co-operative Commonwealth Federation government of Saskatchewan to write a *Bill of Rights*, and influenced the thinking of Pierre Trudeau, which resulted in the current *Canadian Charter of Rights and Freedoms*. Scott also represented the voice of English Canada on the Royal Commission on Bilingualism and Biculturalism. Reference: Djwa, Sandra. (1987). *A Life of F.R. Scott: The Politics of the Imagination*. Toronto: McClelland and Stewart. *See also* **padlock laws**.

secondary deviance As used by U.S. sociologist and anthropologist Edwin Lemert (1912–1996), *secondary deviance* refers to deviant behaviour that flows from a stigmatized sense of self; the deviance is thought to be consistent with the character of the self. A person's self can be stigmatized or tainted by public labelling. Secondary deviance is contrasted to primary deviance, which may be behaviourally identical to secondary deviance, but is incorporated into a "normal" sense of self. One may, for example, get drunk several times because one sees oneself as enjoying a party. However, if one notices that friends are hiding their liquor during visits to their house, one may come to see oneself as a "drunk," and then continue to get drunk because one *is* a drunk. The first acts are primary deviance and the second act is secondary deviance. Reference: Lemert, Edwin. (1951). *Social Pathology*. New York: McGraw-Hill.

secondary group *See* **group, secondary**.

secondary labour market Occupations that tend to be located in the most competitive areas of the economy and are more labour-intensive are considered to be the secondary labour market. These occupations tend to pay lower wages, have insecure employment, be less likely to be unionized, and provide less opportunity for advancement. Typical industries are restaurant and hotel services personnel, cashiers, and retail salespeople. This labour market has been dominated by women and minorities, while the primary labour market has been dominated by white males. The term *secondary labour market* was originally part of what

was referred to as *dual labour market theory*. The term *segmented labour market* is now used, but studies continue to find a significant dualism to the labour market, and this continues to be useful for understanding women's occupational location and their low wages relative to men. *See also* **dual labour market; primary labour market; segmented labour market**.

secondary sexual characteristics Characteristics that are sex-related but are not directly connected with the physiology of reproduction (the sex organs) are secondary sexual characteristics. For example, statistically, men tend to be heavier with more muscle mass and physical strength than women, although there are some women who are heavier, more muscular, and stronger than some men. *See also* **sexual dimorphism**.

second reading *See* **first reading**.

sect Usually contrasted with churches or denominations, sects are thought to be small and inward-looking religious or spiritual groups that reject the values of the wider society. Examples would be the Jehovah's Witnesses, Seventh-Day Adventists, and Christian Science adherents. These groups typically begin with a charismatic leader who articulates a strong rejection of the compromises made with the secular world by other religions. Over time, as leadership is routinized and members experience some upward mobility, there tends to be more acceptance of worldly matters and secular values.

secularization The process of organizing society or aspects of social life around nonreligious values or principles, secularization is linked closely to German sociologist (1864–1920) Max Weber's concept of a growing "disenchantment of the world" as the sphere of the magical, sacred, and religious retreats in cultural significance before the driving force of rationalization of culture and social institutions powered by emergent capitalism. *See also* **rationalization**.

security certificate Available since 1991 under the *Immigration and Refugee Protection Act*, a security certificate allows for the indefinite detention of a permanent resident (not a citizen) of Canada or a refugee, without evidence being reviewed in a public process and usually without the presence of the detainee. Persons detained in this manner can then be returned to their homelands, even if this puts them at risk of torture or death. Since the Act's inception, only 27 people have been so detained, but with the growing threat of terrorism, it appears to be used more frequently. Six men were being held under these certificates in mid-2005. Courts have ruled these certificates to be constitutional. *See also* ***Anti-Terrorism Act***.

Security Council *See* **United Nations**.

segmented labour market *See* **dual labour market**.

self-control One of the aims of all socialization is to place a "police person" inside each of us, rather than relying on external controls. Many experience self-control when a voice inside says: What will Mother think? Will this harm my chances of being accepted as a police recruit? This is effective self-control.

self-determination, right of The right of all peoples or nations to determine their own political status and economic, social, or cultural development, the right of self-determination was first articulated by the United Nations in 1960, when it resolved: "All peoples have the right to self-determination; by virtue of that right, they freely determine their political status and freely pursue their economic, social, and cultural development." This resolution has been helpful for groups struggling for independence and forms one basis of the Québécois claim to a right of self-determination.

self-government In the Canadian context, *self-government* has clearest reference to the aspirations of First Nations peoples. While the term is as yet without a clear definition, as used by the federal government it means something like self-determination. The *Indian Act* replaced traditional Indian governments with band councils that act as agents of the federal government. These councils exercise only those powers granted by the *Indian Act*. Whatever form self-government takes, it would involve legislative changes to give First Nations peoples the tools to be much more self-determining. For some First Nations peoples, the idea of self-government is an acknowledgment of nationhood. For these groups, their status as self-determining nations was never given up through colonization or treaties, so to have self-government recognized is seen as an acknowledgment of this earlier, and continuing, nationhood. As currently envisaged by federal and provincial governments, self-government is not equivalent to territorial sovereignty, although it implies extensive legal autonomy within the general framework of the fed-

eral government's overriding power to make provisions for "peace, order, and good government."

self-report study A method for measuring crime, a self-report study involves the distribution of a detailed questionnaire to a sample of people, asking them whether they have committed a crime in a particular period of time. This has been a good method for criminologists to determine the social characteristics of offenders.

Senate *See* **parliament**.

sentencing circle An adaptation of an aboriginal tradition, a sentencing circle is conducted after an individual has been found guilty by a court or has acknowledged guilt; through the circle, the native community determines what sentence should be imposed. Both the court and the convicted person must agree to having the sentencing phase referred to a sentencing circle. Although there are variations, the judge, convicted person, lawyers, victim, and community members sit in a circle in an informal environment and discuss the convicted person and the harm done to the victim and to the community. In this broad forum and through examination of a wide array of facts, the circle attempts to decide what sentence should be given. The circle has been given some direction by the judge, and limits may be set. The judge will typically impose the sentence arrived at by the circle. Also known as *circle sentencing*. Reference: Green, R.G. (1998). *Justice in Aboriginal Communities: Sentencing Alternatives.* Saskatoon: Purich Publishing.

separation of powers A constitutional structure of government, legal authority is divided among various institutions to effect a separation of powers. In the United States, the *Constitution* divides federal authority among the president, Congress, and the Supreme Court, all of which have separately delimited powers and responsibilities. In Canada and other parliamentary systems, although the judiciary is independent, the legislature and the government executive are joined, since the executive depends on the support of the legislature and government ministers are almost always members of the legislature.

sequential analysis As used by ethnomethodologists, sequential analysis is the same as conversational analysis. Social scientists, for example, have analyzed police interrogations to discover the common-sense methods the police use to obtain a confession.

Reference: ten Have, Paul. (1998). *Doing Conversation Analysis*. London: Sage.

serf An unfree status associated with agrarian economies dominated by feudal social relationships, a serf is a labourer bound to the land and to service to a landlord. In England, the serf status differed from that of slaves in that serfs possessed security of the person, the right to personal property, and customary rights to use land and other resources. In other societies, for example, Russia, serf status was often very similar to that of the slave and serfs could be sold in the marketplace to other owners. Serfdom has occurred in many world societies, including England, France, Russia, China, and Japan. While serfdom first died out in England in the 16th century, it persisted in Russia until the general emancipation ordered by Tsar Alexander II in 1861. A modified form of serfdom, based on indentured or bonded labour, is still widespread in some world societies. *See also* **feudalism**.

seriation A method of relative dating in archaeology, seriation builds on the assumption that many things can be thought of as part of a series. For example, tool technology has progressed from simple to more complex, so one can assume that a site with primitive tools is older than one with more complex tools.

service economy Usually contrasted with a goods-producing economy, a service economy is based largely on the provision of services rather than of manufactured goods. These may include medical, accounting, social work, teaching, design, consultancy, commercial cooking, restaurant table-serving, and taxi-driving services. The shift to a service economy is sociologically interesting because it appears to be associated with different labour market demands, differing educational requirements, and differing wage structures. *See also* **goods-producing economy**.

sex The term *sex* indicates the biological classification of individuals as males and females. Sociologists would note, however, that even though this is a classification based on biological differences, it is a socially constructed classification. *See also* **gender roles**.

sexism Actions or attitudes that discriminate against people based solely on their sex, sexism is linked to power in that those with power are typically treated with favour and those without power are typically discriminated against. Sexism is also related to stereotypes, since the discriminatory actions or attitudes are frequently based on false beliefs or overgeneralizations about sex characteristics and on seeing sex as relevant when it is not. *See also* **stereotype**.

sex typing *Sex typing* refers to stereotypes of the biological sexes and the consequent action of characterizing men and women on the basis of these stereotypes. This is part of the process of the social construction of gender. For example, women are mediators and men are competitive; boys prefer trucks, while girls prefer dolls. *See also* **gender; stereotype**.

sexual assault *Sexual assault* is a broader classification of sexual offence than *rape*, and now replaces *rape* in Canada's *Criminal Code*. Rape was said to occur only when sexual penetration was involved, but the *Criminal Code*'s replacement defines sexual assault as an assault that has as its consequence a violation of the sexual integrity of the victim. There are now three levels of sexual assault that replace the earlier offences of rape and indecent assault. *See also* **rape.**

sexual dimorphism Differences between males and females in size and appearance are called *sexual dimorphism*. Sexual dimorphism in humans is greater than in some animals and less than in many. Evolutionary psychologists and biologists are intrigued to understand the function of sexual dimorphism.

sexual division of labour The allocation of a work task, either in the private household or in the public economy, on the basis of the sex of the person is called the *sexual division of labour*, which is related to stereotyping. Women may cook the meals and men wash the dishes, or women may perform caring roles such as nursing or social work in the public economy, while men perform the tasks of driving trucks, fighting fires, or manufacturing goods. Most societies have had some division of labour by sex. Although this expression seems to have survived criticism from social scientists, it is actually incorrect: The division of labour between the sexes is chiefly *gendered*—it is based on cultural practices rather than any inherent suitability of either sex to perform specific roles.

shaken baby syndrome A form of child abuse, shaken baby syndrome was first recognized in 1972 when it was realized that some brain damage in babies and young infants is caused by a parent or caregiver shaking the baby violently enough to cause brain injury.

shaman A type of religious specialist, a shaman is thought to possess unusual ability for dealing with supernatural beings and spirits. Reference: Kalwet, H. (1988). *Dreamtime and Inner Space: The World of the Shaman.* New York: Random House.

shaming One way that small and intimate societies deal with deviant or unacceptable behaviour, shaming involves creating a sense of humiliation in the offender by disgracing or discrediting that person. This approach to social control maintains a connection between the offender and the society, allowing the person to remain part of the community rather than creating a marginal status. Reference: Braithwaite, J. (1989). *Crime, Shame, and Reintegration.* Cambridge: Cambridge University Press.

Sharia (Sharia'h) law In Muslim teachings, this term was originally a reference to the "path leading to water" or a way to the very source of life, and thus the way in which Muslims were to live. Over time, Sharia became interpreted as law, and traditional Sharia tribunals covered some elements of criminal law as well as what we now refer to as *family law*, conflict mediation over inheritance, custody, and so on. Many provinces in Canada allow for the voluntary use of faith-based arbitration. However, in the name of multiculturalism, there has been growing pressure to have provinces incorporate Sharia law into arbitration acts. In 2005, a Government of Ontario report recommended that voluntary use of Muslim arbitrators be introduced, but in the face of international protest, Ontario premier Dalton McGuinty immediately withdrew the recommendation and said there would be no Sharia law in Ontario and all religious arbitrations in the province would be banned. There is opposition to such a change among Muslims themselves, as some see the law as leading to violation of the equality rights of Muslim women. Others argue that Sharia law is not necessary in order to lead a Muslim life.

Sharpe decision A complex and controversial set of court decisions regarding child pornography resulted from the trial of John Robin Sharpe, who was charged with two counts of possession of pornography (400 photographs) and two counts of possession of child pornography for the purpose of distribution or sale (stories he had written).

Sharpe was convicted on the first charge but was acquitted on the charges of possession of child pornography for purposes of distribution, and this was upheld on appeal. However, on appeal to the Supreme Court of Canada, the court upheld the law and created two exceptions: the right to protect private works of the imagination or photographic depictions of one's self, and the creation for their own pleasure of sexually explicit depictions of children. The court ordered that Sharpe be retried and be provided with the opportunity to argue that his works met one of these exceptions. Sharpe was successful in making this argument. In 2004, the federal government introduced Bill C-2 to address some of the concerns raised by this case and removed any reference to the notion of artistic merit. Members of the arts community then raised concerns that they would be the ones charged under the amended law, citing what they called the *Lolita test*—if the great novel by Vladimir Nabokov would not be permitted under a law, then the law is faulty. Revisions to the Bill included the following defence: The work has a "legitimate purpose related to the administration of justice or to science, education or art" and "does not pose an undue risk of harm." This Bill was passed by both Houses of Parliament in July 2005. Reference: *R. v. Sharpe* [2001] 1 S.C.R. 45.

Shaw, Clifford R., and Henry D. McKay U.S. sociologists Clifford Shaw (1895–1957) and Henry McKay (1899–?) were associated with the Chicago School and its focus on the effects of urbanization on social organization and rates of crime and deviance. Their early research in the 1940s was centred on analyzing whether crime rates in particular regions of Chicago were associated with the characteristics of the citizens who lived there or were related to the situational environment, or "ecology," of their area. By tracking urban migration patterns, as successive waves of urban migrants and immigrants arrived, it was possible to demonstrate that it was areas of the city, rather than particular population groups, that were consistently correlated to crime rates. This result was explained by the long-established "social disorganization" theory of the Chicago School, which proposed that crime and delinquency were caused by social factors and not by inherent characteristics of individuals and groups. The most important of these social factors is the level of socioeconomic stability. Populations subject to rapid transformation of their conditions of life are much more likely to have high crime rates than settled communities. And since social instability affects the lower classes more, they will have higher rates of crime. Reference: Shaw, Clifford R., & McKay, Henry D. (1942). *Juvenile Delinquency and Urban Areas: A Study of Rates of Delinquency in Relation to Differential Characteristics of Local Communities in American Cities.* Chicago: University of Chicago Press [1969].

shifting agriculture *Shifting agriculture* describes a system in which land is cleared and then cultivated until it is exhausted, at which point new land is cleared and the process restarted.

signifier A term from semiology—the study of signs—a signifier can be an expression, gesture, clothing style, form of architecture, or consumer good. The signifier and the signified always exist in some relationship (called *signification*) and the hearer is always decoding this relationship. For example, taking the expression "A pig is coming," in one instance the hearer may "hear" the signifier "pig" and assume that an animal pig is in the area. Another time, the hearer may "hear" that a policeman is in the area, while at yet another time, the hearer may "hear" that the speaker's supervisor is arriving.

Silent Spring Published in 1962, and written by U.S. biologist, writer, and ecologist Rachel Carson (1907–1964), this book was an early call to arms for the environmental movement. Carson portrayed the forces that modern society has brought into being as assaulting nature and human life itself. The title of *Silent Spring* comes from an imaginary community in which "There was a strange silence. The birds, for example—where had they gone? Many people spoke of them, puzzled and disturbed. The feeding stations in the backyards were deserted. The few birds seen anywhere were moribund; they trembled violently and could not fly. It was a spring without voices. On the morning that had once throbbed with the dawn chorus of robins, catbirds, doves, jays, wrens, and scores of other bird voices there was now no sound; only silence over the fields and woods and marsh." When this book appeared and was serialized in magazine form, the chemical industry mounted an expensive campaign to silence Carson. She had done her homework, however, and her facts stood. Reference: Carson,

Rachel. (1962). *Silent Spring.* Wilmington, MA: Mariner Books [1994].

six degrees of separation You may have seen the movie *Six Degrees of Separation* without realizing that the title was based on a piece of research by U.S. social psychologist Stanley Milgram (1933–1984). Milgram sent a letter to 160 randomly selected people in Nebraska, asking them to use the mail to try to have a letter hand-delivered to a specific person in New York. (The first person would send the letter to someone they knew who might have a contact in New York or who might know someone who had such a contact, in the hope that that person could then send it to someone else who might know the person in question and so on.) He was interested in how many hands the letter would pass through before it was delivered. What he found was that the average number of mailings was a little less than six; hence the idea that we are separated from any other person by about six people. Reference: Milgram, S. (1967). The Small World Problem. *Psychology Today, 1,* 60–67.

skinheads This term is commonly used to describe young people who have shaved their heads. Unfortunately, some of them are marginalized persons who hold extreme nationalist beliefs and have frequently attacked and killed immigrants who are seen as threatening the racial purity of their new nation.

slavery A relationship between people in which one person is not free but is treated as the legally owned property of the other is one of slavery. As such, the slave can be sold or exchanged. Slave relationships have been found in many parts of the world and have sometimes been the central economic relationships of the society. It is estimated that 11 million slaves were brought from Africa to the Americas before the trade in slaves was abolished. As legal property of their owners, slaves can be forced to produce goods or services whose value remains with the owner.

Smith, Adam (1723–1790) Scottish economist and moral philosopher Adam Smith's most famous and influential work, *An Inquiry into the Nature and Causes of the Wealth of Nations* (1776), outlined the basic principles of a free market economy and the central importance of the division of labour in enhancing productivity. As a result of the division of labour and comparative advantages of technology and resources, many regions and nations were able to produce far more than their own needs in certain commodities and, therefore, free market trade between these nations could result only in an overall enhancement of wealth as they each concentrated their production on areas where they were most efficient. This argument ran counter to the established precepts of mercantilism, which supported quota or tariff barriers to imports and establishment of regulated monopolies to conduct international trade. Although Smith was a founder of *laissez-faire* economics and supported its central claim that individual self-interested decisions would summate to the common good, his concerns extended to the problems of what Marx was later to call the alienation of labour and the threat of monopoly and manipulative practices inherent in the capitalist economy.

Smith, Dorothy (1926–) Dorothy Smith was born in England and attended the London School of Economics, where her initial interest in sociology developed. She moved to the United States in the 1960s in order to study and teach at the University of California at Berkeley, during which time she was influenced by exposure to the work of phenomenologists and to the growing women's movement. She later accepted work at the University of British Columbia, where she began to reread Marx and was one of a group of women to offer the first courses in women's studies. These forces have shaped her many writings as she struggles to develop a perspective that is shaped by the standpoint of women in society. Smith has been associated with the University of Toronto since 1977. Reference: Smith, Dorothy. (1999). *Writing the Social: Critique, Theory and Investigation.* Toronto: University of Toronto Press.

social bond The degree to which an individual is integrated into "the social" is defined as a social bond. Does the person have binding ties to the family, to the school, to the workplace, to the community? While French sociologist Émile Durkheim (1858–1917) first focused on the importance of the social bond, it has gained wide acceptance in the theory and research of U.S. sociologist Travis Hirschi (1935–). Hirschi argues that as the social bond is weakened, the degree of deviant involvement goes up.

social construction of reality An aspect of many micro-interpretive perspectives in sociology, social construction of reality must be understood as a contrast to positivistic and structural sociology. Rejecting the notion that events or social phenomena have an independent and objective existence, advocates of this microperspective examine the methods that members of society use to create or construct reality. French sociologist Émile Durkheim (1858–1917), for example, was a positivist and a structuralist, and argued that suicide had an objective existence, independent of himself and others. That is, there was something about the way of death that constituted something as a suicide. An advocate of the social construction of reality perspective would argue that suicide is just a label for a death and is constituted, or created, by the accounts that people like police, family, or coroners give of the death. Our accounting methods then construct reality rather than there being some independent reality that we can describe or explain. This phrase was used in 1966 by U.S. sociologist Peter Berger (1929–) and German sociologist Thomas Luckmann. Reference: Berger, P., & Luckmann, T. (1972). *The Social Construction of Reality* (2nd ed.). London: Penguin. *See also* **ethnomethodology; labelling theory; phenomenological sociology; symbolic interactionism**.

social contract theory This term is used metaphorically to suggest that a group of self-interested and rational individuals came together and formed a contract that created society. Each was willing to give up a little bit of freedom to create social rules that would protect self-interest. This theory suggests that intellectually aware individuals were historically prior to societies. It was this view that French sociologist Émile Durkheim argued against in the late 19th century with his claim that society must come before the individual since human culture and communication can arise only in society. Reference: Morris, C.W. (1999). *The Social Contract Theorists.* Lanham, MD: Rowman and Littlefield.

social control theory Social control theory attempts to explain why it is that all of us do not commit crime. Or to put this another way: Why are most people law-abiding? The answer lies in dimensions of social control, or the many ways in which people are controlled by family, schools, work situations, conscience, etc. Most conventional theories, by contrast, try to explain why individuals commit crime. Reference: Hirschi, Travis. (1969). *Causes of Delinquency.* Berkeley: University of California Press.

social Darwinism A late 19th-century social philosophy that unites an interest in social problems (e.g., inequality) with an interpretation of Darwin's work on the origin of species, advocates argue that the central Darwinian principle of evolution, development and progress, is the survival of the fittest and extinction of the weakest. Applied to social affairs, this implies that those who get ahead in society are the most fit and deserve their position. More importantly, perhaps, this perspective suggests that supporting those who fall behind (by providing welfare, for example) interferes with the principles of evolution and obstructs social progress. Sociologists, of course, believe that social problems like inequality must be understood within a social and cultural context, rather than a context of biological competition. Reference: Hofstadter, Richard. (1992). *Social Darwinism in American Thought*. Boston: Beacon Press.

social democracy A general term for political doctrines that claim an important role for the state and the community in shaping and directing a society's economic and social life, social democracy differs from socialism because it is committed to preservation of a largely capitalist and free market economy, but shares with it an emphasis on the importance of redistribution of wealth and income, so that citizens may have social and economic conditions that effectively provide for reasonable equality of opportunity. Modern welfare-state liberalism is closely allied to social democratic ideas. *See also* **socialism**.

social disorganization theory This theory holds that crime and other deviant behaviours are most likely to occur when social institutions are not able to direct and control groups of individuals. It is argued that gangs will arise spontaneously in social contexts that are weakly controlled. Some criminologists think that the concept of social disorganization just reflects middle-class failure to comprehend organization different from their own. Reference: Sutherland, E.H. (1939). *Principles of Criminology* (3rd ed.). Philadelphia: Lippincott.

social formation A term used by critical sociologists, *social formation* has a meaning similar to that of *society*. When we talk of Canadian society, however, we tend to think only of one society and imagine it as being static. Critical sociologists wish to talk about Canadian society being formed in different ways over time. Each would be a different social formation, although all would be called Canada. Each formation would be characterized by a particular organization of economic and political relationships.

social gospel movement An attempt to use the Gospel, the teachings of Christ, to deal with social problems arising in an expanding industrial nation like Canada, the social gospel movement appeared in Canada in the 1880s and was a major force in social and political life through the 1930s. Its central belief was that God was at work in the creation of social change, social justice, and moral reform. This core value can be found in the Social Service Council of Canada (1912), the United Church (1925), and the Co-operative Commonwealth Federation (1932), and played an important part in shaping the nature of sociology in Canada. The movement is particularly associated with the work of Labour MP for Winnipeg North-Centre J.S. Woodsworth (1864–1942), Saskatchewan premier and "father of medicare" T.C. Douglas (1904–1986), BC MPP Grace McInnis (1905–1991), and others. These ideas would now be part of what is referred to as *liberation theology*.

socialism Socialism is a political doctrine that upholds the principle of collectivity, rather than individualism, as the foundation for economic and social life. Socialists favour state and cooperative ownership of economic resources, equality of economic condition, and democratic rule and management of economic and social institutions. *See also* **social democracy**.

socialist feminism A perspective that examines women's social situation as shaped by both patriarchal gender relations and by the class structure of capitalism, socialist feminism sees gender and class oppression as inseparable, and rather than working for the equality of women within a liberal, democratic, capitalist society, it argues for the equality of women within a society that is not dependent on the exploitation of one group by another (i.e., a classless society). *See also* **feminism**; **liberal feminism**.

socialization (1) A process of social interaction and communication in which individuals come to learn and internalize the culture of their society or group, socialization begins immediately at birth, with the conditioning influences of infant handling, and continues throughout an individual's lifetime. Sociologists recognize the limitless variety of individual experiences of socialization, but have given much attention to general patterns of socialization found in individual societies and groups within them. The sociological use of the term refers to the learning and absorption of culture and not simply to the process of interacting with others. (2) The term is also sometimes used to refer to the collective ownership and management of economic resources (e.g., a nationalized industry), or to publicly provided and financed services (e.g., "socialized medicine").

social maps The term *map* is used primarily as a metaphor in this context (although one could actually place data or statistics on a geographic map). Mapping in the first sense means identifying the social characteristics of victims, offenders, or inmates, or other groups.

social mobility Social mobility is upward or downward movement within a stratification system. Liberal theory claims that capitalist societies are open class, and therefore one can expect a high degree of social mobility. According to liberal theory, this movement within a stratification system should result from a person's achievements and should not be based on ascribed characteristics such as sex, race, region of birth, and parent's class position. Social mobility is typically measured by comparing the status positions of adult children to those of their parents (intergenerational mobility), but it can be measured by comparing a person's status position over that person's own lifetime (intragenerational mobility). Sociologists see social mobility as a useful way to measure equality of opportunity. *See also* **demand mobility**; **equality of opportunity**.

social movement A group of people organized outside of institutions established for this purpose, a social movement's goal is to bring about political and social change that will satisfy the participants' shared interest or goal. Political parties therefore would not be social movements, although the New Democratic Party often describes itself as part of a social movement. It is more correct to talk about the environmental movement, the gay rights movement, the women's movement, the labour movement, victim's rights movements, prisoner's rights movements, or movements for drug decriminalization. Sociologists are interested in studying the dynamics of such movements and the conditions or forces that make some successful and others less successful.

social relations of production Another way of referring to the class structure, the social relations of production refers to the social relationships that people enter into in the production or delivery of goods and services. From a Marxist perspective, these relationships are inevitably those of owners and nonowners, or those who control the work and those who do not control the work. In this way of thinking, social class is founded on the economy of any society, and it is the pattern of class relations that gives a society its central character.

social structure The patterned and relatively stable arrangement of roles and statuses found within societies and social institutions, social structure points out the way in which societies, and institutions within them, exhibit predictable patterns of organization, activity, and social interaction. This relative stability of organization and behaviour provides the quality of predictability that people rely on in everyday social interaction. Social structures are inseparable from cultural norms and values that also shape status and social interaction.

society A human community, usually with a relatively fixed territorial location, sharing a common culture and common activities, is considered to be a society. There is cultural and institutional interdependence between members of the society, and they are, to some extent, differentiated from other communities and groups. Societies are generally identified as existing at the level of nation–states, but there can be regional and cultural communities within nation–states that possess much of the cultural distinctiveness and relative self-sufficiency of societies.

sociobiology A perspective on human social behaviour made accessible by the publication in 1975 of *Sociobiology* by U.S. entomologist E.O. Wilson (1929–) and in 1976 by the publication of *The Selfish Gene* by British zoologist Richard Dawkins (1941–), sociobiology begins with the assumption that humans are above all other animals and therefore the roots of human social behaviour can be found in our evolutionary heritage. Since this way of understanding relies on genetics and biological adaptation, it is not a sociological perspective. The term *sociobiology* has been replaced to a great extent by the term *evolutionary psychology*. Reference: Wilson, E.O. (2000). *Sociobiology: The New Synthesis* (25th anniversary ed.). Cambridge, MA: Harvard University Press.

socioeconomic status A term that is often contrasted with that of social class, *socioeconomic status*, largely an American usage, has developed as a way to operationalize or measure social class on the assumption that class groupings are not real groups. It is a rather arbitrary category and is developed by combining the position or score of persons on criteria such as income, amount of education, type of occupation held, or neighbourhood of residence. The scores can then be arbitrarily divided so as to create divisions such as upper class, middle class, and lower class. Sociologists are interested in socioeconomic status, as they are in class, since it is assumed that this status affects life chances in numerous ways. *See also* **class**.

sociolinguistics Sociolinguistics is the study of the structure and use of language as it relates to its social setting. For example, one might study the differences in the forms of address used in speaking to a friend and speaking to an employer.

sociological imagination As used by U.S. sociologist C.W. Mills (1916–1962), this term refers to the ability to imagine and understand the intersection between personal biography and historical social structures. This is indeed the essence of sociology: imagining that every individual's life is given meaning, form, and significance within historically specific cultures and ways of organizing social life. Having a sociological imagination then is identical with being a good sociologist: It is a standard against which to judge sociology. Reference: Mills, C.W. (1959). *The Sociological Imagination*. New York: Oxford University Press.

sociology A social science that examines the structure, organization, and culture of societies and their processes of social change and social interaction, sociology encompasses a wide range of diverse theories and perspectives. Broadly, it can be separated conceptually into critical or conflict versus functionalist perspectives. The former deals with such topics as inequality, class conflict, gender relations, and political economy, while the latter is focused on the social processes that stabilize and maintain existing societies and support social integration. Sociological perspectives differ also in their areas of focus, with "macro" perspectives being interested in the way society as a whole shapes individual experience and institutional dynamics, while "micro" approaches such as symbolic interactionism are centred on the analysis of patterns of social interaction between individuals and within groups. The sociological approach to crime is interested in the social correlates of crime, including issues of class, status, sex, levels of community integration, development of ethnic and youth subcultures, etc., and in the way crime is socially constructed both by the exercise of power and in processes of social interaction and interpretation. While criminology was initially included within sociology departments and often treated as the sociological study of deviance rather than specifically of crime, specialist criminology departments gradually emerged since the focus of criminology became centred on the analysis of the causes of crime and means for its reduction and on penal and correctional policy. Criminology therefore became associated with pragmatism, social experimentation, and social work, rather than the more theoretical and conceptual approach of sociology. Reference: Hiller, H. (2001). The Most Important Books/Articles in Canadian Sociology in the 20th Century. *Canadian Journal of Sociology*, *26*(3).

sociology of knowledge The study of the social bases of what is known, believed, or valued both by individuals and society is known as the *sociology of knowledge*. The essential idea is that knowledge itself, how it is defined and constituted, is a cultural product shaped by social context and history. In this view, knowledge cannot be treated as a thing in itself, as an objective, universally true body of facts and theory, but must be understood in the social context in which it originated. The principal ideas of postmodernism are closely linked to this long tradition in philosophy and the social sciences. Reference: Mannheim, Karl. (1952). *Essays on the Sociology of Knowledge*. New York: Oxford University Press. *See also* **postmodernism**.

Somalia, incident in On March 16, 1993, Shidane Arone, a 16-year old Somali, was beaten to death by Canadian soldiers after being captured. In December of the previous year, the United Nations authorized a peace-enforcement mission to Somali in response to mass starvation as a result of civil war. Canadian soldiers from the Airborne Regiment were sent—a troop, however, with a reputation of having a "bad attitude" and lack of respect for authority. The situation in Somalia was more chaotic than anticipated, and U.S. soldiers were soon harassed. Canadian troops were given permission to shoot at thieves under certain circumstances.

Canadian troops made many "home movies" that showed troops engaging in behaviour that did not bring much honour to Canada. The killing of Shidane Arone resulted in a cover-up by the Armed Forces and eventually in an inquiry. The person thought to have been most directly involved in the beating of Arone attempted suicide three days after the incident, and the resulting brain damage prevented him from going to trial. It was later thought that the behaviour of the Canadian troops may have been as a result of a reaction to Mefloquine, an antimalaria drug that is now known to produce a form of "madness" in many users. Reference: Desbarats, Peter. (1997). *Somalia Cover-Up.* Toronto: McClelland and Stewart.

somatotypes This term refers to body types, and behind this idea lies the belief of early criminologists that there were distinctive body types and that these types were associated with personality and temperament. It was believed that the mesomorph with a well-built, muscular body (note the sexist connotation of this) was associated with an aggressive personality, insensitivity to pain, and a tendency to act impulsively. Reference: Sheldon, William. (1954). *Atlas of Men: A Guide for Somatyping the Adult Male of All Ages.* New York: Harper and Brothers.

Sons of Freedom *See* **Doukhobors**.

Sophonow, Thomas Thomas Sophonow was wrongfully convicted of the 1981 murder of Barbara Stoppel. The jury in Sophonow's first trial could not reach agreement, so he was tried twice more; each time the conviction was overturned by a court of appeal. The Supreme Court of Canada prevented a fourth trial and, in 2002, the police apologized to Sophonow and an inquiry recommended a large compensation package for the almost 4 years Sophonow spent in prison and some 20 years of harassment. Reference: Corey, Honourable P. (2001). *The Inquiry Regarding Thomas Sophonow.* Winnipeg: Minister of Justice.

sororate A marriage tradition where a man marries his wife's sister, sororate usually takes place after the original wife has died or has proven to be sterile. Sororal polygyny takes place if a man marries his wife's sister while his original wife is alive.

soul As used by French historian and philosopher Michel Foucault (1926–1984), *soul* refers to what psychologists mean by the psyche, the self, subjectivity, or human consciousness. Foucault argues, for example, that the development of the penitentiary in the early 19th century resulted in a shift from punishing the body to punishing the soul.

sovereignty Sovereignty is the authority possessed by the governing individual or institution of a society. Sovereign authority is distinct in that it is unrestricted by legal regulation, since the sovereign authority is itself the source of all law. The idea of state sovereignty appears to have developed in Europe in the late middle ages, where it emerged once a division was made between the sacred authority of the church and the secular authority of the state. As long as state power was subject to religious institutions—like the Catholic Church—state sovereignty could not emerge. *See* **Treaty of Westphalia**. In Britain, state sovereignty is possessed by the Crown in Parliament: Law passed by Parliament and consented to by the Crown has unchallengeable legal authority. In Canada, the locus of sovereignty is more ambiguous, since the written parts of Canada's *Constitution*, the *Constitution Act, 1867*, and the *Constitution Act, 1982*, prescribe a federal–provincial division of powers and special procedures for constitutional amendment that limit the authority of the Crown and Parliament. Major changes to Canada's *Constitution* require the unanimous consent of Parliament and the 10 provincial legislatures, thus suggesting that political sovereignty in Canada is shared by the Crown in Parliament and the Crown and legislatures of Canada's 10 provinces. When it is claimed that Canada's sovereignty in the North is being eroded, it is being suggested that Canada no longer has power or ultimate authority over the territory. As the ice melts in the North and the waterways are opened, there is going to be increasing pressure to declare that parts of Canada are international waters.

Sparrow case In a legal case that advanced the aboriginal rights of native peoples in Canada, Ronald Sparrow, a Musqueam, was charged with violating federal regulations while fishing in an area not covered by existing treaties. A 1986 court of appeal ruled that Section 35(1) of the Canadian *Constitution* meant that an aboriginal right to fish for food continued to exist in nontreaty areas of the province. Reference: *R. v. Sparrow* [1990] 1 S.C.R. 1075.

speciesism The attitude that it is naturally right and appropriate to give priority to human interests and demands over those of all other living creatures, speciesism has led to endangerment and extinction of many animal species and to extensive environmental damage and depletion.

specific deterrence As used in criminal justice, *specific deterrence* refers to crime prevention achieved through instilling fear in the specific individual being punished, so that the person refrains from future violation of the law. Also referred to as *individual deterrence*. *See also* **general deterrence**.

specific land claims Claims to land made by native groups covered by treaties but where the terms of treaties have not been met or land has been removed over the years without consent are specific land claims. *See also* **Calder case; comprehensive land claims**.

Spencer, Herbert (1820–1903) British social theorist and philosopher Herbert Spencer was an influential British thinker who developed the theory of evolution in a manner useful to the social sciences. He believed that nothing remains in its pristine or primary stage but always changes. This change is always in one direction as he developed the ideas of movement from simple to complex, from homogenous to heterogeneous. Some of these ideas find their way into the writings of French sociologist Émile Durkheim (1858–1917). This now all sounds rather strange as we worry that the world is becoming more homogenous. Reference: Turner, J. (1985). *Herbert Spencer: A renewed appreciation*. Beverly Hills: Sage.

spirit of capitalism According to German sociologist Max Weber (1864–1920), the spirit of capitalism is rationalization—being methodical and calculating in the pursuit of profit. Weber argued that this drive to organize work to most efficiently achieve the goals of profit or business success had its origins in Protestantism. *See also* **Protestant ethic**.

split labour market *See* **dual labour market**.

sponsored immigrant Under the *Immigration Act*, any Canadian citizen or permanent resident is able to sponsor a range of close relatives as immigrants to Canada. Family class members must meet only the criteria of good health and character. The other two classes of immigrants are refugees and independents (including entrepreneurs).

sponsored mobility This is a British term, contrasted with *contest mobility*, used to refer to a method of identifying people at an early age for social advancement; sponsoring, or supporting, them as they prepare for their rise to the top; and then guaranteeing them a comfortable position. Similarly, those not so identified are not supported or given opportunities and thus are destined for positions at the bottom of the class structure. *See also* **streaming**.

spuriousness Spuriousness is the incorrect inference of a causal relationship between two variables where the relationship is in reality only accidental. Researchers attempt to identify or eliminate spuriousness by the use of random assignment in an experimental design or through the use of control (extraneous) variables in the manipulation of data during analysis. *See also* **causality; control variable**.

Sputnik The first earth-orbiting satellite, *Sputnik* was launched by the Soviet Union in 1957. The successful launching of this satellite shocked Western countries and initiated the space race. To compete with the Soviet Union, Western countries, especially the United States, restructured education at all levels and massively increased funding for science programs and scientific research.

Stalinism This political and economic system was in force during the period from 1926 to 1953, when Joseph Stalin was leader of the Soviet Communist Party and all-powerful dictator of the Soviet Union. Stalinism claimed absolute domination of the Communist Party over all aspects of Soviet life, politics, and culture, and justified mass murder and policies of mass terror in an attempt to establish communism. The Communist Party itself was repeatedly purged, and leading members executed, exiled, or imprisoned. It is estimated that as many as 20 million people may have died in famines as a result of Stalin's policies of forced agricultural collectivization, as well as many hundreds of thousands more in political purges, displacements of populations, and the rigours of the vast system of prison camps established by Stalin's secret police.

standpoint feminism *See* **feminism, standpoint**.

staple As used by Canadian political economist Harold Innis (1894–1952), a natural resource exported to a more advanced economy is a staple. According to Innis, the character of these resources and their export have given shape to the development of Canadian society. Staples such as beaver pelts, cod, wheat, and forest products have each shaped settlement patterns, transportation routes, and the structure of power.

staples trap This term refers to economic or social forces that trap a nation or region in the export of a particular staple. The particular settlement patterns, characteristics of the labour force, methods of capital accumulation, or transportation routes make it difficult for British Columbia, for example, to move away from a major reliance on forest products, even though the richest and most accessible forest resources have been consumed. *See also* **staple**.

stare decisis A key principle of the common law tradition in English Canada, translated from Latin, *stare decisis* means "to stand by decided matters," and embodies a set of rules concerning which court rulings are binding on other courts. In general, the decisions of a higher court are binding on those of a lower court.

state As defined by German sociologist Max Weber (1864–1920), the institution that claims the exclusive right to the legitimate exercise of force in a given territory, through the use of police to enforce laws or the army to maintain civil stability, is a state. Institutions of the state include government and agencies such as the army, police, judiciary, Crown corporations, welfare bureaucracies, and regulatory bodies. While there have been stateless societies, most complex societies have state systems of formal government and administrative bureaucracies. *See also* **Treaty of Westphalia**.

state capitalism A term proposed by critical sociologists and social theorists, *state capitalism* is used to describe the political and economic structure of Soviet-style communist systems. The core idea is that state ownership of the means of production, as in Russia and other previously communist regimes, did not lead to any emancipation of the workers but merely substituted bureaucratic domination by the state and state officials for that of owners of capital. *See also* **communism**.

Statistical School The Statistical School is associated with early social scientists like Belgian statistician and astronomer Adolphe Quetelet (1796–1874) and French statistician Andre-Michel Guerry (1802–1866), who began to explore the structure of emerging European societies with the assistance of statistical methods. While their early use of statistics is important, they also developed a structural explanation of crime and other social problems. Although this work was to become important later, it was overshadowed by the importance given to the more individualistic theories of Italian criminologist and physician Cesare Lombroso (1835–1909). Reference: Beirne, Piers. (1996). The Invention of Positivist Criminology: An Introduction to Quetelet's Social Mechanics of Crime. In Brian C. MacLean, *Crime and Society: Readings in Critical Criminology*. Toronto: Copp Clark.

statistically significant When researchers study within groups or between group differences, they need a technique to determine if this difference would have occurred by chance. Various statistical techniques can determine this, and if it is unlikely that the differences could have occurred by chance, it is called a *statistically significant difference*. Usually a 0.05 level of significance is used (there are 5 chances out of 100 trials that this difference would occur by chance), but other levels can be used.

statistics The term *statistics* refers to a collection of tests or techniques that are applied to the data, or observations, that social scientists have gathered. There are two categories of statistics: descriptive and inferential. Descriptive statistics are used to describe characteristics of the sample or population the researcher is working with; for example, one can calculate a mean, standard deviation, etc. Inferential statistics are used for drawing inferences about a population based on the observations of a sample. For example, reports of opinion polls routinely note that "A sample of this size is accurate to within x%, 19 times out of 20." This is the inference to be drawn about the population from which the sample was drawn.

status A position in a social structure regulated by norms and ranked according to power and prestige, status differs from class in that it is a measure of a person's social standing or social honour in a community. Individuals who share the same social class may have very divergent status. For example, people's status is affected by ethnic origin, sex, and age, as well as their level of recognition in the community. While status is statistically related to class, it is common for individuals to have inconsistent class and status locations. Most sociologists use both the concepts of class and status to describe the systems of social stratification (the way individuals are ranked in various hierarchies of income, wealth, authority, and power) found in societies.

status, achieved A position in a social structure, achieved status is attained by the individual as a result of the individual's abilities, work, and personal involvements. While occupational statuses are generally achieved, often in a competitive process, one can also achieve more personal statuses; for example, "married" is an achieved status. *See also* **status, ascribed**.

status, ascribed Ascribed status is automatically transmitted to an individual at birth or at a particular time in the life cycle. An individual is accorded this status through inheritance or as a result of such characteristics as sex, ethnicity, or physical features.

Status Indian A native person who is registered under the *Indian Act* as an Indian is a Status Indian; a non-Status Indian is one whose ancestors were never registered or who lost status for various reasons. At one time, women and their children lost status, for example, when they married a nonnative man or a native man who did not have status. Under Bill C-31 (1985), these people have been able to regain their status. Court decisions are beginning to make the distinction between Status and non-Status Indians less significant. *See also* **C-31 Indian**.

status offence A delinquency or crime that can be committed only by people occupying a particular status is a status offence. The *Juvenile Delinquents Act* (replaced in 1984), for example, created criminal offences of school truancy, incorrigibility, sexual immorality, and violations of liquor laws. Only young people could be charged with or found to be in a state of delinquency because of these behaviours. It was found that approximately 20% of young girls coming to Youth Court did so because of their sexual behaviour, while few boys were brought to court on these grounds. *See also* **double standard**.

Status of Women Report A Royal Commission report tabled in the Canadian House of Commons in 1970, the *Status of Women Report* is built on the premises of liberal theory, and measures women's status against the values of equality, individualism, and freedom. The Royal Commission on the Status of Women was created in 1967 and, chaired by Florence Bird, held public hearings into the status of women in society and made numerous recommendations to government.

statutes Laws enacted by a sovereign law-making body such as a provincial legislature or the House of Commons are statutes.

statutory rape Sexual intercourse with an underage person, with or without consent, is statutory rape. *See also* **rape**.

steam bath raids On February 5, 1981, 150 police officers simultaneously raided four Toronto gay bath-

houses, arresting 286 clients and 20 staff members. The next night, 3,000 protesters participated in a late-night rally, and on February 20, 4,000 people attended another protest demonstration. On March 12, Toronto City Council established a committee to investigate relations between the police and gay people, and subsequently, on November 3, 1981, the police department was pressured to educate its members about community relations with gay people. Although many individuals were tried and sentenced, this event marks a step in increasing official recognition of the rights of gay people to free association to practise their lifestyle. Reaction to this event led to the development of gay rights movements in Canada. *See also* **Stonewall riot**.

stereotype This term derives from the printing process and refers to a plate made by taking a cast or mould of a surface. A stereotype then is anything that lacks individual marks or identifiers, and instead appears as though made from a cast. In sociology, the stereotype (the plate or cast) is always a social construction, which may have some basis in reality, but is a gross generalization (e.g., women like romance novels). To stereotype is to apply these casts, or gross generalizations, to people or situations rather than seeing the individual variation. *See also* **sexism**.

stigma As used by Canadian-born sociologist Erving Goffman (1922–1982), a stigma is a "differentness" about an individual that is given a negative evaluation by others and thus distorts and discredits the public identity of the person. For example, physical disabilities, facial disfigurement, stuttering, a prison record, being obese, or not being able to read may become stigmatized attributes. A stigma may lead to the adoption of a self-identity that incorporates the negative social evaluation. Reference: Goffman, Erving. (1962). *Stigma: Notes on the Management of Spoiled Identity*. New York: Prentice Hall. *See also* **Goffman**.

stigmata Physical signs of some special moral position are stigmata. While having Christian origins, Italian criminologist Cesare Lombroso (1835–1909) used the term to refer to physical signs of the state of atavism (a morally and biologically inferior person). The stigmata of criminality for Lombroso were things like the shape of ears, length of fingers, and the slope of the forehead.

Stonewall riot On a weekend in June 1969, the New York police, continuing a policy of harassment of homosexuals, visited the Stonewall Inn, charging that liquor was being sold without a permit. As the homosexual clients were being taken to the police wagon, a spontaneous show of resistance erupted, and the police were forced to retreat and call for reinforcements. This resistance is now given substantial symbolic value and is seen as the birth of the modern gay rights movement in the United States. *See also* **steam bath raids.**

strain The strain concept is central to a functionalist approach or to systems theory, both of which assume that society is like an organism or mechanical system. This system is sustained by harmony and integration. However, if something begins to go wrong, this is a sign of a fault in the system, or of strain. The system has to find ways to adapt to this strain or correct it, or it will lead to transformation of the system. American sociologist Robert Merton's (1910–2003) theory of crime (anomie) in an example of strain theory. He claims that there is often a strain between the culturally defined goals we all strive for and the legitimate means provided for us to achieve those goals. *See also* **anomie; Merton, Robert.**

stratification A social division of individuals into various hierarchies of wealth, status, and power is known as *stratification*. There is disagreement about how to describe stratification systems—some sociologists favour the concept of class and others discuss status differentiations.

stratified This term literally means *to be layered*. In archaeology, most sites have remains layered according to the date at which they were deposited. In sociology and anthropology, the term refers to societies or groups with a hierarchy or structure of inequality.

stratigraphy A method of relative dating in archaeology, stratigraphy builds on the assumption that things deposited in the lowest strata of a site are older than those at higher strata.

streaming Assigning students to distinctive streams or programs within the education system is referred to as *streaming*; for example, a university-bound stream and a vocational stream. While schools may think this assignment is based on the cognitive ability of students or on their special needs, sociologists have frequently shown that streaming is based on social characteristics (class, sex, race, etc.).

structural adjustment loan Structural adjustment loans are issued by the International Monetary Fund or the World Bank to nations in need, usually developing nations or those in economic crisis, and always have conditions attached. The conditions are designed to transform the economic structure of the nation receiving the loan. These conditions might include opening of the capital markets of the nation, privatization of some public services, and reduction of government spending.

structural explanation One type of explanation for crime (such as homicide), structural explanation focuses on social structure (usually this refers to inequality, poverty, or power differentials). For example, the patriarchal structure of the family might help explain the abuse of women and children within the family. Canadian sociologist Rhonda Lenton argues that the racial structure of the United States and the depth of its poverty (and the weakness of its welfare state) compared to Canada's, might help explain the difference in homicide rates. Reference: Lenton, R. (1989). Homicide in Canada and the U.S.A.: A Critique of the Hagan Thesis. *Canadian Journal of Sociology*, *14*, 163–177.

structural functionalism A perspective used to analyze societies and their component features that focuses on their mutual integration and interconnection, structural functionalism analyzes the way that social processes and institutional arrangements contribute to the effective maintenance and stability of society. The fundamental perspective is in opposition to major social change. *See also* **Durkheim, Émile; macroperspective.**

structuralism (French) This term refers to the work of French social theorists such as Claude Lévi-Strauss (1908–) and Jean Piaget (1896–1980), who claim that in the most ordinary of events there is a hidden structure or pattern (often called *deep structure*, a term taken from linguistics), which is not immediately apparent, but can be discerned by careful analysis. For example, what can be learned from the names given to pets, from food categories, from the way a child compares volume in two containers? For the early structuralists, the hidden structures in these practices reveal the structure of the human mind. This being so, there should be some uniformity in the pattern found in these practices around the world.

structuralist approach An approach to understanding the role of the state within a conflict or Marxist perspective, adherents of the structuralist approach see the state as having been captured by the structure of capitalism. While having a degree of autonomy or freedom from the dominant class of society, the state finds it must act so as to reproduce the economic and social structures of capitalism. This approach typically sees the state doing this through attending to three functions: capital accumulation, legitimation, and coercion. *See also* **capital accumulation**; **coercion**; **instrumentalist Marxism**; **legitimation**; **relative autonomy**.

structuration This term is used by British sociologist Anthony Giddens (1938–) to capture elements of macro- and microsociology, structure and agency, determinism, and free will. By *structuration*, Giddens means that human actors re-create through their interactions (and this makes social change possible) the very social structures that constrain their actions. It involves the reproduction on a daily basis of the structures and institutions of society.

subcultural transmission Part of a wider theory that argues that behaviour is learned through socialization into the norms and values of the society, subcultural transmission argues that some groups have values that are supportive of illegal behaviour. Those exposed to this subculture are more likely to exhibit deviant or criminal behaviour.

subculture A culture within a culture, a subculture has the somewhat distinct norms, values, and behaviour of particular groups located within society. The concept of subculture implies some degree of group self-sufficiency, such that individuals may interact, finding employment, recreation, friends, and mates within the group.

subjectivism In traditional positivistic and macrostructural sociology, the subjectivity of the researcher and of the subjects is seen as something to be avoided. The preferred stance for the researcher is objectivity, making the assumption that observation of the world can occur in a neutral fashion without being influenced by theory or cultural or personal assumptions. The subjectivity of the subjects being studied is to be avoided, since it is assumed that people's lives are shaped by structural and cultural forces of which the subject may be unaware. More recent sociology is open to acknowledging the subjectivity of both researcher and subjects. One might study, for example, the ways in which the coroner interprets notes, slash marks, family environments, or medical histories in an effort to arrive at an interpretation of a death. The coroner's subjectivity then

is a valid area for investigation. Similarly, one might be interested in how the scientist is also involved in arriving at an interpretation and examining how this is shaped by the subjective assumptions made. Subjectivism, then, is an approach to doing science that acknowledges and makes room for subjectivity. *See also* **macroperspective**; **objectivity**.

Sudanese kinship system In the Sudanese kinship system, virtually all of the members of the primary kinship group are distinctively named. For example, there would a distinctive term for your grandmother on your mother's side and your grandmother on your father's side. This system is associated with societies with substantial class division.

sufficient condition In a causal relationship, a sufficient condition (or variable) is any variable that is sufficient to bring about the effect in question. For example, a growing unemployment rate might be sufficient to cause an increase in the crime rate. Obviously, many other factors (variables) could also cause the increase. Typically, there are many conditions sufficient to cause an increase, or a decrease, in crime. *See also* **necessary condition**.

suffrage Suffragists were early members of the women's movement who protested in order to win women the right to vote in political matters (suffrage). The beginning of the suffrage movement in Canada can be dated to the founding of the Toronto Women's Literary Society in 1877. The Canadian Women's Suffrage Association grew from this organization under the leadership of Dr. Emily Stowe (1831–1903), the first Canadian woman to practise medicine in Canada. Women achieved the federal vote in 1918. Provincial voting rights for women were achieved between 1918 and 1940, first in Manitoba and last in Quebec. Reference: Howard, Irene. (1992). *The Struggle for Social Justice in British Columbia: Helena Gutteridge, the Unknown Reformer.* Vancouver: University of British Columbia Press.

superego This is a concept developed by psychoanalyst Sigmund Freud (1856–1939) that describes one of three components of the individual personality or self: the id, the innate impulses and drives; the ego, the unique and individual self; and the superego, the internalized social norms or conscience. Much Freudian analytical theory is based on articulating the development of these aspects of self and their relationships.

superstructure A term from Marxist social analysis, the idea of superstructure is central to the materialist concept of history and social development. Marx argues that the fundamental base of any society, which permeates and shapes all its other legal, political, and intellectual characteristics, is the social relations of production: the social and technological way that production is organized and carried out. These relations of production provide the social foundation on which the superstructure of legal and political relations and human intellectual ideas and consciousness is developed.

Supreme Court of Canada The Supreme Court of Canada, established in 1875, has been Canada's highest court since 1949, when appeals to Britain's Judicial Committee of the Privy Council were abolished. It is the final appeal court in all areas of law. The court has nine judges, three of whom must be judges or lawyers from the civil law bar of Quebec. With the adoption of the *Canadian Charter of Rights and Freedoms* in the *Constitution Act, 1982*, the role of the court was greatly expanded, as it now adjudicates the validity of laws in the light of these new constitutional guarantees. It is empowered to strike down laws that conflict with the *Charter*. Reference: Bushnell, Ian. (1992). *The Captive Court: A Study of the Supreme Court of Canada*. Montreal–Kingston: McGill–Queen's University Press. For examples of the Supreme Court's judgments see the following judgments: **Butler case**; **Calder case**; **Delgamuukw**; **Latimer, Robert**; **Malott case**; **Morgentaler, Henry**; **Sharpe decision**; **Sparrow case**.

surplus A surplus is the excess of production over the human and material resources used up in the process of production. In simple societies, there was often little if any surplus, since the production from hunting and gathering was entirely used up in subsistence. With the development of animal herding and settled agriculture, production exceeds immediate subsistence needs, and social inequality and class division becomes possible when particular individuals or groups are able to take control of this surplus.

surplus value In Marxist theory, surplus value is created by individual labour that is left over, or remains in the product or services produced, after the employer has paid the costs of hiring the worker. It is this value, which the worker produces but does not receive, that allows the capitalist owner to expand its capital. *See also* **labour theory of value**.

sustainable development Economic activity or growth that does not reduce or deplete the resources available to future generations is called *sustainable development*.

Sutherland, Edwin (1883–1950) U.S. criminologist Edwin Sutherland was a leading scholar in the sociology of deviance and famous for his theory of differential association published in 1934 and elaborated on in 1939. This theory relates the propensity for crime among certain groups to problems of social disorganization and the effects that socialization into deviant lifestyles has on behaviour and normative orientations. If an individual associates with others within a deviant subculture, then that person is more likely to engage in crime.

swidden farming Swidden farming is a form of horticulture in which natural vegetation is cut and burned and a new crop planted in the cleared land.

Sydney Tar Ponds Sydney Steel Corporation of Sydney, Nova Scotia, began to manufacture steel in the 1900s and for 80 years deposited waste in "tar ponds" in areas surrounding the plant and very close to downtown Sydney. These ponds included a great many hazardous wastes from the manufacturing process. These "tar ponds" are perhaps the greatest environmental hazard in Canada, and while efforts to clean up the mess began in the 1980s, little has been accomplished. People in the area now have high levels of cancer-causing agents in their bodies, and many are demanding that governments move them to safe sites.

symbolic analyst Symbolic analysts engage in what Robert Reich (1946–), Secretary of Labor in the Clinton administration and now on the faculty of the Goldman School of Public Policy at the University of California, Berkeley, calls *symbolic-analytic services*. This is Reich's third occupational category and refers to tasks such as problem solving, problem identification, and strategic brokerage services. In short, it is all those jobs that involve the manipulation of symbols (data, words, oral and visual representations). This is a way to talk about a particular form of service worker in what others might call *knowledge work*, and is seen as the area of substantial growth in the developed capitalist nations of the world. Reich also believes that symbolic analysts, due to the nature of their work, develop distinctive lifestyles, social attitudes, and political beliefs. Reference: Reich, Robert.

(1991). *The Work of Nations*. New York: Alfred Knopf.

symbolic communications All communication with others is symbolic and involves the use of language, sound, body language, and expression.

symbolic interactionism A sociological perspective that stresses the way societies are created through the interactions of individuals, symbolic interactionism, unlike both the consensus (structural functionalist) and conflict perspectives, does not stress the idea of a social system possessing structure and regularity, but focuses on the way that individuals, through their interpretations of social situations and behavioural negotiation with others, give meaning to social interaction. U.S. social psychologist George H. Mead (1863–1931), a founder of symbolic interactionism, saw interaction as creating and re-creating the patterns and structures that bring society to life, but more recently there has been a tendency to argue that society has no objective reality aside from individual interaction. This latter view has been criticized for ignoring the role of culture and social structure in giving shape, direction, and meaning to social interaction. Reference: Blumer, Herbert. (1969). *Symbolic Interactionism*. Englewood Cliffs, NJ: Prentice-Hall. *See also* **microperspective**.

syndicalism A political doctrine advocating workers' ownership and control of the productive resources of a society, syndicalism emerged in France in the late 19th century and was influential in much of Europe. Syndicalism (in both French and Latin, *syndicat* is the term for *union*) was founded on the idea that organizations of workers within any particular industry or service provided the organizational basis for the direction and administration of the means of production on collective and cooperative principles. Syndicalists envisaged a revolutionary, but largely nonviolent, overthrow of private property, with the workers seizing ownership and control. The resulting power structure would be highly decentralized, with each industry and service being owned and directed by the workers involved in it. Syndicalism envisaged social revolution being achieved by the complete unification of workers within each sector of the economy, and thus they opposed the craft-specific structure of traditional labour unions and advocated industrial unionism that would bring all workers within

each industry into a one collective organization. *See also* **craft union**.

syntax In linguistics, syntax defines the rules or principles for constructing phrases or sentences.

T

Taber, Alberta In 1999, a 14-year-old student entered his school in Taber, dressed in a black trench coat and carrying a sawed-off rifle, and opened fire on students. One student was killed and a second seriously injured. It was discovered that the young shooter had been mercilessly bullied in school, and for the public, this made bullying a social problem. Cases like this have many interests for criminologists. The most obvious is why these events happen, but less obvious is the question of why these events almost always happen in a small town, the place the public believes is the safest place to raise children. Reference: Newman, Katherine. (2004). *Rampage: The Social Roots of School Shootings*. New York: Basic Books. *See also* **Columbine High School**.

taboo A Polynesian word, first encountered by a European during the voyages of Captain Cook, *taboo* literally means *marked off*. It refers to those special articles or symbols within a culture that are given a distinct status as sacred, metaphysical, or dangerous. Incest, for example, is a familiar taboo.

Taylorism This term is the name given to the work management principles followed by U.S. engineer Frederick Taylor (1856–1915), which were designed to transfer control of the work process to management and to achieve the greatest rate of productivity from workers through dividing labour and having work performed in a manner detailed by management. Reference: Taylor, F. (1919). *Shop Management*. New York: Harper. *See also* **industrial relations**; **scientific management**.

technocrat A technocrat is a person who has power because of a technical capacity or knowledge.

technophile Literally, a technophile is a lover of technology, and is likely to be a person who sees the positive benefits deriving from technology and advocates increased use of technology as a solution to economic, social, and political problems within the society.

technophobia Literally, the fear of technology is technophobia.

teknonymy Teknonymy is the practice of referring to people by the names of their offspring, rather than by their own personal or ancestral names; for example, Jane may be called "mother of John." If John then goes on to have a child and names her Mary, his mother and father will cease being referred to as "mother/father of John" and will now be called "grandmother/grandfather of Mary." There will be another shift of name if the grandparents become great-grandparents. The social result of teknonymy seems to be that precise links between generations of kin are forgotten and this creates a generalized feeling of kinship with others in the community. It also stratifies the community generationally.

terrorism Actions taken with the intent of instilling fear in civilians, terrorism is aimed at achieving political ends. The designation of an act as "terrorism" is, however, more difficult than the definition suggests, since one person's terrorist may be another's freedom fighter. After the events of September 11, 2001, anti-terrorism legislation was passed in Canada and in many other countries. Reference: Ignatieff, Michael. (2004). *The Lesser Evil: Political Ethics in an Age of Terror*. Toronto: Penguin Canada. *See also* **Anti-Terrorism Act**.

terrorists, types of When thinking of terrorism and terrorists, it is essential to draw some distinctions among different types of motivations. Michael Ignatieff provides useful categories, including the following types: (1) Insurrectionary terrorists who undertake acts of violence with the hope of overthrowing the state power to open the way for a more revolutionary form of government. The state may become destabilized if it overreacts to the terrorists (for example using troops against protesters) and in the process appears illegitimate in the eyes of the majority. There are many historical examples of this; for example, the Russian revolutionaries in the 19th century who attempted to overthrow the government even though it was taking steps toward a more liberal form of democracy. This revolutionary activity resulted in the communist revolution of 1917. (2) Freedom fighters are those who are fighting to seek forms of justice for a group of people. Examples of this type would include those fighting for separation from an existing state, those dealing with occupation of a homeland, or those dealing with obvious oppression of a group of people. This is the type of terrorism we were familiar with, especially in the Palestinian–Israeli conflict, before the destruction of the World Trade Center in September 2001. (3) The loner terrorist who takes violent action in order to draw attention to a particular cause. Examples of this would include those who murder doctors who perform abortion and the Oklahoma bomber in the United States. (4) Nihilist terrorists such as Al Qaeda, who appear to have no intention of overthrowing a state, seldom talk in terms of human rights or social justice and do not serve a determinate population, but talk in terms of destroying enemies and finding martyrdom in the process. As they appear to have no internal or community mechanisms of control they are very dangerous and can be met only by counterviolence. Reference: Ignatieff, M. (2004). *The Lesser Evil: Political Ethics in an Age of Terror*. Toronto: Penguin.

textual analysis An analysis of written or spoken texts as a way to understand social life, textual analysis has become more common with postmodern sociology, but it is derived largely from structuralists such as Belgian social theorist Claude Lévi-Strauss (1908–), French historian and philosopher Michel Foucault (1926–1984), and Swiss psychologist Jean Piaget (1896–1980), who studied human thought, myths, story-telling, and texts. Foucault, for example, argues that the way we see and understand the world, which is represented in written or spoken texts, is central to understanding a particular time period or society and the way power is organized.

theocracy Referring to a state ruled by religious authorities where there is no separation of church and state, the term *theocracy* is widely used today to refer to Islamic states like Iran, where the elected parliament and government are subordinate to a council of the nation's leading religious authorities. Theocracy has a long history, and the establishment of the separation of church and state in many European countries required a centuries-long struggle against church authorities and against the monarchs who were often allied with them. The religion-inspired conflicts of 17th- and 18th-century Europe persuaded the framers of the United States constitution to add as a first amendment, in 1791, that the establishment of a state religion or the suppression of any religion was expressly prohibited. Recently, however, the United States has become unusual among Western societies in making the Christian religion a central part of public discussion about political values and policies.

theory All sciences use theory as a tool to explain. It is useful to think of theory as a conceptual model of some aspect of life. We may have a theory of mate selection, or of the emergence of capitalist societies, or of criminal behaviour, or of the content of dreams. In each case, the theory consists of a set of concepts and their nominal definitions, assertions about the relationships among these concepts, assumptions, and knowledge claims. Swiss psychologist Carl Jung (1875–1961) began his theory of the self, for example, by asserting the key concepts—introversion and extroversion—and the relationship between these two components—one is dominant and the other subordinate. It assumes that the dominant characteristic will be displayed in behaviour and the subordinate one in our dreams or unconscious. The content of dreams can be explained by bringing Jung's model to the inquiry. In the classic model of how science is conducted, the scientist begins with a theory, deduces a hypothesis about the real world from the theory, and then engages in the necessary research to determine if the hypothesis is true or false. In this way, science is always about theory testing. *See also* **hypothetico-deductive model of science**.

thick description A term developed by U.S. anthropologist Clifford Geertz (1926–), *thick description* reflects his interest in systems of meaning. He suggested that it is of little value for those in the social sciences to provide only a thin description of behaviour, since it is always embedded in context and the meaning derives from this context. The example he uses is of a wink. One can describe the behavioural component of the wink but a wink can mean several things, depending on the context. So a thick description describes the wink but also describes the context necessary for the reader or observer to understand what was meant by the wink. The anthropological observer then must be very alert to, and knowledgeable of, the context in which all social life is embedded. Further, it can be very misleading to bring the contextual understandings of one culture to the observations of another. *See also* **indexicality**.

third reading *See* **first reading**.

Third Way A relatively new political philosophy having its roots in an earlier period but emerging in a serious way in the 1990s, the emergence of the Third Way was stimulated by the growing awareness that there is no longer a viable alternative to capitalism and to the success of politicians like Margaret Thatcher in Britain and Ronald Reagan in the United States. These two leaders tilted their nations more fully toward programs of neoliberalism. The Third Way philosophy attempts to balance the values of neoliberalism with those of social democracy. From this starting point, it acknowledges the power of the free market and focuses on the creation of wealth for a nation. It also recognizes the potential for welfare dependency and the limits of the state. At the same time, it attempts to encourage social solidarity and the values of social justice. Third Way philosophy is seen in the politics of Tony Blair in Britain and of Bill Clinton when he was the U.S. president. There is also growing recognition that this philosophy is present in the Liberal governments of Canada, although it has not yet been fully accepted by those to the left. Critics argue that Third Way philosophy is just a kinder presentation of a neoliberal program. Reference: Giddens, A. (2000). *The Third Way: The Renewal of Social Democracy*. Oxford, UK: Polity Press.

third world Categorizing societies as *third world* has lost much of its meaning with the breakup of the Soviet Union and the decline of communism as an economic system. *First-world countries* once referred to the developed, capitalist societies, while *second-world countries* identified the developed socialist societies. *Third-world countries* were those large political communities in the initial stages of development, while *fourth-world societies* are those that are traditional communities marginalized from economic development and political power. The concept of "fourth world" has been applied to the aboriginal communities of North America.

torture The inflicting of severe pain on a person as punishment or as a means of interrogation or intimidation is defined as *torture*. Milanese official, Enlightenment Project philosopher, and one of the fathers of utilitarianism, Cesare Beccaria (1738–1794) was responsible for eliminating torture from the criminal justice system, but it is still widespread around the world as a means of intimidation or interrogation and is often used by secret police or soldiers. Courts, however, have had a great deal of trouble in deciding just how much pain has to be imposed for a condition of torture to be established. Reference: Conroy, John. (2000). *Unspeakable Acts,*

Ordinary People: The Dynamics of Torture. New York: Alfred Knopf.

Tory Now designating a member of a conservative political party, the term *Tory* originated in 17th-century Britain and referred to a political party, supported largely by aristocratic interests, that defended royal prerogatives and divine inheritance of the throne. This party was resistant to democratic ideals and the growing political and economic power of the middle class. In modern Canada, the term is used to refer to the Conservative Party. *See also* **conservatism**.

total institution *See* **institution, total**.

totemism The belief that people are related to animals, plants, or even natural objects by virtue of descent from a common ancestry, totemism is still found on the west coast of Canada, where native groups believe themselves to be linked to the bear, raven, or other creatures.

trade liberalization The process of making the international trade of goods and services more open, free, or liberal, trade liberalization is also identified with the concept of free trade. Trade liberalization can also involve the liberalization of capital markets for the free flow of investment capital around the world.

trade unions, state coercion and Several historical examples can be found of the state using the police as instruments of class control. Two important examples of conflict are provided here. (1) A landmark strike of General Motors workers in Oshawa, Ontario, on March 2, 1937, marks the birth of industrial unionism in Canada. American union members, under the leadership of John Lewis, had broken away from the American Federation of Labor over its refusal to consider organizing unions along industrial lines rather than around crafts or trades. As mass production grew (the famous "production line" of automobile plants), the idea of craft unions made little sense to workers. The breakaway U.S. unions created the Committee for Industrial Organization (CIO) in 1935, and made tentative visits to Canada. This new union came to represent the 4,000 Oshawa workers. The union was accused of being a front for communism and its victory was declared to be a threat to the productivity of the province. The Liberal premier of the province became directly involved in fighting against the union and in negotiations. Government links to big business were more than apparent. The victory of the union was a symbolic victory for the CIO and began the creation of unions as we know them today. The Liberals won the next election on an anti-labour campaign, but their shift to the right created a space for the newly emerging Co-operative Commonwealth Federation (CCF) party and, more importantly, pushed the working class away from the Liberals. This legacy was to last for much of the remainder of the century. (2) On September 12, 1945, workers at the Ford plant in Windsor went on strike, perhaps the most important event in Canadian working-class history. Among other demands, the workers wanted the plant to become a union shop and for there to be automatic union dues check-off by the employer. The strike came to a less than spectacular end, but the union did agree to have an arbitrator examine its issues. Ivan Rand was selected for this, and his report indicates that he was open to the evolution of worker rights. His final recommendations turned down the union shop proposal, but did offer a dues check-off procedure. This procedure (now called the *Rand formula*) is still present in most unionized workplaces. The agreement means that workers do not have to be members of the union to work in a shop (they can withdraw from the union if they wish); however, they must pay union dues if they are to benefit from the negotiations carried out by the union. The CCF had taken an unpopular position during this strike (requesting that the government take over the running of the plant) and this damaged the party's links to the labour movement. This fracture was not healed until the creation of the New Democratic Party in July 1961. *See also* **Regina Riot; Winnipeg General Strike**.

transgender *See* **transsexual**.

transnational corporations Corporations whose sales and production are carried out in many different nations are transnational corporations. As a result of their multinational reach, these corporations are often thought to be beyond the political control of any individual nation–state.

transportation In England in 1615, transportation was a punitive sentence, meaning transportation to the West Indies and the American colonies, imposed chiefly for capital offences and as a substitute for the death penalty. In 1718, the terms of transportation were established at 14 years for capital offences and 7 years for a range of noncapital offences. After the American revolution of 1776, transportation to that destination ceased, and in 1787, the new destination of Australia was established. The first voyage left England in May 1787 with 717 prisoners, 48 of whom died during the voyage. Their destination was Sydney Cove and their arrival on January 28, 1788, marked the foundation of the colony of New South Wales. A second contingent left England in 1789, and 278 prisoners died during this voyage. Transportation virtually ended in 1853, although there were some isolated cases until 1868. In all, from 1787 to 1867, a total of 158,702 prisoners from England and Ireland and 1,321 from other parts of the British Empire were transported to Australia.

transsexual An individual who has physically or psychologically crossed the boundary between the sexes and thus becomes the other sex is a transsexual. These people may or may not engage in cross-dressing. While movement may be in either direction, more transsexuals are men who have become women. Western cultures have been criticized frequently for being extremely dualistic in gender or sexual identities, making little—or no—room for a third or fourth gender. Hinduism by contrast has an elaborate repertoire of sexual transformations, bisexuality, and sexual expression. The term *transgender* is now preferred, since it clearly suggests that sexual categories are themselves social constructions.

treaty A treaty is an agreement or contract between two or more sovereign nations, creating obligations and responsibilities for both parties. The British and French colonizers of what is now called Canada and the Canadian government itself have negotiated many treaties with the native nations who occupied the land. These treaties are now protected by the Canadian *Constitution*. *See also* **numbered treaties**.

treaty Indian A native person or descendant of a native person who signed a treaty is a treaty Indian. The registration list under the *Indian Act* was drawn up to include those band members who signed treaties, so all treaty Indians are also Status Indians (unless they have lost their status). Treaties were signed with bands in parts of British Columbia, Ontario, and the Northwest Territories, and most of Alberta, Saskatchewan, and Manitoba. *See also* **C-31 Indian; numbered treaties; Status Indian.**

Treaty of Versailles In June 1919, the *Treaty of Versailles* brought a formal end to World War I and imposed punitive measures on Germans. These punitive terms included a restriction on the size of the German army and on the manufacture of arms, the requirement that all German overseas colonies be given to the victorious powers, and the stipulation that Germany accept responsibility for causing the war and pay civilian damages amounting to billions of dollars. The treaty also realigned many of the boundaries of Europe.

Treaty of Westphalia This 1648 treaty incorporated a number of other treaties that brought about the end of the Thirty-Years' War and the Eighty-Years' War. The importance of this treaty flows from those provisions that laid to rest the idea that the Holy Roman Empire would have secular dominion over the entire Christian world. This principle made the nation–state the highest order of government and led to a world in which wars were between states and not between religious groups.

tribalism The use of this term must be understood against the assumption that citizens of the modern world would develop significant identification only with large groupings that included a plurality of social categories. For example, the identity of "Canadian" would include many ethnic groups, sexual preferences, social interests, and religious groupings. Tribalism is used to describe those situations in which broad social identification has broken down, so that people identify themselves exclusively within a narrower category. For example, people may organize their lives around ethnic identification or sexual preference or religious belief. This retribalization of the society is thought to lead to fragmentation and divisiveness as people identify with an in-group, making a shared sense of citizenship among larger groupings more and more fragile. *See also* **identity politics**.

tribe *Tribe* is a term that has often been used in a derogatory fashion, but for anthropologists, the concept refers to a form of political organization in which a number of bands or villages are integrated in informal and temporary ways. Leadership is informal and bands and villages cooperate on larger issues when it is determined to be in the interest of the smaller groups. The smaller groups retain their autonomy.

Trudeau, Pierre Elliot (1919–2000) Prime minister of Canada from 1968–1979 and 1980–1984, Pierre Trudeau's government established official bilingualism in 1969 as a key part of his strategy to develop a stronger sense of Canadian, rather than Quebec, nationalism among Quebec's Francophones. In 1970, he led an aggressive federal government response to politically inspired murder and kidnapping by the Front de libération du Québec in Quebec, invoking the *War Measures Act*, mobilizing the army, and suspending some civil liberties. He also championed the idea of multiculturalism and was largely responsible for creating the vision of a Canadian society in which individuals can be full citizens yet maintain links with their heritage cultures. In the 1982 *Constitution Act*, he achieved the elusive goal of patriation of the Canadian *Constitution* and the creation of constitutional guarantees of individual and group rights in the *Canadian Charter of Rights and Freedoms*. He was a controversial and charismatic politician, and his vision of a bilingual Canada with a strong federal government, equality of the provinces, and an extensive framework of human rights remains deeply embedded in Canadian law and institutions. Reference: Trudeau, Pierre Elliott. Ron Graham (Ed.). (1998). *The Essential Trudeau*. Toronto: McClelland & Stewart.

Truscott, Steven At the age of 14, Steven Truscott was convicted in adult court in 1959 of the murder of 12-year-old Lynn Harper. Controversy over the quality of the evidence and the legal process dogged the case for many years. Canadian law allowed for the execution of Truscott, but his sentence was commuted by Minister of Justice Davey Fulton. By the end of the century, new evidence revealed that there was a much more likely suspect, but by this time, Truscott was living in the community, having been paroled in 1969, and was not then prepared to push for wrongful conviction. However, in 2001, the Association in Defence of the Wrongfully Convicted filed an appeal with the federal minister of Justice, requesting that the case be reopened, and the case was referred to the Ontario Count of Appeal in 2004, much to the disappointment of Truscott, who wanted a new trial. In November 2005, Justice Fred Kaufman ruled that there was probably a miscarriage of justice in the Steven Truscott case, but not enough new evidence to exonerate him completely. Reference: Sher, Julian. (2001). *Until You Are Dead: Steven Truscott's Long Ride into History*. Toronto: Alfred Knopf.

Type 1 error In inferential reasoning or statistics, rejecting a hypothesis when it is true and should be accepted is a Type 1 error. The probability of making such a mistake is indicated by the level of significance used, so the probability of this type of error can be controlled by altering the level of significance. Types 1 and 2 errors are linked, however, so that reducing one increases the other. A researcher will try to achieve some balance between the two types or alter the balance to meet the needs of a specific situation.

Type 2 error In inferential reasoning or statistics, accepting a hypothesis when it is false and should be rejected is a Type 2 error. Also known as a *false positive. See also* **false positives**.

typification The work of Alfred Schutz (1899–1959), an Austrian phenomenologist, suggests that in all of our encounters with others, with the exception of "we-relationships" (the most intimate of relationships), we experience and understand the other in terms of ideal types. We form a construct of a typical way of acting and assume typical underlying motivations or personality. For example, we make prior assumptions about the personalities and behaviour of a doctor, priest, or judge. Ethnomethodologists have studied the use of this process of typification as a tool for understanding how people such as coroners, prosecutors, police officers, and others achieve a sense of concreteness and predictability in their work. Coroners, for example, may operate with a sense of a "typical" suicide, prosecutors with a sense of a "normal" crime of child abuse, police officers with a sense of the "normal" or typical resident of a particular neighbourhood. Reference: Emerson, R.M. (1969). *Judging Delinquents: Context and Social Process in Juvenile Court*. Chicago: Aldine. *See also* **ideal type**.

typology A set of two or more ideal types, a typology is used for categorizing behaviours, events, societies, groups, etc. For example, French sociologist Émile Durkheim (1858–1917) developed four types of suicide: anomic, egoistic, altruistic, and fatalistic. German sociologist Ferdinand Tonnies (1855–1936) identified two types of society: *Gemeinschaft* and *Gesellschaft*. *See also* **ideal type**.

U

Ukrainian internment In 2005, then-Prime Minister Paul Martin acknowledged that the World War I internment of Ukrainians in Canada and the loss of civil liberties was wrong, and signed an agreement with the Ukrainian community. Between 1914 and

U

1920, 5,000 Ukrainians were interned in Canada and approximately 80,000 were stripped of their civil liberties, including the loss of the right to vote in 1917. The terms of the agreement provided funds to establish road markers and plaques to identify sites of internment and funds to develop educational materials to ensure that this episode in Canadian history is not lost. *See also* **internment**.

ultra vires From the Latin, *ultra vires* means to act beyond the scope of powers. Government powers in Canada are distributed between the federal and provincial governments; each government then must act within its own power. If provinces pass criminal law, for example, this would be ruled *ultra vires*, since criminal law is an exclusive federal power.

underclass A term similar in use to Marx's concept of *lumpenproletariat*, the underclass is a group that is not in a regular economic or social relationship with the rest of the community. It refers to the chronically unemployed, those who live on the proceeds of petty crime, panhandlers, and bag ladies. American sociologists in particular use this term, since a large underclass is thought to pose a threat to the stability of society because they are not adequately connected to the institutional and cultural regulation that is experienced by most social members.

underground economy *See* **informal economy**.

United Empire Loyalists United Empire Loyalists were U.S. residents who remained loyal to the British Crown during the American War of Independence and fled to Canada. Approximately 40,000 émigrés arrived in Canada; most settled in Nova Scotia, although some 7,000 relocated in Quebec to provide the first substantial British population in that province. The attitudes and political philosophy of these new settlers are seen as significant for understanding the subsequent development of Canada. Reference: Stewart, Walter. (1985). *True Blue: The Loyalist Legend*. Don Mills: Collins. *See also* **Constitutional Act, 1791**.

United Nations The *Charter of the United Nations* was agreed on by 50 nations in the closing months of World War II in 1945. The new organization was designed to promote international cooperation and security, and to prevent the outbreak of wars. With the establishment of numerous secretariats and agencies, the United Nations expanded its role to encompass international trade and development, as well as environmental and social issues. The main bodies of the UN are the General Assembly, in which the member states each have one vote, and the Security Council, which has 15 members of whom 5 (Britain, France, Russia, China, and the United States) have permanent seats and the right of veto. Initially, the United Nations was supported by the Western powers, especially the United States, because the United States commanded a majority of support in the General Assembly, which allowed it to circumvent Russian or Chinese exercise of the veto in the Security Council. In recent times, however, with the General Assembly having expanded to include many nation–states either not aligned with the United States and its allies or hostile to them, support for the United Nations and its international role has withered. *See also* **Universal Declaration of Human Rights**.

units of analysis Most social research looks for patterns when comparing "things" to one another. The things that researchers are comparing or examining are referred to as the *units of analysis*, or the units to be analyzed. The most frequent unit of analysis is the individual, suggesting that researchers look for patterns among a collection (perhaps a sample) of individuals. Research can also be conducted in which a pattern is sought among a collection of groups; the group would be the unit of analysis. For example, like French sociologist Émile Durkheim (1858–1917), one might try to determine what social factors are linked to the variation in suicide rates among nations or regions. One can also look for patterns among things like newspaper stories, advertisements, a category of social interaction, social events, or speech utterances. In this case, the unit of analysis would be what U.S. sociologist Earl Babbie (1938–) has called *social artifacts*.

Universal Declaration of Human Rights Following World War II and the horrific experiences of that struggle, many nations joined together to create the United Nations. The original *Charter of the United Nations* contained a general statement on human rights. The need for a more detailed and substantial statement on human rights was recognized, and a commission was established to create such a document. This commission wrote the *Universal Declaration of Human Rights* (drafted largely by a Canadian, John Peters Humphrey (1905–1995, a former lawyer who was then director of the UN Division of Human Rights), which was adopted by the General Assembly of the United Nation on December 10, 1948. This document was described as humanity's response to the death camps of the Nazis, the countless refugees, and the tortured prisoners of war. In 1966, the United Nations adopted two further documents on human rights: the *Covenant on Civil and Political Rights* and the *Covenant on Economic, Social and Cultural Rights*. These covenants contain many of the rights asserted in the *Universal Declaration*, but they differ in that they are legally binding on those nations signing the covenants. The first of these covenants declares that everyone has the right to life; freedom of thought; equal treatment in the courts; and freedom of assembly; and that no one shall be subject to torture, slavery, or forced labour. The second declares that everyone has the right to the enjoyment of just and favourable work conditions; to form trade unions; an adequate standard of living; education; and to take part in cultural life and enjoy the progress of science. In 1989, a third covenant was added, the *Convention of the Rights of the Child*. These four documents together comprise what is called the *International Bill of Rights*.

universality A philosophy concerning the provision of the benefits of the welfare state, universality declares that all citizens have access, regardless of their need. For example, all citizens receive the same access to health care in Canada, regardless of income level. The underlying principle is that less powerful citizens can more easily be deprived of benefits, or benefits can more easily be reduced, if they are not received by most people in the population. In recent years, the principle of universality has been seriously eroded in Canada. The baby bonus, once given to mothers of all children, has been replaced with a child tax credit, which gives income to mothers on the basis of household income. *See also* **means test**.

University of Toronto, anthropology at The first anthropology course in Canada was established at the University of Toronto in 1860 by Daniel Wilson (1816–1892). In 1915, Thomas McIlwraith (1899–1964) was appointed to teach anthropology and created the first anthropology department in Canada in 1936.

University of Toronto, sociology at *See* **Clark, S.D.; Eichler, Margrit; Innis, Harold; Smith, Dorothy**.

unwritten constitution *See* **constitutional convention**.

Upper Canada Established by the division of the province of Quebec in 1791 as a result of the *Constitutional Act*, Upper Canada eventually became the province of Ontario. British colonization of this territory was encouraged. *See also* **Constitutional Act, 1791**; **Lower Canada**.

Upper Paleolithic Period The last part of the Old Stone Age, the Upper Paleolithic Period is associated with the emergence of modern-looking hominines.

urbanism Similar to the notion of modernity, *urbanism* refers to the form of social organization and values typically found in large urban settings. The central values are those of individualism and impersonality, and the major characteristics of social organization are a developed division of labour, high rates of geographic and social mobility, and predominance of impersonality in social interactions, despite the acute social interdependence. *See also* **mass society**.

utilitarianism (1) This theory holds that individuals are best able to define their needs, desires, and goals, and where they have freedom to make choices, the result will be the greatest possible satisfaction for the greatest number. This is an individualistic perspective because it claims that individuals making free choices necessarily leads to a society where satisfaction and happiness are maximized. The theory overlooks the potential for one individual's choice to constrain or remove the choices of others. (2) As a justification for punishment, utilitarianism asserts the utility of the act of punishment or the punishment of a particular offender. *The utility of punishment* refers to any future benefit for the society (or the greatest number) that can be derived from the act. Justifications in terms of deterrence (individual or general), rehabilitation, incapacitation, and crime prevention are all aspects of utilitarianism. Utilitarian justifications are contrasted with retribution. *See also* **retribution**.

utterances These are units of speech that are examined by conversational analysis, a stream of work within ethnomethodology.

V

vagrancy (1) William Chambliss, professor of sociology at George Washington University, examined the historical origins of the first vagrancy law, passed in 1349 as a response to landowners who were having difficulty finding workers because of the Black Death and the fact that many owners had sold serfs their freedom in order to raise funds for military campaigns. Men were not permitted to refuse work and churches were not permitted to give support to those refusing work. This example is frequently used in the sociology of law to show how rule makers respond to the needs of the economically powerful. (2) Canada had vagrancy rules in the *Criminal Code*. Vagrancy "C" was defined as "being a common prostitute or night-walker found in a public place who does not, when requested, give a good account of herself." The Royal Commission on the Status of Women (1970) objected to this law, claiming it discriminated against women. This section was replaced with a soliciting law in 1972. Reference: Chambliss, William. (1964). A Sociological Analysis of the Law of Vagrancy. *Social Problems, 12*, 67–77.

validity This is one of two criteria (the other being reliability) by which researchers judge their results or measurement tools. A valid result is one that accurately measures what it claims to be measuring. Using shoe size as a measurement of intelligence is not a valid measure of intelligence. It lacks face validity, since it is not obvious that it is measuring what it claims to measure. One test of validity might be the extent to which your measurements allow you to make predictions about future behaviour. If your measurement of intelligence does not predict how people perform on exams, then perhaps it is not a valid measurement of intelligence. *See also* **external validity**; **internal validity**; **reliability**.

values Relatively general cultural prescriptions of what is right, moral, and desirable, values provide the broad foundations for specific normative regulation of social interaction. *See also* **norm**.

vandalism Meaning willful and ignorant destruction of public or private property or of works of art or architecture, the term *vandalism* comes from the name of the Vandals, a Germanic people who overran Gaul, Spain, and northern Africa in the fourth and fifth centuries C.E. After military defeat by other warring tribes, the Vandals retreated to Spain in 409 and subsequently sailed to Africa, where in 439 they attacked and took control of the great city of Carthage. In 455, they sacked Rome, bringing an end to the classical period in European history, and ushering in the long period known by many as the Middle Ages. In about 536, after a series of military defeats, the Vandals disappeared as a distinct people.

variables A term central to quantitative sociology and to macrostructural sociology, the term *variables* refers to that which varies, rather than being constant. In particular, its reference is to structural features that vary (things like sex, age, race, social class) and have an influence on behaviour or attitudinal variables (e.g., discrimination or attitudes about abortion). Researchers work out ways to measure these variables (often by asking questions) and determine their importance in understanding human behaviour. Those variables thought to be causal variables are called *independent variables* and those thought to be effects are called *dependent variables*. A variable has two or more values; the variable of sex, for example, has the values of female and male. *See also* **dependent variable**; **independent variable**.

verstehen Associated with the writing of German sociologist Max Weber (1864–1920), *verstehen* is now seen as a concept and a method central to a rejection of positivistic social science (although Weber appeared to think that the two could be united). *Verstehen* refers to understanding the meaning of an action from the actor's point of view. It is entering into the shoes of the other, and adopting this research stance requires treating the actor as a subject, rather than as an object of your observations. It also implies that unlike objects in the natural world, human actors are not simply the product of the pulls and pushes of external forces. Individuals are seen to create the world by organizing their own understanding of it and giving it meaning. To do research on actors without taking into account the meanings they attribute to their actions or environment is to treat them like objects. *See also* **ethnographic research**; **positivism**.

vertical mosaic This term was introduced by Canadian sociologist John Porter (1921–1979) to describe Canadian society. The term *mosaic* is used to capture the multiethnic and multiracial character of the society, and the term *vertical* implies that these ethnic and racial groups are arranged into a hierarchy. A similar term would be *ethnic stratification*. Reference: Porter, John. (1965). *The Vertical Mosaic*. Toronto: University of Toronto Press. *See also* **Porter, John**.

victimization survey This type of survey, in which people in a random sample of the population are

V

NEL   Thomson Nelson Canadian Dictionary for the Social Sciences   **165** asked to recall and describe their own experiences of being a victims of crime, is a valuable tool for criminologists because such surveys provide a measure of unreported crime (sometimes called the *dark figure of crime*). The first such Canadian survey was conducted in 1981. A survey on victimization has been included in the General Social Survey since 1988. The objective of this survey is to gather data on a regular basis in order to monitor changes to Canadian society. Reference: Skogan, W. (2000). Criminal Victimization in Canada, 1999. *Juristat, 20*(10).

victimless crime The conventional conception of crime implies that there is a victim of the criminal behaviour who experiences harm. There are, however, criminal behaviours like illegal gambling, drug use, and selling sex, where those involved do not experience harm and are indeed willing participants. Many argue that crimes of this nature are victimless and should not be regulated by criminal law.

Vold, George (1896–1967) George Vold was a professor of sociology at the University of Minnesota and later at Stanford Law School and a contributor to the development of conflict perspectives within criminology. Instead of viewing crime as an individual's violation of law, Vold seeks to locate it in the dynamics of competing group interests. In social life, individuals inevitably affiliate with groups that will promote their needs, interests, and desires, and these diverse groups engage in interaction and competition with each other over control of power, economic resources, and social status. The groups that are most successful in mobilizing the necessary support and authority are able to pass laws that constrain the opportunities and limit the goals of other groups, thus exerting pressure on them to violate the law. His most important book was *Theoretical Criminology,* originally written in 1958. Reference: Vold, George, Snipes, Jeffrey B., & Bernard, J. Thomas. (2002). *Theoretical Criminology.* New York: Oxford University Press.

Volstead Act Passed by the United States Congress on October 28, 1919, the *Volstead Act* prohibited the manufacture and sale of alcohol in the United States. Since a ready market existed for this prohibited good, organized crime in America easily gained a foothold. Many Canadians also became rich during the subsequent Prohibition Era, making fortunes from illegal cross-border traffic in liquor; however, rather than pursuing organized crime, they became successful businessmen. Canadians were not allowed to ship liquor to the United States legally, but they could ship to Cuba and other countries, from which the liquor could be smuggled into the United States. Not surprisingly, American boats were reported to make four or five trips to Cuba in one day.

W

Wade v. Roe *See* **abortion**.

Waffle Group Established within the New Democratic Party (NDP) in 1969, the Waffle Group, led by Mel Watkins, now professor emeritus of economics at the University of Toronto, and James Laxer, now professor of political science at York University, attempted to move the NDP further to the left by espousing clearly socialist and nationalist ideals. The leadership of the party believed that these ideas were unappealing to the public and would challenge the political legitimacy and electability of the NDP. The group was eventually expelled from the party. *See also* **Co-operative Commonwealth Federation**.

war crimes During World War II, Allied nations were determined to prosecute German war criminals, defining *war crimes* as plotting aggressive warfare and committing atrocities against any civilian population. This definition was used in the trials of war criminals, which began in 1945. In recent years, there have been suggestions that Canada (for its involvement in the fire-bombing of German civilians) and the United States (for the dropping of atomic bombs on largely civilian-inhabited cities), as well as other nations, were also guilty of committing atrocities against civilians, but these nations were never brought to trial. In the 1990s, the United Nations again initiated tribunals to prosecute war criminals in the former Yugoslavia and in Rwanda. It is estimated that there are 4,000 war criminals living in Canada, many of them having entered from Nazi Germany. In 1985, Canada established a commission (under the late Justice Jules Deschênes) to examine the problems of war criminals in Canada. Reference: Deschênes, Jules. (1986). *Commission of Inquiry on War Criminals.* Ottawa: Minister of Supply and Services; Littman, Sol. (1988). *The Rauca Case: War Criminals on Trial.* Toronto: PaperJacks.

War Measures Act A 1914 statute giving emergency powers to Cabinet, the *War Measures Act* allowed it to govern by decree (without the usual approvals of democratic institutions) in times of war, invasion, or real or apprehended insurrection. It was this power that the federal government invoked in 1970 to deal with the Front de libération du Québec crisis, which the government called a state of "apprehended insurrection." The Act had been used in its early years to intern members of the Communist Party, Japanese Canadians, Jehovah's Witnesses, and Italian Canadians. In 1988, this statute was replaced by the *Emergencies Act.*

Watergate Affair When the offices of the Democratic Party of the United States were burgled in June 1972 (the offices were in the Watergate apartment complex), public confidence in elected officials took a decidedly negative turn. The investigation into this break-and-enter revealed the involvement of White House staff and President Richard Nixon's knowledge of the event. It was also learned that the president had kept secret tapes of White House conversations containing evidence of corrupt financial affairs and efforts to evade the truth about illegal (and thus secret) bombings of Cambodia. President Nixon was forced to resign from office under threat of impeachment.

Weaver, Sally (1940–1993) The first woman to receive a doctorate degree in anthropology in Canada (in 1967), Sally Weaver devoted her career to the study of native peoples and to applied anthropology, published an important book on the 1969 White Paper, and was influential in establishing what is now called the Canadian Anthropology Society. *See also* **White Paper (1969)**.

Weber, Max (1864–1920) The work of Max Weber, German political economist and one of the founders of modern sociology, was very comprehensive and diverse but his key sociological focus was on the rise of rationalization in Western society, which he saw as crucial to the development of capitalism. *Rationalization* referred to two social processes. First it involved the expulsion of religious and mythical ideas and their replacement with ideas based on science and empirical analysis. Second, it referred to the systematic organization of social and economic institutions for the efficient and calculable achievement of specific goals. In Weber's view this process was initially encouraged by the transformation of religious ideas that accompanied the Reformation, but with the establishment of capitalism, the momentum toward

rationalization came from the dynamics of capitalist production itself, with its constant competition-driven search for technological innovation and efficiency. Weber's other main contribution to the social sciences is his concept of interpretive sociology, which insists that the observer and interpreter of social action must understand the subjective meaning of the actions for the actors involved. This perspective is seen by some sociologists as the foundation for what were later to become symbolic interactionism, ethnomethodology, and phenomenology. It is doubtful, however, that Weber would have fully sympathized with perspectives that tend to lack an appreciation of social structure and culture as external to the actor and shaping that person's thought and behaviour. Reference: Parkin, F. (1982) *Max Weber.* New York: Tavistock.

welfare state A term that became widely used in the 1940s, *welfare state* refers to the development of state-initiated programs that provide citizens with minimum income, old age pensions, unemployment insurance, health insurance, and universal access to a range of social services. In Canada, the development of the welfare state gained momentum after 1940, when Unemployment Insurance (now called *Employment Insurance*) was introduced. In the next few years, programs to fund hospitals, old age pensions, and old age security were established. The development of the welfare state represents a softening of classical liberalism, which defines the role of the state very narrowly. It is not surprising that as classical liberalism returns (often called *neoconservatism*) there is an attack on the welfare state. *See also* **liberalism**.

Westray mine disaster On May 9, 1992, the Westray mine in Pictou County, Nova Scotia, exploded, killing 26 miners. The federal government was involved in financing the mine in spite of cautions about safety contained in engineering reports. Once in operation, workers feared for their safety and provincial safety inspectors identified numerous safety infractions that were never corrected. Although an inquiry was held and regulatory and criminal charges laid against the owner and four managers, little was accomplished. This event is frequently used by criminologists to illustrate the problems of prosecuting corporations in criminal court. Reference: Comish, Shaun. (1993). *The Westray Tragedy: A Miner's Story.* Halifax, NS: Fernwood Publishing.

Whig A term originating in the 17th century in Britain, a Whig was a member of the Whig political party, which was supported largely by the new commercial interests and defended the power of Parliament against royal prerogatives, thus encouraging the democratic revolution in Britain. The term was transplanted to the American colonies and referred to the supporters of independence from Britain. An American Whig Party was formed and it remained a major party until the 1850s, when it was succeeded by the Republican Party. The term has had little currency in Canada, although the Whig ideal of popular parliamentary government was a strong force in 19th-century Canadian politics. *See also* **liberalism**.

white collar Originally used as a contrast to blue-collar workers (manual labourers), the term *white collar* is intended to capture the distinction between non-manual and manual labour workers. With the rise of the service economy and the shrinkage of manual labour, the term has become less useful.

white-collar crime As originally used by U.S. criminologist Edwin Sutherland (1883–1950) in 1945, *white-collar crime* referred to the illegal activities of businesses and corporations committed to furthering the goals of business. These acts were not regulated by criminal law, but by regulatory laws of various kinds. These acts included false advertising, antitrust violations, environmental pollution, and dumping product on the market below cost. Criminologists now call this *corporate crime* or *organizational crime* and reserve the term *white-collar crime* for those illegal acts committed by people in positions of trust (usually in white-collar jobs) for personal gain. For example, making personal long-distance calls on an employer's account could be defined as a white-collar crime. Reference: Sutherland, Edwin. (1983). *White-Collar Crime: The Uncut Version.* New Haven: Yale University Press.

White Paper (1969) In June of 1969, the Trudeau Liberal government circulated a White Paper that would reform the relationship between natives and the Government of Canada by eliminating all arrangements that applied to natives, including the *Indian Act.* The philosophy behind this dramatic suggestion was the principle that natives should be treated more like Canadians. This was shaped by the U.S. Supreme Court decision in the *Brown vs. Topeka Board of Education* case, which found that the idea that Blacks could be segregated or even separated from society and still be treated equally was in fact a violation of equality provisions. In this spirit, Trudeau felt that all special provisions for natives must be removed and natives treated more like citizens of the nation. The 1969 White Paper, perhaps predictably, created outrage in the native community and created an organizational network of native associations that has since reshaped the way Canadians think about First Nations, and brought about a growing willingness to entertain the idea of self-government. Reference: Kymlicka, Will. (1995). *Multicultural Citizenship.* Toronto: Oxford University Press. *See also* **Brown vs. Topeka Board of Education; Indian Act**.

white slavery A term from the late 19th century, *white slavery* depicts and perhaps explains prostitution. It was believed that sex-trade workers were forced into prostitution by men. While this was true in a small number of cases, most young women entered into prostitution at this time because of their economic marginalization, resulting from changes to the factory system. The term is still used to refer to sex-trade workers in developing nations.

widening the net This sociological thesis claims that as alternative methods of punishment are introduced to the criminal justice system, they simply expand the number of people brought under the control of the state. This is thought to happen because a new measure does not usually replace an old measure, but provides a means for bringing people previously ignored into the criminal justice system.

"Wild Boy of Aveyron" *See* **feral child**.

Winnipeg General Strike This strike lasted from May 15 to June 25, 1919, and resulted from postwar inflation, the influence of the new and revolutionary industrial unionism, and the example of the successful Russia revolution of 1917. When negotiations broke down on May 15 with a wide range of Winnipeg employers over rights to collective bargaining, better wages, and improved working hours almost 30,000 workers struck within a matter of hours. Workers were joined by many public service employees, including the police, municipal employees, firefighters, postal workers, and utility workers. Employers responded with the organization of a "Committee of 1000" and were assisted by the federal government, which threatened to fire all federal employees who participated, arrested strike leaders, and changed the immigration acts to allow for deportation of strike leaders. On June 21, Royal North-West Mounted Police charged a strikers' demonstration, killing one demonstrator and injuring at least 30 more. Federal troops then occupied the city, and on June 25, the strikers had to come to terms with defeat and called off the strike. Reference: Bercuson, David. (1990). *Confrontation at Winnipeg*. Montreal–Kingston: McGill–Queen's University Press. *See also* **Palmer Raids**.

witchcraft All societies hold beliefs that supernatural powers can be influenced to act in particular ways. This influence can be controlled through magic, usually directed at getting the supernatural to do positive things or through witchcraft in which a person believed to have special powers is capable of doing harm. It is this belief that certain people have the power to do harm that leads to witch-hunts. Reference: Lehmann, A. C., & Myers, J.E. (Eds). (1993). *Magic, witchcraft and religion: An anthropological study of the supernatural*. Mountain View, CA: Mayfield.

Wolfenden Report A 1959 British report of the Departmental Committee on Homosexual Offences and Prostitution (chaired by Sir John Wolfenden), the *Wolfenden Report*'s major recommendation was that sexual activity between consenting adults should no longer be a criminal offence. This report had influence in many Western nations, and in 1969, after Pierre Trudeau became minister of Justice, Canada repealed sections of the *Criminal Code* that had made homosexual activity a criminal offence.

Wolfgang, Marvin, E. (1924–1998) Professor of criminology at the University of Pennsylvania, Marvin Wolfgang advanced the theory of a subculture of violence. This theory sought to explain the high rate of violent crime among American Blacks as the product of a uniquely violent subculture in which widely diffused violent values supported and encouraged violent behaviour and gave status to those who engaged in it. This theory has had many critics and it has defied empirical validation. Reference: Wolfgang, Marvin E., & Ferracuti, F. (1967). *The Subculture of Violence: Towards an Integrated Theory in Criminology*. London: Tavistock Publications.

women in Canadian anthropology While women are now well represented as students and faculty in anthropology departments, this was not always the case. Some of the first generation of Canadian women in anthropology include Sally Weaver, Joan Ryan, Elvi Whittaker, Helga Jacobson, and Laurel Bossen.

women in Canadian political science It has taken longer for women to have an impact in the field of Canadian political science than in other social sciences. Although women political scientists are involved in all areas of the discipline, there has been considerable focus on a feminist political economy perspective that relates gender roles and ideologies about gender to the political status and political participation of women. There has also been a lively discussion of a feminist view of the state as a cultural institution. Among today's leading women Canadian political scientists are Heather MacIvor at the University of Windsor, Yasmeen Abu-Laban at the University of Alberta, Jane Jensen at Université de Montréal, Cristine de Clercy at the University of Saskatchewan, and Diane Mauzy at the University of British Columbia. Reference: MacIvor, Heather. (1996). *Women and Politics in Canada*. Peterborough: Broadview Press.

women in Canadian sociology While women are now well represented as students and as faculty in sociology departments, this was not always the case. Some of the first generation of Canadian women in sociology include Jean Brunet (1920–); Helen C. Abell (1917–2005); Grace M. Anderson (1923–1989); Eleanor Cebotarev (1928–); Kathleen Herman (1920–); Helen McGill Hughes (1903–); Thelma McCormack (1921–); Helen Ralston (1929–), the first doctoral graduate from Carleton University in Ottawa; Aileen Ross (1902–1995), the third sociologist to join McGill University; Dorothy Smith (1926–). Reference: Eichler, M. (2001). Women Pioneers in Canadian Sociology. *Canadian Journal of Sociology*, 26(3).

Women's Legal Education and Action Fund (LEAF) This organization was formed in April 1985 to pursue litigation under the equal rights provisions of the *Canadian Charter of Rights and Freedoms* in order to change aspects of Canadian society and to improve women's position in society.

women's liberation thesis In criminology, this theory holds that women's involvement in crime will come to more closely resemble men's as gendered differences between women and men are diminished by women's greater social participation and equality. Although sounding plausible, there is little empirical evidence to support this theory. Reference: Adler, Freda. (1975). *Sisters in Crime*. New York: McGraw-Hill.

women's movement A broad term for a range of social and political organizations and activities such as research, writing, and criticism, the women's movement has the main goal of advancing the status of women in society and overcoming cultural marginalization of women's perspectives and experience in society.

working class This term has been found more frequently in Britain, and while having an imprecise meaning, generally includes skilled and unskilled manual workers (perhaps synonymous with blue-collar workers) and sometimes lower levels of white-collar workers. It is similar in meaning to *lower class*, unless it is used in a more Marxian sense to refer to those who work for a living (i.e., the proletariat).

World Bank The proper name for the World Bank is the International Bank for Reconstruction and Development. (Along with the International Development Association, it is referred to as The World Bank Group.) It has a membership of 184 nations and a staff of about 10,000. The primary purpose of the World Bank is to assist in the reconstruction and development of territories of members by facilitating the investment of capital for productive purposes, including the restoration of economies destroyed or disrupted by war; the reconversion of productive facilities to peacetime needs; and the encouragement of the development of productive facilities and resources in less-developed countries. While the reconstruction of nations affected by war remains important, the World Bank has increasingly moved toward attempting to stimulate growth in less-developed countries. This transition was made necessary when the Marshall Plan was developed to aid in the economic reconstruction of Europe. Indeed, the motto of the World Bank could be "a world without poverty." To achieve these aims, the World Bank can raise funds on the international financial markets and lend these funds to member nations to finance the development of resources planned to stimulate economic growth. It can invest directly in the development of dams, communication, transportation, and other productive facilities. In 2002, the World Bank was working in more than 100 developing nations. The Bank lends approximately $45 billion dollars to developing nations each year. Other groups also lend enormous sums; government-funded export development agencies (such as Canada's Export Development Agency) lend over $100 billion.

World Economic Forum The World Economic Forum is an annual gathering (usually held in Davos, Switzerland) of approximately 3,000 individuals representing the largest corporations in the world.

World Social Forum Begun in 1999, the World Social Forum is an annual gathering of protesters, volunteer workers, citizen organizations, and others intent on countering the dominant economic voice of the World Economic Forum by articulating social values as the foundation for world development.

world systems theory This theory is derived from the work of German-born social philosopher, political economist, and sociologist Karl Marx (1818–1883) and was made into a developed set of ideas by U.S. sociologist Immanuel Wallerstein (1930–), who taught at McGill University in the early 1970s and is now senior research scholar at Yale University. Wallerstein shows that capitalism is not just an economic system bounded by national borders highlighting class inequality. Rather, capitalism must also be seen as involving relationships among nations, and these relationships too are based on inequality. Those nations that developed capitalistic economies early then went on to dominate other nations through colonization or simply through linking the economies of the nations in ways that favoured the more dominant nation and placed the others into a condition of dependency on the dominant nation. This state of dependency tended to hamper the development of the other economies. Reference: Wallerstein, Immanuel. (1974). *The Modern World System*. New York: Academic Press [1980]. *See also* **dependent development; metropolis–hinterland theory**.

World Trade Center, New York The centre of the financial district of New York, occupying approximately 10 square blocks and providing employment for 50,000 workers, both towers of the World Trade Center were totally destroyed on September 11, 2001, when terrorists crashed two hijacked passenger airplanes into the towers. During the same attack on America, a hijacked airplane was crashed into the Pentagon, and a fourth plane crashed into a field, presumably on its way to the White House. Approximately 3,500 people were killed in the two attacks, and the world thrown into uncertainty. The World Trade Center had also been the site of a terrorist attack in 1993, when a powerful car bomb exploded in a delivery area. Reference: National Commission on Terrorist

Attacks upon the United States. (2004). *The 9/11 Commission Report.* Washington: Government Printing Office. *See also* **bin Laden, Osama**.

World Trade Organization (WTO) The International Monetary Fund (IMF) and the World Bank were established because of the concerns of the West that World War II had arisen from the economic policy failures of the previous decades, failures that plunged nations into crisis and opened the door to Hitler's Nazi regime in Germany. The Great Depression of the 1930s and the political reaction against it made it attractive for nations to pursue protectionist trade practices and, in Germany and Japan, to develop policies of industrial economic development that would give them the capacity to act as imperialist national powers. The world was going to have to do better to overcome the economic and political dangers of disrupted and failing economies and the political chaos they created, and the IMF and World Bank were part of a grand design to achieve future stability. As part of this grand scheme, international trade policies would have to be dealt with. In 1948, a group of Western nations met in Havana, Cuba, to formulate plans for an International Trade Organization (ITO). However, the United States felt that some of the policies being advocated sounded too communistic and abandoned the project. With the failure of plans for an ITO, the Western world began the difficult job of negotiating a set of regulations to produce freer trade and a set of predicable conditions for international trade. The rules were called the *General Agreement on Tariffs and Trade* (GATT). Under the GATT, the world (primarily the West) did prosper. In 1994, as part of the Uruguay Round of GATT negotiations, the members created the World Trade Organization (WTO) to become the planning and enforcement arm of the GATT. The WTO is located in Geneva, Switzerland, and has a staff of about 500. Approximately 140 nations belong to the WTO, and membership allows nations to trade with other nations as long as they comply with the large rule book containing all of the trade agreements. Like the IMF and World Bank, the WTO is a made up of member nations, and it is usually the trade ministers who sit as representatives and meet every two years to negotiate new trade rules. China was recently granted membership in the WTO; in return, it was required to open its capital markets to foreign investors.

Reference: Shrybman, S. (2001). *The World Trade Organization.* Toronto: James Lorimer.

wrongful conviction Many prisoners claim they are innocent but it is only recently that this issue has gained public attention, as several men have indeed been found to have been wrongfully convicted for murder. Many names have been added to the list of those known to be wrongfully convicted or those probably wrongfully convicted. Among the first group are David Milgaard, Thomas Sophonow, and Guy Paul Morin; among the second are Stephen Truscott, Romeo Phillion, and James Driskell. Social scientists have an interest in this topic in order to understand the organizational dynamics that may have led to faulty decisions and judgments. Reference: Anderson, Barrie, with Dawn Anderson. (1998). *Manufacturing Guilt: Wrongful Conviction in Canada.* Halifax, NS: Fernwood Publishing; Campbell, Kathryn, & Denov, Myriam (Eds.). (January 2004). Wrongful Conviction. *Canadian Journal of Criminology* (special issue), 46(2). *See also* **Morin, Guy Paul; Truscott, Steven**.

X

xenophobia This is the term for an individual's irrational and obsessive hatred of people perceived as being different and foreign, and is related to the concepts of racism and ethnocentrism. All of these can be overcome by the study of the social sciences and coming to appreciate the ideas of culture and social structure as tools for understanding ourselves and others.

Z

zero tolerance A philosophical approach to violence and drug use, zero tolerance gained popularity in schools and other institutions during the 1990s. As the name implies, institutions were to adopt a policy of no tolerance for specified behaviour. This would suggest, for example, that those engaging in violence on the school property would be expelled from school. The removal of discretion from authorities would ensure a consistent practice and eliminate inequality in its application. While the policy sounds good in its simplicity, research has shown that the policy has escalated the number of young people excluded from school and has demonstrated a pronounced racial bias in its enforcement.